THE TV SHOWRUNNER'S ROADMAP

101 Things I Learned in Film School
with Matthew Frederick
Grand Central Press, 2010

The Screenwriter's Roadmap:
21 Ways to Jumpstart Your Story
Focal Press, 2012

THE TV SHOWRUNNER'S ROADMAP

21 Navigational Tips for Screenwriters to Create and Sustain a Hit TV Series

Neil Landau

Routledge
Taylor & Francis Group

LONDON AND NEW YORK

First published 2014 by Focal Press

Published 2019 by Routledge
2 Park Square, Milton Park, Abingdon, Oxon OX14 4RN
52 Vanderbilt Avenue, New York, NY 10017

Routledge is an imprint of the Taylor & Francis Group, an informa business

Library of Congress Cataloging-in-Publication Data

Landau, Neil.
    TV showrunner's roadmap : 21 navigational routes to creating and
sustaining / Neil Landau.
        pages cm
    1. Television authorship.   2. Television—Production and direction.
3. Television writers—United States—Interviews.   4. Television producers
and directors—United States—Interviews.   I. Title.
PN1992.7.L36   2014

ISBN 13: 978-0-415-83167-3 (pbk)

Typeset in Minion Pro and Stone
Sans By Apex CoVantage, LLC

I've been an Executive Producer on twelve scripted TV Series and I can honestly say that everything I've learned about how to sell, create, and operate a show is contained in Neil Landau's *The TV Showrunner's Roadmap*. Anyone with the ultimate goal of becoming a Creator/Executive Producer of a television series should read this book, as should anyone interested in knowing how their favorite show came to be.

— **Gavin Polone, television and film producer,** *Curb Your Enthusiasm,* *Gilmore Girls, Twisted, Zombieland, Panic Room*

The ultimate "how to" guide for anyone working in TV. Whether you're a writer, an executive, or just a TV watcher, Neil highlights every aspect of the unrelenting task of producing television, leaving us with even more respect for the process and those who do it successfully. It's the most comprehensive guide I've ever read, supported by interviews with the most talented writers working in the business today. A fantastic and insightful read!

— **Maira Suro, Executive Producer of the Emmy nominated series** *The 4400,* **former Senior Vice-President of Development and Current Series at NBC-Universal Cable Productions, former President at American Zoetrope Television, and former Director of Drama Development at CBS**

Neil's book is a must-read for anyone serious about the craft of writing for television. His analysis of the fundamentals is clear, precise, and entertaining. But it's his one-on-one conversations with showrunners currently working at the top of their game that makes this book a true gem, giving the reader fly-on-the-wall access to some of the best minds in the business.

— **Channing Dungey, Executive Vice-President, Drama, ABC Entertainment Group**

If I had my wish, I would insist that every TV writer—from the youngest "baby" staff writer to the most experienced showrunner—read this book! Then I'd get every producer, studio honcho, development executive, and summer intern to read it, too ... because Neil's book really IS the roadmap to TV series in the 21st century!

— **Tana Nugent Jamieson, Senior Vice-President, in charge of all scripted programming, A&E** (*Bates Motel, Longmire, The Glades*)

Neil has not only beautifully and succinctly tackled an enormous subject — what it takes to be a television showrunner — he also has provided a blueprint for any writer forging through the turbulent and ever-changing waters of producing a TV series. He gives good common sense information and advice on working in television. And he writes in a clear, understandable, and entertaining way. But the unique value of the book is the interviews from an impressive list of top showrunners, who recount their own experiences. I'd recommend this book to anyone looking for a career in the television business.

— **Stephen Tao, Television Executive, Bad Robot Productions**

Neil's is the book that finally demystifies the process of breaking into <u>and staying in</u> the business. It's an invaluable guide filled with step-by-step advice about how to navigate the not-always-obvious industry pitfalls. Ignore his advice at your own risk!

— **Elizabeth Wise Lyall, Current Programming, CW Television Networks**

Neil Landau, screenwriter, producer and one of Hollywood's best writing teachers, has blessed us with this amazing guide to the world of television writing and show running. I wrote and produced television for twenty-three years and I learned invaluable skills from this book that I never even acquired on the job.

— **Fred Rubin, veteran TV producer; UCLA Professor of Screenwriting; and Instructor for the ABC/Disney, Warner Brothers, and Nickelodeon Writers' Fellowships**

Bound to Create

You are a creator.

Whatever your form of expression — photography, filmmaking, animation, games, audio, media communication, web design, or theatre — you simply want to create without limitation. Bound by nothing except your own creativity and determination.

Focal Press can help.

For over 75 years Focal has published books that support your creative goals. Our founder, Andor Kraszna-Krausz, established Focal in 1938 so you could have access to leading-edge expert knowledge, techniques, and tools that allow you to create without constraint. We strive to create exceptional, engaging, and practical content that helps you master your passion.

Focal Press and you.

Bound to create.

We'd love to hear how we've helped you create. Share your experience:

For my brother, Michael, who always
watched TV with me, back then.
And to Trent, who always watches TV with me now.

CONTENTS

---

* Interview on companion website: http://www.focalpress.com/cw/
landau.

ABOUT THE AUTHOR

Neil Landau is a screenwriter, producer, author, and professor in the MFA in Screenwriting and Producing Programs at UCLA School of Film, Television, and Digital Media. His movie credits include the teen comedy *Don't Tell Mom the Babysitter's Dead*; his TV credits include *Doogie Howser, M.D., Melrose Place, The Magnificent Seven, The Secret World of Alex Mack, Twice in a Lifetime,* and MTV's *Undressed* and pilot deals at CBS, Disney, Freemantle, Lifetime, Spelling, and Warner Bros. Television. He served as Executive Script Consultant for several years for Sony Pictures Television International, is a faculty member in the Academy of Television Arts and Sciences, and just won a Spanish Academy ("Goya") Award for best screenplay adaptation for the animated movie *Tad the Lost Explorer* (2012); he is currently working on the sequel and on a new animated movie for Paramount: *Capture the Flag.*

ACKNOWLEDGMENTS

I am most grateful to the illustrious showrunners interviewed in this book for generously and graciously taking the time to share their knowledge, insights, and hard-earned wisdom.

To my crackerjack editor, Trisha Chambers, who always makes it fun because (1) she's so organized; (2) she's so smart; (3) she loves TV, too.

It takes a village, and I certainly couldn't have built this one without these industrious associate editors: Spencer Ballou, James Morris, and Tom Austin.

Enormous amounts of respect and gratitude to these friends and colleagues for their encouragement and support: Hal Ackerman, Alexander Akopov, Eyal Alony, Cary Brokaw, Channing Dungey, Sorche Fairbank, Jordi Gasull, Ben Harris, Jennifer Johnson, Sergey Kaluganov, Allison Liddi-Brown, Pamela K. Long, Denise Mann, Laurie Megery, Cory Miller, Irina Pivrovna, Janis Richardson, Mike Stein, David Stern, and Richard Walter.

Thanks to Dennis McGonagle and Carlin Reagan at Focal Press.

And special thanks to my sons, Noah and Zach, just for being awesome.

FOREWORD

Writing this book was like stepping into quicksand. My last book was about writing movies, which are finite; once a movie is finished, it can be dissected, analyzed, and interpreted by audiences. But sequels aside, a movie is intended to end—its story set in stone. A classic movie is an indelible, singular sensation.

A television series, on the other hand, is a fluid, continuously unfolding story. The plot thickens. Mysteries deepen. Characters evolve. The end of one episode presents us with more questions than answers. The detectives may catch this perpetrator, but tune in next week for more crime and punishment.

We forge ongoing relationships with our favorite TV series that can often run for a hundred episodes over many years or even decades. As we watch iconic TV characters win and lose, struggle and endure, we feel what they feel; we root for them, pass judgment, yell at the TV screen— and come back for more. They become part of our lives. And when a long-running series ends, we collectively feel the sense of loss.

This book isn't just about classic TV series of yesteryear. Sure, I pay homage to those shows, too. But this is the New Golden Age of Television, so I wanted to stay current. And yet, with the sheer volume of TV series on hundreds of channels, watching *all* the shows on the air—let alone keeping abreast of their latest plot developments—is a virtually impossible task.

I could have narrowed the playing field by solely focusing on pilot episodes, but I also wanted to explore how series build, evolve, and sustain over time. And so I found myself catching up on long-running series and falling down many rabbit holes. The overwhelming challenge was selecting the best TV series to analyze and which showrunners to interview, along with the trepidation of overlooking someone's favorite show (I apologize in advance for that). And even as I'd complete an interview with a current showrunner and discuss the show's latest developments, that series would keep forging ahead, making it harder and harder to get a foothold (hence my quicksand analogy).

When I was a kid and we got our first color TV, there were only three channels: ABC, CBS, and NBC. Now there are almost a thousand. The technology has substantially changed, prompting a steady migration away from the big broadcast networks and the creation of hundreds more niche cable channels (many owned by the parent companies of broadcast networks). If you go by a college dorm, you won't see many TV sets in students' rooms; if they're watching TV, it's probably on their iPads and laptops and smart phones. Regardless of *how* they're watching, I'm confident that the best storytelling today exists not in movie theaters but on TV. Sure, reality shows can provide us with a sense of spontaneity, immediacy, and voyeurism. But only great scripted dramas and comedy series can transport us on a journey that transcends real life. Stay tuned.

INTRODUCTION

What Is a Showrunner?

In movies, the director is king. In the television series business, the show-runner calls the shots. A showrunner is almost always the head writer and executive producer (EP) of a TV series. Very often, but not always, the show-runner is also the creator of the series. In many cases, a TV network will buy a series "pitch" or a completed pilot script that's already been written specu-latively (on "spec") by a screenwriter who has little or no producing experi-ence. In such cases, the studio and network will work together to assign an experienced showrunner to supervise all the writing on the series, and this Executive Producer will also be the last and final word on all production decisions, including casting, locations, art direction, the hiring of the direc-tors for each episode, and all final cuts in postproduction for the series. Not all EPs are showrunners, but all showrunners are credited as EPs.

Non-showrunner EPs can either be directing producers, impresarios from the series' production company, or perhaps the producer who packaged the pilot by discovering the writer or nurturing the project from its inception. Blockbuster screenwriters who transition into writing and producing TV series (which has become more and more prevalent in the last few years) will often be awarded an EP credit and might also be entrusted with run-ning the show. EPs might also earn their title from a series that originated in another format (movie to TV) or a series that was successful in another country (called "incubation") and then exported to the United States.

Showrunners can be one person in the leadership position or writing partners who have ascended to the highest levels on a TV series. Although there are exceptions, most showrunners earn their positions after many years of paying their dues, working their way up the food chain. On a TV series, all upper level writers on staff receive the title of "producer" with a prefix added according to his/her relative position on the food chain (which most higher level writer/producers take very seriously). In addition to breaking stories and writing scripts, many high level writer/producers will participate in pre-production decisions (casting, locations, on-set supervision in respectful collaboration with the director, post production, network note sessions). Depending on the showrunner, some story editors and staff writers may or may not be invited to participate in extra producer responsibilities. If you're fortunate enough to be included in the whole process: seize the opportunity! It's an invaluable learning experience. But make sure that you're an unobtrusive observer, and only offer your opinion when asked for it.

Here's the hierarchy:

- Showrunner (credited as EP; customarily also head writer)
- EPs (who are not the actual showrunner): writer/producer
- Co-executive producer: writer/producer
- Supervising producer: writer/producer
- Producer: writer/producer or supervisor of production.
- Consulting producer: writer/producer
- Co-producer: writer/producer (with very few, if any, producer responsibilities)
- Executive story editor: highest level staff writer
- Story editor: promoted from "staff writer"
- Staff writer: often called "baby staffer" (this is an entry-level writer position)
- Freelance episode writer: hired to write a script but not on staff

Suffice it to say that the showrunner can earn millions of dollars per season and, if the series is successful, garner all the credit and accolades. By the same token, if the series gets cancelled after its first few airings, the showrunner will take all—or most of—the heat.

Every member of the TV series (actors, writers, directors, producers, crew) works under the auspices of the showrunner who must answer to the senior executives at the studio and the TV network.

The Successful Showrunner Checklist*

According to my informal showrunner poll, the following are the most essential qualities and skills for the successful management of a scripted, episodic TV series:

- **Staying on time and on budget:** According to veteran showrunner, Jeff Melvoin (*Early Edition, Alias, Army Wives*) and cofounder/director of

---

* Remarks quoted are excerpts from the showrunner roundtable discussions sponsored by *Variety* and *Hollywood Reporter* (2013).

the Writers Guild of America Showrunner Training Program, a show-runner's first responsibility in episodic television is *quality scripts, on time.* Time is money. Keeping a series running on time and on budget—from script through post-production—is essential for all showrunners.

- **Forecasting:** The ability to anticipate future story needs and production problems. According to Kevin Williamson (current showrunner of *The Following*), "You can map it out all you want, but when you come up with better stuff, you start changing things." For this reason, many showrunners prefer to break story for no more than five episodes at a time, giving them the opportunity to course correct. For *Homeland* co-creator/showrunner Alex Gansa, "We didn't even know at the beginning of the year that Carrie and Brody would spend time in each other's company very often. In episode 3 or 4 of the first season, I was in dailies and it was as if the word 'chemistry' was flashing on top of the screen [. . .] and we had to go back and look at scripts we'd already written and figure out a new way to tell the story." According to *Mad Men* showrunner Matthew Weiner, "I didn't know Don [Draper] and Roger [Sterling] were friends until episode 9." For *Suits* showrunner Aaron Korsh, "The most fun is when we surprise ourselves. If a plot discovery shocks us in the [writers'] room, then we know we're really on to something." For *The Americans* showrunner Joel Fields, "We thought we knew everything from the beginning, but then about half of it dropped out [in service of better, juicier ideas]. . . . It was an unintentionally hybrid process."

- **Vision and Scope:** Showrunners are involved with every facet of the series, making decisions on casting, locations, lighting, music, production design, and everything in between. Mood and tone are vital showrunner decisions from the get-go. According to *The Americans* showrunner Joel Fields, "The standard for television series is really high now. Today's audiences are expecting a cinematic experience." According to Kevin Williamson, "We're creators. We paint a picture."

- **Development and Adaptation:** Many current series are based upon shows from other countries (*Homeland, The Killing, The Bridge, House of Cards*), books (*Game of Thrones, True Blood, Orange is the New Black*), and even classic movies (*Bates Motel*). In developing/adapting source material, the showrunner must evaluate what to retain from the original and what to change. Putting a new spin on Sherlock Holmes and his many iterations, *Elementary* showrunner Rob Doherty's vision was of "Sherlock Holmes in repair; the man [who was] always ten steps ahead of everyone [is] now secretly maybe only two steps ahead." Doherty's intention was/is to honor the spirit of the original without being a slave to it. For showrunners Carlton Cuse and Kerry Ehrin on *Bates Motel*, "Our goal was not merely to do an homage; that wasn't interesting to us. We wanted to create our own *Psycho* franchise." And since Norma Bates was already dead in the film, they were wide open. For *House of Cards* showrunner Beau Willimon, regarding his adaptation for Netflix, "The voice [of the series] is way more powerful than the actual mechanics of what you're adapting; that's what people really connect to."

- **Wizardly Writing (and Rewriting and Rewriting) Talent:** Even Aaron Sorkin admits that he has many more "off" writer days than days when he's totally on and in the zone. And yet, a TV series is like a monster that must constantly consume new story and new scripts . . . so you need to keep writing to meet the schedule no matter what. Having a well-toned writing muscle and the discipline to crank out new material and "bring up" scripts in need of revision—and fast—is a crucial skill for every writer and/or producer on staff. I always tell my TV writing students that the best way to succeed on a writing staff is the ability to hand in *solid first drafts* (that require only minimal revisions). Showrunner Kevin Williamson, a self proclaimed "control freak" (so you know it's true) doesn't care about your personality to be on his writing staff—*if* you can deliver a great script every time you're up at bat—which is extremely difficult to accomplish and a rare commodity in the episodic TV business.

Here are the basic steps for staff writers:

- Some shows require their lower-level writers on staff to submit a brief outline (called a "beat sheet") and once that barebones structural document is approved by the showrunner, the writer will proceed to a more substantive (eight- to eighteen-page) outline. Series with all senior writers on staff (at co-executive producer level and higher) usually forego the formal outline and delve directly into a first draft.
- In general, once the outline is approved by the showrunner and/or senior-level producers, the writers on a one-hour drama series will have anywhere from two weeks (usually only occurs at the beginning of the season) to as short as two days (during the crunch time of production) to write a first draft of the teleplay. On a cable series with a short order of, say, only twelve episodes, sometimes *all* the scripts are written before production even starts. Other series can't afford that luxury. A critically acclaimed basic cable drama series' showrunner told me that even under the best of circumstances, her writers only get five days plus two weekends to hand in a first draft—and usually less. She runs a tight ship.
- These steps in the writing process are determined by the comfort level of the particular showrunner, studio, and network. A major challenge for staff writers at every level is keeping up with the myriad notes that continue trickling in from the studio, network, showrunner, other writers/producers on staff, production department heads (known as "keys"),

and the actors. The showrunner or co-executive producer will dissemi-
nate those comments to you as you're working on your script. Suffice
it to say that it can be a tracking nightmare for each scriptwriter and
for the show's script coordinator,** as every episode written before and
directly after yours will impact your teleplay. It's a fluid process necessitating a showrunner to possess not only great writing skills, but also a
sharp memory.

- On sitcoms, the schedule differs. The writing staff collectively "breaks" a
story and the writer(s) will write up a beat sheet and/or outline in a couple of days, get feedback from the showrunner, and then go write a first
draft in about a week. Script deadlines can vary quite a bit from show to
show. According to a veteran, Emmy Award–winning sitcom showrunner, "It depends what time of the year it is. If it's early in the season, they
might get even two weeks. At the end of the season, maybe only four
days, but they probably would split a script with someone." Once written, this first "writer's draft" will be discussed and collectively rewritten,
then punched up in time for the table read (with all the actors, writers,
producers, and network execs present).

- With sitcoms, the table read will often occur on a Monday. Based on the
feedback from those present at the table read, the script will be rewritten during the same week. On a multi-camera sitcom, as the script is
being revised, the director and cast will rehearse the episode (with script
changes arriving daily), so that the best possible script will be ready in
time for the live taping on Friday night of the same week.

- On single-camera sitcoms, after the table read, the script will also be
rewritten, but there is much less latitude for script changes, as scenes will
be rehearsed and shot in the same day. If the script changes substantially,
the scenes already shot will necessitate reshoots (known as "pick ups").

- **Patience:** It can take a new series time to find both its creative legs and
connection to an audience. For Carlton Cuse (*Lost, Bates Motel*), "The
first season is exploratory," [analogous to] "putting out an apartment
building fire with a garden hose." Getting the audience emotionally
invested in the characters trumps everything. Or as Kevin Williamson
puts it, "All stories need to be emotional or no one will give a shit."

- **Delegation and Collaboration:** All showrunners must wear many hats
and become skilled at multitasking, but it takes a village to run a show.
Some showrunners, such as David E. Kelley (*The Practice, Ally McBeal,
Boston Legal*), surround themselves with producers who can take care of

---

** The script coordinator is the person in charge of continuity on all *scripts*. This job
differs from the script supervisor, who is the person in charge of continuity on set
between takes, among other major production responsibilities.

all production issues so that Kelley can sit in his office and write virtually every script—longhand—and then his assistant types it all up and distributes it. For showrunner Matthew Carnahan (*House of Lies*), having both a nonwriting EP on his team and a strong postproduction supervisor eases the strain on his time, so he can primarily focus on the writing. For him, this is the key to efficiency. Delegation is only possible when showrunners have a strong team to hand things off to—with the confidence that they can deliver. Aaron Sorkin is always looking for young, smart, new writers that he can mentor. Working on one of his series, writers are not going to be doing much script writing—"But they will get a one- to two-year paid apprenticeship. If you hire eight to ten writers and three are left by midseason, that's a good haul, and you'll hold on to those people for the rest of your life." Michael Schur, *Parks and Recreation* showrunner, (facetiously) claims to have "delegated as much as possible without getting fired."

- **Diplomacy:** Otherwise known as managing egos with actors, writers, studio and network execs, and production staff. According to showrunner Mindy Kaling (*The Mindy Project*), to keep the morale up on a writing staff, "finding the good in a draft" is important. Showrunners receive notes from many sources. The newer the show, the less experienced the showrunner, and the lower the ratings: the greater the volume of notes. Successful showrunners know how to filter the plethora of notes down to their staffs for the best net result. A harsh, unvarnished note can only serve to shut a writer down—when the showrunner (ideally) wants to inspire and not tear down a writer's confidence. Sometimes this can be accomplished with a degree of handholding; in other instances (depending on the specifics and the proficiency of a particular writer) being blunt without bullshit can be the best way to go. Bottom line: the notes almost always need to be disseminated—and not verbatim—from the network or studio execs. Writers speak the language of writers and can usually determine the "note beneath the note" and are better equipped as to how to address the critique. And strong showrunners will have a conversation with the network and/or studio execs to fight for or against notes before getting the writer involved. Not every note from the network/ studio *always* needs to be addressed; often it's a simple clarification and the note goes away. But there are also those times when an entire outline or script is "kicked out" by the network or studio. It's costly and has an enormous ripple effect on the production machine, but it happens. From my own experience on writing staffs, a little praise goes a long way. Yes, you're getting paid an enormous amount of money every week, but that can only ease the strain of harsh criticism and outline notes WRITTEN IN ALL CAPS (as if they're SCREAMING at you) to a certain degree.

Showrunners need to be good role models for the rest of the team—and need to develop a thick skin to handle criticism from execs, production staff, and detractors on social media. One of the biggest changes in the TV business in recent years is the role of social media, from Twitter to fan sites and message boards. Virtually all showrunners I interviewed follow some of these threads—and most admit to being influenced by strong (viral) reactions to their series' latest plot developments. In the past, showrunners and writing staffs worked in a vacuum and their only barometer of audience reaction was Nielson ratings. And while TV ratings are still calculated by networks and advertisers to determine viewership numbers and ad rates, ratings are only part of the picture—not the be all, end all. A showrunner needs to trust his/her gut and not be too swayed by ratings and immediate fan reactions.

- **Organization Skills:** For *Anger Management*'s showrunner, Bruce Helford, who writes and executive produces two episodes per week, plus runs two writing rooms simultaneously to keep up with the staggering demand for material: having a writing staff packed with showrunner-level talent is crucial to meeting their script deadlines. For production budgets, schedules, writing timeframes and deadlines, I highly recommend an excellent book on the subject: *The One-Hour Drama Series: Producing Episodic Television* by veteran TV producer Robert Del Valle (Silman-James Press).

- **Fortitude and Stamina:** Running a TV show is tantamount to running a marathon. It's not a sprint, so you've got to pace yourself. It's a daunting, overwhelming, monumental task. For veteran showrunner Aaron Sorkin, "It's a whole year of always having a term paper due every week." Right after you finish one episode, no matter how good it is, you immediately need to start on the next one. In the positive column, a showrunner like *Mad Men*'s Matthew Weiner is at the point in his stellar career where everything he writes gets shot and aired. In the negative column is the Sisyphean task of cranking out brilliant scripts over and over and over. Or as Weiner puts it, "It's like winning a pie-eating contest and the prize is more pie."

- **Homework:** Remarkably, showrunners tend to watch each other's shows—with a mixed reaction of respect, competitiveness, and awe. And most showrunners work nights and weekends to stay on stop of the workload. Or as former *Walking Dead* showrunner Glen Mazzara so aptly put it, "Showrunners don't sleep."

1

PREPARE THE PERFECT PITCH

Before we get into what and how to pitch your original TV series, first we need to discuss where to pitch it—and that means *branding*.

Once upon a time, in the old, pre-cable, pre–satellite dish TV, pre-Internet download days, there were three major TV networks: ABC, CBS, and NBC. Decades later, FOX TV became the fourth major network, followed by the WB and UPN—which then merged to become the CW.

And then cable TV exploded—fast and furious—and now we have hundreds of cable networks, each with their own niche audience and content. Niche broadcasting means that each network now has its own signature brand tailored to its core demographic. For example, Lifetime is "Television for Women"; Spike is geared toward men; Nickelodeon is geared to kids; Logo to gays and lesbians; MTV to high schoolers and collegiates; SyFy to science fiction geeks and women who love them; HGTV to house hunters and designers, and so on.

Premium (pay) cable channels, like HBO and Showtime, were once known for showing movies several months after they left the multiplex, but then the premium channels started producing their own original series—*The Sopranos, Deadwood, Weeds, Homeland*—sans commercial interruptions plus profanity and nudity. AMC, FX, and Starz followed with darker, edgier content than the major broadcast networks—which still reach the biggest, most diverse audience and tend to keep the content of their series safer for a more universal, more conservative viewership. But ABC, CBS, NBC, and FOX all have their own niche brands that cater to their loyal audiences which in turn appeal to big, national advertisers. The sweet spot for broadcast networks is located at the intersection of Madison Avenue and Main Street USA. If they're fishing for viewers, they're casting the widest net.

Meanwhile, if you have cable or a dish, your TV surfing possibilities are now virtually endless. Of course this doesn't stop most TV viewers from routinely grousing that "there's nothing on!"

The niche of each channel is what's known as branding, or what's in their "wheelhouse." Each network has its own specific programming needs based upon what's working for them ratings wise; which audience they're targeting; which advertisers they're trying to attract; and what's compatible with their current hit series.

For many years now, CBS has dominated the primetime landscape with their procedural crime series, the *CSI* and *NCIS* franchises, along with their hit sitcoms: *Two and a Half Men, The Big Bang Theory, 2 Broke Girls*— and their programming strategy has mainly been "if it ain't broke, don't fix it." With so many of their shows delivering relatively big ratings, CBS has had very little real estate to fill in their schedule. Sure, CBS—and every network—is always on the prowl for that rare, groundbreaking, outside-the-box juggernaut series, but mainly they know their core audience, which tends to be over forty years old and salt of the earth, politically conservative, blue collar, and families.

Of course this can and will change for CBS in the near future as their CSI franchise begins to fade and competition at the other networks challenges them to evolve. But CBS serves as an apt example of branding. They know who they are and what they want. They tend to gravitate toward positive heroes and heroines who fight for truth and justice—and usually prevail. You're not going to see an antihero like Walter White (from *Breaking Bad*) on CBS anytime soon. CBS may have a slew of slickly shot crime-procedural series that feature societal deviants and serial killers—but not in the leading roles. And that's OK by them because CBS also happens to be the parent company of Showtime that offers up *Dexter, Homeland*, and *Weeds*. Consequently, if you were going to pitch a dark, edgy, subversive series featuring a heavily flawed, cynical, antihero as protagonist, CBS wouldn't be the place to do it—at least for now.

When developing a pitch for a new TV series, one of the first questions to ask yourself is, Which networks would be a good fit for the genre, tone, lead characters, and premise? If there is only one possible network, then your premise might be too narrow—too niche. It's the law of averages, so why not increase your odds for a sale by creating a series that has the potential to play on more than one network?

This translates to, perhaps, preparing different variations of the same pitch. For example, let's say you're planning to pitch a series about a family living in a Utopian master planned community—where mysterious occurrences begin to infringe on their idyllic neighborhood. In the version of this series geared to ABC—which tends to cater to women in their twenties and thirties (think *Grey's Anatomy*), you would probably want to emphasize the sexy female characters in their twenties, thirties, and forties. In the CW version of this series, you would want to focus on the rebellious, angst-y teenagers in the community. In the FX version, you'd want to push the envelope and delve into the dark, twisted, and perverse.

There are different variations on the same theme for many TV series concepts, so don't limit yourself by putting all your eggs in one basket. Have a strong vision of your series, but be open to the needs of the marketplace at any given time.

Ann Donahue, Emmy Award–winning writer/producer/showrunner/co-creator of *CSI: Miami*, once offered me this advice on pitching and selling an original series, "Find out what they're looking for and bring it to them."

Great advice, right? But how? Part of navigating the branding marketplace is doing your due diligence before you go in and pitch (and I'll get to strategies of how to pitch further in this chapter). Before you craft your pitch—or write your speculative ("spec") pilot—you'll want to do some reconnaissance ("recon"). If you're fortunate enough to have an effective agent or manager, that's a big part of their jobs; if they're good, they'll always have their eyes and ears to the ground ferreting out what buyers are seeking for the new development season. This might be a show that would be compatible with and complementary to an existing series following the cancellation of an underperforming series. Or maybe the network has a new mandate from a new network president.

Pitching Research

Can you do your own recon and due diligence without an agent or manager? Absolutely. Once you come up with an original idea for a series that you're incredibly passionate and excited about, here are my recommended steps:

1. Determine other current and past series that have a similar tone and feeling of your original series. On which networks do/did they appear? Does that network still have the same programming niche and profile? If yes, do they currently have a series that's too similar? If not, then that network could be a good fit for your series and a great place to pitch.
2. Determine the programming profile and brand of a particular network. Tune in for their shows and stick around to watch the commercials. If you're seeing lots of cosmetics and feminine products being advertised, then you know that network is primarily targeting women. If you're seeing lots of beer and truck commercials, chances are they're targeting men. Commercials are advertisers "pitching" their clients' products to you; to the advertiser, the show you're watching is actually just a delivery mechanism to sell their products to as many consumers as possible. Your job as a TV series creator is to pitch to the network whose advertisers

are pitching to their niche audience. It's a food chain and your show is viewer bait. Sure, you're an artist who wants to dedicate your craft to the making of art, but if you're writing for television, it's all about targeting the eyeballs and delivering the ratings for the buyer. Absent that, no matter how critically lauded your series may be, it's going to get axed.

3. Do your research. What shows are doing well in the ratings for their particular network, and which shows are struggling to attract viewers? A niche network like SyFy isn't going to get the same ratings shares as one of the major broadcast networks, but what's considered a "hit" for that specific network? If you're planning to pitch an original series that evokes one of their struggling or recently cancelled shows, you've already shot yourself in the foot.

4. When you go in to a TV studio or network, be mindful of the credits of the executives to whom you're pitching. Have they been at this studio/network for a while, or did they come over from another niche cable network? Which shows did they champion? Which shows are they most proud of? What kind of taste do they have? Don't assume that they love all of the network's current hit list. They might deplore the current slate of programs and want to shake things up with new concepts and new voices. Conversely, they might want more of the same. Surf the web for interviews and sound bites from these execs. I'm not suggesting that you blatantly pander to them. I *am* suggesting that you appeal to their proclivities. ("Work smarter, not harder" is another Ann Donahue aphorism.)

5. Know your genre inside and out. If your ambition is to create a new, groundbreaking sci-fi series, do your homework and know about every sci-fi series past, present, and on the horizon. Remember, you're not just competing with what's currently on the air, you're also competing with every series in the same genre from the past decade or more. You don't want to be blindsided in a pitch meeting when an exec points out that your "original" series is actually a retread of a cancelled series from last season, or maybe it's too similar to a series that's currently on another network. Know what's fresh and unique about your series. How is it different than what's already out there? How is it the same—but with a twist? You don't need to reinvent the wheel every time. In fact, if you study the TV landscape, most shows are variations on their precursors. *Deadwood* was an edgy, much darker version of countless westerns from *Gunsmoke* to *The Magnificent Seven*. For example, *Lost* was a dark, supernatural, serialized version of *Gilligan's Island*—with a *Twin Peaks* spin. *House, M.D.* turned the heroic doctor show formula on its head with a brilliant physician who has contempt for his patients; *House* was also a new wrinkle in the crime procedural franchise—but instead of criminals, the doctors were investigating and thwarting diseases.

6. Some recon might involve casting. Is there a particular movie star who's seeking a role in a TV series with specific parameters? Is there a network actively developing series concepts for a specific actor?

7. Seek out TV production companies that are actively developing series for the new pitching season. The producers to target are ones with deals at studios and networks, and it might be a good idea to suss out a producer who had a hit series recently, but doesn't currently have any shows on the air; these producers are always aggressively looking for The Next Big Thing and might be more open to hearing pitches and reading spec pilots. The hottest production companies in town, such as J.J. Abrams' Bad Robot Productions, are unlikely, if not completely foreclosed, to hearing unsolicited pitches because they're inundated by top agents pitching projects from their hot clients with proven track records in TV and film. You don't need to shoot for the top tier; you just need a producer with some solid contacts who can help get you in the door. This business is cyclical, so yesterday's hot producer might be weathering a cold spell—and that means he/she might be open to making new relationships with new talent.

8. Know who's reading what and when. For decades, the major broadcast networks have opened their doors to hear new pitches about a month after the up-fronts.[1] The up-fronts are traditionally held in May in New York. New series orders (anywhere from six to thirteen episodes) are placed in mid-to-late May. And then network execs are wont to take vacations before resuming the new development season in June. More recently, the network pitch-buying season has come even later—in July. The networks have budgets of how much they can spend on buying and developing new series pitches, and once they exhaust these budgets, their shopping spree is over—usually by the end of October (although, occasionally, a pitch will sell in November, but that's rare). Based on this schedule, studios and producers are in the development pitch and planning mode for many months prior to June. The suppliers to the networks (i.e., producers and TV studios) like to get their ducks in a row at the beginning of the new year; they'll be watching indie films, reading screenplays and spec pilots, watching graduate student shorts, hunting for hot new playwrights all year round, and then zeroing in on the talent (writers, show creators) they'd like to be in business with for the new network pitching season. If you're trying to get in the door to pitch your original series to a network, producers with a proven track record are the key. The trick is getting them to read your very best work and,

---

[1] The marketplace where networks present new series to their affiliates and, based upon their enthusiasm or lack thereof, decide which pilots will be picked up (green lit) to series.

hopefully, they'll become fans, anoint you at the studio and networks, and become your business partner and advocate in the marketplace. Their job is to find and develop talent and new series concepts. Your job is to make noise and get them to notice you with your impressive body of work.

Once you've determined *where* your new series might be a good fit, the next step is for you to prepare a viable, cohesive, indelible pitch. If you consider yourself a reclusive, reticent, tongue-tied, prone to stage fright writer, then pitching is not the venue for you. Selling a TV series is about showmanship and the creator's passion and charisma. A strong pitch is a performance. It needs to be tightly scripted, rehearsed, timed, edited, memorized, and then come off as effortless, spontaneous, and a whole lot of fun to watch. A good pitch is like a great movie trailer: it entices, teases, and succinctly articulates to the audience what the show is going to be about—all in about fifteen minutes or less.

Pitching Guidelines

Here are my guidelines for preparing and delivering a great pitch for an original series. Every pitch needs to be customized, so these guidelines are not rigid and do not have to be in this precise order. In fact, depending on genre and format, some of these rules may not apply.

1. **Your pitch presentation should have the same tone as the genre of the series.** If it's a comedy, your pitch had better be laugh-out-loud funny. If it's an edgy thriller, it needs to offer suspense, thrills, and chills. If it's a family drama, the pitch needs to evoke empathy and pathos. If it's a crime, legal, or medical procedural series, the pilot story needs to offer a surprising, emotionally resonant mystery.
2. **Set the stage for the pitch before delving into the basic story points ("beats") in the pilot episode.**
   a. What's the basic format (i.e., half-hour dramedy, one-hour drama)?
   b. What's the genre and tone?
   c. What's the principal time period?
   d. What's the main setting? If you were pitching *Once Upon a Time*, you would need to establish two realms.

3. **Make eye contact with everyone.** Don't just pitch to the most powerful player in the room; you're going to need other advocates. Not making eye contact with a junior executive can alienate him or her and cause him or her to torpedo your pitch after you've left the meeting. Be democratic, respectful, and diplomatic.

4. **Once the stage is set, start with a killer teaser to pique their interest.** Everyone loves to hear a great story told by a master storyteller, so start off with a provocative cold opening. Maybe it's facts and stats. Maybe it's a provocative question. Maybe it's a joke that captures the flavor of your comedy.

5. **Once you've effectively grabbed their attention with the teaser, pitch out the basic A and B stories of the pilot episode.** I've found it's best to describe the cast of characters on a need-to-know basis within the context of the story versus as a laundry list. But do not give short shrift to the characters. No matter how delightful and innovative your series' premise might be, a series is only as compelling as its leading players. Present a thumbnail sketch of who's who—but don't snow blind them with too many names and specifics. Do tell them how and when and why we're being introduced to this group of characters at this particular time. How are they uniquely flawed and engaging? What are their primary strengths and weaknesses?

6. **Present the basic structure of the pilot episode.** I like to delineate the act breaks so the execs can get a sense of the tone, pacing, style, and mini-cliffhangers at the end of each act—leading up to the big, climactic cliffhanger at the end of the pilot episode. Ideally, the ending of the pilot episode will be surprising, organically earned, and resonant.

7. **End your pitch of the pilot episode on a high note that portends future conflicts versus too much resolution and harmony.** The primary difference between a TV series and a movie is, by and large, that a movie is intended to be finite; "The End" is intended to be the end of the movie. In contrast, the end of a TV pilot is just the beginning of what is intended to be an ongoing journey for the characters.

8. **Make them care.** Get them invested in the plight of your characters. Keep them on the edge of their seats with suspense—which is generated by their *emotional investment in the characters!* You want your series to get under their skin. You want it to haunt them. You want them to talk to their colleagues and bosses and significant others about it. You want them to lose sleep over it. They say yes, and you make the sale when they simply can't say no.

9. **Clarify the week-to-week of your series.** In other words, what's the franchise? As you'll read in my interview with *The Walking Dead* showrunner, Glen Mazzara, "Great TV is about cool people *doing* cool shit." So it's not enough for you to introduce and describe your characters, it's also essential that you specify what they're going to be doing in each episode.

10. **Show them your series is set on fertile ground. Have at least three examples for future episodes.** This will probably not be necessary, but

be prepared with brief loglines in case they ask. Avoid lots of plot details, but do let them know where the series goes from there. What are the "story engines," that is, what is the series going to be week to week? Is it going to be serialized with an ongoing plotline for the whole season? Or are the episodes going to be closed ended and resolve by the end of each episode by divulging whodunit or the verdict or cure or truth? In a purely serialized series, such as *24, Dallas, Gossip Girl, Breaking Bad, Mad Men, The Walking Dead, Lost, Friday Night Lights,* and *Parenthood,* the ongoing stories in the lives of the characters are the week-to-week franchise. These ongoing, cumulative character plotlines and subplots are called "character arcs."

11. **What is your intention for your series?** Let them know in your pitch so they have a framework for the story you're trying to tell. In a purely procedural series, such as *Law & Order, CSI, Bones, House,* the franchise will be the case of the week. And then there are *hybrid* series that are both serialized and also offer closed-ended A stories, such as *The Good Wife, Grey's Anatomy, Scandal,* and *Once Upon a Time.* The series, *Touch,* featuring Kiefer Sutherland, started out as a character-driven procedural in its first season and evolved into a serialized series in season 2. Know the network's brand and what's working within their wheelhouse. Currently at ABC, hybrid shows are working quite well, while purely serialized shows (such as *Revenge*) are starting to lose steam with viewers.

12. **Briefly and succinctly pitch out the basic mythology of the series.** Keep it simple! Your series' mythology will take the form of a *central mystery*—secrets from the past that are actively hidden or obscured. Mythology is about how the past (aka "backstory") affects the present and future of your series' characters. *Lost* was a serialized show with a deep, rich, ever-expanding mythology that dealt with the mysteries of the island. No need to tell the execs *everything* you know. Not knowing what's going to happen invokes the *central questions* of your series—which is the lifeblood of good television. Even in a sitcom in which nothing fundamental ever really changes and the characters very often stay the same, the fun is knowing not *if* they're going to get out of trouble—but *how*. A good pitch will entice them to ask you questions. If you can end your pitch and then they're brimming with curiosity about what's going to happen next to these characters, they're probably going to buy your pitch just to find out.

13. **Let them know if it's a "premise" pilot or a "non-premise" pilot—** although this should be fairly obvious from your pilot episode.

    A *premise pilot* means that episode 1 is essential to start the series; a premise pilot establishes the premise from day one. *Lost* was a premise pilot because it started with the plane crash. *The Killing* was a premise pilot because it's the first day that Sarah Linden (Mireille Enos) starts investigating the murder of Rosie Larsen and partners up with Stephen Holder (Joel Kinnaman). *Grey's Anatomy* was a premise pilot because it started with the first day of internship for the new residents. *The X-Files* was a premise pilot because it began with Dana Scully (Gillian Anderson) being introduced to Fox Mulder (David Duchovny) and the inception of their partnership. *Homeland* was a premise pilot because it started with POW Nicholas Brody (Damian Lewis) returning home and Carrie Mathison's (Claire Danes) accompanying suspicion of him.

In contrast, a *non-premise pilot* simply drops us into the world of the *series that's already in progress*. It's the first episode for the audience, but it's *not* day one for the characters. It's just *now*. *Mad Men, Game of Thrones, Downton Abbey, Parenthood, Modern Family, E.R.,* and *The West Wing* were non-premise pilots. *The Mentalist, Rizzoli & Isles, Law & Order,* and most of the plot-driven procedural dramas are non-premise pilots. There are also hybrid franchises that begin with a climactic moment and then either flash-forward (such as in the pilot for *The Good Wife* and *Royal Pains*) or flashback (such as in the pilots for *Breaking Bad, The Walking Dead,* and *Damages*). To me, *Friday Night Lights* was a premise pilot because it ends on the debilitating injury of star quarterback Jason Street (Scott Porter) and its effects on not only Coach Eric Taylor (Kyle Chandler) and his family, but also on the whole town of Dillon, Texas. *The Sopranos* was a hybrid pilot because it's Tony Soprano's (James Gandolfini) first day of therapy with Dr. Melfi (Lorraine Bracco).

14. **Think about casting—networks are all about getting the widest audience possible for their brand, so it's always a good idea to have diversity in your cast.** A big exec at a major TV studio recently told me that, given the size of the Hispanic audience, it's now impossible to pitch a series without at least one major Latin role. This isn't about pandering. TV viewers like to see their lives reflected in some way on their favorite series, so think about a multi-ethnic, multigenerational cast. Are their exceptions to this rule? Of course, *Seinfeld, The Sopranos,* and *Friends* immediately come to mind, but times are changing. P.S.: Sometimes it can be useful to offer a casting suggestion even if it's a movie star who's not going to be doing a TV series any time soon or ever—just to create a picture in their minds, "she's Jennifer Aniston with a briefcase." This strategy can also be risky because you might end up choosing someone the exec hates.

15. **If you have a huge canvas of characters for an ensemble series, it can be helpful to prepare a visual aid—such as a chart—to refer to each**

character. I've cut out pictures from magazines and prepared such a chart so they don't get confused about who's who. However, I dissuade you from giving them a printout of a Cast of Characters because then they'll spend the whole pitch looking down at the handout instead of up at you.

16. **A short (three minutes or less) "sizzle reel" can be effective if it's really provocative and well executed.** Beware of anything that looks amateurish and have a contingency for technical snafus.

17. **Props can be a useful selling tool, but don't use them as a crutch.** A gimmick like a bar of FIGHT CLUB soap to sell *Fight Club: The Series* and coming into the meeting with a black eye and bruises might make for a memorable pitch, but their decision to buy the show will be based on the story and characters, not the marketing gimmick.

18. **Finish the pitch, and don't buy it back.** What this means is, when you're done with your rehearsed pitch, shut up. This is crucial to (potentially) closing the sale. After you're done pitching, there's always that excruciating silence in the room that every fiber in your (insecure, neurotic) being will want to fill with embellishment. *Do not give in to this temptation.* When you're done pitching, try to embrace the silence with confidence. Think about having a winning hand in poker. Don't act all arrogant or jittery. Just sit there and let them make the next move. Anything you say beyond your proposed pitch that's not elicited by them can and will be used against you, so don't equivocate. If they have any questions, they'll ask you. If they're ready for you to depart, they'll say thank you. Don't act desperate and ask them when they're going to make their decision. Don't ask them for feedback on the pitch or how you can improve it. Insecurity does not invoke confidence in a buyer.

19. **Hollywood is built on relationships.** Obviously, talent plays a significant part, too, but good relationships close the sale. Any time you sell a pitch, the executive who advocates for it is placing a bet on you. If the executive is unsure that you can deliver the product—a kickass pilot script—then he/she is going to hedge their bets and spend their limited discretionary funds on a more confident, tried and true series creator. If you're a total neophyte, they can always pair you up with an established showrunner should the series go into production. However, for this initial step of ordering the pilot script from you, they need to feel comfortable in their relationship with you and/or place their confidence in your producer to shepherd you through the script development process. Every pitch meeting is a learning opportunity for you, and not the be all, end all of your career—unless you get angry and rude for their not immediately embracing your brilliance and storm out. Be a team player, not a diva. Be magnanimous and flexible even when they take a phone

call or answer an email right in the middle of your pitch. Keep your ego and T.V.C. (thinly veiled contempt) in check. It will only hurt you, not them.

20. **Be a professional.** Show up on time and be prepared. *Never begin a pitch with a disclaimer!* If you're having a terrible day and got a speeding ticket on the way to the meeting, pull yourself together and leave your troubles outside the door.

21. **Don't discuss finances or price quotes in the pitch meeting.** Be the artist and tell them to discuss that stuff with your rep. You're a storyteller, not a lawyer or a haggler.

22. **I generally recommend that you have three pitches prepared when you're meeting with a producer.** If you strike out with one, move on to the next one. However, when you're going in to pitch at a TV studio or network, only pitch one project. You need to project an air of being fully committed, passionate, even obsessed with getting this one project on the air, as opposed to a shoe salesman.

Don't burn any bridges. When you go into a network or studio executive's office, it's extremely important to remember that your first priority is *not* to make the sale. Your first priority is to establish rapport with the exec. They granted you the meeting because they read a sample of your work—and they liked it. Maybe this particular pitch is not for them (for an infinite number of reasons). It's your job not to be crushed by their lack of enthusiasm and/or rejection and to keep the door open. Never argue. Don't try to change their minds; you'll look desperate (the kiss of death in a pitch meeting).

INTERVIEW: Kim Moses and Ian Sander

Kim Moses and Ian Sander Credits

Best known for:

Ghost Whisperer (Executive Producers/ Ian Sander—Director) 2014
Ghost Whisperer (Executive Producers/Directors) 2005–2010
Ghost Whisperer: The Other Side (Web Series)
(Executive Producers/Producers; Kim Moses—Writer) 2007, 2010
Profiler (Executive Producers/Directors/Writers) 1996–1999
I'll Fly Away (Ian Sander—Executive Producer/Producer/Director)
    1992–1993

Emmy Nominated (Drama Series) 1992–1993
Emmy Nominated (Made for Television Movie) 1992
Equal Justice (Ian Sander—Producer) 1991

NL: We are talking about selling, pitching, and packaging, as well as, what makes a viable series and franchise. I'd also like to hear where you think the TV business is heading—and maybe a little on new media. It might be helpful initially to talk about how *Ghost Whisperer* came about since it has been so successful. How did you position that and sell it?

IS: We've been in the network and cable television business. Let's talk first about network which, here in the United States, is CBS, NBC, ABC, FOX, and CW. My father once asked me, "How does your business work?" I thought about it and said, "In drama alone, and you could say the same thing for comedy, every network and/or studio exec, between the months of July and September, is going to hear anywhere from three hundred to five hundred pitches. Of those three hundred to five hundred pitches—and they're from real people, from Kim and I, David Kelley, John Wells, J. J. Abrams, lawyers, agents, they're likely to commission anywhere from fifty to seventy-five scripts. Of those fifty to seventy-five scripts, they're likely to commission ten to twelve pilots. Of those ten to twelve pilots, they will probably pick up three to four. Of those three to four, one, maybe two will be on a second season. When I said that to my father who was at the time eighty-five, he said, "What the hell kind of business is that?" Those are real odds, not to scare, but to challenge. When you go in to pitch, you must find a way to lift your material above those other three hundred to five hundred pitches because they're only going to order fifty of them. And, that's the art of selling for television.

KM: I think the odds that you've given are more for network. But the other thing that has become very difficult, and it feels like there's an insatiable appetite for it, is what they call "loud" as opposed to excellent. The best is that you get both. But "loud" right now is very important because the network model is basically in a different place. It's not as empowered as it was—particularly because there's so much competition. First, there were three networks, then there were four, now there are five . . . plus the DVR. And the DVR is quickly becoming the number one network, believe it or not, because people want to watch their shows when they want to watch them—not when the networks are programming them. And now there's cable. Cable has become the place where a lot of talent wants to work. There's the platform of cable, the platform of video games, the platform of online, and all the digital media competition which is giving the networks a run for their money. But because there's so much money to be made, these platforms are pushing up against the networks and the studios. What *is* giving the networks a run for their money are networks like Univision which are often beating networks like NBC. And that's a new phenomenon which is not going to change because the Latino demographic is very young and very fluid. It is a growing culture which is influencing music, fashion, design—pop culture—with an insatiable appetite for content. The other thing that's happened is that the cable networks have started branding themselves, like Bravo and the History Channel, and are beating out the broadcast networks with brave content swings like the *Hatfields & McCoys*.

IS: If I'm not mistaken, more people saw the History Channel those three nights than watched anything scripted last year on NBC. I think maybe *Sunday Night Football* and maybe *The Voice* or a couple other unscripted shows might have higher ratings, but the reality is that no scripted show beat the History Channel which until that night, most people you talk to didn't know existed.

KM: What's interesting is the *Hatfields & McCoys*' success has empowered Bravo and the History Channel and smaller networks like Ion and other cable outlets. All these cable channels which were solely doing reality programs are now shifting to developing, selling, and programming scripted. That's more competition for the broadcast networks which is an enormous challenge for them—but more opportunity for content creators.

IS: And, now with digital, you have even more people entering, although there's some question as to whether they're successful to begin with. Whether it be YouTube or Hulu—who's going to be doing original programming? We all know that Netflix is already into original programming—and DirecTV. It's obviously growing and you have to think that people aren't jumping into this because it's a loser. These are businesses, these are big corporations that are looking at the business model and saying, "Maybe there's an audience we can reach. Maybe there's a business model there that we could make money on and if there isn't, let's see if we can create a new one." And, therefore, they want to jump in. It's great. In terms of where television is going from a practical sense, that's where it's going.

KM: It's a really exciting time to be in the TV industry because of all of the evolution. It's also a challenging time if you're just being tactical and not strategic—and tactical means creating a great show and just putting it out there. For us as a company, we spend a lot of time talking to futurists and cultural specialists and decoders, networks and studios and chief participant officers of fan groups. But we also go outside of the industry to get lots of points of view. What we've learned is that you have to be tactical *and* strategic. Tactical is creating and developing, selling, and launching a great show, and then making sure that you're continuing to grow that show, not just the show itself, but also the universe of digital platforms which we'll talk about in a little bit. You can't just put a great TV show out there anymore. You also have to be strategic which is having to go out and find that audience, engage with that audience, and create a trust. You do all this before you even launch the show; after the launch, you continue to nurture and grow the relationship with the audience. The biggest mistake I think that Hollywood makes—and it's all of us—is saying, "Well, I don't like this. I wouldn't watch that," because it's not about us. The fan world is all about what have you done for me lately. It's about the people across the country and around the world—the fan bases and the potential viewers. So, when we go into a pitch, that's what we're always thinking about: how to focus the content for that fan base.

We have to make sure that we have a process in place that drives the creative, so at the beginning of every development season, we create what we call a "point of view" document, which is about two hundred pages. It's an analysis of the world for the year: the economy, the culture, how people relate to each other, the interconnectedness . . . We start very broad and narrow the focus more and more, drilling down into the entertainment industry and what's going on with features, books, and television. Then, we go to the networks, studios, cable, and digital media. It's a snapshot of the world at this point in time. We do it through a lot of research, analysis, and relationships with all kinds of experts within and outside of the Entertainment Industry— it's our "discovery" phase and we love it! We meet with the heads of the networks and discuss their programming needs, then we meet with their programmers, research people and creative execs. Once we put the information together, we use this POV as the lense through which to look at all the material we consider developing that season. We see two different things: there's the marketplace in the entertainment industry and there's the global marketplace which is becoming more and more important because of how technology has stitched the world together. Once we have the POV doc in place, we start working with concepts, arenas, pieces of material and writers to match them up—like intricate jigsaw puzzles. Once we feel like we have one plus one equals one thousand, that's when we start working with the writer to craft the pitch. We don't want our material to be residual because that's the "been there, done that" category equals old new. We don't want to be dominant because by the time the networks get ready to order pilots, if your material is dominant, it will appear dated. And if it's emergent, then it may be too early to take the material out and people won't get it. So the halfway mark between dominant and emergent is where we aim to be in development—that's our sweet spot. The thing that gives pitching structure is having a process and a strategy—this will protect the creative.

IS: With *Ghost Whisperer*, Kim and I and John Gray were working on developing another project. We've known John for twenty years. I produced his first television movie in 1989 and I met Kim on the same movie. John and we had the same agent. At that point, we had already been in the series business: *Profiler, I Fly Away, Equal Justice, New York News, The Beast,* and more. We convinced John that we should try to come up with a series which had a paranormal aspect to it. At which point, John Gray gets a call from an executive at CBS, Bela Bajaria who at the time was the Movie of the Week and long form executive. John had recently directed a movie there called, *Helter Skelter*, which did quite well. Bela said she had done a movie with a guy named James Van Praagh called, *Talking to the Dead*, which also did well. It was a four-hour, mini-series (Ted Danson played James). She said, "There's this woman that James introduced me to named Mary Ann Winkowski. She's a real life ghostbuster. She'll come to your house and get rid of the ghosts haunting it. She's amazing! Do you think there's a series in that?" He said, "To tell you the truth, I don't know anything about series, but I'm working on something with Kim Moses and Ian Sander, would you mind if I talked to them?" "Well, if they want to do it, that would be great," she said. And, when John came to us to say, "Do you think this is a series?" We said yes.

KM: We discovered through a Gallup Poll that 70 percent of people between the ages of five and sixty-five believe in ghosts (It starts at age five because of Casper.) And then, we googled *Talking to the Dead* and got 60 million hits, so we said, "That's a show with a built-in audience and it has legs."

IS: So the three of us came up with a pitch for doing a show about a ghost whisperer. Kim and I had a deal at ABC, so we had to pitch it to them first, but sure enough, they passed and we went to CBS. Van Praagh came with us. We had Mary Ann Winkowski on the phone from Ohio while we were in the room, and we said, "Mary Ann's going to talk about what she does." In the middle of her talk on speakerphone, she says, "Am I wrong or is there a file cabinet in there with a plant that's dead on top of it?" We all looked up at the file cabinet and there's a dead plant on it. I looked at Kim and I whispered, "It's sold." And, sure enough, CBS bought the show. It was lots of fun to develop and then John wrote a wonderful script. The pilot then got ordered into production, but it was cast contingent, meaning because it's a single female lead show we have to find the star that the network will approve before we go forward. The thing is that even if a show is not cast contingent, it's cast contingent. If you're doing a single lead show and you don't find the right actor, they're not putting you on. Jennifer Love Hewitt happened to also have a development deal at that time down the hall from us at the studio. We had gotten to know her over the past six months and had talked about doing a show together, but she had just shot a sitcom pilot and was waiting to hear if it was being ordered into series. So, in the meantime, we went out and offered the *Ghost Whisperer* lead to a couple of different actresses—fortunately they passed—and then Love's show did not get picked up.

KM: We knew she was the girl—we knew all along.

IS: We gave her name to CBS, and they said maybe because she had never carried her own series. So we put her in a room with Les Moonves and we believed they would charm each other—and they did. Finally, we offer her the show, and she reads it and loves it. So we went into production on the pilot, John directed it and did a beautiful job. CBS said, "We love the pilot, but we have a lot of great pilots," which I took to be French for "if CBS owned half of it," we're in. So we (the Endeavor Agency and I) brokered a deal between ABC Studios and CBS Studios. The show got on the air, but CBS hated the title. We had title contests to try to come up with a new one, but in the end, we got to go back to *Ghost Whisperer* which we're so glad we did. The show got picked up for Friday nights at 8:00 p.m. on CBS. We did research and found out that 18 percent of the shows from the previous ten years that had premiered since *X-Files* on a Friday night went to season 2. Eighty-two percent did not. And we were on CBS which had *CSI, CSI: Miami, Without a Trace, Cold Case*—all procedurals. And our lead character was a twenty-five-year-old girl who sees ghosts. Now, ever since we did *Profiler*, which was 1996, we have been creating online assets at the intersection of TV and digital media and we learned that's where the real magic is. So to launch *Ghost Whisperer*, we started producing interactive games, newsletters, videos, and lots of other assets which we distributed to *Talking to the Dead* sites, paranormal sites and Jennifer Love Hewitt fan sites. By the time the show came on the air, we were the most buzzed about show of any show coming on that year according to Trendums. The season before it was *Lost*. Over the next five years, we continued to do more and more of this for our show. Every week for every episode, we would create new assets and distribute them to our audience, including bloggers, websites, fansites, etc. Through this process (there's that word again), we built a database which drove the ratings up. Eventually it developed into what we call the "total engagement experience" (TEE). Basically, it's taking a television show and making it the most important component of a more comprehensive entertainment experience. Including multi-platforms which will ultimately drive viewers from one platform to the other in what we call an "infinity loop" that does a number of things: (1) builds ratings, (2) gets press buzz, and (3) creates revenue sources.

An example of a new revenue source happened during the first season when we got a lot of e-mails saying, "We know what it's like to be a ghost whisperer, but what is it like to be a ghost?" So, Kim and I, but really Kim, came up with the idea of doing a web series from the point of view of a ghost. We pitched it to CBS, and they said, "Can you put a car in it?" So we said sure. One thing we've learned is if the network asks you a question, yes is usually the right answer. We went to Detroit and pitched it to General Motors (GM), and they agreed to pay for it and we put a car in it—and the web series ended up winning "Best Web Series" of the year from TVGuide. com. It was called, *Ghost Whisperer: The Other Side*. Not only did GM pay for the web series, but they also became a sponsor of the show's second season. That was a big deal for CBS and us because GM had not been a sponsor the first season. We also did product integration by switching all of our regulars' cars to GM cars for which GM paid the studios for the product integration. It was the first time that a blue chip company got to test drive a prime time network series through an original web series, and eventually, *Wired* and *Forbes* did stories on it. Whether it was mobile apps, graphic novels, our companion book *Ghost Whisperer: Spirit Guide*, or the four years of web series, all of these platforms ended up giving the show a branding presence that ultimately helped keep it on the air for 107 episodes, drive it into syndication on three networks and cable outlets, and be broadcast in 169 territories around the globe.

NL: Do other producers, studios, or networks come to you now to create this "total engagement" for their series?

IS: Yes, we now do it for other TV shows including *Desperate Housewives*, *Ugly Betty*, and *Ghost Whisperer* in syndication on the Syfy Network and WE. Often it's "one-offs" instead of the whole multiplatform approach. What is important, which is much harder though, is to have this holistic approach to marketing—it takes a lot of creative energy but it's worth it. And the other component that's really valuable is our "AOP: Audience Outreach Program." So now, when we go in to pitch a pilot, we will not only bring material for the pilot, like the agenda, the show description, visual aids, and an expert, but we also bake into the pitch the TEE. As twenty-first-century producers, we feel it's our job to develop the show, pitch and sell it, produce it, and then deliver the eyeballs through our TEE.

KM: The first time we did the TEE, we did it as a matter of survival to keep our show on the air and build an audience. But then it was so successful that we started doing it for other shows and then we started doing it for feature films—we just worked on *Hotel Transylvania* and *Happy Feet II.* Delightful! We've done it for Warner Bros. and Sony, as well as some of the other major studios. People have asked us, "Isn't it hard to run a show and do all these other things?" Interestingly, it is not because it's all a creative process and it's all going the same way like spokes in a wheel moving at high speed but in perfect sync.

What it's really like is putting your show on steroids. When we go in to pitch, we do the traditional pitch, but then we bring in the whole back end as well with social media. We believe that entertainment companies have three points of engagement: (1) the content, (2) the technological device, and (3) the social conversation.

For us as a company, we have a stake in the ground for Smart TV. We've been talking about second and third screens forever, and finally the entertainment industry is starting to value it. Because viewers are in the habit of using second or third screens, we want to give you an experience on those complimentary platforms which doesn't draw your attention away from the TV show or feature film, but rather enhances the experience.

IS: Kim gave a lecture at MIT about two or three years ago, and one of the things that the people said was, "We've heard this before—why bother doing it? It only helps the studio and the network." And she said, "No, I'm here to tell you that I have a kid in private school thanks to the TEE." *Ghost Whisperer* ran for five years and *Profiler* for four. Both shows got to syndication. Obviously, you have to have a good show. The actors, the writers, the directors are the most important part, but sometimes it's not enough. So I'm not saying that *Ghost Whisperer* was only a hit because of the TEE and all our transmedia storytelling, but I don't know if it would have been as big a hit without all of this either.

KM: Launching shows seven or eight years ago, when all those shows were monster hits, is different than launching a show now. Today, you can't just launch a show.

NL: When you hear a concept initially, because you two must hear a lot of pitches, and you say, "That sounds interesting to me." The very next question is, "Where can I sell it?"

KM: Ian brought in several books the other day, and when I heard the second one I thought, "That's a series!" because I knew through the POV lens that we had created—we knew we could sell it to CBS who wants to hold on to the mother lode of what they're doing, but they also want to appeal to a younger audience, so they're looking for cop shows with a twist.

IS: Last fall they came out with *2 Broke Girls* and now they have a younger female audience. So now the question for them is, "What's the drama version that can platform off of that which will give us a female hit that keeps the *2 Broke Girls*' audience?" It will be a subtle change. Just like how *Survivor* led to *Amazing Race* and *CSI* beget the other two *CSI*s. Wherever they've had a hit, they knew how to build from it.

NL: *The Good Wife* has been a big hit for them.

IS: They like that they have a show which is getting buzz and is up for awards because there aren't that many network shows that are competing with those cable companies for awards. *The Good Wife* is one of the ones that is. It's a very highly respected show. To be able to hit the quality mark twenty-two times a year as opposed to twelve or thirteen with a year off like some of the cable shows have—that's impressive.

NL: What are the essentials of a pitch? I would imagine that you need a very strong logline.

KM: Yes, and you need a *great* title. Last year started the year of you've got to have a great title.

NL: What's the difference between a logline and a hook?

KM: A logline is a marketing tool for the network and the studio. They need it to sell up (to their bosses and sponsors) and to sell out (to the press and viewership). Now everyone knows you can't summarize a great show in one sentence. There are supposed to be so many different levels and nuances, but the logline needs to tell you what world you're in and what the characters represent in that world—and it has to communicate the tone too.

IS: Keep in mind that usually when you're pitching a show, you're not pitching it to the person who's ultimately going to put it on the air. It will have to be re-pitched. So you have to give them something they can use. Sometimes it's a logline, sometimes it might be material like a book, or it may be a poster or an expert. You want to give them as many tools as you can, so they can pitch up.

NL: What about a hook?

IS: A hook is almost like a copy line: "Just when you thought it was safe to go back in the water."

NL: Now, franchise is tied to the question of, what's the element each week? With *Ghost Whisperer*, it was a new spirit each week.

IS: For the most part, the best network television shows are shows where the audience can be satisfied by the end of the show with some closed-ended element. There are exceptions. *Lost* being one of them. Underneath that, we have what we call a mythology which gets people to come back every week. Often that's an ongoing quest or a mystery that's unfolding. So, you want something that is satisfying, self-contained, but has an underlying mythology. With *Profiler*, for example, you had the case of the week, but you also had the fact that our lead character, Sam [Ally Walker], was being stalked by someone who killed her husband, and he was manipulating her life in strange and fascinating ways. She wanted to catch her stalker and he wanted to catch her—a great cat and mouse game on both parts. If you have both of those things going, that's a home run.

NL: When you pitch in the network room, are you going to pitch all of these out: the arena, the tone, the world, the characters, the tease, and maybe the basic elements? How much will they present? A basic, bare-boned pilot episode?

KM: The best pitches are when we set the project up with why its culturally relevant, why here/why now and why this writer specifically. Then the writer does the world, the characters, the triangles between the characters, the themes and then launches into the teaser and first act of the pilot, ending with some juicy cliffhanger. From there on, the writer does not pitch from beat to beat to beat. It's more of a broad pitch of the A, B, C stories and why we're supposed to care about those stories and the characters and why they're relevant to the series. During the pitch, there's a little bit of dialogue and maybe a scene or two which dimensionalizes the characters. Then, the pitch ends with the pilot finale. Finally, we go into a couple of episode ideas to demonstrate the "legs" of the show, and an arc for a couple of the main characters to demonstrate how this fits into the mythology. I always feel it's important to get two things across with writers: (1) setting up the world before you go into the characters and (2) why this writer is passionately connected to this material. We sold a show to NBC last year, and they told us that the reason they bought it was because both ourselves and the writer were so passionate about the material. When we go into the pitch in the first place, Ian and I always clearly set up the room because you never know when they're running from room to room if they remember what all the loglines are. We set it up with the title and the logline and why we're there. I think it's unfair for us to assume that the executives are going to be able to embrace the material without you setting the table.

NL: Can an unknown first-time writer without staff experience or movie cred sell a pitch?

IS: It's hard. You have to make your pitch and your show unignorable. If there's any way to ignore it, they will—how can they not with hundreds of pitches swirling around them? Maybe you do this by attaching a book that went through the roof or the writer of a book or feature film that went through the roof. Or an expert or director they can't ignore. Or even if you can attach a star, but that's harder to do.

KM: I don't think it's fair to say that you can't roll the dice in this business or look for your entrée. It's only because over these last two years (and I think it's going to change again because everything is cyclical) it's been all about: Who are the eight-hundred-pound guerillas and how do we get into business with them? The Internet has made our business a much more democratic process. We have a friend, Kevin Tancharoen, who was a dancer and a choreographer, and then he directed *Fame*. But instead of doing another movie right away, he took *Mortal Combat* the game and shot a web series, which was about six or eight minutes long, that he paid for out of his own pocket. He was so smart because he picked this material where there was a huge following—every kid in America was playing *Mortal Combat* at the time. The reason we know about it is because he is a friend of our son, Aaron, and he shot some of it at our house. One morning, a few months later, our youngest son comes running into the house and says, "Kevin's video is on the front page of YouTube!" By the time Declan told us that, it had already had 1.2 million hits on the first day's posting. In the next two days, it had 6 million hits and was building. Then, Kevin got a call from Warner Bros., who owns the property, and was scared to death that he was going to get sued. But they had called to ask him if he would direct the *Mortal Combat* feature. It's hard—the odds are against you, but there are still opportunities, if you're clever and industrious. You don't have to get in line like we had to get in line when we started in the business.

2

EXPLORE A NEW ARENA

Great television series provide us with a glimpse into an unknown world or a world we *think* we know—until we see it from an insider's perspective. I always tell my feature film screenwriting students to think of the principal setting of their screenplays as another character in the story. This guidance applies equally, if not more so, to the world of a TV series. The "arena" of your series is its setting, but also encompasses time period, geography, weather, local customs, vernacular, style, traffic, values, social mores, and cultural, political and religious influences.

Sons of Anarchy, created by Kurt Sutter, shows us the inner workings of an outlaw motorcycle club based in the fictional town of Charming (in the Central Valley of California). As we discover more about the characters and the almost-Shakespearean power dynamics of the show, we get a closer look at protagonist Jackson "Jax" Teller (Charlie Hunnam) as he begins to question his position in the club and, by extension, his humanity.

The Sopranos invited us into the work life and family life of Tony Soprano and provided us with a glimpse into the New Jersey mafia. *Breaking Bad* shows us how an unassuming high school chemistry teacher, Walter White (Bryan Cranston), learns to cook and distribute crystal meth. In this case, we're inside Walt's head. As he learns, we learn.

Six Feet Under granted us an all-access pass to the Fisher family through their funeral home business. *Big Love* showed us the quotidian existence of a polygamous family.

There is validity to the ol' writing axiom to *Write what you know*. But I think that's way too limiting. Sure, write what you know, but what you don't know, *research*! Whether you're a naturally curious person or not, the only reason for a writer to avoid research is sheer laziness. For me, research can be invigorating, fun, and, let's face it, much easier than writing. Instead of staring at the blinking cursor on your computer, you get to go out into the field, explore new places, and interview real people (instead of dauntingly inventing them from whole cloth).

Researching a New World

When I decided to write a pilot about the Federal Witness Protection Program (officially known as Witness Security or WitSec), I knew virtually nothing about this branch of the U.S. Marshals Service. What intrigued me about this series concept was the thematic question of whether or not a person can ever truly escape the past. I also liked the high stakes of danger and reinvention for survival. I knew this was a ripe arena to explore because, at the time (before *In Plain Sight* was developed and picked up by the USA network), there had never been a TV series about WitSec. I also knew it was viable because it was extremely difficult to penetrate the veil of secrecy that hangs over the WitSec program. I knew if I was going to be able to write about the specifics of WitSec, I would need to become an expert on the subject. Easier said than done. How does a screenwriter get an inside view of a branch of government dependant on secrecy? I did months and months of extensive research via websites, non-fiction and fictional books, and interviews with FBI agents (U.S. Marshals and WitSec, for obvious reasons, declined to talk to me). The more I researched, the more fascinated I became with the arena. In addition to impressive stats about WitSec—such as the fact that not a single protected witness *who has followed WitSec's stringent protocol* has ever been killed since the inception of the program—I also needed a window into how it all worked. Who got into the program, under what kind of circumstances, and how did they manage to stay alive? I also needed to decide on the POV of my arena. Should the series be from the perspective of the witness and his family, or from the perspective of the U.S. Marshals (known as WitSec field inspectors)?

Once I felt confident that I could effectively capture the verisimilitude of this world, I then needed to find a way into my pilot episode. For example, I knew that the canvas for my intended arena was much too large. WitSec is a national organization with thousands of witnesses and field inspectors. I knew I had to narrow the field to one regional office, and I decided that my series would work best from the POV of a chief inspector so that each episode logistical could focus on a particular witness. In doing my research, I also learned that the majority of the witnesses are relocated to the Midwest for both logistical and safety reasons, and that most, if not all, of the witnesses in the program were guilty of something; at best, they were angels with dirty faces. At worst, they were murderers and drug dealers who the U.S. Department of Justice was willing to use as bait to reel in bigger fish: drug lords, mafia capos, and terrorists.

My research showed me how a typical protected witness enters the program. But I, more or less, already knew that it would include: new names, new social security numbers, new zip codes, new jobs, new schools, etc. It was my deeper research that revealed lesser-known aspects of the program—and I knew that was my vein of gold. I wanted my audience *to discover something new* in my pilot. For example, what would happen to a protected witness whose new identity is inadvertently compromised? I'd read about a protected witness's wife who accidentally ran into an old friend at the supermarket. And when the witness and his family had to be immediately airlifted out of their new neighborhood and relocated for the second time—new identities redux—I got excited. I had legal pads filled with these kinds of discoveries about my arena. What if a protected witness's teenaged daughter turns eighteen and decides to leave the program? (She'd never get to see her family again.) What if a protected witness wanted to attend the funeral of a beloved relative not in the WitSec program? (They'd need to resign from the program permanently if they chose to compromise their new identity.) Could a protected witness who also happens to be a concert pianist ever be allowed to publicly play again? (No. Never.) I also found humor in unexpected places: like the WitSec agents tasked with getting a morbidly obese former mafia kingpin into shape (à la *The Biggest Loser*), so he would be less conspicuous and easier to protect.

I cannot encourage you enough to dig deeper and mine the specifics of your intended arena. Not only will it provide you with character quirks and possible story ideas, it will also make you an authority in the network executives' offices. When you conclude your pitch and they start bombarding you with questions about the world of your series, you're already succeeding. When they read your pilot script and are captivated by the tip of the iceberg of your series' arena, they just might hire you to continue on the path of discovery.

Analyzing Popular Settings

Some TV series emerge from the creative marriage between a unique, iconic protagonist and an intriguing setting. Placing Sherlock Holmes in present-day London gives you a fresh take on the mystery genre. Taking neurotic former San Francisco police detective, Adrian Monk (Tony Shaloub), a man who developed severe OCD and phobias following the death of his wife—and making him a private investigator with a caretaker nurse as his partner— gave us a new spin on the police procedural (*Monk*). The one-hour drama series *Justified* features Deputy U.S. Marshal Raylan Givens (Timothy Olyphant) whose swagger and quick draw suggests the 1870's Wild West—only he's in present day. Then uproot him from Miami (where he killed a mob hit man) to a backwoods coal mining town in Harlan County, Kentucky—which happens to be Givens' hometown to which he vowed never to return. As the hard-living, womanizing Givens metes out his unique brand of cowboy justice, he becomes the target of criminals and incurs the rancor of his U.S. Marshals superiors.

The arenas of some series are no-brainers: *Boardwalk Empire* is set in and all about the infamous heyday of Atlantic City; *Northern Exposure* dropped a New York physician into a quirky Alaskan outpost (the fictional town of Cicely) as he faced culture shock amidst its quirky denizens. *Mad Men* is as much about the epicenter of American lifestyles—New York in the 1960s—as it is about Madison Avenue ad execs; *NYPD Blue, CSI: NY, Law & Order, Rescue Me* are all about New York's finest and bravest; *L.A. Law, Entourage, The Shield, The Closer,* and *NCIS: LA* are all steeped in the socially and racially diverse Hollywood culture. *Nip/Tuck's* arena was a plastic surgery clinic in a city propped up by beauty and sunshine: Miami, and later Los Angeles. *Scandal, Homeland,* and *Bones* are embedded in and around Washington, D.C., as was *The West Wing,* for obvious reasons. *Scandal* is about a political image consultant; *Homeland* is about a former POW with national political aspirations—who may be a "turned" terrorist; *Bones* centers around a forensic anthropologist who works out of the fictional Jefferson Institute (a stand in for the Smithsonian). For each of the preceding shows, the setting is intrinsically linked to the premise.

When it comes to hospital shows, it can be argued that the hospital is the arena, and its zip code is more random. *ER, Grey's Anatomy,* and *Chicago Hope* (despite its eponymous title) could all easily be relocated to different cities and still be dramatically satisfying. Because hospitals tend to be their own mini-cities or microcosms, they offer unlimited story engines—which can be influenced by specific settings—but tend not to be wholly dependent upon their locales.

The Killing could have been set in any city, but the dark, wet, and brooding weather and geography of the Pacific Northwest certainly added an ominous layer to the proceedings—which was based upon a Danish series.

In *Friday Night Lights*, high school football is like a religious experience for the citizens of the fictional, rural town of Dillon, Texas. As kickoff nears, businesses close early, the streets empty out, and everything revolves around the big game. While the economy sputters and families struggle to make ends meet, these football games provide the people of Dillon with a cathartic experience. They cheer for victory or vow to bounce back from a crushing defeat. Football isn't just a game; it's a metaphor for hope in their lives. The series could have been set in any number of small towns across America, but the series remained faithful to its inspiration from the non-fiction book *Friday Night Lights: A Town, A Team, and A Dream* by H. G. "Buzz" Bissinger and the 2004 film based on it. Published in 1990, the book documents the 1988 football season of the Permian Panthers in Odessa, Texas. The movie was directed by Bissinger's second cousin, Peter Berg, who developed the TV series, and wrote and directed the pilot episode. To protect the privacy of the real life Odessa residents, Berg and his producers chose to rename the town

Dillon, but local texture, nuance, and inspiration emerged from Odessa. What makes this such a groundbreaking, emotionally satisfying TV series is its documentary, *cinéma vérité* style. The handheld camera is our POV, so when it *darts* and *weaves* and *participates* in the action, it provides us with the sensation that these characters are our friends and family—that we're sitting in the bleachers watching every game, making Dillon our town, too.

The phenomenally successful showrunner, David E. Kelley, has rooted many of his one-hour drama series in Boston: *The Practice, Ally McBeal, Boston Public,* and *Boston Legal.* This was not a random choice. While Kelley was born in Waterville, Maine, he was raised in Belmont, Massachusetts, and is the son of legendary Boston University Terriers and New England Whalers hockey coach, Jack Kelley. David E. Kelley received his law degree from Boston University and later worked for a Boston law firm. Kelley's four most popular shows are not generic legal dramas set in Anytown, USA. Boston is a city that Kelley knows inside and out which adds a layer of verisimilitude to the fictional court cases—even when the verdicts come too quickly and tax our willing suspension of disbelief. While most of the court proceedings take dramatic license in service of humor and suspense, the legal jargon and specifics of setting keep us rooted in—and tuned in—to what feels like a real place.

Don't try to fake these details. Sure, the Hamptons setting in the USA series *Royal Pains* embellishes and idealizes this playground for the rich and powerful on the eastern seaboard, but it also successfully captures many of the real hangouts and traditions of the place. The premise of this series: a handsome "concierge doctor" and his business partner/brother cater to and make house calls at the beachfront mansions of elite Long Islanders. But these aren't merely generic millionaires and billionaires, they're a specific breed of privileged, wired New Yorkers who venture out from the city to "relax" in their weekend and summer homes. Their manner of speaking, sense of entitlement, and interactions with regular residents who keep this place running all year round, not only ground this series in a playfully exuberant reality, but also provide the show with a multitude of "story engines." The fun of this blue-sky series is its elements of fantasy and escapism, but the true-to-life stakes of its medical cases also serve to remind us that rich people have problems, too, and that while money can certainly make life more luxurious and easy, it certainly doesn't buy you happiness. If you're going to set a series in the Hamptons (*Revenge* is also set there), it's your duty to visit the place. Go and see for yourself.

Setting also plays an important role in wholly fantastical series. *Game of Thrones,* based upon a series of fantasy novels by George R. R. Martin, is set on the fictional continents of Westeros and Essos at the end of a decade-long summer. The series weaves together several plotlines, encompassing three different arenas: the civil war for the Iron Throne of the Seven Kingdoms; the threat of the impending winter on the mythical creatures of the North; and the banished last scion's desperate scheme to reclaim the throne. Each realm offers its own geography, rules, and power structures—and yet demonstrates how their destinies are intertwined.

In *Once Upon a Time,* there are two separate realms: the fairy-tale world from a legendary medieval time, and Storybrooke, USA—which feels all at once current, anachronistic, and frozen in time. Both settings are magical realms where wishes can come true, evil curses can overshadow happy endings, and virtually anything imaginable can happen.

What's essential in conjuring up supernatural and magical realms is to keep the rules of each world simple, clearly defined, and consistent. The landmark series *Lost* was challenged—and many would say compromised by—an ever-expanding rulebook. There were flashbacks in season 1, followed in subsequent seasons by flash-forwards and *flash-sideways*. For fans of the series (this author being among them), the unpredictable storytelling was thrilling, but for detractors, *Lost* had "jumped the shark"[1] by that point, reading like a bumper sticker that says: *Don't follow me, I'm lost, too!* Evolving and expanding the rules of fantasy and supernatural series is par for the course of a super successful series. Dr. Frankenstein may have created the monster, but, at some point, the monster develops a will of his own. And so, even though the brilliant co-creators of *Lost* (J.J. Abrams, Damon Lindelof, and Jeffrey Lieber) may have known how their series was going to end from the beginning, they were overwhelmed by the longevity and enormous popularity of their creation. How do you expand a finite series concept into one that could run indefinitely? Their choice was to expand the world—and sometimes that includes quantum leaps of time and space.

See interview with **Steven S. DeKnight** on the companion website: http:// www.focalpress.com/cw/landau

---

The best fiction is inspired by real life—and each setting exists in its own bubble of reality. If the world of the series is gritty and dangerous, we might watch the show hoping for someone to break free; if the bubble is elitist and materialistic, we're watching to see when it's going to burst. Without a spiritual and/or moral center, the arena of a series, just like any real-life environment, is unsustainable. For first-rate evidence of this decree, see also *The Wire, Deadwood, Breaking Bad, The Sopranos,* and *Boardwalk Empire.*

---

[1] When a series steps outside the confines of its conception and taxes the goodwill of its loyal audience. The term originated in an episode of the classic sitcom *Happy Days,* when the Fonz (Henry Winkler) attempted to jump over a shark on water skis.

3
SERVICE YOUR FRANCHISE

W hen I think about a franchise, I immediately think of McDonald's and Starbucks. And that's not too far from the context of how "franchise" is used in the TV development business. I travel a lot, so I can tell you firsthand that a McDonald's is pretty much the same in most cities across the globe.

The McDonald's corporation serves around 68 million customers daily in 119 countries. The language and alphabet on the Golden Arches sign may differ from country to country, but the McDonald's trademark colors, décor, logo, management styles, and menu options are virtually always intact. Even in India where cows are sacred, you can order a Big Mac—but instead of getting a beefy Big Mac, you'll get a veggie *Maharaja* Mac. Using this analogy, the definition of *franchise* is "the same, only different."

If each McDonald's across the globe is similar in design, menu, and function, then what's the difference? The most obvious answer is geography. Location.

The deeper answer is humanity. People. You can dress the employees in identical uniforms, but no two will ever be exactly the same. You can interview the customers who might order the same items, but their taste in fast food doesn't dominate or define their unique personalities. You can eavesdrop on conversations from the kitchen to the dining area, and you'll get as many different, highly specific variations on the human experience as there are hamburgers sold. Billions and billions.

To summarize my extended analogy, the most substantive difference between the original prototype for any chain restaurant, coffee house, or retail store is not its menu items or products sold, it's the unique *stories* that emerge from under their roofs.

In the TV business, the original prototype for a television series is called the "pilot." Each episode that follows this first episode is an extension and gradual exploration of the basic circumstances, characters, and themes established in the pilot. In this way, all pilots are origin stories. They set up a world and then invite us to drop in and bond with its inhabitants over an extended period of time.

In general, the main difference between a movie and a TV pilot is that a movie is intended to have a beginning, middle, and end; it's designed to be finite. A TV pilot, on the other hand, is conceived and constructed to be infinite—or last for as long as loyal viewership and solid ratings continue.

In conceiving a TV pilot, your initial creative process might be very similar to writing a screenplay for a feature-length movie: premise, setting, character development—but the tricky part is recognizing that you're not writing toward the ultimate payoff at the climax anymore. Instead, you're getting your audience up to speed on the "arena" (setting, logistics, characters) of your series—and then setting the stage for what your series is going to be from episode to episode and week to week.

In other words, the end of a TV pilot is just the beginning of your series.

The Promise of Your Premise

A pilot is a promise you make with the viewer—call it a marriage contract—that tacitly lets them know what they're going to be getting when they decide to commit to watching your show every week. You're *not* promising them abject predictability and repetition. You *are* promising them that you are going to love, honor, and obey what you set up in your pilot episode. In TV writing parlance, this is what's known as *servicing your franchise*.

Successfully servicing the franchise of your series means that you're going to present your loyal viewers with a show that's fundamentally the same, only different. The basic setting and premise of your series genre will remain mostly unchanged, but the particulars of the stories will, it is hoped, change and surprise us each week. In many series, the main characters (aka series "regulars") will also remain the same from episode to episode, but in other series, the characters will evolve from episode to episode and from season to season.

When a TV executive or producer asks you, "What's the franchise?" of your intended TV series, what they're really asking you is, What are your main characters going to be *doing* each week? What are the "story engines" that keep your plotlines moving forward? Like a shark, a TV series must keep swimming or perish.

Franchise Types

Case of the Week

The most basic type of series franchise is *case of the week*, which is why there are so many shows about doctors, lawyers, and cops. In a medical drama, these are the medical cases for each new patient. In a law show, these are the legal cases of the plaintiffs and defendants. In a crime show, these are the police and other law enforcement cases.

The franchises in case of the week shows are inherently procedural. In each new episode, we're going to get a new client, patient, or perp, and by the end of the episode, our devoted team of specialists has worked hard, overcoming external and internal conflicts, to solve the case.

In trying to determine the specific franchise of your new TV series, focus on the verbs. What are your characters doing each week: they're investigating, discovering, uncovering, diagnosing, healing, litigating, prosecuting, confronting, arresting, indicting, avenging, killing, and so on.

Most series regulars on the four broadcast networks (ABC, CBS, FOX, and NBC) are wholly positive, more or less heroic characters. Sure, they're flawed and wrestle with their internal demons, but they're seeking justice—whatever that means to them in their field of expertise.

Some of these series offer us closed-ended cases with fast, dependable resolutions (diagnosis/cure, proof/verdict, arrest/justice) in the same episode. Just as many series offer open-ended cases with more oblique, gradual, serialized resolutions over the course of the whole season.

The X-Files was a paranormal procedural that offered case of the week with a twist: more than one possible explanation for otherworldly phenomena and resolutions that were provocatively inconclusive.

Scandal centers on a high-powered Washington, D.C., public relations firm run by the indomitable Olivia Pope (Kerry Washington). Her specialty is getting politicians and Beltway power players out of trouble. She and her associates are not lawyers or cops; they're spin doctors who diagnose and manage political scandals through any means necessary, including subterfuge. Failure is not an option for this team. Olivia Pope is labeled a "gladiator in a suit" in the pilot episode. The cases of the week are always appropriately scandalous, provocative, morally complex, and often both salacious and controversial. Nevertheless, in season 1, *Scandal* offered closed-ended cases that resolved by the end of each episode. Meanwhile, the personal stories, such as Olivia's passionate affair with the President of the United States, Fitzgerald Grant (aka "Fitz"), along with the myriad of subplots for Olivia's team, are ongoing and heavily serialized, as are most current episodes.

The primary goal for each showrunner is to meet its audience's expectations of the types of cases and basic tone of his or her given series. New cases need to be fresh and even break new ground—but within the wheelhouse of that particular show. In other words, a series can break new ground with a new case without breaking the entire mold for the show itself. Audiences tune in to their favorite programs with a relative comfort level for what that show is going to deliver to them. If you're watching a scary/creepy cop procedural series, such as *Law & Order: Special Victims Unit*, you know what you're going to get: hard-edged, perverse, dark crimes. Yes. But you also know that the violence and sexual content is going to stop short of gratuitous, graphic, and pornographic. And even though the detectives are going to prevail, it's not a show you're going to want to watch with your kids.

When you tune in to watch *House, M.D.*, you already know the new patient's illness is going to be a medical mystery that defies a cure. But what you don't know is just how the misanthropic Dr. Gregory House (Hugh Laurie) is going to solve it.

Effectively servicing the franchise of a given series puts a new, unpredictable, provocative spin on a case. Ideally, this new spin will emerge from the characters' relationship to each new case. What psychological "buttons" might a new case push in a character? What are the main challenges to solving the case? If the case is too easy, it's not viable. It must challenge the series regulars in some way and serve up an inconvenient truth.

The difference between a mediocre series and a great one is the showrunners are always digging for a new vein of gold. Depending upon the genre of the series, the gold within each episode will be the moral dilemmas and gray areas of the main character(s).

Hybrid Procedural–Serialized

While case of the week series are franchises most easily grasped and serviced, not all TV series follow this procedural "formula." Some series, such as *The Good Wife*, are hybrid series—equal parts legal procedural and serialized drama.

The hybrid one-hour drama series has followed the playbook from many successful cable TV series, such as *Dexter* and *The Following*, in which cases can play out over a course of several episodes or even a full season (or as *The Killing* painfully learned via viewer exodus, over two seasons). The television business is rapidly evolving to embrace new technologies and to meet its audience's viewing habits, so serialized series, are now much more easily digestible than they were a few years ago.

The advantage to a franchise that offers closed-ended cases is that viewers can watch each individual episode in any order and still feel satisfied.

Serialized shows, on the other hand, require much greater viewer commitment, and if you miss more than a few episodes, it might feel daunting to tune in (the way many viewers started to feel after missing too many episodes of *Lost, 24,* and *Game of Thrones*). Of course, nowadays viewers can DVR and download episodes, so that they can catch up at their convenience.

A huge challenge for all shows with a serialized element is pacing. How much plot progression needs to happen from episode to episode? If the story unfolds too slowly (as was the case during the first half of season 2 of *The Walking Dead*), the audiences might grow grumpy and restless. If the story moves too quickly (such as, arguably, the second season of *Homeland*), the audience may cry foul about credibility or complain about rushed, sloppy plotting at the expense of character depth.

Servicing the franchise of a series is not only about choosing which cases and/or plotlines to explore, but also about the pace of delivering new information, clues, discoveries, and resolutions.

A big part of servicing a franchise is hitting the "sweet spot" of your series. I'll have a whole chapter dedicated to this very question later on. For now, suffice it to say that it's imperative that you identify the major currency of your series' franchise—and spend it wisely.

In *Homeland*, the currency of the series is our *not* knowing whom to trust. Who's the good guy? Who's the bad guy? How do they coexist? Who will prevail and at what cost?

In *The Walking Dead*, the currency is a core group's survival against seemingly insurmountable odds.

Central Question

Central questions explore the potential of the *future*. A good central question stokes the audience's curiosity and their need to know more. How is this problem going to be solved? What's going to happen?

All great TV series present us with strong central questions. *The Sopranos* makes us wonder how long Tony and his cohorts can prevail in the organized crime business, along with Tony's sanity and the impact their dirty dealings continue to have on their lives and the lives of their loved ones.

Central questions are the key ingredient in "must-see TV." We're waiting to see how a crime story or a love story is going to play out. As long as we keep wondering and anticipating and discussing and posting—we're going to keep watching. As soon as all questions are answered, the series is forced to either introduce new central questions or end.

In *Girls*, the central question—aka franchise—is, Will Hannah (Lena Dunham) and her twenty-something friends ever find a lasting sense of fulfillment in their lives?

Parenthood is a nuanced, bittersweet saga about three generations of the Braverman family, with an emphasis on the POV of the three siblings. Arguably, the *Friends* theme song, "I'll Be There for You," applies to this brood where blood is thicker than water.

Parenthood can be equal parts lighthearted and intensely emotional, in contrast to its similarly themed ensemble sitcom cousin, *Modern Family*—which also explores three generations of family, but goes for laughs, with a much broader (albeit grounded) tone and zanier situations.

Modern Family's stylistic interview format provides the show with faster, slicker pacing which highlights each episode's theme. I would also argue that the interview format (borrowed from *The Office*) makes *Modern Family* a higher concept show. The franchise, in this case, becomes the exploration of what happened and why—like family therapy. Sure, it's a gimmick, but it enables the audience to feel like we're confidants. And these interviews not only "break the fourth wall" by having characters talk directly to the unseen, unknown interviewer (aka the camera, aka the audience), they also provide us with an added perspective on the weekly proceedings—which heightens the humor and drives home the central question/unifying theme of each episode.

In a softer concept series, the basic franchise is the exploration of the main characters' quest for the ecstasy of success versus the agony of defeat—and coping with the interstices. A useful way to articulate the franchise of a "soft" concept show is, "Each week, the characters will struggle to achieve _____." The specific struggles of the characters are the source of drama and comedy. The potential for failure, existential pain, disappointment, regret, and humiliation provide the stakes.

In *Friday Night Lights*, the central question/franchise was, Will they win or lose the big game and will it help them overcome their quotidian problems?

In *The Big Bang Theory*, the central question/franchise is, Will these geeks and nerds ever fit into the mainstream and feel like "winners"?

Game of Thrones offers us the ongoing power struggle between two kingdoms, so the central question is, Who will win?

In *Breaking Bad*, Walter White incrementally builds a crystal meth empire, and then struggles to protect it. The central question for Walter is, Will his megalomaniacal hunger for money and power ever be enough?

Walt had been such a milquetoast "loser" in his life that now he'd rather die than suffer defeat. Following his terminal cancer diagnosis, Walt's desperate need to provide for his family motivated him to cross the line into the drug trade. What started off with good intentions has gradually devolved into winning at all costs—even if it means losing his wife and son. As Walt's physical health improves and his cancer goes into remission, he becomes addicted to the danger and power. He peddles crystal meth, but he's an adrenaline junkie. When I interviewed creator/showrunner Vince Gilligan (see Chapter 5), Gilligan commented that Walter White's "superpower" is his ability to delude himself in order to justify his actions. I suppose it's only a matter of time before antihero Walt becomes a tragic hero. From the heights of his wealth and power, Walt has nowhere to go but down.

In determining the franchise for your series, you might conceive both the overarching, "umbrella" central question for the long haul, as well as the more finite season arcs—also in the form of questions—from season to season.

In some series, these questions are thematic. Season 1 of *Mad Men* seemed to examine the theme of living and selling the American Dream, while season 2 shattered that dream, coming to terms with truth in advertising and in life.

Each season of *Dexter* offers a new super villain (aka "Big Bad") who challenges and defies Dexter Morgan's (Michael C. Hall) vigilantism. The central "umbrella" thematic question of this series remains constant: What is justice?

In *Revenge*, the central theme is, Can vengeance lead to peace of mind? For *Homeland*, the series theme is, Can the war on terror ever be won?

Central Mystery

The franchise of some series lies in unraveling a central mystery about the past. What happened? How, when, where, and why—and what will be its impact on the present and future of our series regulars?

In *Lost*, the series *mythology* was its franchise. The astute creators/showrunners instinctively knew that a series franchise that relied solely on whether or not a group of castaways would ever get off the island wouldn't be enough. *Gilligan's Island* depended on wackiness and stupidity, which made being shipwrecked look like a whole lot of fun. (The laugh track helped us suspend our disbelief as to why movie star Ginger Grant brought her entire wardrobe on a "three-hour tour" and why the millionaire Howells brought along all their cash.)

Yes, *Lost* offered us the central question of how the jet crash passengers were going to survive, but it also quickly presented us with aberrations of nature, paranormal activity, and the ever-expanding mysteries of the island itself. The central question may have initially been, How are we going to get off this island, but soon morphed into bigger existential questions, such as What the hell is this place? Why are we here? Who *else* is here? And even if we can find a reliable source of daily sustenance, can we ever overcome our sins from the past? And even if we do, does time even exist? Did our existence ever matter? Why are we still alive? Are we still alive?

Once Upon a Time is a fable that exists in two worlds: the mythological land that exists long ago in the pages of a storybook and in the "present-day" small-town slice of Americana known as Storybrooke, Maine. This enormously inventive and imaginative series alternates between the present "reality" and the past "fantasy," and the impact the past has on its present characters who have a doppelganger (or double) in Storybrooke. The series borrows this conceit from *The Wizard of Oz,* in which the Scarecrow, the Tin Man, and the Cowardly Lion all have a counterpart in the "real" world back in Kansas.

The main franchise of the series is based upon the central question of whether love can be stronger than fear (aka magical spells/curse). In season 1, the Evil Queen placed a curse on the enchanted storybook characters that followed them to Storybrooke. The Evil Queen (Lana Parrilla) felt robbed of love and fulfillment, so she cursed Snow White (Ginnifer Goodwin) and Prince Charming (Josh Dallas) to a land where there would never be any happy endings—which, ironically, was the Evil Queen's greatest desire and therefore *her* happy ending. The pilot of this series set up this franchise: each week we'll see if the evil spell can be broken and if our characters will transcend the curse and find love—or not. There is also the underlying thematic question of what's real and what's illusion.

The present-day story centers around Emma Snow (Jennifer Morrison), who manages to pierce the bubble of the once frozen in time, hermetically sealed Storybrooke. Emma starts out in the series as a cynic in counterpoint to the earnest young believer, Henry Mills (Jared S. Gilmore)—who is her biological son given up for adoption. We root for Emma and Henry to reunite. As mother and son, they belong together, but not if Henry's adopted mother, Regina Mills (also Lana Parrilla), has anything to say about it. Turns out that Regina is not only the two-faced, villainous mayor of Storybrooke, she also happens to be the Evil Queen. Snow White and Prince Charming have counterparts in Storybrooke, who are also meant to be together, but that's another huge struggle and part of why we watch each week.

In the much darker, perverse anthological miniseries *American Horror Story,* each season begins with a new tale of fright set in a new location with a new cast of characters. As in all haunted house or asylum horror stories, the safety and sanity of the characters in the present is played against the ominous mythology from the past. The sins of the past obliterate any chance for a happy ending. It's not a coincidence that season 2 was set in an asylum ruled by a tyrannical nun, Sister Jude Martin (Jessica Lange). There was no atonement or catharsis, and the only escape from existential pain was lobotomy or death.

> TV characters need positive goals in the specter of negative consequences. Without this positive/negative charge, there is no conflict. And without conflict, there is no drama or comedy. In this way, all TV series are about winning and losing.

INTERVIEW: Michael Rauch

Michael Rauch Credits

Best known for:

Royal Pains (Executive Producer/Writer/Director) 2009–2012
Life Is Wild (Executive Producer/Creator) 2007–2008
Love Monkey (Executive Producer/Creator) 2006
Beautiful People (Executive Producer/Creator) 2005–2006
Wake Up and Smell the Coffee (Executive Producer/Director) (film) 2001
In the Weeds (Writer/Director) 2000

NL: The franchise of your show is medical cases, so I'm wondering how you approach each medical mystery. Do you start with the ailment or do you start with character?

MR: There really isn't a specific formula for us. We always have an A medical story and usually have a B medical story also. The episode will begin with a blue-sky period where you start with a completely empty white board and you end with an outline. On this show, I would like that to happen within two weeks. And, oftentimes we'll come in with a medical condition that feels like this is a fun one that we haven't done and that will work in the show, and then sometimes we'll come in with a theme or a character and work the medical condition around that. So, there's a lot of different ways it works. We have a medical consultant who sits in the room with us a couple days of the week. We have two on set medical consultants, and after fifty-six episodes of this show we are well-versed in where to find—whether it's from an ad or from a magazine or from a website, we are just always noting down very cool medical stories that we hear about or read about. Usually, the writer of his/her own episode will come in with something and sometimes we'll feel like, "You know what, this is a great A story," and sometimes, "You know what, it feels more like a B story. It has three or four beats in it and not six or seven beats in it. So, let's use this as a B story and work an A story around the theme."

NL: So, you're a seven-act show, if it's a teaser, plus six acts?

MR: We're actually six acts. We are a teaser, four acts, and a tag. That structure was given to us by the network and it's worked pretty well for us. We've had some situations where our tags are shorter than the network wants them to be. We had an episode last year where we had our first death on the show. It was very important to us to have the announcement of the death be the entire tag, but it was about a minute and 20 second scene and the network basically said, "You can do it, but our research shows that if you hold a tag off that long, people will think the show is over." They're not going to stick around to see the commercials. They see it's 9:56 and that's it. So, we were swayed to take a scene from act four and put it at the top of the tag which built the tag into about four minutes. And, it didn't really hurt our original intention at all.

NL: So you're a showrunner who adheres to having A, B, and C stories connected by a unifying theme?

MR: Absolutely, and sometimes the unifying theme is self-evident to a viewer, and sometimes it's just something we talk about for a larger arc in the season. But, it does feel like the storytelling is more organic and more cohesive if there's one single theme, even if we have to stretch it a little bit. But, there is something that is holding all the various stories together. With season finales and usually the last two episodes and the first two episodes, themes just kind of pop up because we know where we have to get to. So, it's often easier for us to begin the blue-sky process with a theme and start tying in the other stories around that. And, right now, we're breaking our twelfth episode and a theme has occurred to us toward the end game of breaking it as all the stories have started to rise to the surface.

NL: Do you ever approach a whole season or arc of episodes with a thematic?

MR: We do. In fact, the episode I was citing about the tag where there was a death, it was a storyline about a character that we had no intention of bringing back, but we wanted to have a patient die and this felt like a good character to do it with. He was played by Tom Cavanagh, a character named Jack O'Malley, because he was such a likeable character and he connected very well with Hank [Mark Feuerstein] and it felt like if we're going to kill someone, we should kill someone who we really care about and really like and we won't expect it. Jack's death and his story about Lupus connected to Hank, in terms of Hank never having lost a patient since he's moved out here. It happened once when he was in the E.R. in Brooklyn in the pilot. But, it was about his growth of learning to let go and to let himself open up emotionally to patients and what the risk of that is. So, that kind of theme is what helped us find the Lupus story which then brought us to the death of the character. It was an arc that we played throughout the third season.

NL: And very unpredictable for your viewers.

MR: It was—it was very unpredictable. We were concerned about what the feedback from our most loyal viewers and, overall, it was very positive. The people who were upset by it seemed to be upset by it in a good way, in a way that was unexpected and satisfying and let them believe that we're not quite sure if what we think is going to happen is actually going to happen. Which has happened to us this season too; we ended season 3 with the brothers getting into a big fight. And everyone expected that in the first episode of season 4 that they'll kiss and make up. We decided that we would play almost the entire third season building to this fight. And, if in one episode, we just resolved it, it would feel cheap and it would feel unearned in terms of our storytelling and in terms of the integrity of the show. So, we've stretched it out to the first few episodes, and I know there have been fans who have been unhappy with that because to them *Royal Pains* is everyone getting along and Hank and Evan getting along. But, we feel good about being able to play this out because it feels real and authentic to what happens when people who love each other—whether professional colleagues or brothers—get in a big fight; it takes some time for them work it out.

NL: I love the choice you made because now they're rivals and you get new kinds of stories. I would imagine that anytime you come across a story that has tentacles, and you go, "Now, we can go here, and here, and here" and it will enable us to go different places, story-wise.

MR: That's absolutely right, and what it allowed us to do was to introduce this new character, Dr. Jeremiah Sacani, played by Ben Shenkman, who never would have existed if these guys hadn't split. What you said is completely true which is we have found new ways to tell stories, and of course, the brothers will get back together, but with it we now have this fresh real estate where we have a Dr. Sacani and we have Kyle Howard playing Dr. Van Dyke. And, after our fifty-something episode, it gives us new places to go without feeling like we're recycling the same stories.

NL: I think that the heart of the show works so well because for every case, you infuse a strong emotional investment for Hank. He genuinely cares— which makes us care about the outcome. But I would imagine that one of the biggest challenges for you and your writers is not being too predictable— because we know that everything's going to be OK in the end. I mean, basically, it's a feel-good show. The mystery is not whether they're going to solve the case, but rather *how*. But every once in a while you'll throw us a major curveball, such as in the episode titled "After the Fireworks" that ended with a scary explosion, lives hanging in the balance.

MR: That was the season premiere, and it was unusual for us to have something that big and that dramatic and also to play as a cliffhanger at the very end of an episode. Usually our cliffhangers are more character oriented. You know, the one where Evan lost all of the money, or where their father, Henry Winkler, shows up. It felt both as a premiere, it was a fun way to kick things off and also, in a way, that action was a microcosm of the fireworks that we're happening between the brothers. It felt like something we could play out dramatically that also touched on the theme of what we were doing in the opening of the season.

NL: When you're in your writers' room with your team, are you thinking about cliffhangers within each episode as you're structuring your act breaks?

MR: We are. We have an amazing writers' room.

It's funny because we began the show thinking that every act in every episode had to have a medical cliffhanger. We worked so hard for that, and finally, at some point, the network said, "You guys are so strong with character—don't feel the pressure to have to . . ."—and it was such a relief to us.

And, now we do try to balance, so we don't force anything, and if we have a great—obviously it's a medical show and we need to have strong medical stakes, but we've built up enough of a character series now where there is that soap element and now people truly care what's going to happen to Divya [Reshma Shetty], what's going to happen to Hank, Evan and Paige [Brooke D'Orsay], and we can end acts with Campbell Scott [as Boris Kuester von Jurgens-Ratenicz]—not is he going to die, but what's going to happen in this world he's now entering. It takes the pressure off us medically and helps balance the tone of the show because tonally USA network has a very specific thing which now they're trying to change because they're growing so much. But, for us, the tone of the show is where we live and it's a sweet spot of as you said, "happiness is buoyant," but at the same time people get sick. When we've done things that are dramatically very extreme, like in season 1 Andrew McCarthy, his character was in drug rehab, we balanced it with a very silly storyline of a woman who was turning blue. That's how we try to manage to keep the tone in a comfortable spot where the audience knows what they're going to get and all of a sudden we haven't turned into *CSI: Miami* or something.

NL: Because you're a cable show and you have a shorter season, do you arc the whole season at one time or is it more—a lot of shows it will be according to how many members are on staff—you'll go maybe five or six?

MR: We try to have a sense of where we're going to go. Inevitably that changes because you start writing a story that you thought was so wonderful and then you cast it incorrectly or it's not coming to fruition like you thought it would, so you shift. Traditionally, we've been a summer and winter show with two-thirds of our episodes in the summer and one-third of our episodes in the winter. So, what we've done is we've structured the summer season as one season and the winter season as another. This year [2012] in season 4, we're actually doing fourteen episodes in the summer and a double episode in the winter. This has been very different for us. We've been breaking the fourteen as one long arc. We started this year at the end which was very helpful for us and then went back to the beginning, but having a very strong sense of where we wanted to take each character. We have these flags we've planted that every three episodes or so we want to hit. We have preemptions for July 4 and for the Olympics, so it breaks our season up into little mini-seasons: we have a four-episode season, a six-episode season. So, we build little mini finales and premieres into this larger being.

NL: And, because your A stories always close or I think almost always . . .

MR: Almost always, yeah . . .

NL: They're self-contained enough that you can just tune in and watch them—and if you have a break you're not going to be lost like in *Lost*.

MR: Exactly.

NL: When you're arcing, do you have a central question? I know that with Henry Winkler as Hank and Evan's father, there was that mystery with what happened with dad. With Boris' illness, there's a central question of is he going to live or die and what's going on. Do you think of that in terms of arcs as well?

MR: More often than not, we do. We will raise a question for ourselves as with this new character, Dr. Sacani. He's someone who came in with very high social deficits. Now, we have to be, as a medical show, especially authentic to what that means if someone's on the spectrum or not. We don't want to fudge that for dramatic purposes, but the challenge that we raised is how does someone like that fit into a practice like HankMed? And, how much growth can a character like this have when he rubs up against Hank and Divya and Evan. So, for this character, that was the question we raised and that we're playing out and developing throughout, and so far, we think very successfully. Ben's done an amazing job of bringing it to life with nuance and subtlety, but still drawing you into this person and hoping that they can overcome or manage some of the deficits.

NL: You've used the term *blue sky*, and I've heard it used in different contexts: one is you just sort of blue sky the whiteboard thinking about where you're going this season; but I've also heard of blue sky as kind of the tone of the show which is not dark storm clouds, but more a blue-sky kind of show—that's sort of been USA's brand. Can you clarify and elaborate on what it means to you?

MR: Yes, I think both of those things are true in this case. USA is a blue-sky network. This show is specifically a blue-sky show; it exists in the Hamptons—in a make-believe Hamptons where the skies are always blue and where the houses are always beautiful. I think USA has successfully defined that tone for the network. As they are expanding, they're moving probably into semi-blue skies now because they don't want to repeat the same thing over and over again. So, I think the skies can be a little cloudier at times and the tone a little bit edgier as they evolve as a network. But, for us, it really is a very nice way of describing what the tone is and, in fact, Henry Winkler's company that he was a part of when he first came in was called Blue Sky. It was just a nice way to call attention to the fact that this is what we're doing. And, yes, in terms of breaking episodes, the beginning is that it's all just clear blue skies until you start filling it in. And how, at times, unfortunately, the clouds do roll in.

NL: When you and your writing staff gather at the beginning of the season before you start production and you're just tossing around possible story ideas and arcs and character things, how involved is the network in approving stories? Do they ever kick something out or kill it? Or, probably by now, because they trust you and you have a hit show, are they less involved?

MR: The way this network works is that they're incredibly respectful of our creative process. On this show, during the first couple of weeks of a new season, we'll just talk big picture. We'll talk about what worked in the previous season and what didn't work in the previous season. What we owe from the previous season to this and what we want to try to do that we haven't done before. And start trying to put some things up of places we'd like to go, and then we start getting into specific story ideas and episode ideas. Usually about four to six weeks after we've started, Andrew Lenchewski (who created the show) and I will go into the network to Jeff Wachtel [Co-President, USA Network] and Bill McGoldrick [Senior Vice President, Original Scripted Programming, USA Network] and Michael Sluchan and the studio will come with us and we'll pitch in about fifteen or twenty minutes, "here's where we want to go this season. Here's where we want the show to go; here's where we want Hank to go, Evan, Divya, Boris"—and then they'll chime in. Usually in a very supportive and helpful way and sometimes in a less enthusiastic way which is their job and their right—they're paying for the show. Just to make sure that if there are any course corrections to be made, they're made before we get too far down the line. They, as a network, are incredibly good at knowing their audience and know the shows and the details of the show in a way that is remarkable when you think about how much work they have and how many shows they have on the air. I mean Jeff Wachtel can literally quote lines from season 1 from the sixth episode which Andrew and I have forgotten about, "Didn't this character once say this or how can they do that?" So, they keep us on our toes, but yes, that's what happens and then once we start handing out outlines, we'll get notes and then we'll do a script and we'll get notes and it's usually nothing too destructive, and then the next time we'll get notes, it's in a cut, and then we'll go on from there.

NL: What's the page length range of your outlines?

MR: The outlines we do on this show are usually ten to twelve pages. They're pretty detailed. Because we're a summer show and we air in the summer, we also have to shoot in the summer. So, a lot of cable shows are able to finish all their scripts before they go into production. Unfortunately for us, we are always battling air dates with our scripts because we're airing the same time we need to be shooting. So, it's a pretty quick turnaround, and therefore, the outline needs to be a very good jumping off point for the script. So, a writer doesn't go off and spend four days writing an outline and then three weeks to get the script done. We do it more as a team—we get the outline to a good place and then the writer takes it over, puts it in his or her voice and then within a week, there's a script. And, that keeps us on schedule. With the schedule we have here, we can't fall behind, we just can't afford to.

NL: And do you do a polish on each script?

MR: It's important that the scripts have a singular voice. We have a very senior staff and a very talented, experienced staff, so that the amount of polishing every season gets reduced. Sometimes a script comes in that doesn't need to be touched. Sometimes it just needs some polishes here and there, and, of course, there are times when a script needs more work. But, we're very lucky to have the writers' room that we do, and, more often than not, the scripts come in in fantastic shape unlike any show I've ever been on.

NL: And therein lies the longevity of your franchise.

4

DELIVER THE VERDICT

In the old days, the verdict at the climax of an episode would strictly adhere to a tidy resolution because that's what TV audiences wanted: truth, justice, and closure. A good TV series was like putting on a comfortable pair of slippers; viewers wanted to be entertained, not overly taxed with moral complexity. Networks were notoriously controversy-averse. The bad guys always got caught. Crime never paid off with anything but a prison sentence. Scumbags were always prosecuted to the full extent of the law. Nice guys and gals didn't always succeed at their missions, but love and friendship always saw them through in the end.

But then something happened: as technology progressed, audiences became more restless. Attention spans shortened. Channel surfing and Internet downloading/streaming became the national pastime. And audiences wanted to be challenged, surprised, even shocked. The proliferation of reality TV is based upon the unpredictable outcome happening *live*. Contestants have the potential to win big, but are much more likely to suffer some form of humiliation. The appetite for TV audiences shifted from complacency to participatory. Kids don't just want to sit there and watch—they want to interact and play along on their PlayStations and Xboxes.

Influenced by reality TV and provocative news reporting, dramatic programming across the board became more edgy and envelope pushing. Heavily flawed protagonists combating their neuroses and addictions popped onto our TV screens. These protagonists didn't need to be wholly positive role models—they could be antiheroes (Dexter Morgan, Walter White, Don Draper, and Patty Hewes). And series centering on dark, edgy, flawed characters from both one-hour dramas (*Dexter, Breaking Bad, Mad Men,* and *Damages*) and half-hour dramedies (*Weeds, Nurse Jackie,* and *Enlightened*) are too complex to shoehorn into a predictable, closed-ended episodic formula. If a case can be setup and resolved that easily, then the world of the series starts to feel too easy or too black and white as opposed to more nuanced shades of gray.

Defining Series Type

Episodic television can be categorized by the following three types of endings:

1. **Closed-ended episodes:** The main plotline (aka A story) is set up in the teaser or act 1, complicates in the middle acts, and is resolved by the end of the episode. Viewers can tune in at any time and easily be able to follow the action without a crib sheet explaining all the backstory and series mythology. It's not essential that they watch each episode chronologically because each show features a self-contained mystery.

   In a *legal procedural* series (*Law & Order, Boston Legal, Ally McBeal, The Practice*), the closed-ended episode is usually the verdict of the trial (guilty, not guilty, or a settlement).

   In a *police procedural* series (*CSI, Rizzoli & Isles, Bones*), the closed ending comes in the form of revealing the perpetrator of a crime (*who-dunit*) as the solution to the crime of the week mystery. The story resolves when the perp confesses or is brought down by irrefutable evidence.

   The phenomenally successful *CSI* and *Law & Order* franchises are not shows about criminals; they're shows about *justice*. In the old days, the prosecutors needed eyewitness testimony; now they just need DNA. The science lends itself to closed-ended A stories because these kinds of plotlines, based on forensics and ballistics, are truly irrefutable and absolute. Open and shut cases.

   The CSI franchise has been so durable because, at its inception, it broke new ground. It wasn't a *who*-dunit; it was a *how*-dunit. CSI gives us a glimpse into the science of crime solving. We know the team is heroically going to solve the case by the end of each episode. It's never a question of IF the criminal is going to get away with murder. Instead, we get to watch how our slick, resourceful, super smart investigative team tracks clues and gathers incriminating evidence to nab the perp.

   Our interest in these kinds of cases hinges on our emotional investment in the outcome. Maybe the perp is sympathetic and his actions were mitigated by special circumstances. Frequently, there will be some dissension among the team about the case.

At times, the case of the week will trigger some kind of personal, emotional reaction from someone on the team. However, if this strategy is too on-the-nose or author convenient and happens in every episode, the writing can start to feel contrived. Ideally, the case of the week will resonate within the cast of regulars, but in subtle, oblique ways. The case may resolve in a tidy fashion, but even in closed-ended procedurals, there are going to be ripple effects that emerge in subsequent episodes.

In a *medical series* (*House, M.D.*, *Grey's Anatomy*, *Royal Pains*), the closed-ending usually comes in the form of *healing* (diagnosis, treatment, or possibly a cure).

In the majority of *situation comedies*, the A-story situations have a beginning, middle, and end. The problem(s) of the week resolves without having any substantive, lasting impact on the characters, and then next week's episode features another tremendous trifle. For decades, *the golden rule of sitcoms was that characters do not change*. Audiences would tune in each week to see their favorite sitcom character face new challenges based upon their quirks and character flaws, but they fundamentally would *revert to form* by the end of the episode—and that's OK because of the second golden rule of sitcom characters: we love them not only despite their unique flaws but also because of them. It's their imperfections that make them fallible, also vulnerable, and funny. In fact, sitcom characters tend to become more rooted in their identities when they're under stress—and if it's a viable, funny comedy series, they'll be under stress every week. Of course, there are exceptions to these rules as single-camera sitcoms evolve: the jury is still out on Jay Pritchett (Ed O'Neill) on *Modern Family*, but he does seem to be changing with the times and becoming more tolerant.

2. **Serialized, open-ended episodes:** Multiple plotlines play out over the course of several episodes or the entire season before reaching a cliff-hanger type "resolution" which might be the answer to an extended mystery. Most serialized TV series track the progression of each main character's love life and (possibly) work life with an emphasis on the relationships between characters. Character progression is what is known as a "character arc." Where does he or she start off at the beginning of the season and where does he/she end up at the end of the season? What dramatic conflicts does he or she face? Serialized series borrow from the playbook of daytime soap operas—with the marked difference being that nighttime serialized dramas (such as *Desperate Housewives*, *Mad Men*, *Breaking Bad*, *Homeland*, *Revenge*, and *Dexter*) air once per week

(versus five times per week for a daytime soap), tend to move much faster (versus daytime, where a character might be pregnant for several years!), and are much more nuanced when it comes to character development.

Damages is an example of a legal procedural series told in a serialized form: one main case per season.

The Killing is an example of a crime drama serialized over the course of two seasons (at its own peril) but is returning from cancellation (licking its wounds), and the revamped series will now resolve by the end of the same season.

Lost, Game of Thrones, Once Upon a Time, and *The Walking Dead* explore an actively unfolding central mystery that's heavily linked to each series' mythology. These shows use a serialized structure that tends to leave viewers with more questions than answers by the end of each episode.

3. **Hybrid series (also referred to as "semi-serialized"):** This type of series seems to be the most prevalent in today's marketplace. The hybrid series offers an A story that reaches some kind of resolution, but the more personal stories unfold slowly as extended subplots over the course of the entire season. The rules of the structure are much looser. Sometimes a case or plotline will resolve by the end of an episode, but even as one element is resolved, there will often be fallout that will spill into subsequent episodes.

The Good Wife is a good example of a hybrid legal series. In the early episodes, Alicia Florrick (Julianna Margulies) would work on a case which would be settled by the end of the episode. But, as this series has progressed, the single-case, closed-ended episodes took a backseat to the more serialized personal drama stories. You could say that the A stories became the B stories, and vice versa.

Grey's Anatomy tends to offer closed-ended medical cases at the forefront of each episode, but the characters' love lives are the core of this series.

Scandal is another series that started out with "scandal of the week" A stories that Olivia Pope (Kerry Washington) and her associates managed to resolve by the end of each episode. But, as the show has developed, the ongoing scandals inside the White House and the accompanying political machinations have taken center stage. I suppose this was to be expected given that Olivia was having an affair with the president of the United States. *Scandal* doesn't seem to be foreclosed on returning to closed-ended cases from time to time, but the show has evolved into one of the juiciest political intrigue shows on television. See also: *House of Cards*.

As you can see, hybrid and serialized series are much more complicated than their closed-ended counterparts. The truth is subjective depending on point of view. Walter White operates according to his own moral compass, so *Breaking Bad* is never about good versus evil or right and wrong. It's all a matter of perspective. When you play by your own rules, you can always win.

Similarly, Dexter Morgan on *Dexter,* Don Draper on *Mad Men*, and Nancy Botwin on *Weeds* are skilled liars and manipulators, justifying their actions to suit their needs—often motivated by good intentions. They're antiheroes because they're not ruled by conscience; they're ruled by impulse. And if the show is going to be "must-see" TV, their impulses must override our impulse to change the channel.

Predicting the Future of Television

Up until 2010, the broadcast and cable networks tended to prefer closed-ended, self-contained episodes to retain viewers who may have missed an episode from time to time. The conventional wisdom was that it's hard enough to launch a new series, so why make it even harder by airing a series that's dependent upon loyal, dedicated viewership? Broadcast networks were always skittish during premiere week in September because they were concerned that if an audience didn't tune in for the pilot episode, would they be able to follow the action in episodes 2 through 22? Networks were also able to rerun series with closed-ended episodes and post decent ratings. Conversely, if viewers missed too many episodes of a serialized series like *Lost*, then ABC ran the risk of alienating and losing their viewers.

But audience trends have changed significantly in the past few years—and continue to evolve even as I write this. Viewers don't need to make an appointment with their favorite shows anymore when they can watch them on their DVRs or download them on Hulu or Amazon or even via the broadcast and cable networks' own websites. Rather than being daunted by a serialized story, viewers seem to like making the time investment and even look forward to "binge viewing" many episodes back to back. For decades, networks would offer "marathons" of *The Twilight Zone* during the winter holidays, showing every episode in a twenty-four-hour cycle. Now it's Christmas all year long.

In 2013, most networks and TV studios are still partial to closed-ended episodes because they sell better and more reliably in foreign television markets. Outside the United States, audiences are more likely to watch series in their predesignated time slots (without the benefit of a DVR). Furthermore, closed-ended episodes can be watched in any order and easily understood and digested—even if the foreign broadcaster arbitrarily places commercial breaks at dramatically inopportune times.

> No matter the format—closed-ended, serialized, hybrid—all compelling TV characters in all genres share a common denominator: we tune in to see them get into and out of trouble.

INTERVIEW: Michelle and Robert King

Michelle and Robert King Credits

Best known for:

The Good Wife (Creators/Executive Producers/Writers/Director—Robert King) 2009–2012
  Emmy Nominated (Outstanding Drama Series) 2010–2011
  Emmy Nominated (Outstanding Writing for a Drama Series) 2010
  WGA Nominated (Drama Series) 2012
  WGA Nominated (New Series) 2010
In Justice (Executive Producers/Writers) 2006
Vertical Limit (Screenplay—Robert King) 2000
Red Corner (Screenplay—Robert King) 1997

NL: This chapter is about crafting an inevitable, but surprising conclusion. I also want to discuss the specific challenges of working on a legal series. But before we even get into that, I wanted to talk to you about the pilot. You made very specific choices in the pilot in that you started with the scandal and then cut ahead six months. How did you decide that that would be your way in to the series?

RK: Our spark for this series, and what we initially pitched to the studio and network was that first image of the political scandals—that would usually involve a candidate at a podium talking to reporters. Then, there would always be this cosmetic attachment—this wife who was there to share his shame—even though she was this innocent party. Is there anything more sympathetic in this world than this woman who is being dragged through the mud even though she didn't do a single thing wrong? In fact, she was just as injured, if not more injured, than anyone else. And yet, she had to swallow her pride and do this. We felt that (1) this was a character that we couldn't help but sympathize with and (2) that this was an opening that you could get hooked into the situation even without knowing what was going on in the woman's head because you were so drawn in by that image and knew it from the news.

MK: And in terms of the next scene [jumping ahead six months] of Alicia [Julianna Margulies] as with almost everything in the series, it's Alicia driven. And what is the reality? How long would it take this woman to recover her bearings, find a position, and get her life in order to start work? So that was the reason behind that choice.

NL: Obviously, you could have decided to have her wake up the morning after that scandalous press conference and show her slowly picking up the pieces of her life. But you chose to cut to six months later, I would imagine, in order to launch the legal franchise of the show: getting her in a courtroom, getting her first legal case, and getting her first verdict.

MK/RK: Yes, that's right.

NL: My favorite thing on the pilot teaser is that little piece of thread in Peter's (Chris Noth) sport jacket and her instinct to reach out. It's just such a wonderful detail. When I teach Writing the One-Hour Drama Pilot at UCLA, I always show that scene. It's just beautifully shot.

RK: What's fun is that TV is becoming more cinematic where you can do things like that. What we find fun with it is that old TV shows might have had a monologue about the woman being a housecleaner or the wife as care-taker to this husband and she was worried about his wardrobe or that it's the moment where she's trying to remove herself from her surroundings because they're so embarrassing. But if all you do is show this little image—it does tell you everything you need to know in that moment.

NL: When the series first went on the air, I know that at CBS, in particular, they were very much interested in closed-ended A stories. Their wheelhouse is procedurals, but what seemed to happen with *The Good Wife* pretty early on was that the personal stories and the love stories started to take over. While you still have the case of the week, the serialized elements became much more pronounced. Did that shift from the original intention of the show? Are A stories still your cases or have A stories become more of the personal stories?

MK: For the most part, even in the fourth season, we still think of the case as the A story. Very occasionally, we'll speak in the room in terms of twin A stories where a personal story will rise up in significance.

RK: I think part of the reason for that is that it's easier to talk about it that way in the room. Writers' rooms are built on talking about very specific logical aspects of the story. That's what we find most helpful and I'm sure the writers themselves find the most helpful. Usually the best way to access emotion and character is by starting with what is the most concrete aspect of your story which then allows you to put flesh on it. Regarding whether we moved from cases toward emotion, there was a very great moment in development with CBS where we got notes from Nina Tassler [President of CBS Entertainment] where she asked for more emotion out of the scene. She asked for an additional scene that showed Alicia's mindset now that it's six months later. We added a scene which was not in the original script, where Alicia talked to the Mary Beth Peil character playing her mother-in-law, Jackie, who was this Eisenhower-type wife who thought Alicia was being a little bit rebellious and dismissive over her husband and dwelling on his interlude with prostitutes. It was a good scene, but what was really great for us was to hear the executive say, "Could you go in more of an emotional direction?" Because there was a split personality up until that point where some executives said, "You've got to do more with the case," which usually means you've got to explain more. It felt like we could get away with a lot because everyone is so fucking familiar with the genre of the courtroom, so that they could fill in the gaps with anything they've seen. What that gave us was the freedom to do less with the procedural. TV is all about real estate. You only have forty-two minutes to tell your story. So if you do less with the procedural, it opens the door to do more with character.

NL: Starting with the pilot, you also seem to structure your shows differently. The pilot has a sixteen-page teaser, and your teasers tend to be quite long—almost like first acts. Where did that come from?

RK: With the pilot, before our first commercial break, we wanted to set up all the main characters. And I think all of the characters, except for Chris Noth's character, were set up in the teaser and we wanted to establish relationships. It's not enough to say he works in the office and that he's garbage. It's more about, "What is the relationship?" You need to set up that it was Will [Josh Charles] who brought Alicia in and that Cary [Matt Czuchry] is a little suspicious of Alicia because they're going for the same job. All of that needed to be done which meant that it had to be a fairly long teaser because if they go away on commercial break . . . you kind of have to bring them along kicking and screaming into what you're trying to entertain them with.

MK: In terms of calling it a teaser, that's really just a remnant of what studios and networks call it. As far as we're concerned, it's an act.

NL: So it's like a five-act structure?

RK: Yeah, I think so. You know that ABC and even NBC are doing a six-act structure because they don't want to have a commercial between the end of one show and the beginning of another. When we were at ABC that was a nightmare. You should talk to Damon Lindelof about that. The six-act structure, I think, is sort of killing drama on other shows. Just because each act out . . . they say they don't mind soft act outs, but when you do one, they say, "Oh, that's not a very good act out." It keeps you from getting a rhythm going.

NL: When you're breaking your stories, you're very cognizant of where those act breaks need to be, right?

MK: We are.

RK: That's the first move. After we decide what the case is, we ask, "Where are the highpoints in the story?" If you have two highpoints right next to each other, there needs to be some drama that leads up to one another and that's clearly an act out. We're a little traditional that way.

NL: Do you sometimes start with the verdict? Knowing who done it?

MK: I don't think we've done that even once.

RK: We're doing a law show, but we kind of hate law shows. The usual predictability of there's a case that comes through the door, you're in court, and "oh, oh," the witness is not working for you, then another witness collapses on the stand, and then the jury goes away and comes in with a verdict. So bullshitty. It's either guilty or not guilty and it's just what the screenwriter wants it to be. We've always tried to avoid it. I think we've had a verdict maybe four times over four years.

NL: And also in reality, those verdicts would not come within one or two days that the episode is taking place.

RK: Yeah, I know.

MK: That's the other thing. What we've tried to do is suggest that sometimes justice or the lack of justice is accomplished through the negotiations of the lawyers while the trial is going on which feels a little bit closer to life. We try to honor the fact that lawyers are often not just waiting for the jury to come in, they're trying to negotiate a plea bargain or, in a civil case, reach a financial settlement. Some of our shows are just about the depositions because those are interesting and have their own sort of verdict, in that if you reach a settlement, that is the verdict. Also, then the verdicts don't have to be yea or nay. They can be about whether this is a financial amount that is good for us or there can be more split verdicts where we lose something financially or there's a gag order. Just gives you more options to make it surprising for the audience.

NL: Do you have a legal consultant on staff or do either of you have a law background?

MK: Neither Robert nor I are lawyers. However, we're very fortunate. There are eight other writers on the staff this season, and four of them are attorneys. In addition to that, we have a legal consultant in Illinois.

NL: Right, because it is so specific to Cook County. I was thinking about other metaphorical verdicts on the show which are more like central questions for each season. There's always the one about whether Alicia and Peter are ever going to get back together which, with the current state of things, it looks like yes, they are going to. Then you have Peter's campaign and where that is going to go. Do you map out a whole season in broad strokes on where you want to take each character? Or do you do it in blocks of seven episodes or thirteen? What's the strategy?

RK: We split the year in two. The first part of the year usually goes to episode 13, but that varies. This is based on the first year when you never were sure you were going to go past episode 13. We wrote toward knowing that we could end a story by episode 13. Our years have been both twenty-two and twenty-three episodes. We've been putting the back nine or back ten as their own self-contained arc. After our first year, we plotted out for a big reveal somewhere within the second half of the show which was the milestone we needed to build toward. In the second year, it was the discovery that Kalinda [Archie Panjabi] slept with Peter which was episode 17. So you could then have the first half of the year build up toward that. What we're trying to give the audience is a sense of completion when they reach the end of the story. But what we have found is as much as we want to be like cable, we have such a long year. Instead of their eight, ten, or thirteen episodes, we know our years are twenty-two and twenty-three episodes, that's why we've split it up into two. What we're trying to do is tell two seasons worth of cable stuff in one year. Again, so that the audience doesn't get lost in the idea of where is the beginning of the story and where is the end. There's always something tending to conclusion or coming from the beginning. You're always within reach of one or the other, no matter where you are in the year. We do have a very big roadmap for ourselves of what the year is. It's complex though because there's one for the first thirteen and one for the back ten.

NL: Because you're doing so many episodes, can you talk about the challenges of pacing—how much story you reveal at one time? I don't know if you're watching *Homeland*, but I'm amazed by how they're burning through story. I would imagine that would be incredibly dangerous for a network show because you'd start to run out of story quickly when you have to spread things out over so many episodes.

RK: I think that's right, and the difficulty in network is network tends toward melodrama because there are so many events you have to have happen. The bottom line is no matter how complicated somebody's life is—it would never be as much as happens on a network show. You just get exhausted by the end of the year with how many events have to happen in twenty-two episodes. That's the advantage of cable of telling a little more self-contained stories. You can tell a story that is more mimicking reality. We get around that by playing characterization really slow. We're trying to juggle a lot of balls at the same time. A lot happens in theory, but a lot happens across five characters. Alicia is not ripped from place to place every episode. Sometimes it's Cary's problem or Kalinda's.

MK: You mentioned the question of pacing and how we make those choices. Yes, we do have a roadmap, but we are also forced to deal with scheduling issues that suddenly make one slow things down or speed things up depending on when one can get a cast member to tell a particular story. That impacts pacing.

RK: This may be something interesting for the writers and readers of your book to understand that network TV on the casting front is a little bit of a clusterfuck—that might be too strong. You're struggling to get actors who really want to do the show, but are now on *Sons of Anarchy* or are doing a three-episode arc on *Private Practice*. We find ourselves pacing based on the knowledge of when we can get an actor back.

MK: Again, that is because we're choosing to do some serialized storylines. If we were only telling closed-ended stories, casting would not be the same kind of problem. You would need your new defendant and your new attorney. You can find those people. There's no shortage of good actors—particular since we cast out of New York. Because we want somebody specific, that's when we run into difficulty.

NL: How important is theme when you're mapping out the personalized stories? When you're coming up with the A legal cases, are you trying to marry them to a theme from the B or C stories?

RK/MK: No.

RK: Actually, we go out of our way not to. Whenever there's thematic resonance, it feels more organic if it's actually the writer bringing it out in the writing process. So if you have three very different stories, when you start marrying them on the board in the writing process, you'll start to see echoes and resonance that you start dragging out as you're writing. If you do that prosaically, it starts to feel imposed. It's not arising out of these specific events. It feels more like the thematic resonance is built. The only time we marry stories is when events help in a domino effect. One story would start a beat of a second story.

MK: We always try to work from the reality of how things would feel to Alicia. So in that sense, she might feel at the end of the day that this week was all about X, but it's not as though she created that, it just might feel that way to her in retrospect.

RK: One last thing I'd say, too, is that it allows the characters in this meta way which isn't meta to comment on thematic connections. If it's imposed on the writers' room, it feels like it's the long hand of the screenwriter. But, in fact, if the events are not similar at all, but the character starts to see thematic resonance, they can talk about it because I think in people's lives more than on TV, people actually talk about when their lives are seeming like a TV show. The bottom line is that there's such a fear of being meta on TV, but in fact, in real life if you have these things that thematically connect and you're surprised by it, you'll talk about it to a friend or a husband or a wife. And that's what we want characters to have the freedom to do.

NL: What's the internal process with story documents? Do you do beat sheets, outlines? How extensive are the outlines? What's your process with your writing staff?

RK: Pretty dysfunctional. (*laughs*)

MK: In terms of what goes to the studio, it's changed. Initially, we were doing a one- or two-page story arena which was just a brief synopsis of what the case and then the personal story would be. Then, we would give them an outline.

RK: The point of the arena document was just that if they knew of other shows in their wheelhouse that might be doing something similar, they could warn you off or if there was some legal difficulty. We're doing one on the FCC, for example. It wasn't to steer you away from it, but just to be a little more conscious of what to avoid.

MK: Then we would do an outline that was somewhere between twelve and eighteen pages. And then a draft of the script. But that was the first three seasons, and it is pared down, so that now what the studio gets is a couple page arena document and then the draft of the script.

RK: The only other thing that we do internally beyond that is that Michelle and I draw up a fairly extensive beat sheet which is not all that readable, but is to us and the writer of the sequence of events. Because the structure you put on the board is pretty bare bones. Sometimes the beat sheet will juggle those events or add elements. It's just to see how the scenes would dovetail together.

NL: And you two are based in New York, is that right?

RK: We're bi-coastal people. Our writers' and editors' room is in L.A. and production is in New York.

NL: When you bring in directors, do you have extensive tone meetings with your directors?

RK: Yes. Our tone meetings go on for four hours. They're just nightmare affairs.

MK: But they're done over videoconferencing.

NL: I'm sure you've been asked this question a million times, so I apologize if it's boring. It's fascinating that you're doing a show about marriage and you're married showrunners. How do you delegate your responsibilities, and how is it working together?

RK: I think it's good because showrunning is very complicated. You have to multitask all the time, network-wise. I don't know if this is the same for cable, but network-wise, there's three operations happening at the same time, which is the writers' room, production, and all the editing and postproduction. Those three things are happening simultaneously, but on different episodes. You might be building in the room episode 4, shooting episode 3, and editing episode 2. There's this multilayered effect that to have another head who shares your problems and can multitask while you're multitasking is essential. You're probably hearing that from the other showrunners.

MK: There's so many little avenues of this stuff. There's casting that must be dealt with, there's standards and practices and the legal element. All these things have to be looked at, so it's useful to be more than one person. Candidly, I don't know how one person does the job.

RK: Then to be married on top of that has the added benefit of it's really someone you don't mind being with—at least with our marriage but not all marriages. They kind of share your same taste and instincts. So if I'm in a meeting, Michelle hopefully trusts that I will make decisions that she'll approve or at least won't grimace too big about it afterward. And I think the reciprocal is true. The only thing that I would say is complicated is that we have a thirteen-year-old daughter and that is a full-time job. Luckily she's not bored by it, I think she's amused by what we do. There's never really a completely home life. We try to dovetail things nicely, but look, it's a hard job.

NL: So much of it gets mirrored in Alicia's life.

RK: You are so right.

MK: We're lucky with that.

NL: That's why it comes off so real. What's the best thing about being the showrunners on *The Good Wife*, and what are the biggest challenges for you individually?

MK: I'll start with the challenges. The challenge is the time. It's trying to do this for twenty-two episodes. The benefit is that, just speaking for myself, I love the show, love the characters, the actors are spectacular; the writers are really some of the smartest, nicest people I've ever met. It is such a pleasure to spend time with them. The producers we work with happen to be people who are very smart and ethical and have a good sense of humor. It's an amazing bunch of people we get to work with and that for me is the positive.

RK: I was in features for a while, and features always felt like you were clawing through mud to try and get your story on the screen. You rewrote the same script hundreds of times just to even get a listen. It never felt that you were actually telling the story to anybody other than your own head and a few studio executives. The amazing thing about TV is that before you were desperate for a drop of water and now you have a fire hose shooting at your face. What we have is final cut. I don't think anyone gets final cut except Spielberg and some other people in features. In TV, the showrunner is given final cut on twenty-two to twenty-three little movies every year. People appreciate your opinion and don't question it because they don't have time to question it. There's nothing better in the world for writers than current TV production because there is so much handed over to the showrunner to say, "Here. Now go do it." I think the only downside for me is time, as Michelle said, which is also the time that you want to make something perfect and they don't give you time to make it perfect. It's not about financial costs, although that's a part of it, but it's more that you don't have the time to edit it for another week. The other aspect is ratings, which is hard because, for the best reasons, they take it very seriously. Our show is a moderate hit, which I think doesn't fall correctly in the demo, which can be tough. I would say that, and not having a life, are the down sides.

NL: How has the newer role of social media—in being able to get feedback, not just from ratings, networks, and studio executives, but from people writing in and blogging and immediately tweeting—affected you? Are you aware of these things coming after episodes? Does it influence the storytelling?

RK: I think it's probably a very comfortable pose to say no, but unfortunately, the answer is yes. I'm very aware of it. First of all, I think it's fantastic. As a writer and a reformed screenwriter for features, every day was procrastinating by participating in social media. Now it has the added aspect of being slightly an echo chamber because the people that participate are usually hardcore fans who have sometimes similar opinions and sometimes not. What you're looking for is very intelligent analysis that you don't get from mainstream media, but you might get the loner in some Brazilian town who saw the show and has exactly crystallized the thoughts that you were thinking. What you do is you take that Brazilian kid in that town and you make that who you're going to write the next episode for. I think social media is not about the mass of people. It's finding those people in the audience that I think Groucho Marx was talking about. There was someone he'd always look at and know that he made that person laugh. Otherwise, you don't have real access to the audience. I think it's the best thing that happened to TV since the product. I think the only danger of it is it becomes an echo chamber. I'm someone who, unlike someone like Kurt Sutter [Executive Producer on *Sons of Anarchy*], doesn't get involved by answering back or having a Twitter account. I think it's much more where the voice of the show is the show itself and the voice of the audience—[because now you can] get a sense of what people are saying.

5

MAKE US CARE

A s writers, we find ourselves creatively "in the zone" when the characters start speaking for themselves on the page—as if they've taken on a life of their own. As readers, this same process happens when we forget that we're reading words on a page and feel as if we've been transported into the world of the story.

Cultivating Viewer Investment

For a TV series to prosper and become a classic, the audience needs to become *emotionally invested* in the lives of its characters. We need to worry about their problems, big and small. We need to care about their hopes and dreams, triumphs and misfortunes. We need to bond with them, consider them part of our lives: as friends or coworkers or family members.

In a sitcom, we need both to laugh *with* them and, at times, *at* them. When they suffer humiliation, we need to cringe, not only because of the awkward situation, but also because we can identify with the universal feelings of shame, best intentions gone wrong, heartbreak, disappointment, and insecurity.

Must great TV characters be likeable? Not necessarily. Must they be compelling? Absolutely, yes. But what makes for a compelling, iconic character at the center of a TV series?

Well, it depends on genre, tone, and the network's wheelhouse. As we explored in Chapter 1, CBS has successfully remained faithful to its brand of wholly positive, heroic characters on its one-hour procedural dramas by relegating the outcasts, underdogs, and flawed protagonists to its sitcoms:

The Big Bang Theory, 2 Broke Girls, Two and a Half Men, Mike & Molly. Other networks have their own viewer and advertiser needs, and therefore "cast" their programming models accordingly.

What makes a character compelling to an audience for the long haul? If you're thinking he or she must merely be likeable and "save the cat," you'd be wrong. If a character's main personality trait is being "nice," then you're probably going to have a boring, superficial protagonist. Why? Because "nice" is generic and suggests harmony, whereas good comedy and drama is all about *conflict*.

Sure, a great, iconic character can have a heart of gold, but he/she also needs to have a streak of inconsistency or contradiction. Maybe she had always been the nicest person in the world, but in each episode she's going to be tested and forced by circumstances beyond her control to get mischievous or jealous or competitive or petty or selfish or greedy—every color in the spectrum—over the run of the series.

If all movies are, on some level, coming-of-age stories—no matter the age of the characters—then I would argue that all TV series are about characters struggling to succeed in life on their own terms—and usually butting up against the expectations of others, causing the protagonists to recalibrate, reconsider, and reevaluate.

Generally, in sitcoms, this recalibration results in nothing fundamentally changing in the characters' universe. In other words, most sitcom characters do not change. We embrace them for their flaws and foibles, and faithfully watch as they consistently make the same mistakes and repeat their same psychological patterns—and we love them for being so thoroughly rooted in *who they are*.

Creating Iconic Characters

In the classic TV series *All in the Family*, Archie Bunker (Carroll O'Connor) was a stubborn, petty, mean-spirited bigot from start to finish. He was maddening to watch every week, but also very funny because he (almost always) unwittingly became the butt of the joke.

If the common link between all iconic characters is a core contradiction—both positive and negative traits—then Archie's iconic status was his ability to be simultaneously bombastic and befuddled. He hated that his little corner of the world in Queens, New York, was being invaded by his "little goyle" Gloria's (Sally Struthers) husband, Michael ("Meathead") Stivic (played by Rob Reiner). It wasn't just that Gloria and Mike would be living under the same roof with Archie and his dimwitted, but surprisingly wise wife, Edith (Jean Stapleton). It was also what Mike and Gloria's younger generation represented to Archie's ideology.

If Archie was the self-anointed king of his castle, then anyone who didn't agree with Archie was viewed as an adversary. Ironically, Archie—and all iconic characters share this trait—was his own worst enemy.

And even though Archie ostensibly loved his family and worked hard to support them, he was so narrow-minded and intolerant that he'd invariably find himself swimming against the tide, trapped in his own belief system, and (humorously) drowning in his own misery. His gruff side was his defense mechanism against all perceived threats. His "nice" side was his soft spot for his daughter. You always got the sense that Archie would do anything for his daughter—anything but accept Meathead in her life. Gloria was his soft spot; Mike was his Achilles' heel.

In order for us to root for iconic characters, we need to have a grasp of their vulnerabilities.

In *Cheers*, Sam Malone (Ted Danson) was a recovering alcoholic. On *The Sopranos*, Tony Soprano (James Gandolfini) suffered from clinical depression. On *Mad Men,* Don Draper's Achilles' heel was/is his past. On *Homeland*, Carrie Mathison's (Claire Danes) vulnerability is due to Nicholas Brody (Damian Lewis) as well as her struggle with bipolar disorder. It's these characters' vulnerabilities that help stoke the fire of our rooting interest.

All iconic characters are willful and possess strong desires. They're *driven.* They're control freaks. Sometimes they succeed, but if they always got their way, the lack of turmoil and struggle would cause the series to dramatically flatline. What's much more important is that they continue to strive for success as they define it. It's usually their inability to redefine the meaning of "success" that gets them into trouble.

In Archie's world at the time, women, minorities, and gays were gradually being liberated, and his inability or unwillingness to accept change marginalized him both inside and outside of the Bunker household. With his ever-loyal wife by his side, Archie the misanthrope became the underdog of the series. And American TV audiences can't help but root for the underdog—even when their own actions and belief systems are what undermine their ability to evolve and grow up.

If Archie Bunker ever became a self-actualized Zen master, he would cease to entertain us.

In the wry HBO series *Enlightened*, Amy Jellico (Laura Dern) bounces back from a nervous breakdown and attempts to live the next chapter of her life as a nonjudgmental, unconditionally loving being of light. Having been a live wire of anxiety and ambition, Amy aspires to remain serene, forgiving, and to transcend the petty disturbances of daily life. Unfortunately, she also needs to get back in the saddle and make a living, so she goes back into the workforce—at the same corporate behemoth that had brought her down. In spite of all the psychological tools Amy had learned in rehab, she's always just a trigger point away from a full-blown panic attack. Amy can be delusional and ridiculously sanguine, but we continue to root for her because she's trying to be authentic and strong, even as she suffers humiliation, puts on airs, and remains incredibly fragile. The last thing Amy wants is to end up like her mousy, pragmatic, lonely mother (played by Diane Ladd). Amy is an idealist and, like her spunky predecessor Mary Richards (Mary Tyler Moore), she might just make it after all. But in the meantime, it's going to be a rough road—and that's good news for fueling the story engine.

No one wants to watch a TV series about a freshly paved smooth road. We're drawn to the potholes and speed bumps and perilous curves. We like our series characters to zoom through the intersection as the traffic light turns from yellow to red. We're drawn to characters who are, at the very least, *tempted* to speed up. Some characters will get a moving violation ticket; others will get a lucky break; others will be able to talk themselves out of trouble; and still others will get into a wreck and face the consequences.

In *True Blood*, Sookie Stackhouse (Anna Paquin) desperately wants to be with vampire Bill Compton (Stephen Moyer) despite admonitions and interference from friends, family, Bill's powerful cohort of vampires, and other antagonistic forces, including Bill's sire Lorena (Mariana Klaveno) who's still hung up on him. Sookie never takes the path of least resistance. That's her thing. That's what defines her.

In a perfect TV universe, no two characters will react exactly the same in the same situation. *Who they are* dictates how they'll behave—and if they're compelled to act out of character, our investment in them will spike our curiosity and cause us to wonder why.

That's what good TV series do: they show us how beloved characters perform under pressure. Based on their backstories, we try to anticipate how iconic characters will behave in a given situation. But the trick is to avoid predictability and to find highly specific small moments that serve to intensify the situation and surprise us. And so, the bigoted Archie Bunker may reluctantly acquiesce to having his picture taken with an African American celebrity (Sammy Davis Jr.), but the writers push the envelope and blindside Archie—and us—by having Sammy plant a kiss on Archie's cheek as the photo is snapped. It's one small step forward for Archie's tolerance, but he's so out of step with the ever-changing world that he'll never be able to catch up—*and we don't want him to.*

There's a purity and integrity to all iconic characters whether we like them or not.

All great sitcom characters suffer from myopia because they're limited by their past experiences and project the past onto the present and future. They fear the unknowns of a strange new world. Better and easier to stay within the relatively safe confines of the show's universe than to break out of its bubble and start anew. We've seen evidence of this when sitcoms spin off supporting characters into their own brave new world—with mixed results. Frasier Crane (Kelsey Grammer) successfully managed to quit his day job and segue from the Boston bar called *Cheers* into his Seattle-based radio psychologist career on *Frasier*—but mainly because Frasier stayed fundamentally rooted in his Crane-ness. The locale and supporting characters may have changed, but Frasier was still the same persnickety yet loveable gasbag he'd always been.

Creating Antiheroes

While most TV series leads are iconic heroes and heroines who struggle to be trustworthy, well-intentioned, dependable spouses, parents, friends, neighbors, and colleagues, there are many cable series that feature *antiheroes* who test the limits of society. If you'll notice, virtually all "groundbreaking" TV series are about rule breaking characters: Walter White on *Breaking Bad* was a mild-mannered science teacher turned megalomaniacal drug lord; Dexter Morgan is a vigilante serial killer; Carrie Mathison (on *Homeland*) not only consorted with a suspected terrorist and got him to let his guard down but she also fell in love with him; Don Draper *appears* to be the idyllic family man and knows how to sell the perfection of the American Dream to his advertising clients (on *Mad Men*), but in actuality, Don is a lying, cheating manipulator; Vic Mackey (Michael Chiklis) was supposed to be a law enforcer, but in the pilot episode of *The Shield*, Vic shot an unsuspecting undercover cop in the face, point blank.

In *Justified*, deputy U.S. Marshal Raylan Givens (Timothy Olyphant) breaks the law, as much as it he enforces it, in his Kentucky hometown. In the pilot, Raylan gives a criminal an ultimatum: "If you don't get out of town in twenty-four hours, I'm gonna shoot you on sight," and he delivers on his promise.

In some of the preceding examples of antiheroes, the characters' ends serve to justify the means. Dexter seeks justice. Vic Mackey feels he needs to break the rules in order to defeat the scumbags on the streets of Los Angeles and to overcome the restrictive bureaucracy within the police department.

Other shows have an array of dissolute characters, but they remain empathetic because of a relatable code of ethics. In *Sons of Anarchy*, Jax Teller (Charlie Hunnam) has committed assault, extortion, murder, and even injected his reformed addict ex-wife with heroin to ensure custody of his son, and he's arguably the moral compass of the show! However, Jax would do anything to protect his family and his motorcycle club.

In *The Wire*, Omar (Michael Kenneth Williams) is a shotgun-wielding outlaw whose specialty is robbery, but he only steals from drug dealers.

However, in the case of *Breaking Bad*, as the series has progressed, empathy for Walt has become more dicey. Walter White may have started off as a terminally ill, high school chemistry teacher, loyal husband, and loving father of two (including a handicapped son), but Walt has evolved into a self-centered, greedy, power-obsessed criminal mastermind. The only thing stronger than Walt's convenient self-delusion is his hubris. Even his mountains of wealth have become immaterial. What Walt loves most is being feared and respected. Any shreds of human decency that Walt may still possess have been overshadowed by his need to stay at the top of his game.

What's most fascinating with the case study of *Breaking Bad* is how the audience continues to root for Walter White—even as he's progressed from white knight family man into a pitch-black murderous monster. This raises the question: Is Walt just an anomaly expertly crafted by showrunner Vince Gilligan and portrayed by the brilliant, supremely likeable actor, Bryan Cranston? Or is there something else that compels us to continually root for such a bad guy?

I believe that all iconic characters need to possess both positive (+) and negative (−) characteristics. This +/− polarity provides all series with the right amount of dramatic heat to sustain it over many seasons.

- Walter White begins as a novice in the crystal meth drug trade, but he's also an expert chemist with a unique skill set. He's simultaneously naïve and smart.
- Walt has strong leadership qualities, but he also grows increasingly paranoid and is unable to trust anybody, so he becomes a lone wolf.
- Walt is a loving family man who will say anything to hold his family together, but his actions become more and more dangerous and reckless, placing his wife and kids in greater danger.
- Walt is greedy and power hungry, but his secret double life prohibits him from showing off his power and wealth, so despite his growing ego and fortune, he continues to live small.

Perhaps we root for him—and Archie Bunker, Frasier Crane, Vic Mackey, Nancy Botwin, and dozens of other iconic series leads—because we all possess both light and dark impulses—and there's a vicarious thrill to watching characters veer into the dark side. Some of our rooting interest might come from wanting to see just how much they can get away with or from our desire or curiosity to see if they will find redemption or a tragic demise.

> We dread driving past the destruction of a train wreck, but somehow we can't look away. Our interest isn't in the carnage. Our rooting interest is in the *survivors*. We all know that life is complicated, difficult, heartbreaking, relentless, and precious. Great iconic characters engross us because no matter how many times they get knocked down, they never give up.

INTERVIEW: Vince Gilligan

Vince Gilligan Credits

Best known for:

Breaking Bad (Executive Producer/Writer/Director) 2008–2013
  Emmy Nominated (Outstanding Directing in a Drama Series) 2008; 2012
  Emmy Nominated (Outstanding Drama Series) 2009–2010; 2012
  WGA Award Winner (Drama Series) 2012
  WGA Award Winner (Episodic Drama) 2009; 2012
  WGA Nominated (Drama Series) 2010–2011
  WGA Nominated (Dramatic Series) 2011
  WGA Nominated (New Series) 2009
  AFI's Top 10 TV series 2009, 2011–2013
  TCA Award 2010, 2012
  Peabody Award 2008
Hancock (Film) 2008
The X-Files (Executive Producer/Co-Producer/Supervising Producer/Writer/Director) 1996–2002
  Emmy Nominated (Outstanding Drama Series) 1997–1998
  Emmy Nominated (Outstanding Writing for a Drama Series) 1997
The Lone Gunmen (Executive Producer/Writer) 2001

NL: The toughest thing for most screenwriters is creating original characters. People come up with ideas for what might be an interesting show, but creating complex characters is extremely difficult to do. What's your process when you're starting with the pilot? Walt (Bryan Cranston) is all about the choices that he makes in life. How do you make your creative choices?

VG: It's interesting because each new project is a bit like a snowflake. It has its own shape. The best way to explain it is to talk specifically about *Breaking*

Bad. When the idea first struck, it intrigued me. I think in hindsight what struck me in one of those rare Eureka moments of inspiration was not a plot or a big idea; it was a character who I found very intriguing—the character I didn't even have a name for who became Walter White. The idea of a previously good man—an inherently good man—a guy who is a loving husband and father who works hard for his family—who strives to do the right thing and does not break the law. Who suddenly, for external reasons, decides to very much veer off course off the path of goodness and become a bad guy. That intrigued me. It wasn't the idea of cooking meth or putting a lab in the back of an RV; it was the interesting trappings that came with it. What intrigued me was the possibility of telling a story where the protagonist, by force of will, decided to become bad and would eventually become the antagonist, that idea of sand shifting beneath the character's feet via a process that he put in motion. I'd love to say that it always works out that way. You start with a blank pad of paper and a pencil, your chin in your hand, saying, "OK, what interesting character can I write about today?" The trouble is they don't appear to you that often, unfortunately. But when they do, it's a wonderful thing.

NL: Some writers construct these lengthy backstory biographies for their nascent characters before they even know how they're going to fit into a show—which can feel arbitrary, and yet also necessary. I've read in other interviews that you started with the idea of turning Mr. Chips into Scarface. When you're trying to develop his character and put him into a world, choices of making him a chemistry teacher, and when did you hit upon the idea that he was going to cook meth? And, setting it in Albuquerque and choices about his family and son?

VG: I was on the phone with a buddy of mine that I've known since NYU Film School back in the mid-1980s who is actually one of my writers on *Breaking Bad* now. He was a writer on *The X-Files* with me. This was a year or two after *The X-Files* had ended and we were talking about what we were going to do next because good writing jobs were hard to find at that point. He told me a story that he had read in the New York Times, I think, about a guy who had been caught with a meth lab in the back of a Winnebago going around cooking crystal meth. My friend Tom [Schnauz] said, "Hey, maybe we should try that and make a little dough." At the moment he made that joke, a character who would do such a thing flashed in my mind and became very interesting—the idea of a good man willfully going bad. This was a man who was doing bad things for ostensibly good reasons. It's interesting if you had told me in that first week or so to sit down and write a biography of this man, I would have written something very different from who Walt ended up being. Not to say that that's a bad exercise. Anything that you can put on paper that can help focus your thinking and gets you closer to the goal of creating something is to the good. If it's looking through a phone book until you come up with the right combination of first and last names that helps you picture the character, so be it. But, you have to stay flexible. The really interesting things about Walter White only came to me a season or two later once the show had progressed and once I had the benefit of working with Bryan Cranston who truly helped create the character and embodies it. And once I started working with my excellent writers who helped me see the potential in what it was that I had come up with and helped me make it so much better than what it would have been if it was just me alone working on it.

In those early days for instance, I realized what Walt's superpower is. I didn't realize what a world-class liar he would be. That's really his superpower. He lies most ably to himself. He is able to convince himself of anything. First and foremost, that he is a good man, that he does what he does for his family—the huge, awful lie that's at the center of *Breaking Bad*, long past all reason and any evidence to the contrary.

NL: Like any superhero, they have a superpower, but then they also have an accompanying weakness or Achilles' heel. In his case, it appears that they are one and the same.

VG: Indeed. His Achilles' heel is his pride. His ability to lie is his power. He has made so many bad choices out of a sense of pride, when his ego is wounded, and it's a very fragile ego. There's a great expression I heard years ago when someone was described to me as being "the piece of shit at the center of the universe." When I heard that, it stuck with me. I think it describes Walt. He does not see himself as the piece of shit. He sees himself as the center of the universe, but it's a very fragile universe that can crack very easily when he is presented with evidence that he is not the be all and end all.

NL: I was thinking about the film *The Social Network*, and how Mark Zuckerberg gets that rejection from that girl early on in college, which shapes all of his grandiosity and ambition. In your pilot, Walt hits that rock bottom moment with, besides his illness, when he's at the car wash and the student from school shows up with the girl and Walt's scrubbing a tire rim. He feels so completely humiliated and it's like his Scarlett O'Hara, "As God is my witness, I'll never go hungry again" moment. No matter how much he has, Walter seems to have this insecurity when it's ill-gotten and you're fearful that it could all be taken away. The last episode that aired, your mid-season cliffhanger, when Skyler (Anna Gunn) says, "How much is enough?" It's not about the money. What would you say he's afraid of?

VG: That's a good question. The obvious answer would be death. The motivation that got him off his keister in the first place to becoming a criminal was the fear of imminent death. He was facing an end-of-life crisis. It's a very existential show. Walt faces many existential moments that he so far has managed to surmount. And, yet, he doesn't seem to spend a lot of time pondering death—maybe in the early going in the first season he did. He's gotten past that. We even had an episode a few seasons back where he said to his brother-in-law, "You know, I used to worry about everything, it used to keep me awake at night. But, since I got my cancer diagnosis, I sleep like a baby." I think Walt's big fear is insignificance. Whether he's here or not, that's not the issue, but once he's gone, he fears he'll be instantly forgotten—that he won't have mattered or counted for anything. This is a man who in a later episode lets Jesse [Aaron Paul] and the audience know that he could have been somebody. He could have been a billionaire or at least a millionaire many times over as a founding partner of Gray Matter. This company that his girlfriend and his best buddy from college founded with him. He stepped away from that and he has intense regret about it. The stock price every week shows him how much money he could have had, if he had stuck with the program. This is a very damaged man who fears that he is irrelevant and insignificant. And decides ultimately, I think it's from *Paradise Lost* that Satan says, "It's better to reign in Hell than serve in Heaven." It's the realization that Walt can stand being a criminal. It wouldn't have been his first choice, but it gives him something that he needs. It gives him power and potency and relevance. It's better to be somebody negative than nobody.

NL: There's a great line at the end of season 4 where he says to his wife, "I'm not in danger, I am the danger." He never thought he could become this guy. He's cooking meth, but he has his own addiction to this power.

VG: His addiction to power and the money, I think, becomes a yardstick of sorts. That huge pile of cash that we see in that eighth episode of season 5 is a yardstick nothing more. Walt and Skyler could never spend it all without garnering the unwanted attention of the IRS and the feds. It's just an enormous pile of paper in a U-Store-It facility. That scene you mentioned earlier shows Walt's ability to lie to himself. When he says, "I'm not in danger, I *am* the danger," he could not be more wrong.

NL: How much research did you do going into the pilot? Do you have meth consultants? How do you come up with some of this stuff?

VG: The thing I loved about this show when it first started was that Walter White was essentially me. In other words, the thing that held me in good stead when I wrote the pilot before I had a staff, including folks with the DEA and oncologists and professors of chemistry. All these folks that help us out with the various facts and information. Before we had any of that, Walter White was just a guy who one day woke up and decided I'm going to start cooking crystal meth. He was very much me at that point in the sense that he didn't know any more about a life of crime than I did. So, as a writer, it worked out very well for me. I do not have any of the chemistry knowledge Walt possesses. He is a brilliant chemist and I barely know how soda pop is made. Having said that, the thing that held me in good stead in those scenes where he was teaching chemistry is that he's talking to a bunch of knuckleheads and they're barely listening. He has to dumb it down and speak in laymen's terms. That got me through—the ability of Walt to pick his audience. And then, Walt bumbling his way into a life of crime is pretty much the way I would have done it, if I had the desire and I wasn't too scared of the police which is what made it so fun to write. I'm better with writing characters who are a little closer to me because I'm not very good at research.

NL: As you started to get into cooking meth, he's kind of a neophyte in that world. How did Jesse enter onto the canvas for you?

VG: I got so very lucky that we cast Bryan Cranston and Aaron Paul in these two lead parts, and of course, all of our other wonderful actors as well. These actors have truly inhabited these roles and more than that, they've shown us just how deep and rich and complex these characters could truly be. It's a large part of what makes them iconic. They have shown both me and my writers the way to make them iconic. A good example is Aaron Paul as Jesse Pinkman who, I hate to admit, in the early going was just a plot mechanism. There was a lot about that pilot that was somewhat mechanistic. Hank Schrader's [Dean Norris] character was a logistical element who existed to prod Walt in a certain direction. Hank was this bold, brassy, "hail fellow, well met" frat boy of a character who was everything Walter White was not. You could tell that Walter was secretly jealous of this guy and had this contained animus toward him. Jesse Pinkman existed to show Walt the way into this criminal underworld at which point in the beginning, and then I was just going to kill off his character.

So, I'd love to tell you that I had the whole thing figured out from day one, but that would be a lie. I, for instance, was ready to kick Jesse to the curb as soon as he had downloaded his somewhat limited knowledge of criminality to Walt. And, then I was going to create someone more interesting for season 2. Or, beyond that, I'm not even sure that I saw the necessity of Walt having a partner to begin with. I thought he would have various underlings. This is where luck takes a hand because we cast this outstanding actor, Aaron Paul, who in the early going added so much value to the show that there was no way I could kill off this character. Conversely, if we had cast somebody who was a bit of a dud, I wouldn't even have questioned it. I would have just edited around him and then killed him off in some spectacular fashion. It's a good lesson to writers that if you really want the writing itself to be the be all and end all, you should be writing novels—which someday I would like to try myself—but when you're working in TV and movies, it is very much a collaborative effort. Your writing will live or die—no matter how good it is—based on the quality, talent, and enthusiasm of the actors who inhabit the role and on the quality of the director directing them. It works both ways. The actors and directors can fill in some gaps in your writing and make it better. Or they take some of your good stuff and make it worse, unfortunately. There's a certain amount of luck or fate that takes a hand when the casting happens or the director is hired. You always keep your fingers crossed and hope for the best. You never know how it's going to turn out. That's what makes it terrifying and exciting.

NL: It's also ironic that Walter starts out as a teacher, but then he's such a great student. He learns from everybody and takes a little bit from each of them.

VG: That's a good way to put it. I never really thought about it that way. Walt is an excellent student. He drinks in this criminal world around him very quickly. Yet, he is arrogant enough that he has trouble thinking of himself as a student. He prefers to think of himself as the master. That is what chafed so much in the season where Walt was under Gus Fring's (Giancarlo Esposito) thumb. I think what chafed him the most was not that Gus wanted him dead, but that Gus was the master and Walt was the indentured servant.

NL: When you're breaking stories in your writers' room, are you doing traditional A, B, and C stories? Are you structuring a half a season at a time according to any specific theme? Or is it episode by episode?

VG: It is very much episode by episode. I had never done a series before this that had involved A, B, and C stories. I had certainly seen my share of TV which contained them. I should preface this by saying there's no right way to do television. All that matters is that you find a way that works for you. The way we do it on *Breaking Bad* is that we make it an all hands on deck affair. I have six writers and I want them all in the room with me every minute of the day. I hate it when they get up and go to the bathroom, for instance, because I want everyone there to listen and to contribute. I want everyone there helping to move the ball down the field. This show is so serialized that you really need that.

On *The X-Files*, you did spend a lot of time by yourself. You'd go off and ponder or go to your office or walk around the FOX lot trying to come up with a stand-alone episode. But with *Breaking Bad* you have to be in that room. You almost have to have a mantra where you ask over and over again, "Where is Walt's head at? What does he want right now? What is he afraid of? What is his goal right now? What does Skyler want? What does Jesse want?" That is what we do. We build these episodes brick by brick. We don't think in terms of A, B, and C stories. We think of *Breaking Bad* as Walter White's story. A character study of one man. This is a world where Walter White's choices and actions lead to difficulties and problems for all the other characters within that universe of the show. He is the A story. He is the main taproot from which branches out all other limbs and leaves of the story. He's the acorn that's set it all in motion.

Even though it's a show ostensibly about a man dying of cancer, metaphorically speaking, Walter himself is cancer. Walt is the malignancy at the center of the show that affects others to their detriment—his family first and foremost.

NL: When you're doing a serialized show, one of the challenges is that you don't want to burn through story too fast. If you're doing them episode by episode, what are your instincts for revealing story?

VG: My instinct is that there's a very interesting dynamic that occurs when you're creating a serialized TV show, although this could occur in more episodic shows as well. You want to swing for the fences. You want to give the audience a reason to stay tuned in. It's hard keeping folks' attention. In other words, sometimes the faster you tell the story, it becomes problematic in and of itself and you risk losing viewers by the very fact that you are working too hard and the sweat is showing. The best philosophy I have on that subject, and one that, admittedly, I have at times not heeded myself is to give the audience the bare minimum. Give him just enough that the show is interesting. Don't give them any more than they need to keep watching. Try to keep the show moving as slowly as possible, so that it is still interesting and moving in a forward direction. This is a terrible phrase, but it fits. You've got to be careful not to shoot your wad. It's a real crude way of putting it, but I can't think of a more apt expression. You've got to keep people right on the edge. Keep telling your audience new things about your character. You've got to keep them invested and learning. On the other hand, if you're moving like a rocket, eventually you're going to tire them out. It's a very tricky thing—pacing. I'll be honest with you—I've fallen prey to this myself—during the first season of *Breaking Bad*, I was ready to throw the kitchen sink at the audience. I was ready to give them everything I had and then some. By the end of that first season, because I was desperate for the show to be loved and to stay on the air, I was all set to do crippling damage inadvertently. But the luckiest thing that had ever happened to me on *Breaking Bad* was that it coincided with the Writer's Guild strike and we were unable to do our last two episodes of that season. If we had done them, we would have absolutely swung for the fences, we would have killed off a couple of major characters that I realized, in hindsight, that we could not do without. And we would have crippled the show. So I understand that feeling of wanting to keep the audience satisfied. Sometime though the best way to do that is not to be frantic in your storytelling, but in fact to slow it down a bit. It was a hard lesson to learn and really one I learned from sheer luck.

It helps to know how many episodes you'll have. However, the TV business is not geared that way, you don't know for sure unless you're doing a miniseries. I think that's an underrated form. I wish that the miniseries would make a comeback. It seems to me that it could be poised to. We have so many things vying for our attention and a miniseries allows us to say to ourselves, "I'm going to watch six hours of this and then it will be done." I would be first in line to work on something like that because it's an investment that people can more readily make nowadays.

NL: When I interviewed Damon Lindelof, he said that they knew how *Lost* was going to end. Do you know how *Breaking Bad* will end?

VG: I'd be lying if I said I knew from the get-go how it would all end. There's so much about the character that I didn't know going into it or things that I thought I knew, but better things came along. For me, I find that what works best is not to be too rigid in your thinking. Very often, I have what I thought was an excellent idea and then someone else comes along and says, "Why don't we do it this way?" and I think, "Damn, I wish I had thought of that." So it seems to me that TV at its best is a living, breathing thing. It's organic. And if you're organic in your storytelling which means letting your characters tell you where they need to go, instead of trying to force them into directions that they don't want to take; if you can maintain that organic form of plot evolution, then that will always hold you in good stead. If you're honest with your characters, if you let them behave as human beings would, then you'll never stray too far from the right path.

One last thought, your original question was, "Who do you root for?" It's very hard to root for Walter White the deeper you get into the series and that was a big concern for me early on. I thought I've got to hire a very likeable actor. I've got to stack the deck in his favor. He's got a wife with a surprise pregnancy. He's got a son with cerebral palsy. He's treated miserably in his second job and is laughed at by his rich students. I was very worried. But I'm happy to say that as the series progressed I've relaxed in my thinking. I don't worry as much about Walt being likeable. It surprises me actually that people still root for him at all. I kind of stopped rooting for him as his creator quite a while back. He's a guy I wouldn't want to know if he was a real person. There are people in the audience who have said, "You know, I can't take this guy anymore. I have to stop watching." Hopefully, the show remains interesting even though I don't sympathize with Walt anymore. But then there are good, smart, law-abiding people who still root for the guy, and I find that a very interesting sociological study, because the process for my writers and me is almost to shake off the viewers' sympathy to this main character, to help them see that he really is on a journey from being a good guy to a bad guy. At some step along that journey, you say to yourself, "He really is the bad guy." The show from the beginning was a bit of experimental television, I wanted to tell a story in which the main character was undergoing constant change. But as far as rooting for the character, there are many who do not, but hopefully there are other things that make them tune in.

NL: I think it's a vicarious thrill. You kind of root for him because it's one guy railing against the system. And he's always vulnerable. No matter how strong he seems to get. Plus you always have somebody worse than Walt.

VG: Interesting. That's well put. I like that take on it.

6
VALUE FAMILY DYNAMICS

Every television series is about a family—whether they're related by
blood or not.
Some series are literally about a family: *Modern Family*, *Parenthood*,
The Sopranos, *Breaking Bad*, *Dallas*, *Downton Abbey*, *The Good Wife*, *Friday
Night Lights*, *Homeland*, *The Americans*, *Weeds*, *The Killing* (seasons 1 and 2),
American Horror Story (season 1), and *Brothers & Sisters*.

The Americans is an example of an arranged marriage between two Soviet
KGB agents, Elizabeth and Phillip Jennings (Keri Russell and Matthew
Rhys), who are posing as an American couple in the Washington, D.C., area.
In order for them to blend into their suburban bedroom community and not
arouse suspicion, their deep cover assignment necessitated having children.
The clever twist on this family drama meets espionage thriller is that their
kids have no clue that mom and dad are Cold War spies. This is a marriage of
convenience with a family unit based on secrets, lies, and the ongoing decep-
tion of everyone Elizabeth and Phillip encounter.

The Americans puts the family unit to the test in unique and extreme
ways—with the highest stakes possible should their cover be blown. We're
talking life and death espionage missions set against a backdrop of domestic
harmony.

While sitcom families tend to argue over small stuff that feels big to the
characters (I call them "tremendous trifles"), there is never any doubt of the
unconditional love that belies every quip and wisecrack.

On the other hand, families in one-hour drama series usually deal with
more substantive problems and hardships. The tone can range from relation-
ship/communication issues (such as in *Parenthood* and *The Good Wife*) to
light, humor-tinged jeopardy (*Castle*, *Elementary*) to much darker, edgier

problems (such as in *Breaking Bad* and *Homeland*). The goal for every new TV series is for it to feel fresh in its own right—which means that all TV families need to be imperfect and, on some level, discontent. Or as a famous Russian author once stated, "Happy families are all alike; every unhappy family is unhappy in its own way."

Today's audiences may not be able to relate to what it's like being a KGB spy in the 1980s, a meth cooker in present-day Albuquerque, a mafia kingpin, or a football coach—but we can *all* relate to what it feels like to be in a family. This supports the main point of this chapter: *family stories are universal.*

Expanding Family Types

In some of the preceding examples, there is both a related-by-blood family *and* an extended workplace family. In *The Good Wife*, Alicia Florrick's troubled husband and their two kids are the "home" family, and Alicia's colleagues at the law firm comprise her "other" family (see examples of how later).

Some series are about extended families: *Once Upon a Time, Two and a Half Men, Game of Thrones, Mad Men, Spartacus, The West Wing,* and *Sons of Anarchy.*

Other series focus on colleagues in the workplace that interact as a family unit might, encompassing the dynamics of authority figures (mom and dad), siblings (sibling rivalries and bonding), spouses, wise elders (grandparents), prodigal sons and daughters, black sheep outcasts, and some characters act like children: from tantrum-prone toddlers to rebellious teenagers.

Family dynamics outside of "normal" (related by birth) family units are often based on the same psychological and logistical power dynamics as a "typical" American family. In some cases, friendships forged at work, school, and at play can be even more intense than a traditional family bond because as the old adage goes, you choose your friends, but you can't choose your family.

Blended and nontraditional families are much more pervasive now. Divorce is extremely common these days. Marriage tends to occur later in life for many—if at all. Life moves faster now and most people spend more time with their coworkers than they do at home with their own families.

With such an emphasis outside the home, people naturally gravitate toward coworkers and friends who fulfill their psychological and emotional needs. Consequently, seeking approval from your boss might supplant seeking the approval of your parent(s)—and the former comes with a paycheck for added validation.

Confiding in your colleagues and/or best friends may be preferable to confiding in your sibling, cousin, or aunt and uncle. Our friends and coworkers seem to "get" us better than our immediate relatives anyway—and probably with far less judgment because we share less backstory (aka "baggage") with our newer friends and acquaintances. We're more likely to edit out some of the familial details to present a more ideal version of ourselves. Our actual family members, on the other hand, know us all too well—often choosing to dwell on our old patterns instead of seeing us as we are now.

However, all "family" members, including friends and colleagues, can be adept at "pushing each other's [psychological] buttons." The better someone knows you, the more familiar they are with your weaknesses and vulnerabilities. In other words, the people who love you most, also know how to hurt you the most. Trust in close relationships is built out of respect for these boundaries. When breached, all relationships need to go through the negotiation process of forgiveness, making amends, and wiping the slate clean (unlikely) or holding a grudge (more human).

Intensifying Family Dynamics

All familial relationships are rife with conflicting allegiances and agendas. Household finances are one of the biggest stresses in families. For many men, the ability to bring home a paycheck is still hardwired into their psyche, while at the same time, women are increasingly "leaning in" and not only supporting their families, but also out-earning their husbands—which can create new friction at home. These power dynamics influence the choices characters make in order to feel worthy of love, respect, and validation from season to season.

Many of these choices are pragmatic concerns of basic survival. For example, this is how Walter White got into the meth trade at the outset of *Breaking Bad*: he had a terminal cancer diagnosis, mounting debt, and a pregnant wife, Skyler (Anna Gunn). Walt's initial choices were to provide for his family in his absence. However, as *Breaking Bad* nears its series finale, Walt has more money than he and Skyler know what to do with—they're filthy rich. But it's dirty money and Walt is on a collision course with the police, the DEA, and a growing list of enemies. *Breaking Bad* began with Walt's (misguided) good intentions as he faced his own mortality. There is no question in my mind that this series will end in tragedy for Walt. His megalomania has alienated everyone who once loved and cared about him. Showrunner Vince Gilligan set out to create a series about a Mr. Chips character who turns into Scarface by the end. And like Tony Montana (played by Al Pacino), chances are that Walter White will die alone.

Examining TV Families

Consider these examples of family dynamics from several TV series, with their workplace role juxtaposed against what their more traditional role might be within an actual family:

The Good Wife (Season 1)
Home family:

Alicia Florrick (Julianna Margulies) as wife, mom
Peter Florrick (Chris Noth) as estranged husband, father
Zach (Graham Phillips) and Grace (Makenzie Vega) (their kids)
Jackie Florrick (Mary Beth Peil) as judgmental mother-in-law

Work family:

Diane Lockhart (Christine Baranski) as senior partner, in the role as matriarch
Will Gardner (Josh Charles) as Alicia's on-again-off-again lover—with marital dynamics
Kalinda Sharma (Archie Panjabi) as the wild sister
Cary Agos (Matt Czuchry) as the younger sibling in need of experience and guidance

Grey's Anatomy (Season 1)
Work family:

Dr. Miranda Bailey (Chandra Wilson) as strict matriarch
Dr. Richard Webber (James Pickens Jr.) as patriarch
Dr. Meredith Grey (Ellen Pompeo) as neurotic, insecure daughter seeking approval
Her "sisters": Cristina Yang (Sandra Oh), Izzie Stevens (Katherine Heigl)
Her "brothers": George O'Malley (T.R. Knight), Alex Karev (Justin Chambers), Preston Burke (Isaiah Washington)
Dr. Mark Sloan (Eric Dane) as a cousin
Dr. Derek Shepherd (Patrick Dempsey) as an uncle to everyone except Meredith, who is his on-again-off-again lover (spousal dynamics)

LOST (Season 1)
Strangers as family:

Jack Shephard (Matthew Fox) as leader, patriarch, and healer
Kate Austen (Evangeline Lilly) as co-leader, nurturing mom figure
Hugo "Hurley" Reyes (Jorge Garcia) as lethargic, lazy son
Charlie Pace (Dominic Monaghan) as rebellious druggie son
James "Sawyer" Ford (Josh Holloway) as enterprising brother with anger issues
Boone Carlyle (Ian Somerhalder) as brother
Shannon Rutherford (Maggie Grace), who was Boone's actual stepsister, but also had sister dynamics with other cast members

Mad Men **(Season 1)**

Home family:

Don Draper (Jon Hamm) as philandering, mostly absent husband/father
Betty Draper (January Jones) as narcissistic matriarch (aka bad mommy)
Sally (Kiernan Shipka) and Bobby (Jared Gilmore) (their kids)

Work family:

Bertram Cooper (Robert Morse) as the Wise Grand Patriarch
Don Draper (Jon Hamm) and Roger Sterling (John Slattery) as brothers to
each other and uncles to their staff and colleagues
Peggy Olson (Elizabeth Moss) as the smart eldest sister
Joan Harris (Christina Hendricks) as workplace mom
Pete Campbell (Vincent Kartheiser) who behaves at times like a spoiled brat
son and then at other times as the pariah brother
Ken Cosgrove (Aaron Stanton), Harry Crane (Rich Sommer), and Paul
Kinsey (Michael Gladis) as sons to Don and Roger and as brothers to
each other

Scandal **(Season 1)**

Work family:

Olivia Pope (Kerry Washington) as powerful, glamorous mom; the boss
Cyrus Beene (Jeff Perry) as the president's chief of staff; Olivia's equal in
political power, but also serves as her uncle/father figure
U.S. Attorney David Rosen (Joshua Malina) as Olivia's know-it-all brother;
sibling dynamics
President Fitzgerald Grant (Tony Goldwyn) as Olivia's secret lover, best
friend; spousal dynamics, even though he's married to Mellie
First Lady Mellie Grant (Bellamy Young) as Olivia's archrival stepsister
Harrison Wright (Columbus Short), Abby Whelan (Darby Stanchfield),
Quinn Perkins (Katie Lowes), and Huck (Guillermo Díaz) as the children

Defining Character by Familial Role

Family dynamics are especially useful when assembling an ensemble cast.
It's not that you'll need to cover every gender, age, or familial role. But it
is helpful to determine how each character might relate to one another
in both positive and negative ways. Police detective partners, even if
both heterosexual and male, will invariably relate to each other as fighting spouses at times. Professional colleagues might jockey for position

to impress the boss, and thus struggle through the jealousies of sibling rivalry.

Notice how age and gender is not always the main determining factor of family dynamics. In season 3 of *The Walking Dead* after patriarch Rick Grimes' (Andrew Lincoln) wife, Lori (Sarah Wayne Callies), dies in childbirth, their prepubescent son, Carl (Chandler Riggs), is forced to grow up fast. He becomes so confident with his marksmanship and fearless zombie killing skills that he evolves from innocent child to resourceful survivalist adult in a matter of months. And when his father, Rick, starts hallucinating (seeing the ghost of his late wife) and losing his sanity, it's Carl who (temporarily) emerges as the patriarch of the prison group until Rick can come to his senses and lead again. This transfer of power occurred when the elder leaders were occupied elsewhere—with Daryl Dixon (Norman Reedus) trying to rein in his loose cannon brother Merle (Michael Rooker) and Hershel Greene (Scott Wilson) dealing with his impaired.

In later episodes, Andrea (Laurie Holden) seeks normalcy and traditional community life by moving to the "secure" township of Woodbury. The patriarch of the town is the Governor (David Morrissey). As Andrea and the Governor become romantic partners, she essentially becomes the First Lady of Woodbury (its matriarch). Meanwhile, outside Woodbury and inside the prison compound, Carol Peletier (Melissa McBride) and the Greene sisters move into matriarchal roles. Glenn (Steven Yeun) and Maggie Greene (Lauren Cohan) become "spouses." While Beth Greene (Emily Kinney) and Carol tend to Rick's new baby as new mommy figures. Toward the end of the season, Michonne (Danai Gurira) returns to the prison and bonds with Carl as his new maternal/big sister protector figure.

When populating your series or creating guest characters for a particular episode, ask yourself not only who is this new character, but also, how will the arrival of this new character impact your regular characters?

All relationships are like mirrors, and each new person we encounter reflects our sense of self right back to us. They can also remind us of someone else either in appearance, attitude, or how he/she makes us feel. This causes characters to project their past onto new individuals—perhaps overreacting to a quasi-judgmental remark that (usually subconsciously) reminds them of a judgmental parent.

The sub-subtext of virtually any scene is familial power dynamics, psychological wounds from the past, and subtle movements that reaffirm clan position. The show's family may spend most of its time in a house, office, police precinct, hospital, prison, or any other arenas where people rely on each other, challenge each other, learn, struggle, and, hopefully, mature.

Great series are about great relationships that are consciously and/ or unconsciously based on family dynamics. Where does your series "live"? What's its primary arena? What's its "sweet spot"? As you ponder these questions, bear in mind that *home is where the heart is.*

INTERVIEW: Shonda Rhimes

Shonda Rhimes Credits

Best known for:

Scandal (Executive Producer/Creator) 2012
Private Practice (Executive Producer/Creator) 2007–2012
Grey's Anatomy (Executive Producer/Creator) 2005–2012
    Emmy Nominated (Drama Series) 2006–2007
    WGA Nominated (Dramatic Series) 2006–2007
    WGA Award Winner (New Series) 2006
    PGA Nominated (Drama) 2008
    PGA Award Winner (Drama) 2007
    PGA Nominated (Drama) 2006
Off the Map (Executive Producer) 2011
The Princess Diaries 2: Royal Engagement 2004
Introducing Dorothy Dandridge (teleplay) 1999

NL: My first question has to do with the fact that your series are so addictive. They're compulsively watchable, and I believe it stems from your characters. So, in addition to the brilliant casting, what do you think is so magnetic about your characters? Because all shows have characters, but yours have that extra something that compels us to tune in every week. Do you have any theories as to why?

SR: When I wrote *Grey's*, it was the first television project I had ever worked on, so I wrote it as if I was writing in my diary. It felt very personal. I was very surprised to discover that people responded to these characters in this way. What I learned is that as long as I'm writing as if it's personal, as long as these characters are alive to me—that I dream about them—then those characters remain compelling for an audience. I don't know why that is. I just know that I have to make sure that they feel alive to me and that what's happening to them feels real and not like television.

NL: Right. I think that is so true. And part of that premise is that they're flawed. You show all their vulnerabilities and their fears and their insecurities.

You put them under a microscope. So, I'm wondering when you're conceiving them do you picture them in your mind physically or from the inside out? What were your inspirations for Meredith Grey (Ellen Pompeo) or Olivia Pope (Kerry Washington)?

SR: I think I pictured them from the inside out. There was no physical type. Generally, my scripts come without physical descriptions for the characters at all, which I think is important. I feel like I have an idea of what my characters are and then actors come in and read for the role. With every actor who sits down and reads, my idea of who that character is changes. I wonder is this person the idea that's right or is the next guy the idea that's right? Or, do we keep going until we find the person for whom I think, "Well, they add something fantastic and that fantastic something is perfect for what I'm thinking."

NL: One of the recurring themes in each of your shows seems to be loners or rogues who come together with a team and form this extended family. There's even a line from *Grey's* and, I think, in all three shows that I've watched that says, "I need you to be my somebody." I know there was one about putting down an emergency contact on a form. They do form these metaphorical families, and the theory of this chapter is that there's these archetypes: where there's a mom and dad, sibling rivalries, and spoiled children. Do family dynamics come into play when you're creating an ensemble?

SR: I'm actually creeped out that you've noticed that the characters have said that in all three shows because I've never noticed it before, and when you said, "It's a group of rogues who have come together to form a family"— I was about to go, "No, they're not," but then I thought, "Oh, they are." I've never thought of it that way. I've tried very hard not to examine it that much. I come from a really large family. I have five older brothers and sisters. I was always a quiet person and I spent a lot of time watching them and figuring out what the world was because of what my five older brothers and sisters were doing and saying and being. But, I never thought about it in terms of my writing because I feel like if I try to examine it too hard, I wouldn't be able to do it anymore.

NL: Right. I just thought that Olivia is like the mom to everybody. She actually took in all these damaged people and then we discover that she's damaged in her own way. And Miranda (Chandra Wilson) is that character in *Grey's*.

SR: As is Meredith, who has also become the mother of a bunch of damaged people. I think the incarnations are different. I think *Scandal* is informed by *Grey's* in a lot of ways, and it's the show that I can examine the most because there's a lot of me in Olivia Pope. In that being a showrunner and being Olivia Pope are not that different. For me, there's something about the fact that Olivia has taken in all of these people that are damaged, and she fixes everybody's problems. It's a lot like being a showrunner.

NL: But, hopefully, you allow people to cry sometimes.

SR: Yes.

NL: Although what I also admire about your pilot is that you boldly state things up front that are etched in stone and then often by the end of the pilot, you've debunked everything. "Nobody ever cries, ever," and then you see the vulnerability.

SR: Yeah, Olivia crying. That was important to me.

NL: In terms of point of view when you're conceiving a show, I know Grey's mainly uses Meredith's voice-over. Although there were some episodes where it was somebody else.

SR: It does happen, but it is very rare.

NL: The one that I was watching last night was the episode of *Grey's* with the shooter.

SR: That's the episode that I'm most proud of having written.

NL: It's so suspenseful when Miranda is underneath that bed and the killer's feet are there. It's such sharp writing because to me the best writing is always filled with so much suspense. So, with point of view, we began with Meredith who, even though she comes from a mother who was a famous surgeon, is insecure. In *Private Practice*, as in *Scandal*, you decided not to do the voice-over. And the Quinn (Katie Lowes) character is kind of the Meredith character in *Scandal* because she's the new one coming in. Does the point of view for your show come to you pretty early, or is it once you've laid everything out on the canvas that you start to think about who is going to be the main point of view to unify everything?

SR: It's interesting. For *Grey's*, it was very clear to me that Meredith had to be our way in. Going into a world where we didn't understand its rules. How do you do a medical show about surgery and make it accessible to an audience? That audience, when I was writing the pilot, was me—how do I make it accessible to me? I need somebody for whom the rules get explained on a regular basis who also feels the same fears and nervousness I would feel if dropped into that situation. To me, that's why Meredith ended up being the narrator. With *Scandal*, it really was that I thought I had created an iconic character with Olivia Pope. She is somebody who everybody has heard of. Her name is on people's lips and she fixes things. I needed somebody on the outside to come in and show us what that world was. It very quickly switched from Quinn's point of view to Olivia's point of view because Quinn clearly had secrets up the wazoo. For me, it was just making sure that we had a way into the world, so that you understood how powerful Olivia Pope was, and then having Quinn step back and letting it become Olivia's world.

NL: Right. And, the advantage is that now everyone has a legitimate reason to explain to this new person how their world works because it's an unusual kind of firm. "We're attorneys, but we don't prosecute or defend." It's a very organic way to naturally get a lot of exposition out that's also filled with conflict because she's overwhelmed by it, but also fascinated and drawn to it. Secrets and lies are a natural currency of all your shows, but especially *Scandal*. The big question that remains at the end of the season is, who is Quinn Perkins really? I didn't see that coming, that there was something more about who she is. Then, that supersedes what was the overarching plotline about Amanda Tanner (Liza Weil). I don't know if you would call it storytelling strategy, but when you're breaking story and pulling out and revealing information and people are making discoveries—how are you making decisions about when you're going to reveal things? Is it mathematical or do you say, "At the end of this midseason point or at the end of this season, I'm going to reveal all of this"? And then, reverse engineer it? I think a lot of people get overwhelmed by how they're going to break it all down.

SR: I think it's two things. Part of it is instinctive. I generally walk into the writers' room at the beginning of the season and say, "Here's how the season's going to end." And I pitch the end of the season. I don't call it reverse engineering because it doesn't work that way. Everyone knows where we're going, so we work on finding a roadmap to get there. That roadmap is generally not super planned; it's more instinctive. Things feel right; things don't feel right. Amanda Tanner wasn't necessarily supposed to die at all, but at a certain point, I was like, "Amanda Tanner should die today," and we all went, "Yeah, that feels right." There was a point in, I think it was, episode 3 or 4 where you have the guy giving details about the people who work at Pope & Associates, and we got to Quinn, and everyone was like, "What's Quinn's backstory, Shonda?" And, I said, "Quinn did not exist before 2008." It wasn't because of anything other than when I wrote the pilot, every time I got to the scene where Quinn is crying in the bathroom, the idea of Quinn telling her backstory felt weird. Plus, Quinn kept asking, "Why did she hire me? Why did she hire me?" So, to me, I thought, "Well, that's a mystery." That mystery became much more important as we headed toward the end of the season because Quinn Perkins didn't exist before 2008.

NL: I read an article that with *Grey's Anatomy*, you did all thirteen episodes before it started to air.

SR: We did thirteen episodes the first season but only aired nine. So the remaining episodes aired the second season. But we finished the thirteen episodes, and literally that Sunday after we wrapped production, the first show aired.

NL: What's your barometer as a writer and a creator of a series when you're essentially working in a vacuum? Is it just that you're working from your gut?

SR: Yeah. What I try to stick to even now is how I answer these questions: "Am I into it? Am I compelled? Am I excited? Do I give a crap if anybody watches?" I remember saying with Betsy Beers [Executive Producer] regarding the first few episodes of *Grey's* that "if nobody watches this show, that's fine, we'll just sell it out of the back of our car." That's how much we loved it. As opposed to feeling like, "It's really important to me that other people watch." I was so proud of what we'd done that I didn't need the validation of the network. And that's how I feel about *Scandal*. I was so excited by those first seven episodes that even if nobody had watched them, I still would have been like, "Some of the best work that I've done. I'm proud of that."

NL: It's terrific and, I think, groundbreaking for network television in that Kerry Washington is just so gorgeous and likeable walking into a room, but also so tough, initially, because she's such a "gladiator in a suit" and she's having an affair with the president of the United States (!)—a lot of things which would come under the category of "unsympathetic" or "not likeable." And, then we start to see much more of her vulnerability as the show progresses. I think it's in episode 4 that we actually understand the circumstances of her affair with President Fitz (Tony Goldwyn) in a completely different light. How important is it for the main character to be likeable?

SR: It's fascinating because I get that note a lot. A lot. I sat in a room with an executive who is no longer with the network who basically said to me with regard to Meredith Grey that "nobody is going to like a woman who sleeps with a man the night before she's supposed to start work. That makes her completely unlikeable—you should change that fact." And, I thought, but that's who the character is, it doesn't change that fact. And then, I sat in the same room years later with somebody else who said, "Can Olivia not be having an affair with the President?" Someone else who is no longer with the network. And, I remember saying, "Olivia Pope's going to have sex with the president in the Oval Office on his desk—on the Resolute desk—by episode 4. If you all can't get behind that, then I don't want to make this show." And what I meant by that was I really like flawed characters, but I also feel very strongly that flawed people can be likeable. I feel like cable has shown that time and again—and the networks have been afraid to show that. I mean *Dexter* is a freakin' serial killer, but we love him and we want to watch what he does next. I don't think you have to be kind to be interesting. I think that especially with female characters people want that to be true. I feel like there's something great about being unapologetic about who you are and being flawed and fucked up. It's all those things that make TV worth writing, frankly, not just worth watching, but worth writing for a writer.

NL: What I tell my students about flawed characters is that they don't have to be likeable, if we can see a vulnerability, we can connect to them. There's a great Lily Tomlin quote I read recently where she said, "In private, we're all misfits." The idea that none of us is perfect. That we all make mistakes. To me, it all goes back to the first question I asked you which is why your characters are so magnetic. People watch TV and see that other people have problems and flaws.

SR: The idea that we're going to watch perfect people live perfect lives perfectly that just makes me depressed. I don't want to watch that. I always say *Breaking Bad* is my favorite example—that's such a flawed world and I can't get enough of it.

NL: Back to the family idea, there's a Tolstoy quote that says, "Happy families are all alike and unhappy families are unhappy in their own way." Arguably your ensembles are extended families, it seems that their unhappiness or their imperfections are what make them so fascinating.

SR: I've always said there is a sense for Meredith Grey that she's the mother of these people. She's always trying to keep everyone together. If you look at Olivia Pope in that way, as somebody who is trying to hold everyone together, there's something there, too. There's literally a quote in *Private Practice* at the beginning of season 2 or 3 that says, "Our family becomes your family."

NL: That's right, I wrote that down from the promo video that they made.

SR: We are, in fact, creating them as families. In that sense, we have family drama happening, and, in that sense, that's interesting.

NL: I wrote down that tagline, and then I wrote, "At worst, dysfunctional and, at best, coming together as a team to solve problems." Even the most dysfunctional family will come together when there's a crisis, and it will bring out that strength and resolve in each person.

> *What's interesting is that there aren't any healthy biological families in a lot of ways. That's true with Meredith, and Olivia seems to spring from nowhere. Mellie [Bellamy Young] and Fitz are the most disturbing family in the world. Meredith's got the mother; Addison's [Kate Walsh] got the mother who's secretly a lesbian and the father who drinks too much ... but the families they've created are the families that work for them.*

Now, you've forced me to examine it and now I'm not going to be able to write it anymore! (*Laughs.*)

NL: Two more questions. It seems like your A and B stories usually dovetail and there's kind of a thematic, but the most polarizing question from my last book for movie screenwriters was about theme. Half said it's everything and the other half said you should never consciously write about it. It seems in *Grey's* with the use of voice-over that theme is pretty upfront. When you're breaking story in the room—whether it's a theme for a season or a theme for each episode—are you consciously thinking about it or is it more subliminal?

SR: It's different for every show. It's very interesting because people always say to me that all three of my shows feel like they're run by different people. *Grey's* is thematic both season long and episodically, and it's very important to me that the stories fall into that theme. *Private Practice* is thematic in a season-long way. There's no rule that says that each episode has to fall into a specific theme. Although last season, we fooled around with Addison doing a voice-over when she's in therapy and that's a little bit thematic, but it's not thematic for every character. With *Scandal,* there's no theme for each episode and there's no theme for the characters, and yet, somehow whatever's happening in our A story dovetails with our B story, but it's not necessarily purposeful. We don't sit in the room and talk about it; we just do it.

NL: Last question. What's the best thing about being a showrunner and what's the worst?

SR: I think the best thing about being a showrunner is I write, "INT. OVAL OFFICE—DAY," and then eight weeks later, I go down to the stage and I walk into an exact replica of the oval office and I sit behind an exact replica of the *Resolute* desk and I pretend to be the president. Or, I sit in an O.R. that someone built for me because I wrote, "INT. O.R. GALLERY—DAY," and I pretend to do surgery. And, every single time that's happened, I've gone down to the stage and sat down on that set and played for like forty-five minutes. That's the best part. You're the god of your own world in a way that is not healthy for anybody, but it's fantastic. The worst part is feeling responsible for the jobs of hundreds of people. I don't want to fuck up my job and ruin the ability of hundreds of other people to make a living. There are like eight hundred people who have jobs because I wrote these pilot scripts—that's serious and I don't want to put anybody out of work. I feel an extraordinary sense of responsibility for everyone. It keeps me awake at night.

NL: That's what Shondaland is all about.

SR: It's probably why *Grey's* has gone ten seasons, because I really refused to let the show get boring because we've got to keep going. This is family. The crew is my family. And I want them to keep having jobs. I want us to stay together.

7

FUEL YOUR STORY ENGINE

W hy are most new shows cancelled after a few episodes and others become cultural phenomena? No one knows how to catch lightning in a bottle or else every series would be a hit right out of the gate. The best prognosticating tool we have is to examine series which have endured for the long haul to seek out their commonalities as indicators of success.

In the TV business, when a new series has the touchstones of a long-running show, we say that it "has legs." If you're getting a mental picture of Forrest Gump running a long-distance marathon, then you've got the right idea. TV is a longevity business. Any new series isn't about a quick sprint. The show has to endure and outrun the competition—or it's going to get sidelined, shifted to another timeslot, or more likely, axed. In the TV business today, second chances are rare. A new series must start strong and sustain by either holding steady from its initially strong ratings or, better yet, *building* momentum from word of mouth as it moves toward the finish line. However, in TV, the finish line keeps marching forward. You can be king of season 1, but will the ratings stay up in season 2 and beyond? Yes, it's a super-competitive industry, not for the weak of heart or those with a delicate stomach. No matter how great your success last year, the TV networks are always looking ahead and wondering . . .

What Have You Done for Me Lately?

When a new series concept is pitched, one of the key factors TV executives are considering are the show's chances for long-term survival. Bottom line: they're not apt to buy, develop, or green-light a new series that doesn't have the potential to run for at least five seasons (or more than one hundred episodes). Investing in a new series requires a giant leap of faith on the part of the studio, which has to deficit finance it, meaning that they can only recoup their costs if the show becomes a long-running series. A critically acclaimed, award-winning series only has value for a TV studio and network if it translates into relatively solid viewership ratings. I'm using the word "relatively" because a basic cable show is usually only going to garner a fraction of the viewers of a big broadcast network, so the numbers for a successful series, such as *Mad Men* on AMC, are not going to rival the numbers for *NCIS* on CBS. But the elite *Mad Men* demographic is coveted by many high-end advertisers, so this business model makes sense for AMC. (If *Mad Men* aired on CBS, it would have been cancelled within its first season for low ratings, but on AMC, it's a modest hit compared to AMC's juggernaut series *The Walking Dead* which nabs four times the ratings points and kills scads more zombies—albeit with considerably less Emmy awards—than *Mad Men*.)

Keeping It All in the Family: Infinite Family Plots

In terms of longevity, the current champion is *The Simpsons* with more than five hundred episodes over twenty-five (?!) seasons. Now *that's* a cultural phenomenon. Endlessly inventive and genuinely funny, this series has the genius of Matt Groening, James L. Brooks, and a roster of ridiculously talented comedy writers. But, at the core, this is a show about a crazy, dysfunctional family. Now let's look at some other long-running series about crazy families, and we can discern that series about families provide us with the potential for unlimited "story engines," because as long as each family member has a problem, the show has the potential for new conflicts and new storylines.

All series specifically about families are serialized, as family lives continue to evolve week after week. But one of the main differences is that drama series offer us cliffhangers at the end of each episode to keep us coming back for more, while sitcoms tend to bring each episode's self-contained storyline to a thematic conclusion (often with a subtle moral) to highlight a specific lesson learned. The stakes on family series tend to rest on power dynamics within relationships. In some cases, the serialized dramas gave us life and death stakes—especially after the blockbuster cliffhanger on *Dallas* hinging on the mysterious murder of J. R. Ewing (Larry Hagman) that hatched the iconic cliffhanger question: Who shot J. R.? *Desperate Housewives* and many other serialized dramas about families have also centered around a murder-mystery season arc. These darker, edgier, more provocative dramas about families should not to be confused with softer, G-rated "family dramas," such as *7th Heaven*, which are labeled "family dramas" because they're intended to be watched by parents and their kids.

I'll Be There for You: Enduring Friendships

Series about complicated, layered, and often funny friendships—including BFFs (best friends forever), bromances, and frenemies—also offer the potential for unlimited story engines. But these shows live or die based upon their iconic characters and fresh storylines (aka, fortunate casting + great writing).

Most friendship shows are heavily dependent on their arenas. *Desperate Housewives* was rooted on Wisteria Lane and we, as viewers, felt as if we lived there, too. *One Tree Hill* and *Friday Night Lights* have/had their respective basketball and football games to anchor their plot lines with the formula of: friendship + rivalry = suspense.

Most of these series orbit around two to three main "regular" locations. We know their (often bizarrely upscale) apartments intimately, as if we live there, too. Archie Bunker's chair is permanently ensconced in the Smithsonian in Washington, D.C. And the "M" on Mary Richard's wall is as iconic as her soaring hat in the Minneapolis wind. And, naturally, these friend ensembles enjoy their favorite hangouts. *Beverly Hills, 90210* had the Peach Pit. *Friends* had Central Perk. *How I Met Your Mother* has MacLaren's bar.

The durability of *shows revolving around friendships* also depends upon additional possibilities for story engines, such as each cast member of *Friends* and *Sex and the City*'s workplace antics, new love interests, and new sources of internal and external strife or forces of antagonism to upset the harmony.

Sex, Power, and the Search for "True Love"

There's a tacit understanding that friendships and familial relationships go through ups and downs but eventually return to the status quo; we learn to accept each other's shortcomings because we've seen each other through good and bad times. Intellectually, we know we're not going to change each other, but we still offer our well intentioned yet unsolicited advice and insinuate ourselves at inopportune times. We embrace and endure all of this from our family and best friends because there's a comfort level that allows it. When we negotiate vacations and holiday dinners and special events, we might experience feelings of resentment or animosity from past hurts, but we're usually able to gather around the turkey together and put aside our differences for the sake of the family or friendship. Yes, I'm oversimplifying and generalizing in order to make a point—which is that when you add *sex* to any relationship, all bets are off.

Oh, the agony and ecstasy of romantic relationships—especially on television! Of course there's a big distinction to be made between infatuation, sex, lust, passion, intimacy, commitment, marriage, and love. But for the sake of discussion, let's start with the physical act of two naked bodies letting down their defenses and being open to the intimacy of another's touch—coupled with the *power dynamics* that go along with it. There is dominance and sub-mission in negotiating who's going to do what to whom and where and when and how. And the post-coital negotiations. Spend the night or vamoose? Cigarette or no cigarette? Is breakfast together "taking the next step" or just a meal? Is he or she going to call? Is he or she going to say yes? Are his or her friends and family going to approve of his/her friends and family? And do we approve of each other's wardrobes and hairstyles and pop culture references or lack thereof and where/if we went to college or how much money he or she makes, not to mention spiritual and political beliefs and how we want to raise our kids and do we both even *want* kids—and we haven't even gotten to our music playlists and favorite movies and TV shows yet. You know what, this just isn't going to work out. It's not you; it's me. Can we just be friends?

Suffice it to say, in romantic (sexual) relationships, everything counts in large amounts. We tend to cut our friends and family a whole lot more slack in pretty much every department because what they do is much less of a reflection on us. Or, to put it another way . . .

Romantic Love Tends to Bring Out the Best and Worst in All of Us

Romantic love makes us feel most vulnerable. Sex turns us on, but the pros-pect of "true love" can just as easily shut us down. Love pushes us to the edge of reason. It makes us cry. It breaks our hearts. It terrifies us.

And yet, with few exceptions, *we all want it*—and that's why it's so essen-tial to a great TV series. It's the intersection between desire and fear—the core of all good drama (and comedy). We long for someone "special" to help enhance our existence, to help us feel less alone, to make us feel worthy and attractive and loveable. At the same time, romantic love is *chemical*. You could meet Mr. or Ms. Right and everything looks perfect in their profile—but if there's something missing, it's a lack of *chemistry* which is that vital link that's tangible when it exists and indefinable when it doesn't. In a TV series, some of this is written on the page, but most of it depends on *casting*. It's either there or it isn't, and it's rare, and often ephemeral, especially on TV.

As TV viewers, we're voyeurs. We seek titillation and escapism, but also find ourselves enraptured by the vicarious thrill of TV couples and their on-again/off-again tempestuous relationships. If there's no heat between them, we tune out—but we also can't resist the simmer of the *slow burn* between two people who can't be together for so many reasons and yet, those lips, those eyes. Animals emit scents and make mating calls. Humans flirt, charm, and seduce.

Following are examples of different subcategories of romantic love (as opposed to platonic love) on hit shows.

Happily Married

Hey, it happens. And not just as a form of punishment on *Married . . . with Children*. *Parenthood, Friday Night Lights, Modern Family, The West Wing, How I Met Your Mother, Everybody Loves Raymond, Home Improvement,* and *Downton Abbey* all feature functional couples. Sure they argue and get on each other's nerves from time to time, but there is never any doubt that they're partners in love and fully committed.

Unfaithfully Yours

Always involves the conflict of secrets and lies which is often accompanied by separation, couple's counseling, and sometimes eventually divorce. On *Breaking Bad*, Walter White initially gets into the meth drug trade for the sake of his family—ironically, it's what tears them apart. See also *The Sopranos, The Good Wife, Scandal, Mad Men, Desperate Housewives, Homeland, Nip/Tuck, Rescue Me, The Americans, House of Cards,* and *Boardwalk Empire*.

In one of my all-time favorite movies, *Moonstruck*, the answer to the ongoing central question "Why do men cheat on their wives?" is "Because they fear death." I believe there's quite a bit of truth in that. The specter of mortality is omnipresent, and so is temptation.

It's usually the men who cheat on their wives, but *Nurse Jackie* (Edie Falco), Nancy Botwin (Mary Louise Parker) on *Weeds,* and Betty Draper on *Mad Men* negate that gender bias—for better, for worse.

The Slow Burn

Primarily based on the commonly accepted wisdom that *opposites attract*, this relationship dynamic is all about sustaining the question of "will they or won't they ever get together?" for as long as possible. These couples tend to clash over almost everything, but there is an undeniable attraction—despite protests to the contrary. "Methinks the lady [or man] doth protest too much" usually applies.

On *Castle*, best-selling mystery author Richard Castle (Nathan Fillion) is initially foisted upon hardboiled homicide Detective Kate Beckett (Stana Katic) to help solve a copycat murder case (based on one of his novels). At first, she's infuriated to have a writer shadowing her on the job—and attempts to dump him. But she gradually succumbs to his charms, especially when he breaks through his writer's block and decides to base his new novel's heroine on her. And he just may be able to help her solve the unsolved murder of her mother.

Examples of slow burn relationships: *Cheers* (overeducated barmaid and brutish, handsome saloon owner); *The X-Files* (believer and skeptic); *Moonlighting* (uptown former fashion model and enterprising smartass); *Who's the Boss?* (career woman and her housekeeper/manny); *The Big Bang Theory* (socially awkward physicist and sexy blonde neighbor); *Bones* (slick, cheeky FBI agent and uptight forensic anthropologist). For *Cheers* and *Moonlighting*, keeping the love interests apart was a huge draw for the audience, and getting them together was detrimental to the future of the series; in the case of *Moonlighting*, the ratings dropped precipitously. In the case of *Cheers*, persnickety Diane Chambers (Shelley Long) was out, and new slow burn love interest, the tougher ball-busting manager, Rebecca Howe (Kirstie Alley), was in—and the ratings climbed accordingly.

Conversely, on *New Girl*, creator/showrunner Liz Meriwether decided to speed up the pace of Jess (Zooey Deschanel) and Nick's (Jake Johnson) budding romance. To Meriwether: "It felt like holding it off way longer would have been playing with the audience. It felt organic and the right time to do it [have them kiss]. I don't believe that they kiss and the whole show is over. I believe it creates new opportunities for stories and conflicts and things going wrong. We kind of felt it helped our show and gave it focus."

Showrunner Greg Daniels (*The Office*) points out that you can "miss your window" (by doling out a slow burn romance) "by delaying it for too long." By giving a potential couple other partners to keep them apart, you run the risk that the audience will get more invested in these new couples instead—and will be averse to going back to the original couple.

Burn Notice inverts the slow burn formula. The title of the series refers to the "burn notices" issued by U.S. spy agencies to expel intelligence operatives or sources now considered leaky/defective and therefore expendable (and in one fell swoop expunging their entire work history, support network, and finances). The protagonist, former covert operations agent Michael Westen (Jeffrey Donovan) gets "burned" and finds himself in Miami (his hometown) in the care of his estranged beautiful ex-girlfriend, a former IRA operative and explosives expert, Fiona Glenanne (Gabrielle Anwar). Michael basically needs to lay low in Miami or risk being abducted by former allies and persistent enemies. Whereas most slow burn relationships start off platonic and are fraught with tension, Michael and Fiona's torrid romance is in their past, and the question is "will they or won't they get *back* together?" For the roguish Michael, Fiona is too volatile and high maintenance. Sure, they have great chemistry, but theirs was a romance that ended badly, so he's reluctant to go there again. Fiona, on the other hand, still carries a torch for Michael and enjoys their dangerous missions together. To Fiona, violence is like foreplay, so their partnership is more of a gradual thaw than a slow burn.

Forbidden Love

This subcategory can include a taboo romance between a human and a supernatural being, such as *Buffy the Vampire Slayer* + *Angel* (a vampire who gets his human soul back via a gypsy curse and becomes Buffy's unattainable true love); unfortunately, when they finally consummate their passion, Angel loses his soul again and returns to the dark side as an evil vampire, relegating himself into exile. See also *The Vampire Diaries, True Blood, Being Human,* and *Smallville.*

It can also encompass a romance in which one or both parties are unavailable—physically and/or emotionally. On *Scandal,* political fixer Olivia Pope (Kerry Washington) is having an affair with the married president of the United States (Tony Goldwyn). On *Desperate Housewives,* trophy wife Gabrielle Solis (Eva Longoria) is having a casual affair with her studly teenaged gardener, John (Jesse Metcalfe); it's not just naughty—it's illegal.

The Love Triangle

On *Homeland,* returned POW/U.S. Marine sergeant Nicholas Brody is still in love with his estranged wife, Jessica (Morena Baccarin), but is also rapidly succumbing to his strong feelings for CIA agent Carrie Mathison (Claire Danes). Complicating matters is Jessica's serious relationship with Nicholas' former best friend, U.S. Marine captain Mike Faber (Diego Klattenhoff), because, after Nicholas' seven-year absence, she had presumed that her husband was dead.

On the second season of *Parks and Recreation,* Ann (Rashida Jones) broke up with Andy (Chris Pratt) after living with him because he was irresponsible and self-absorbed, but finds him alluring after he gets a job and becomes more stable. However, by that point, Andy has his eyes set on April (Aubrey Plaza), who just broke up with her two gay boyfriends (who were dating each other) to pursue Andy.

On the first season of *True Blood,* Sookie Stackhouse (Anna Paquin) falls in love with "young" vampire Bill Compton (Stephen Moyer), but when an elder vampire, Eric Northman (Alexander Skarsgård) appears, Bill gets surly, and Sookie and Eric hook up.

On the first season of *Friday Night Lights,* after star quarterback Jason Street (Scott Porter) suffers a debilitating injury on the football field, his steady girlfriend, Lyla Garrity (Minka Kelly), finds herself drawn to sexy bad boy Tim Riggins (Taylor Kitsch), testing both her loyalty and spirit—ultimately leading Lyla from capricious Panthers cheerleader to faithful Christian youth leader.

On season 1 of *Once Upon a Time,* Snow White (Ginnifer Goodwin) and Prince Charming (Josh Dallas) from the Enchanted Forest fairy-tale realm seem destined to be together in their reincarnations as Mary Margaret and David Nolan in Storybrooke, Maine. Unfortunately, he's engaged to another woman, Kathryn (Anastasia Griffith), who was also his unrequited love interest, Princess Abigail, in the fairy-tale realm.

In season 4 of *30 Rock*, Jack Donaghy (Alec Baldwin) is in love with both Avery Jessup (Elizabeth Banks) and Nancy Donovan (Julianne Moore)—both of whom don't know about each other. He tries to date them both while he figures out his feelings. Nancy—Jack's high school love—gets a divorce for him, while Avery—Jack's female Republican/battle axe counterpart—fights her instincts to be independent of men. The triangle is resolved when Nancy finds out inadvertently that Avery is pregnant with Jack's baby, unbeknownst to him. Jack realizes that Avery can offer him everything he wants, and Nancy releases him. Jack and Avery get married, have a baby (in season 5), and end up getting happily divorced later.

Casual Sex: Looking for Love in All the Wrong Places

Even though it's the twenty-first century, on TV series, the old double standard tends to apply here: men can have casual sex, take a shower, and move on, whereas women on TV tend to get emotionally involved. Mainstream TV audiences are still fairly conservative, and seem to have a much easier time accepting men as aggressors seeking conquests and women as guardians of virtue. Of course, as times are changing and TV series are evolving, there are a great number of exceptions. But for women on TV series, the thrill of the one-night stand is often mitigated by reality in the cold light of day, followed by neurosis, remorse, and/or a pregnancy scare or even an STD. And men get off (literally) scot-free. Naturally, this all depends on the perspective of the specific characters. For Samantha Jones (Kim Cattrall) on *Sex and the City*, women can have casual sex to their heart's content—just like men!—with no justification or neurosis required. But even the flagrantly naked and promiscuous Hannah Horvath (Lena Dunham) of *Girls* needs to deal with *some* emotional fallout and equivocation.

See also *Girls, Entourage, Sex and the City, Grey's Anatomy*. This subcategory can also include sexual addiction: *Californication, Nip/Tuck, Queer as Folk*, and *Mad Men*.

Sex for Money, Power, and/or Political Gain

This subcategory includes prostitution on *The Secret Diary of a Call Girl, Hung*, and *The Client List*.

More nuanced versions of sex as part of the job include Elizabeth and Phillip Jennings (Keri Russell, Mathew Rhys) on *The Americans* who pretend to be a happily married couple for the sake of their covert KGB assignments.

On *House of Cards,* Frank Underwood (Kevin Spacey) has sexual encounters with a deceitful, ambitious reporter for his own political gain (and her career advancement).

On *Mad Men,* buxom office manager and struggling single mom Joan Harris (Christina Hendricks) makes a strategic career move to break through the glass ceiling into the boys' club when she agrees to have sex with an all-important client. But it's a bittersweet victory: she wins the prize, but suffers the shame of having slept her way to the top.

On *Homeland,* we're not sure at first if CIA operative Carrie is seducing war hero/possibly "turned" terrorist as a strategy to break him or if she's genuinely falling in love with him. And vice versa. It's a cat-and-mouse love story, and the jury is still out on who's playing whom and why.

Serial Monogamy

This subcategory encompasses characters searching hard for Mr. or Ms. Right, not because they are promiscuous but because they're seeking their "soul mate." And so, they're in a perpetual cycle of dating/hoping/rejecting/being rejected (rinse, repeat).

On *Girls,* Hannah Horvath and her best friends, Marnie (Allison Williams), Jessa (Jemima Kirke), and Shoshanna (Zosia Mamet) endeavor to snag their respective men, and then systematically self-sabotage their relationships due to insecurity, neuroses, fear of intimacy, abandonment, and self-loathing. It's all relatable, often very funny, and heartbreaking—but how long can this smartly written series sustain this trajectory?

30 Rock: If there's one thing for sure about Liz Lemon (Tina Fey), it's that she does not give up. From mystery man at the dentist (Wesley Snipes) [Michael Sheen], to nice guys from Cleveland (Floyd DeBarber) [Jason Sudeikis], to handsome pilots with the name of a comedy legend (Carol Burnett) [Matt Damon], Liz has gotten close several times, but something always happens to ruin the dream—including discovering that one boyfriend had been on *To Catch a Predator*—until she meets Criss Chros (James Marsden), a fellow Star Wars enthusiast, and she finds a way to be a wife, a mother, and a happily working woman.

The Mindy Project: Mindy Lahiri loves romantic movies and big romantic gestures. Her encyclopedic knowledge of popular films fuels her desire to find Mr. Right. She thinks she's found him in Josh (Tommy Dewey), a sports lawyer who has everything—including another girlfriend and an addiction to drugs. Like Liz, she is undeterred and meets a cute minister, Casey (Anders Holm), who promptly tells her that she's too self-absorbed for him and in an effort to prove him wrong, she agrees to go on a one-year mission to Haiti with him. Meanwhile, the audience wants to know when she and Danny (Chris Messina), her copartner in their ob/gyn practice, are going to realize that they're meant for each other. Will the timing be right next season? Will she go to Haiti? Stay tuned.

See also *Ally McBeal, Sex and the City.*

The Crush

Subcategory for young love. The iconic series *The Wonder Years* got the nostalgia of puppy love just right—providing us with a dual perspective of Kevin (Fred Savage) as an insecure, flailing kid in love with the seemingly unattainable Winnie (Danica McKellar), and Kevin's adult self looking back on his life via voice-over.

My So-Called Life, a short-lived ABC series, has now achieved cult status for its nuanced, realistic depiction of romantic high school angst. Its heroine was Angela Chase (Claire Danes) who pines for smoldering, aloof, laconic Lothario Jordan Catalano (Jared Leto). Their intense, slow burn relationship was a complicated courtship of fleeting glances and awkward pauses. There was also Angela's childhood friend, Brian Krakow's (Devon Gummersall) underdog/puppy love attraction for Angela further confusing her coming-of-age. The touchstone of *My So-Called Life* was telling as little story as possible and digging deeper into every small moment.

On MTV's *Awkward*, social misfit Jenna Hamilton (Ashley Rickards) has a freak accident in her bathroom that everyone at school misconstrues as a suicidal cry for help. So Jenna decides to turn her misfortune into a blessing via her blog. Soon, she loses her virginity to popular hunk Matty McKibben (Beau Mirchoff), who privately likes offbeat Jenna but publicly wants to keep their relationship a secret to preserve his image on campus. Their arrangement works until Jenna develops feelings for Matty's best friend, Jake Rosati (Brett Davern), and now has a secret of her own. The show's sensibility is reminiscent of the films made by the late, great movie director, John Hughes, who had an uncanny ability not only to make us laugh and cringe, but also to genuinely move us.

See also *Gossip Girl* for its depiction of cynical, entitled rich kids and their soapy *Dangerous Liaisons* machinations; and *Pretty Little Liars.*

Pushing the Envelope

Whether it's the Dionysian orgies on *Spartacus, Game of Thrones,* and *The Tudors* or the promiscuity on *Entourage, Girls, Nip/Tuck, Mad Men, True Blood,* and *Hung,* these sex scenes range from graphic and (arguably) gratuitous to simply implied. These are all edgy cable series that get around the censors (aka "Standards and Practices") at the broadcast networks with the requisite nudity and provocative sexual situations. See also *Queer as Folk, The "L" Word, Dexter, Weeds, Sex and the City, American Horror Story, Nip/Tuck, The Americans, Red Shoe Diaries,* and *Secret Diary of a Call Girl.*

While the love story component isn't the *only* reason for a series' success, it's certainly a major factor to their longevity. Remove the sexual chemistry from the series and most, if not all, would quickly fizzle. Or as iconic film director and screenwriter Paul Mazursky once said: "All stories are about people trying to get laid."

I gave at the office

The workplace ensemble (excluding procedurals). Notice how each of the following series has its own internal story engine which gives it the potential for unlimited plotlines:

- *M*A*S*H:* eleven seasons (mobile army hospital as backdrop to Korean war satire)

  Story engines: army doctors and nurses' lives; wounded soldiers

- *Cheers:* eleven seasons (Boston bar buddies)

  Story engines: bartenders, waiters, and barflies

- *The Office* (U.S. version): nine seasons (mockumentary set at the fictional Dunder-Mifflin Paper Company in Scranton, Pennsylvania)

  Story engines: Incompetent personnel and steady office politics

- *Mad Men:* six seasons (Madison Avenue ad execs, secretaries, wives, and mistresses set in 1960s New York City)

  Story engines: office politics, cronyism, sexism, racism before and during the civil rights and feminist movements; marital and familial strife

- *Murphy Brown:* ten seasons (The "FYI" political news program in Washington, D.C.)

  Story engines: behind-the-scenes office politics, fresh news stories set against Murphy's (Candice Bergen) messy personal life

- *The Mary Tyler Moore Show:* seven seasons (WJM newsroom in Minneapolis)

  Story engines: Incompetence covering fresh news stories at WJM; Mary's romantic life and friendships at work and at home

It's a Mystery to Me: The Longevity of Law and Order and Medicine

After *The Simpsons*, the next ratings champ is showrunner/impresario/ producer Dick Wolf's *Law & Order*—which spanned twenty seasons and launched multiple spin-offs (*Special Victims Unit, Criminal Intent*, and the short-lived *Trial by Jury*). The global success of *Law & Order* with many cases being "ripped from the headlines," paved the road for every scripted procedural drama, especially *CSI: Crime Scene Investigation* (set in Las Vegas), which is at thirteen seasons and counting. Plus its spin-offs: *CSI: Miami* (recently cancelled after 11 seasons) and *CSI: NY* (recently cancelled after nine seasons). The following are procedural series that offer closed-ended cases of the week in each episode as A stories, with serialized personal stories that tend to arc over a full season.

The Truth Is Out There: Phenomenal Anomalies

The following long-running series and recent hits defy categorization. Each show serves up iconic leading characters and unique storytelling styles (that aren't just gimmicks) which manage to tap into the zeitgeist. Each series is a hybrid of one or more other genres, as specified in the following:

* **Supernatural:** nine seasons and counting—two brothers seek out the paranormal and their missing father in this bromance/family drama/ sci-fi/mystery series with otherworldly thrills and chills
* **The X-Files:** nine seasons—"crime" procedural, but the cases revolve around the paranormal
* **Dexter:** eight seasons—"crime" procedural, but our protagonist is a police blood spatter expert by day and a vigilante serial killer by night; also contains elements of family drama with his sister and late father in the mix
* **Burn Notice:** seven seasons—"crime" procedural, but Michael Westen (Jeffrey Donovan) is a discredited former spy and no longer a sanctioned government agent
* **Lost:** six seasons—post–plane crash/Twilight Zone-esque happenings on a mysterious island; survivors form an extended family drama
* **True Blood:** six seasons—friendship ensemble/family drama/supernatural horror show; proof that audiences seem to have an unlimited appetite for vampirism
* **The Walking Dead:** four seasons and counting—friendship ensemble/ family drama/supernatural horror show; further proof that audiences seem to have an unlimited appetite for zombies

A valuable litmus test for a new episodic TV series is trying to come up with at least six future episode ideas beyond the pilot. Ideally, at this early blossoming phase, the basic premise should trigger so many possible episode ideas that it will make your head explode. On the other hand, if you're having trouble coming up with episode ideas for season 1, this is a strong indication that the premise is too limited and/or flawed. Step back, re-tool, revise, rejigger, and then re-launch.

See interview with **Pam Veasey** *on the companion website:* http://www. focalpress.com/cw/landau

8

IDENTIFY CHARACTERS' WEAKNESSES

We all have strengths and weaknesses. On TV series, these special abilities and liabilities are essential to both comedy and drama. Our primary goal as storytellers is to make our characters so relatable and accessible to an audience that they become emotionally invested in what happens week after week after week. We need viewers to cheer for their successes and lament their disappointments. We need the audience to *worry* about our characters and feel what *they* feel on a visceral level. And the key to this entry point is through character vulnerability.

In general, people tend to feel vulnerable due to physical and/or psychological limitations, such as

- lack of basic survival resources and safety (*The Walking Dead, Lost, Revolution*)
- feeling trapped/lack of freedom (*Prison Break, The Americans, Once Upon a Time*)
- lack of money (*Breaking Bad, Weeds, 2 Broke Girls*)
- lack of physical and/or mental health (*House, M.D., Dexter, Boss*)
- lack of qualifications or readiness in a crisis (*The Good Wife, The X-Files, Damages, Deadwood, Friday Night Lights, Parenthood*)
- lack of trust and/or self-confidence in a relationship (*Girls, Sex and the City, Scandal, Grey's Anatomy*)
- lack of a loyal support system of friends/family/allies (*Mad Men, The Sopranos*)
- lack of time (*The Killing, 24, Homeland*)

If character flaws are organic to character backstory, they tend to work best over the long haul of a series. This backstory is often just obliquely hinted at in the pilot or the first few episodes—which is a good thing for both writers and viewers because what we *don't* know about a character is often more compelling than what we *do* know.

Using Plot as Revelation

The goal in a TV series is to gradually peel away the layers of their characters' defenses and metaphorical masks so that the audience can participate in the ongoing discovery about each character. As a series progresses, characters evolve from season to season. Depending on the series, character evolution ranges from almost imperceptible (Dr. House) to subtle and nuanced (Don Draper on *Mad Men*) to tectonic (Walter White on *Breaking Bad*). The genre, tone, style, and pace of the series will dictate the level of character evolution over time. Procedural series, such as *Law & Order* and *CSI*, are wholly plot driven and tend to have very little character development. Serialized dramas feature gradual, incremental character growth from season to season—sometimes with an endgame in mind and sometimes opened-ended—with new plot developments swinging the pendulum according to character needs and audience expectations (every showrunner I interviewed reads their online message boards).

Sitcom characters are their own species, and usually become more rooted in *who they are* as each episode's situation challenges, taunts, and tempts them. They might fall in and out of love, but almost always *revert to form*, back to their comfort zones—which are also *our* comfort zones as viewers. We laugh with them and at them because they're so familiar and keep ending up back in the same humiliating situations.

But in drama series, as soon as the audience feels that they know *everything* about all of the characters, the series often becomes stale. For these reasons, whether you're working on a series that's been on the air for a while or writing a "spec" episode of an existing series as a writing sample, it's advisable to seek out the *unexplored* aspects of those characters. What kinds of very specific emotional and physical challenges have we *not* seen the characters face? What kinds of dormant fears might they have that get triggered by new characters and situations? Do these new challenges feel organic to the setup of the series? Can we see a clear relationship between cause and effect? Is this new situation *earned* based upon what came before in the characters' lives or is it something that's feeling imposed by the writer as a gimmick and too contrived?

By the end of season 2 of *Girls,* Hannah's (Lena Dunham) OCD (obsessive-compulsive disorder) seemed to emerge from out of nowhere which felt like an unnecessary embellishment to an already very quirky character—and viewer backlash soon followed.

Ideally, a character's major flaw or weakness will be evidenced—either emphatically or obliquely—in the pilot episode. But that's only half of what makes a memorable character.

Maximizing the Pro and Con

Each potential weakness or minus (–) needs some kind of positive strength (+), for all iconic characters enthrall us based upon their +/– contradictions. Dr. Gregory House (Hugh Laurie) has a bum leg, is addicted to pain meds, lacks empathy and sympathy for his patients, and is an incorrigible misanthrope. But we put up with him because he's a brilliant doctor. Dr. House says things the audience wishes it could say ("You can think I'm wrong but that's no reason to quit thinking.") Such is the beauty of drama, in that watching becomes an act of wish fulfillment. We can't say such things in our real lives, but we can vicariously watch as Dr. House does. Will Dr. House ever change? Nope. But it's the precarious dance he's able to do, week after week, pissing everyone off but managing to keep on grooving and succeeding on his own terms as a physician. He's *that* good.

Meanwhile, Tony Soprano (James Gandolfini) from *The Sopranos* is a classic example of a strong, powerful, and complex mafia boss with a major flaw: he's clinically depressed. From moment to moment, the viewer doesn't know if he'll have a nervous breakdown or break someone's kneecaps. It keeps us—and him—on edge. And while he does terrible things—repeatedly cheats on his wife, neglects his children, kills enemies and former allies—we relate to him because even in the midst of all his power and influence, *he's a lot like us.* He ponders death and the meaning of life. He feels guilty for neglecting his kids and for lying to his wife. He sees himself as a devout Catholic and patriot. Sometimes he has remorse when he's forced to honor mafia code, even when it clashes with his own personal ethics. He's often compelled to behave like a monster, but manages to cling to his humanity via visits to his (usually) impartial shrink, Dr. Melfi (Lorraine Bracco). And Tony's also not all bad: he loves animals, such as a prized horse and the ducks in his swimming pool, and deep down we know that he loves his wife and kids, but he's permanently scarred by his own upbringing.

Mad Men's Don Draper (Jon Hamm) is great looking and seemingly always in control. He has money and an interesting career, and yet, he is deeply unhappy. From the moment he took the alias Don Draper (the name on his birth certificate is Dick Whitman), he has lived a life of deceit, promiscuity, and hypocrisy. However, the audience follows his journey because he, like Dr. House, is brilliant at what he does: he gives advertising depth. But let's face it, he's not saving lives. There needs to be more. And there is: we sympathize with him because deep down he hates himself. Don Draper does not *want* to be the cheater that he is, and like the sinner in all of us, we relate and give him absolution. There is always a danger, however, of making a character flaw too flawed before the audience begins to not care about the character anymore. Don Draper, as the series continues, is towing the line between antihero and apathy.

Olivia Pope (Kerry Washington) on *Scandal* is always smooth and in control, fierce and intelligent, and yet her character flaw is that she had an affair with a married man, the then-governor Fitzgerald "Fitz" Grant (Tony Goldwyn), now president of the United States. Some would criticize her as a glorified mistress. At this point in season 2, the affair is over, but she still carries feelings for him. We relate to and accept Olivia not only because she's good at her job as a crisis-management fixer, but also because we know what it's like to love someone unrequitedly. Her flaws reinforce to the audience that we are greater than our biggest mistakes.

In the pilot for *Breaking Bad*, Walter White is a high school chemist facing inoperable lung cancer, the ultimate underdog. But soon Walter starts manufacturing methamphetamine to provide for his family after his death. While we hate what he does (make drugs), his reasons are altruistic: for his family. His character flaw is his hubris and the ability to lie to himself about his "good" intentions. It becomes clear his journey isn't about family—it's about *him*. It's about him ascending from a previously mediocre life into a life of power. The meek shall inherit the earth, and indeed, he has. Why do we follow him? Again, wish fulfillment, as many of our lives are spent, as the saying goes, in quiet desperation.

In *Homeland*, Carrie Mathison's (Claire Danes) insecurity about her hidden bipolar disorder (in season 1) causes her to be hypervigilant in her counterterrorism responsibilities for the CIA. She's willing not only to break protocol and put herself in harm's way, but she also throws herself into an extremely risky and inappropriate tryst with Brody (Damian Lewis) who is potentially a dangerous, "turned" terrorist operative. What makes Carrie so good at her job: trigger-fast instincts and intuition—are also her chief liabilities: too impulsive, paranoid, and renegade. Yet, we admire her doggedness and how she makes the case for what she believes in the face of severe obstacles, for example, when she threatened to pull a Saudi diplomat's favorite daughter from Yale unless he played ball. She is the Voice of Truth in a bureaucracy more concerned with politics than performance. She's a lone wolf, an outsider—just like Brody. We may not condone it, but we can certainly understand her connection to Brody, who is as confused and bifurcated as she is—and somehow we empathize with their taboo attraction. Maybe love can conquer all?

Identifying Weaknesses through Strengths

What's your main character's weakness? Does he use his strength to (over) compensate for it? For example, in *The Big Bang Theory*, Sheldon Cooper (Jim Parsons) is an egotistical scientist who, even though he is the smartest person in the room, has no understanding of irony or sarcasm and can be very annoying. His character flaw is tempered by his complete lack of social skills, which makes him endearing. Even as brilliant as he is, he didn't have a girlfriend (due to his fear of germs and physical contact) until his mid-twenties—something many in the audience take for granted. While he may be smarter than us, he is not *better* than us, and thus, relatable.

In *Elementary*, Sherlock Holmes (Jonny Lee Miller) is a deductive genius who is also terrible in social situations and like Sheldon Cooper is always the smartest person in the room. Obnoxious to a fault, he's not someone to invite to a dinner party. His flaw is acceptable to us because he's a broken man—a former drug addict trying to piece his life back together. He's eaten some humble pie, and while still a difficult personality, we know he is at least *trying* to connect to Joan Watson (Lucy Liu), his sober companion as they solve some of the hardest cases in New York City.

On *Bones*, Dr. Temperance "Bones" Brennan (Emily Deschanel) is once again akin to Sheldon Cooper: intelligent but lacking in social skills. Even her name gives a major clue to her flaw: temperance, which means restraint and control over excess. Not someone that sounds like too much fun. And even as bright as she is, she often says, "I don't know what that means," in reference to pop cultural references. Her flaw is that she's so smart, she's almost outside the realm of our culture, and for that, we accept her.

With these examples, a theme begins to emerge: the audience may not have as much patience for a character that is mediocre at their job. Human nature is such that we give more leeway to people we perceive as geniuses.

Pacing Flaw Revelation

Character flaws gradually expand and deepen over time. We know that Don Draper is a philanderer in the pilot of *Mad Men*, but we don't discover that his mother was a prostitute when he was a kid until season 6.

From the first five episodes of *Scandal*, we presume that Olivia Pope is a home wrecker by participating in her affair with the married president, but we don't learn until episode 6 that Fitz's marriage was one of political convenience. We also presume that Fitz is in the driver's seat and certainly in a more powerful political position than Olivia—but in season 2 we discover that Olivia was actually instrumental in getting Fitz into office—via a rigged election—which he was unaware of. As Olivia's network of (well-intentioned) secrets and lies unravels, she becomes increasingly vulnerable in both her love life and professional life. Her prior strength in handling covert manipulations may now just circle around and destroy her—which raises the stakes.

Most iconic TV characters will continually battle against their flaws and inner-demons in an attempt to transcend them—while other protagonists will live in a bubble of denial. Still other series leads are actually *fueled* by their flaws (*House, Dexter, The Shield, Breaking Bad*). And some will succumb to those flaws.

By the end of a long-running series, some protagonists may overcome their main flaws and learn to believe and trust and love. At the conclusion of *The X-Files*, Mulder and Scully finally see the truth in Area 51 and stop denying their feelings for one another. And in *Lost*, they literally see the light.

On a TV series, there is nothing more satisfying to character development than when a character's greatest strength also becomes his or her greatest liability. This push and pull and internal/external struggle will help sustain a series over many seasons. The trick to dramatic sustainability is keeping your main character in this form of limbo. When the external demons are temporarily suppressed, it's time for the inner demons to rear their ugly heads.

INTERVIEW: David Shore

David Shore Credits

Best known for:

House, M.D. (Executive Producer/Writer/Creator/Director) 2004–2012
    Emmy Award Winner (Outstanding Writing for a Drama Series) 2005
    Emmy Nominated (Outstanding Drama Series) 2006–2009
    WGA Award Winner (Episodic Drama) 2010
Hack (Executive Producer/Writer) 2002–2004
Family Law (Executive Producer/Co-Executive Producer/Writer) 1999–2002
Law & Order (Producer/Supervising Producer/Writer) 1997–1999
    Emmy Nominated (Outstanding Drama Series) 1998–1999
Due South (Writer) 1994–1998
The Practice (Writer) 1997

NL: We're talking about eight seasons of *House, M.D.* Part of the reason that the show has been so beloved and enduring is that you started with a great central character: an iconic, flawed, often maddening, fascinating, complex man. And, it seems to me, that what defines your series is that everyone evolves, *except* Dr. House remains the same. Can you speak to your initial story strategy?

DS: When I first started writing the pilot, it wasn't completely clear in my mind who this character was—although it became clear fairly quickly. I feel strongly that the character is only as strong as the challenges presented to him. So a detective who solves a really obvious murder is not really a detective. It was important to me that you'd have these extremely challenging mysteries, but it was also important that the characters around him be challenging. I certainly feel that some of them have been overshadowed by him a little bit. They needed to be really smart and really interesting and really challenging because what we're judging him on are the judgments he makes and the relationships he establishes. They all have to challenge him in a way which is worthy of him. They were all, hopefully, very specific. You try for that.

NL: So he would bring out different facets of them?

DS: I'm not sure it's quite so calculating that this guy was assigned to bring out this asset or that, but clearly it was the fact that he had this team that was challenging him from below. How did they respond to him and how did they resist him or not resist him? His best friend—same questions—how does he resist him or not resist him, but from a different point of view. That is sort of his conscience. And who would be this guy's friend is also something that is constantly challenging. Obviously Wilson [Robert Sean Leonard] had to have his own demons. He's not as obviously screwed up, but he had to be basically as complicated as House on some level. In some ways, the most challenging one was his boss, Cuddy [Lisa Edelstein]. When you create a character such as House who is just such a steamroller and doing incredibly inappropriate things. What do you do with the boss? Because if the boss actually shuts him down, he's not doing anything. And if he steamrolls over the boss, then she becomes Colonel Klink [from *Hogan's Heroes*] who is just a wonderful sitcom character, but not a good, interesting character for a one-hour drama series. Very early on, we made this decision because it's interesting, but also because it works dramatically for the long term that she should be a character who challenges him, but understands what he's worth and is therefore much more about managing him. She doesn't always shut him down, but she doesn't always let him go. He gets around her when he needs to, but she surprises us when she allows him to do something. She also has to win some battles, but obviously, not all of them.

NL: Did you know from the beginning that you would get a slow burn relationship going?

DS: It was written in the pilot. I think Wilson makes some smart-ass remark about there being a thin line between love and hate. However, even if I hadn't written that in, when I saw Hugh Laurie and Lisa Edelstein working together, it was pretty obvious that there was going to be sexual tension in a big way that we were going to have to deal with. That was fun.

NL: What is your process for constructing story in general? Do you start with character? Do you start with a thematic within an episode? Do you start with the medical mystery?

DS: There was no hard-and-fast rule, but I tried to have a hard-and-fast rule. The hard-and-fast rule was that I needed both: character, but theme basically got subsumed into the patient of the week. Who is this patient of the week? Going back to the whole point of having an interesting team, what's interesting about House was how he reacted to people. What he reads in people. Is he right? Is he wrong? What does that say about that person? What does it say about him? That applies to the patient of the week as well. Somebody comes in who claims to never lie. What is House's opinion on that? What is his opinion on lying? Obviously, he says everybody lies. Is it a good thing? Is it a bad thing? Does he think the person is lying in saying that? Why are they lying? Is it a pathological thing? Is it a medical thing? It was that notion of character that I needed right up front. I also needed a good medical story. I needed both. Every now and then, a writer would come in with just a really interesting medical story. And I would say, "That's great, but you need to find some character thing too." Likewise, they'd sometimes come in with a really great character with some medicine to go with that. Then you would also try to match it up with where you were in the story arc. I wanted both in a way that was thematic, but not obvious.

NL: So your A stories would generally be the medical cases. What would make a worthy A story? When you came up with a medical condition that had to be rare and mysterious, I would imagine what would make it worthy is that there would have to be twists and turns to it.

DS: In that regard, it was like a cop show. You needed twists and turns. You need to be going down a road and have that road be wrong. That was the formula for the show, and I don't apologize for that at all, which we did depart from on occasion.

NL: If it was too obvious of a medical solution, then it was not a worthy story?

DS: The type of conditions that we were attracted to were the ones that were serious enough that they could cause life-threatening symptoms, but vague enough that they could mask as a whole bunch of things which is why it became a running gag that Lupus kept getting mentioned. Unfortunately for those Lupus sufferers, it can be very serious, but it is also very difficult to diagnose. If there's one crazy condition in the world that causes your left ear to fall off, on the face of it, that's fascinating and very visually dramatic, but if there's one condition that does that, that's not going to work for us.

NL: Did you take dramatic license, or did you try to stay true to science and medicine?

DS: We tried very hard to stay true to science. We tried to make it as much about the character and as little about the medicine, but you needed that medical core and that medical spine. That was an excuse to do the story that we wanted. You do have a responsibility. You have millions of viewers. Even if it's a disease that afflicts 0.1 percent of the population, then that's still thousands of people watching your show. You don't want to give false hope or false fear. There are also all sorts of studies now that indicate that people are getting a shocking amount of their medical knowledge from watching TV.

NL: Did you know a full season arc for each character when you would start?

DS: We would usually arc half a season—more or less. We would meet as a group for a couple weeks and figure out where we wanted to take the characters in the first half of the season. Hopefully, as far as we could take it, but it usually ended up being a half a season. Then, as we were getting closer to the end of that arc, we would discuss what we wanted to do next. So, if it's after House and Cuddy breaking up, what is the follow from that breakup and where do we take them next?

NL: Because this chapter is called "Who Changes?—what's interesting when you look at all the seasons from Dr. House that "nobody changes." In your mind, did your characters change or was it just temporary challenges that got them to adjust behavior?

DS: The tricky thing in TV, particularly if you're doing a show that's 100 percent procedural, it's very easy in that regard, you don't have to worry about that. If you're even a hybrid, then you run into this difficult territory of "Well, how did that affect him? How does he change?" Hugh used to say that the difference between TV and movies was that with movies the main character changes while everybody around him stays the same and with TV it's the exact opposite. There's some truth to that. My characters didn't change that much and I have multiple excuses for that and I'm not sure excuse is the right word, maybe explanations: (1) it was the theme of the show that "nobody changes," I believe that, I believe that people don't really change that much. (2) I didn't want them to change. The show was about him and I didn't want him to change because I liked him. So people think they want him to change, but they don't really. They want to see him find love and happiness, but they don't really.

> *I* do circle back to that I truly don't believe that anybody changes, and I think it's more interesting to watch somebody strive to change and maybe . . . maybe in tiny little ways and then maybe fall back.

But we are who we are in how we react to the challenges in that moment. I don't think that writers should quote themselves, but there was a line that I liked from one of the earlier seasons after Foreman [Omar Epps] almost died where House says something along the lines of, "Almost dying changes everything forever for two months." How do people react to not changing and the disappointment with themselves? It's about treading water and not falling back. Not being miserable and staying just above miserable.

NL: In terms of addiction and AA, they say, "Hitting rock bottom is that you change or you die." That was always a tightrope he was walking as well.

DS: You can change your actions, but even that's so difficult to do. With AA, it's not that you're no longer an alcoholic, you're just an alcoholic who doesn't drink. Changing who you fundamentally are is possibly impossible.

NL: In terms of vulnerability of characters and finding new places to take them, there was a season when House fired virtually his entire staff, and when he hired new people, it gave him new opportunities for him to abuse them.

DS: That was exactly it. Having House explore new people and new situations and analyzing them and making them learn something about themselves in the process.

NL: House could always find someone's Achilles' heel and then exploit that weakness. Did he ever do things that just shocked and surprised you—like when he drives into Cuddy's house?

DS: That was the most controversial thing we did—more than I expected it to be. I knew it was shocking. People seemed to react that he was trying to kill her. I never thought of it that way which maybe was stupid on my part, but I never thought of it that way. It was scripted and shot that way: that he looks through the window and sees her leave the room and then he does it. It was intended to be an act of violence, but not an attempt at murder. It was also an irrational act by a very, very rational man. The other thing that I think said quite clearly that he was not trying to kill her is that he walks away with a smile on his face feeling better which tells me that he accomplished what he wanted to accomplish. So clearly injury was not part of what he wanted to accomplish. Stuff that he did that shocked me . . . there were moments where you go, "Yeah, I think he would do that," and the whole idea was that it would surprise the audience and yet make sense. That's fundamental with all the twists and turns you do on a show like this. It gets tricky as you're going along. It's about trying to find that third way. When you have House do exactly what everybody expects anybody to do, you could have him just do the exact opposite, but for the sake of doing the exact opposite, it doesn't make any sense at all. Or you find something that is a different take on it, but that makes sense. Surprising an audience that expects to be surprised is a bit of a challenge. I'm proud of that. It was very satisfying. I wish I could give you a specific example, but let's say you had a patient who felt one way and House had a certain attitude that you would not have expected, but then he's got this defense of it. And then you go, "Oh, yeah."

NL: One that comes to mind was the death row episode where there was a guy who was going to be executed, but House wanted to treat him and yet he's going to die. That patient was more of his priority than another patient who is terminal. That was a controversial episode because of the surprising position that he took. He had this interesting bond with the guy because it was somebody who had been so condemned by society and he related to that on some level—which provided more insight into House's character than I'd seen before. It was a great moral gray area and reinforced House's one-man-against-the-Establishment sensibilities.

Regarding the Establishment and dealing with network or studio guidance and interference, did they leave you alone as you got more successful or did they continue to give you notes?

DS: Very, very few notes. We would get *a* note on every single script. Well, that's not even true—there were some scripts where we wouldn't get a single note. But there would be a call set up after every script went out, and they would give us notes. They were invariably very small which actually started to worry me because you want notes, you don't *want* notes on some emotional level, but you want an outside source to look at it and be objective. And, hopefully, you have executives who can do that and have an honest reaction to the script.

NL: I was asking Veena Sud about *The Killing* and Sarah Linden (Mireille Enos), who was very unlikeable. She has some dark traits which she shares with House, and yet she is also very good at her job. Any interference early on about House or on any of your past or future shows about character likeability?

DS: I think every writer in the world has an attitude about that. I got surprisingly little interference on that. I think there were some internal battles that went on at FOX, but I was protected somehow there. Maybe on some unconscious level I made him nastier than I needed to, so I'd have some place to fall back on. He is nastier than what you'd typically see on network TV. They do say they want likeable characters. Every writer in the world wants to write complex characters. We want to write characters who we want to watch. We're not idiots. You have to have a commercial sensibility, but you have to write it in a way that people want to come back to. That's the job we're in. We want to tell stories that people want to hear. Unfortunately, the networks interpret likeable too often as nice. Nice is just boring. I had very little resistance. I think I would have had more resistance on another network. FOX was still in the glow of Simon Cowell.

NL: But you also paved the way because after House and its success, all of these cable shows sprung up with these dark, heavily complex characters.

DS: If I can take credit for that, I'm happy to do it. If I somehow made it easier, then I am thrilled. Because that's what every writer wants to write and audiences want to watch if it's done well. He's good at his job. He's not simply lining his pockets. He's miserable. And he's saving lives. Whatever the reason—which is something we discussed a lot was, what matters, intentions or actions? And his intention, for example with that death row guy, was that he found that more interesting and therefore he did it.

NL: I'm sure I read this somewhere in my research, but would you say that he cares more about solving the puzzle than the patient?

DS: I think he absolutely cares more about the puzzle. Having said that, it is a good thing for the show that the audience wanted to believe that it was more than that. And the audience may have been right to a certain extent. Because they liked him, the audience wanted to impose a positive viewpoint on him. Had he just been going around saying, "Damn it, I'm saving lives," it's not as interesting. A guy who says, "I could give a crap about saving lives," is too fundamentally horrible and boring. But this is an interesting case and maybe he learns something about the person. And maybe . . . maybe on some level grows to respect that person and save their life. That's much more interesting and compelling.

NL: Was it your perspective that he wasn't capable of empathy—maybe even borderline autistic?

DS: That was speculated out. I never wanted to pigeonhole him quite that much—probably there was something of that nature going on. His reasoning was that it didn't help. There's no reason to do that. It doesn't make the case easier to solve. If anything, it makes it more difficult. Objectivity is your friend in trying to find truth. Truth is truth. So he just wanted to take a very clean look at everything. I always hated when people would ask why this happens. It starts with the writers being interviewed. Just don't answer those questions. Number one, I don't want to take that away from the audience. Number two, I don't think any simple answer is true. I think I can have a reason House did something and the writer of that episode could have a reason that House did something and Hugh Laurie could have a reason why the character did something. By the way, the three of us should be basically in agreement, but Wilson could have an attitude about why House did something and the team can have an attitude why House did something and Cuddy can have an attitude why House did something and so can the audience. And every one of those should be true. It should never be as simple as he did it for X. House says he did it for X. Wilson says he did it for Y. His team says he did it for Z. And all three of them are part of why he did it.

NL: It sounds like part of what sustained the show itself for so long is that House was so mysterious. You didn't answer some of those questions. If you show the wizard behind the curtain, it's not as interesting.

DS: It's not as interesting, but it's also not true. The answer is never going to be true. The expression "everybody lies," which is used all the time on the show. I never meant it as people say black when the answer is white. The answer is always gray and people see it as dark gray or light gray. People see the truth they want to see. We all have biases. That's what it really meant to me and House is trying to rise above that.

9
DETERMINE THE POV

There are many ways to tell a story, and each approach differs depending on what your series is about and around whom the series orbits.

So let's start with this basic question: *whose story is it?*

You have several options. Following is a breakdown of different types of POVs employed on one-hour dramas, sitcoms, and half-hour dramedies. Please note that there is a great deal of overlap between several of these categories:

Single-lead protagonist POV. Primarily utilized to show the world of the series through one dominant perspective. In the cases of *Dexter*, *Revenge*, *The Big C*, and *Nurse Jackie*, this limited POV is particularly important because each of these series' leads has something to hide. *Dexter* is a police blood spatter expert who moonlights as a vigilante serial killer. *Revenge* centers around a beautiful young socialite (imposter) with a ruthless vendetta. In *The Big C*, Cathy Jamison (Laura Linney) had a terminal cancer diagnosis that she prefers to ignore in order to live the rest of her life to the fullest without pity or remorse. Nurse Jackie Peyton (Edie Falco) is a supereffective E.R. nurse, wife and mother—who also happens to be a drug addict, fueling her propensity to regularly cheat on her husband and lie to her kids.

In each of the preceding examples, the audience is privy to their vulnerabilities whereas all or many of the people in their daily lives are (mostly) presented with a façade or persona of the protagonist versus a more open character willing to disclose their secrets and ulterior motives.

See also *Enlightened, Justified, The Following, My So-Called Life, Rescue Me, Californication.*

Single main protagonist with one main sidekick. Series such as *Sherlock* (U.K. version) and *Elementary* (U.S. version), *Breaking Bad, House, M.D.,*

The Killing, and *Royal Pains* feature a brilliant yet flawed lead character who is usually socially awkward, misanthropic, and/or lacking an essential skill—necessitating the need for a partner in business, love, life, and/or crime. Sherlock Holmes needs his Watson to help him navigate the technological world and to compensate for Sherlock's key "blind spot" in life: his lack of empathy. Sherlock is an expert at figuring out riddles and mysteries, but he's lousy at interpersonal relationships—which tends to be Watson's strong suit. Watson also serves as a vital sounding board for Sherlock's hypotheses, as well as being Sherlock's (only) true friend and confidant. Sherlock *needs* Watson but he's loath to admit it, which fuels their *bromance* with humor and conflict.

In *Breaking Bad*, Walter White (Bryan Cranston) begins as a milquetoast, high school chemistry teacher, loving husband and father—a far cry from the badass drug lord with delusions of grandeur that Walt will eventually become. For the first few seasons, Walt is completely dependent upon Jessie Pinkman (Aaron Paul), a young hotshot renegade drug dealer who also happens to be one of Walt's former students. These two guys have zero in common, except their mutual goal to cook the purist, most potent crystal meth on the black market. With Walt's brain and Jessie's street smarts, they're a match made in heaven.

Dr. Gregory House (Hugh Laurie), another brilliant pariah, relies on his one main confidant, Dr. James Wilson (Robert Sean Leonard) to be his moral compass. Dr. House routinely butts heads with his supervisor, Cuddy (Lisa Edelstein) who, invariably, is as ready to dismantle House's hubris and insubordination as he is to undermine her authority. House is able to perform his job with such precision *in spite of Cuddy*, whereas his professional friendship with Dr. Wilson actually helps fuel his effectiveness.

In *The Killing*, Homicide Detective Sarah Linden (Mireille Enos) is fiercely driven and single goal-minded—often going to self-destructive extremes. But it's her unconventional, irreverent partner Stephen Holder (Joel Kinnaman) who simultaneously challenges and supports her out in the field. As good as she is at her job, she wouldn't be nearly as proficient without Holder in her corner—and they both know it. There's a tacit respect and trust between them that ebbs and flows with the highs and lows of the murder case(s).

In *Royal Pains*, two brothers, Dr. Hank Lawson (Mark Feuerstein) and Evan Lawson (Paulo Costanzo) run a thriving "concierge doctor" practice in the form of discreet house calls to the rich and famous. In the pilot episode, Hank is essentially exiled to the tony beachside playground of the Hamptons after being accused of fatally botching the surgery of a wealthy hospital benefactor in New York City. As the series progresses, Hank is an easy-going, down-to-earth physician with an excellent bedside manner, but he lacks the business acumen and spontaneity of his younger, wheeler-dealer brother. Together, these brothers are a dynamic duo, even though Evan is often more of a liability than an asset. And, after all, Evan is the one who came up with the idea of HankMed in the first place. Like most brothers, the two can bring out the best and worst in one another because they know each other's weaknesses so well. But, when the chips are down, they've got each other's backs.

Dominant lead character surrounded by ensemble. The following series are examples of how a leader is only as strong as the team he or she guides, chastises, empowers, and inspires.

In *Scandal*, Olivia Pope (Kerry Washington) is a gorgeous, wicked smart, savvy public relations and damage control expert. The best in the biz—she's a cunning, charming, always impeccably dressed and discreet Beltway insider with a flawless reputation. But behind the scenes, she's also a micromanaging control freak whose personal life is usually spinning out of control. Olivia has super sharp political instincts, knows how to play the Washington power game, and very rarely loses because she has an elite group of specialists on her staff. What makes Olivia so good at her job is she knows she can trust her staff implicitly because they were each "wounded birds"—hand-picked, rescued, and trained by Olivia. She essentially saved their lives and now there is no doubt that there is nothing they wouldn't do to protect and serve their boss.

On *Mad Men*, Don Draper (Jon Hamm) begins as the agency's creative director and the driving force of its success. With the uncanny ability to perform his job best after too much debauchery, Don is equally adept at impressing hard-to-please clients and alienating his bosses and colleagues. Don is a self-destructive genius. For a time, he was able to keep up appearances in the office and at home despite his crumbling marriage to Betty (January Jones). And after his fall from grace, Don manages, once again, to rebrand and reinvent himself with a new (younger model) wife, Megan (Jessica Paré).

Don Draper is the glue of *Mad Men*. The conceit of the series works so well because it is based on the central question: Who is Don Draper really— and will he ever truly change? While each of his main colleagues (Roger, Peggy, Pete, Joan, Ken, Harry, and big boss Bertram) has his/her own aspirations and desires and plotlines each season, they mainly serve as the prism through which we view the many facets of Don Draper. If Don weren't so good at spinning his version of the truth, he wouldn't be such a rock star in the ad world. Advertising is designed to sell us stuff we don't really need, based upon the illusion that a product will fill the void in our lives and make us happy. Don may be too cynical to believe in the idea of lasting happiness; he knows what it's supposed to look like and sound like, but he may be too numb to feel it.

Sex and the City, Girls, and *Entourage* all focus on one main protagonist (Carrie, Hannah, Vince) and her or his three best friends. Whereas *Sex and the City* and *Entourage* embodied the slick, materialistic excesses of Manhattan and L.A., *Girls* revolves around four besties who are struggling in their careers and love lives. What differentiates each of these series from being pure "ensemble" dramedies is the dominance of their lead character's POV. *Sex and the City* begins and ends with Carrie's newspaper column, told via V.O. and setting up each episode's main theme. *Girls* is about Hannah and her three friends. And while we follow art gallery assistant Marnie (Allison Williams), and cousins Jessa (Jemima Kirke) and Shoshanna (Zosia Mamet) into their separate plotlines, Hannah is the nexus of the series. Everyone reports back to Hannah, and the series is as much about how their lives impact Hannah's narcissism as it's about the actual lives of her friends.

Entourage (creator/showrunner Doug Ellin) is based upon the real-life exploits of Mark Wahlberg as he and his buddies moved from Boston to Los Angeles to pursue fame, fortune, fast cars, and femmes. Wahlberg's alter ego from Queens, New York is Vincent Chase (Adrian Grenier). He may not be the most dynamic or noisy character in the series, but he's the sun around which his friends' and colleagues' lives all orbit.

A good litmus test for this type of POV paradigm is this: if you remove the dominant protagonist and just leave the ensemble, would the series still sustain and continue to exist? Vince is the ideal blossoming movie star precisely because he's so laid back and indifferent to fame. His super agent Ari (Jeremy Piven) requires power and money like a vampire needs blood, whereas Vince is a simple, humble guy who could take it or leave it, as long as he's got his buddies, good weed, and gets laid. Of course, Vince *likes* the fame and money, but his life doesn't depend upon it. Vince is the star and the moral center of the show's universe. Everyone around him is a social climber: Vince's best friend, Eric Murphy (Kevin Connolly) ambitiously manages Vince's career; Vince's elder half-brother Johnny "Drama" Chase (Kevin Dillon) is an aspiring actor; even pothead slacker Salvatore "Turtle" Assante (Jerry Ferrara) is an entrepreneur with big dreams. But Vince's POV enables us to recognize the absurdity, pretension, and phoniness of show business. Ari is, by far, the loudest, showiest role in *Entourage*. His shallowness, greed, thirst for power, hysteria and hubris, shocks, provokes and makes us laugh out loud, and yet Ari is best in small doses. To prove my point, if you remove Vince from the ensemble, what you're left with is a series about selfish, soulless Hollywood players. Ironically, Vince makes us care because he doesn't.

See also *Sons of Anarchy, The Mentalist, The Good Wife, The Sopranos, The Shield, Weeds, Veep, Boardwalk Empire,* and *True Blood.*

Voice-over (VO) narration as running commentary on current action. Generally used to widen perspective and place events in a thematic or ironic context.

Sex and the City used Carrie Bradshaw's (Sarah Jessica Parker) magazine column to articulate (via V.O.) each episode's thematic question. In a season 1 episode ("Secret Sex" written by creator/showrunner Darren Star), Carrie poses this thematic question:

CARRIE (V.O.)

How many of us out there are having great sex with people we're ashamed to introduce to our friends?

In this episode, Carrie goes out on her first date with "Mr. Big" (Chris Noth), but he's reticent to introduce her into his social circle and just wants to stay in (bed) with her, leading Carrie to believe that he's somehow ashamed of her. Should she withhold sex in this context or just go for it? Meanwhile, Miranda (Cynthia Nixon) meets a hunky guy at the gym who seems to be hiding something from her. When she discovers a "spanking" video in his apartment, she has to decide whether she should dump him or walk on the wild side and tell no one. At the same time, Charlotte (Kristen Davis) divulges to her girlfriends that she's having sex with a rabbi. Samantha, at the other end of the spectrum, has no issues with broadcasting her *sex-capades* with anyone, anytime, anywhere, and believes that sex should not be delayed for moral reasons. In *Sex and the City*, Carrie's quest is always the A story, and her girlfriends' plotlines are the corresponding B, C, and D stories that are all on the same theme.

In the pilot episode of *Grey's Anatomy*, titled "A Hard Day's Night" and written by creator/showrunner Shonda Rhimes, we're introduced to the dominant main character of the ensemble. We know she's the lead character because her last name is "Grey," the episode begins and ends with her, and it's her voice in the teaser—in which we also witness Meredith as she tries to gracefully depart from last night's one-night stand with a handsome but more or less anonymous stranger—who, to her mortification, will later turn out to be her boss: Dr. Derek Shepherd aka McDreamy (played by Patrick Dempsey).

MEREDITH (V.O.)

The Game. They say a person either has what it takes to play, or they don't. My mother was one of the greats. Me on the other hand . . . I'm kinda screwed. Like I said I'm screwed. I can't think of any one reason why I want to be a surgeon. But I can think of a thousand reasons why I should quit. They make it hard on purpose. There are lives in our hands. There comes a moment when it's more than just a game. And you either take that step forward or turn around and walk away. I could quit, but here's the thing . . . I love the playing field.

As the pilot episode unfolds, Meredith Grey (Ellen Pompeo) begins her residency at Seattle Grace Hospital. She encounters her fellow interns: tough perfectionist Cristina (Sandra Oh); introverted George (T. R. Knight); ex-model Izzie (Katherine Heigl), and arrogant Lothario Alex (Justin Chambers).

They're all introduced to their supervisor, Dr. Miranda Bailey (Chandra Wilson) who's unaffectionately referred to as "The Nazi." During their first long, grueling, exhilarating and intensely challenging shift, each intern grapples with personal demons and the fear that he/she isn't good enough to succeed. And if life and death stakes at every turn aren't high enough, we learn that Meredith is living in the shadow of her mother, Dr. Ellis Grey (Kate Burton) who was a prominent Seattle surgeon in her heyday. At the conclusion of the pilot episode, Meredith visits her mother in an assisted living facility, and we discover that Meredith's voice-over was actually a one-sided chat she was having with her mother—who is now suffering from Alzheimer's and barely even recognizes her daughter. In the touching grace note to the pilot, Meredith realizes that life is hard and offers no guarantees of success. But if you don't play, you can't win; the risk offers its own reward.

While each intern has his/her own specific challenge as a newbie doctor, every medical case is linked to Meredith as our guide. In season 1, this series focused first and foremost on Meredith. However, as the series progresses and other regular characters became more popular (and some left the series to pursue other opportunities), Meredith became less prominent and a more equal member of the ensemble.

In *Dexter*, Dexter Morgan's (Michael C. Hall) voice-over narrative is crucial to our deeper understanding of his motives. We can see with our own eyes who, how, when, and where he kills. But it's the articulation of his inner psychology in voice-over which enables us to grasp at *why*.

Unlike *Sex and the City*, *Grey's Anatomy*, and *Enlightened*, Dexter's V.O. is less thematic and more of an examination of his psyche. Dexter lives by his own (secret) code as taught to him by his late, adoptive father, Harry. Dexter is incredibly smart, but fastidious, emotionless, cold, calculating, and trusts no one (at least not in the early episodes). He maintains a double life: by day, a hardworking blood spatter pattern analyst for the Miami police department; by night a vigilante serial killer who metes out justice and punishment on his own terms. The V.O. keeps the audience inside Dexter's head and tries to help us reconcile his violent actions. His emotionless voice lulls us and draws us in. And, even though, his killing sprees compel us to turn away— we keep watching again and again—because while Dexter is a monster, he's a *well-intentioned* monster.

He also has a dry, funny, droll wit, so while we're repelled by his actions, we're also in on the joke. He disposes of miscreants and societal douche bags. Sure, it's dead wrong. But it's human nature to have thoughts of getting even—and Dexter acts out the fantasy of getting away with murder. Sure, he's a sick puppy and his actions are reprehensible, but in Dexter's world, that's entertainment.

See also *Enlightened*.

Dual leads POV. Another POV option is a dual focus. In *Homeland*, we spend an equal amount of time with Carrie Mathison (Claire Danes) and Nicholas Brody (Damian Lewis). She's a CIA agent in the antiterrorism unit; he's a former POW soldier who's returned to Washington, D.C., as a war hero. Or maybe he was "turned" (brainwashed) by Islamic extremist Abu Nazir (Navid Negahban), while being held captive for eight years, and is now a terrorist. Or maybe he wasn't brainwashed at all, but instead has come to see the value of retribution against the United States for its hawkish imperialism? Carrie suspects the latter, but her POV is unreliable because she has no hard proof, coupled with her erratic behavior caused by her going off her bipolar medication. Is Carrie's commitment to U.S. Homeland Security so devout that she's willing to have sex with the married Brody to earn his trust? Or is she actually falling in love with and sleeping with the enemy?

The brilliance of season 1, in particular, of *Homeland* was how much we did not know. Each episode presented us with different perspectives and theories as to Carrie and Brody's motives—but then the next episode would demolish our expectations and send us back to trying to predict the next plot development. *Homeland* exists in the moral gray areas, and so Abu Nazir's vendetta against the vice president of the United States is rooted in Nazir's heartbreak of losing his son in a U.S. drone attack. And Brody, who is also a father, can completely empathize and relate to Nazir's grief. *Homeland* proves that well-developed "good guys" are flawed, complex, and possess dark sides, and well-drawn villains also have sympathetic points of view. The challenge in such a dual focus is shifting the pendulum of our sympathy from one character to another without alienating the audience or making us feel manipulated.

In *The Americans*, the dual POV is not just written as "us" (United States) versus "them" (USSR), which would have been too simplistic for this smart series. Instead, we are treated to the distinctive points of view of Elizabeth (a Soviet loyalist who's committed to her mission) and Phillip (who has started to question his mission). We also get to witness scenes from this arranged marriage as their true feelings surface, as their kids mature and rebel against parental expectations, and as neighbors and KGB cohorts start to become suspicious. If this were a series solely depicting moles and espionage, it would probably flatten out and flat-line fast. Fortunately, the astute series creator (Joe Weisberg knows that all great series are about families. Cold War espionage plotlines can start to feel repetitive and limited, whereas family dramas are universally relatable and can provide unlimited story engines).

The *Americans* also expands its POV to include Elizabeth and Phillip's new neighbors, the Beemans, along with the added tension that Stan Beeman (Noah Emmerich) is a counterintelligence agent in the FBI; this provides us with a secondary POV as counterpoint to Elizabeth and Phillip's—when they're aligned—and further expands the POV when they're all at odds. This added layer and POV affords us the opportunity to experience how unsuspecting neighbors Stan and Sandra (Susan Misner) get to know Elizabeth and Phillip. We get the sense that, if not for their backstories, these two couples would become good friends. (I'm looking forward to the episode when they all go camping together.) At this early point in this new series, Stan and Sandra, along with Paige and Henry, are all totally clueless about Elizabeth and Phillip's double duties. The "sweet spot" of the show is that the couple of spies Stan is hunting for are right under his nose. This is a series about keeping your friends close and your enemies even closer.

Dual protagonist POVs are almost always improved and enhanced when each of the equal protagonists have different opinions, values, and perspectives, as well as their symbiotic, complementary strengths and weaknesses. The basic idea behind this theory is that if you put two incomplete people together you get one whole, perfectly well-rounded individual.

Examples:

In *The X-Files*, FBI special agent Fox Mulder (David Duchovny) believes in paranormal phenomena, while his partner, Agent Dana Scully (Gillian Anderson), is a skeptic.

In *Bones*, FBI special agent Seeley Booth (David Boreanaz) is paired with forensic anthropologist Dr. Temperance "Bones" Brennan (Emily Deschanel). Booth represents the law, while Bones represents science; together they form a powerful investigative team. The dynamic is even more richly delineated as Booth believes in faith and God, while Brennan believes in science, evidence, and atheism.

In *Castle*, Richard Castle (Nathan Fillion), a best-selling mystery author, is teamed with NYPD detective Kate Beckett (Stana Katic). Their dynamic is represented by their sexual tension and differing approaches to criminal cases.

Rizzoli & Isles pairs Boston detective Jane Rizzoli (Angie Harmon) with medical examiner Maura Isles (Sasha Alexander) to solve crimes. Mirroring the *Bones* dynamic of law and science, the characters play different halves, as Rizzoli is a tomboy and Isles is more of a girly-girl.

In *Nip/Tuck*, plastic surgeon Sean McNamara (Dylan Walsh) is a straight-laced, married-with-kids type, while his partner, Christian Troy (Julian McMahon) is the show's charming bad boy.

While an ensemble, the strongest dynamic in *The Big Bang Theory* is between roommates Leonard Hofstadter (Johnny Galecki) and Sheldon Cooper (Jim Parsons). Both are brilliant, yet Leonard is functional in society, while Sheldon is so trapped in his mind that it makes him a social misfit.

2 Broke Girls follows roommates Max (Kat Dennings) and Caroline (Beth Behrs) as they try to start up a cupcake business. Max is from a poor, working-class family while Caroline was born rich. While both are now broke, they have differing points of view based on their upbringing.

Whether it's the Ashton Kutcher character or Charlie Sheen's, *Two and a Half Men* follows the tried-and-true "Odd Couple" dynamic: it mixes Alan (Jon Cryer), an uptight father, with a hedonist, charming bad boy. Each one is right and each one is wrong. The truth lies somewhere in the middle.

Ensemble cast/multiple POVs. *Desperate Housewives, Grey's Anatomy, Shameless, Downton Abbey, Burn Notice, The Walking Dead, Friday Night Lights, Parenthood, The Wire, Entourage, Six Feet Under, Glee, Dallas,* and *How I Met Your Mother*

In these series, there are often more than A, B, and C plotlines. There are as many stories as necessary to "serve" each of the main characters. However, the A story will often encompass more than one character.

In *The Walking Dead* episode "I Ain't a Judas," the A story revolved around Rick Grimes (Andrew Lincoln) debating what they should do next in the face of dwindling food and supplies; the B story involved The Governor (David Morrissey) as he prepared Woodbury for battle; and the C story involved Andrea (Laurie Holden) as she decided to travel to the prison to negotiate with Rick. All of the stories, however, involved other supporting characters. This storytelling device is used more often in serial dramas, rather than self-contained episodes.

Downton Abbey tells the story of the wealthy upper class who live in the grand estate of the same name, as well as the servants who work there. In episode 6 of season 2, a badly burned Canadian officer comes to Downton claiming he is their lost heir, but the family isn't sure whether to believe him; Matthew Crawley (Dan Stevens), still in a wheelchair, is cared for by Mary (Michelle Dockery); meanwhile, Carson (Jim Carter) debates whether to work for Sir Richard Carlisle (Iain Glen). These are but three stories in a tapestry of many other character threads.

Parallel or Multiple Worlds

Once Upon a Time takes place in two parallel worlds; one in Storybrooke, Maine, and the other in the fairy-tale world of the Enchanted Forest. What happens in one affects the events in the other.

Game of Thrones is an example of multiple worlds, as well as a sprawling fantasy epic set on the continents of Westeros and Essos. Within each realm are a world of characters, settings, and rules.

Parallel time periods, sporadic or consistent use of *flashbacks* to inform on present action. *The Americans, Revenge, Any Day Now,* and *Lost*. The main purpose of flashbacks is to inform present day dilemmas or provide the key to solving a central mystery. They can also be used to provide subtext.

Examples:

Revenge is a retelling of *The Count of Monte Cristo*, where Emily Thorne (Emily VanCamp) returns to the Hamptons to take revenge on those who wronged her late father when she was a little girl. The show utilizes flashbacks to reveal character secrets and motivations.

The series *Any Day Now* revolved around the long-term friendship between women of two races, Mary Elizabeth O'Brien Sims (Annie Potts) and Rene Jackson (Lorraine Toussaint). They became friends in Alabama in the 1960s during the civil rights movement. Though set in present time, every episode wove a current story with one from their shared past.

In *Cold Case*, a show in which Detective Lilly Rush (Kathryn Morris) sought closure for longtime, unsolved cases, the use of flashbacks helped dramatize the testimony she got from interviewees.

Synergistic/complementary arenas. *Law & Order* franchise

Law & Order, in which the first half-hour revolves around the NYPD tracking a case and arresting a suspect, and the second half-hour shows the prosecution of the defendant by the Manhattan District Attorney's office. The show dramatizes the conflict between catching a criminal and the legal hurdles to prosecute one. In an episode titled "The Collar," a priest refuses to cooperate with the authorities, claiming that his communication with the killer was "privileged."

Subjective or objective POV. *CSI, Numb3rs, Bones, Ally McBeal, The Ghost Whisperer, Wonderfalls, Twin Peaks,* and *Battlestar Galactica*

A subjective POV example includes *The Ghost Whisperer*, in which Melinda Gordon (Jennifer Love Hewitt) has the ability to communicate with ghosts.

In *CSI*, audiences see the "*CSI* shot," an extreme close-up of forensics, whether a gunshot, hair, or injury. It is a completely objective view of evidence.

In *Bones*, the team often debates alternate theories as to how a crime happened, giving the audience the chance to witness the possibilities and go inside "the mind" of the team.

In *Ally McBeal*, Ally (Calista Flockhart) has visions of a dancing baby, which serves a metaphor for her biological clock.

In *Battlestar Galactica*, audiences witness Dr. Gaius Baltar (James Callis) as he interacts with Cylon Number Six (Tricia Helfer). Number Six appears only to Baltar and no one else, which leaves the audience wondering: is it all in his mind? Or is it really happening?

Documentary/Interview Commentary

Breaking the Fourth Wall. Another POV option is "direct address," in which a character talks directly to the camera (aka the audience). *Modern Family* uses this technique to great comedic advantage in its confessional interviews as commentary on the present action; in many cases, two characters will participate in these interview segments. *The Office* also uses this device. The benefits of this type of storytelling are twofold: one, it allows the audience to see characters "captured" in moments when they don't think they're being filmed, which gives the audience a true sense of the characters, and second, it provides an important counterpoint to when they are "interviewed" and shows us how the characters *want* to be seen.

In *House of Cards,* we get a different, more theatrical commentary from Francis Underwood (Kevin Spacey) who will often "spontaneously" turn to the camera—just as he's about to enter the action of a scene and/or in the middle of a scene—as an ironic, wry "wink wink" aside to bring the audience in on his Machiavellian agenda. It's an artificial, stylized approach that suits the often duplicitous, insider world of D.C.

Omniscient POV

In *Desperate Housewives,* a dead woman, Mary Alice Young (Brenda Strong), narrates the show, aware of all that's happening on Wisteria Lane.

In *Joan of Arcadia,* the title character, Joan Girardi (Amber Tamblyn), is a teenager who can speak and see (an all-knowing) God.

In *Gossip Girl,* the show is narrated by an omniscient blogger "Gossip Girl" (Kristen Bell). While the voice is a woman's, the blogger is ultimately revealed on the series finale as Dan Humphrey (Penn Badgley). Talk about unexpected.

External Narrator from the Future as V.O.
Observer Looking Back

In *How I Met Your Mother,* the show is narrated from the future as a man looks back on his life, ostensibly telling his kids (and us) the story of "How I Met Your Mother." Narrated by Ted in voice-over by Bob Saget, but portrayed in "present time" by Josh Radnor, the device allows the audience to hear the wisdom gained after an event, along with the event itself.

The Wonder Years was famous for using this device which worked perfectly for this story of a man (Daniel Stern) looking back with nostalgia on his coming of age during the late 1960s.

Playing with Time

The series *24* is famous for condensing an entire season into a story that takes place over the course of only twenty-four hours. Thus, each episode is told in the near-real-time of one hour, compressing events and heightening the stakes.

In *Early Edition,* Gary Hobson (Kyle Chandler) mysteriously receives an edition of the *Chicago Sun-Times* one day before it's actually published, so each day, he makes it his mission to stop terrible events before they happen.

Lost uses flashbacks (to provide character motivation) but also uses flash-forward (to show the future) as well as flash-sideways (which were alternate realities based on the actions the characters took in the present).

> Once you have a unique, original, inventive, and provocative idea for a TV series that's populated with cool people *doing* cool stuff, your next big challenge is to find your way in to the series. And that means point of view.

INTERVIEW: Alex Gansa

Alex Gansa Credits

Best known for:

Homeland (Executive Producer/Developer/Writer) 2011–2012
Peabody Award 2011
AFI TV Program of the Year 2011
   Emmy Winner (Outstanding Drama Series) 2012
   Emmy Winner (Outstanding Drama Writing) 2012
   Golden Globe Winner (Best Drama Series) 2012
   WGA Award Winner (New Series) 2012
   WGA Nominated (Drama Series) 2012
24 (Executive Producer/Co-Executive Producer/Writer) 2010/2009
Entourage (Consulting Producer) 2007
   WGA Nominated (Comedy Series) 2008
Numb3rs (Executive Producer) 2005
Dawson's Creek (Executive Producer/Writer) 1999–2000
Maximum Bob (Executive Producer/Writer) 1998
The X-Files (Supervising Producer/Writer) 1993–1994
Sisters (Supervising Producer/Writer) 1991
Beauty and the Beast (Producer/Co-Producer/Writer) 1989–1990/
   1988–1989
   Emmy Nominated (Drama Series) 1989
Spenser: For Hire (Writer) 1986–1987

NL: Because *Homeland* is based on an Israeli series, *Hatufim*, what are the primary differences between the source that inspired it and where it's gone?

AG: I think the first major difference between the source material and *Homeland* is the genre. *Hatufim* is very much a family drama and *Homeland* is a psychological thriller. That's a huge difference. At the same time though, there are many things we borrowed from the source material that are central to the story, so we owe a huge debt to that show. But, there are significant differences. The main one being that returned prisoners of war in Israel are national figures from the moment they're taken prisoner to the moment they're exchanged and returned home. When Gilad Shalit was returned, he was traded for, I think, about a thousand Palestinians. The calculus that goes into making that political decision in Israel is enormous, and so once those people are returned, they are at the least the center of the debate and at the worst in the middle of a firestorm. There was a certain charged quality about the prisoners of war coming back to Israel which we knew would not hold in America. A prisoner of war who comes home to America would be on the twenty-four-hour news cycle, and then everyone would forget about him. Our feeling was that we had to introduce another element into the show, so what we did was reduce the number of prisoners of war coming home. In *Hatufim*, it was two and in *Homeland*, it's obviously one. In place of the second prisoner of war, we added another point of view character and that was Carrie Mathison [Claire Danes].

NL: And, obviously the whole CIA and the structure of that organization, so it's a whole new series inspired by the germ of *Hatufim*.

AG: I'd say that's true. There is an intelligence apparatus in the Israeli version, but it's much more in the background. The thrust of the Israeli intelligence aspect in *Hatufim* was, "Did those guys give up any information seventeen years ago when they were captured prisoner?" And obviously the thrust in *Homeland* is, "Is this guy going to commit a terrorist attack on American soil right now?"

NL: Since the main focus of this chapter is on point of view, did you start with Carrie as your way in to approach the material or did you start with Brody (Damian Lewis) as the prisoner coming back?

AG: It's so interesting because the point of view question was the question that perplexed [Executive Producer] Howard [Gordon] and me as we began to develop the show. There was a lot of debate and a lot of very vigorous disagreement about that. On the one hand, can you tell a story with two points of view? What kind of show was this going to be? Was this going to be a show about a CIA intelligence officer chasing a bad guy or was this going to be something a little more interesting? Those debates took place among many different people—not just Howard Gordon and me, but also the studio and the network, regarding where we were going to wind up. Were we going to be on FOX or Showtime? I honestly think that if we had wound up on broadcast television that it would have been a much more straight ahead story with a single point of view—with the good guy, Carrie, in her point of view, chasing the bad guy, Brody. Luckily and through serendipity, we ended up on Showtime and were able to tell a much more nuanced, binary story.

NL: The gray areas are so pronounced in the direction that you went because you've created sympathy for Nazir (Navid Negahban). It's a very controversial element. And the vice president becomes the villain in a way. What was your approach to antagonists?

AG: We always felt that our antagonist remained Brody. So, if we were trying to develop sympathy for him, we did that by inhabiting his point of view and making his reasons for turning and carrying out an attack against America as understandable as we possibly could. You could look at the season of *Homeland* as two parts: the first part with the central question: "Was he or was he not turned in captivity?" Then, once we answered that question, the second question for the remainder of the season became, "Is he or is he not going to go through with what he's agreed to do?" The second question, in my opinion, was the more interesting one because now we were able to inhabit Brody's point of view. We had to make the reasons for his action legible and sympathetic. That was our mission as storytellers: To get inside Brody's brain to understand why he had chosen this path and watch him wrestle with the decision to actually go through with it or not.

NL: In your mind, does he suffer from Stockholm syndrome? Was he literally brainwashed—like in the classic film, *The Manchurian Candidate*? Because one of the things that I loved about the season finale was how his daughter and his paternal familial responsibilities were the things that thwarted that suicide bombing.

AG: I don't think he was brainwashed. We didn't want to tell a psycho-tropic, unintelligible brainwashing story. We thought that would be dishonest, but we did want to believe that he was a broken man. By that I mean, years and years of torture and psychological abuse will strip you down to the studs, and Nazir did that through this extreme capture and torture. And then re-humanized Brody, in a way, by introducing him to his son Issa. It was that human relationship and the introduction of religion through the Koran which built Brody into something different than he was before. We didn't view that as brainwashing. We viewed it as Nazir searching for a way to use this man as a political tool in this world. And, Nazir wasn't aware that Issa was going to be killed. He didn't sacrifice his own son to do this. Nazir used what happened in that drone strike to radicalize Brody in a way that he probably wasn't aware he could have before that. Nazir was improvising at that point. And, Brody was probably on board to do something that Nazir didn't think he would ultimately be able to do.

NL: Brody is split in half between his American identity and his Muslim extremist identity, so I'm wondering if there was a parallel to his dual identity and Carrie's bipolar disorder? How was she conceived?

AG: Initially the show was written on spec, but Howard had a big deal at FOX. We were servicing that deal by writing this pilot. So, it was originally written with the intention of selling it to a broadcast network. Not that we wanted it to go to a broadcast network, but that was our first mission statement.

NL: Like a follow-up to *24*?

AG: Yes. So the first iteration of the pilot was much more along the lines of what I told you earlier. Carrie was an intelligence officer. She had some problems, but she was not bipolar. She was just a little reckless and unreliable. She was chasing Brody because she believed he had been turned overseas. And then, once we realized we could do this show for cable, the whole world opened up for us. Actually, Showtime was the first to say, "We love the story. We love the setup, but we'd really like the character of Carrie Mathison to be more cable-worthy. She doesn't have to be such a straight-ahead hero." But, they had no idea what that should look like. Was she a sex addict? Was she a pill popper? In what context were we going to make her a cable heroine? Howard and I wrestled with that for a long time. And, ultimately, we began to see the merits of making both characters unknowable and damaged in a way. To put them on equal footing in that sense.

We look at Brody as someone who is damaged by his experience as a soldier and prisoner of war, and Carrie as someone who is damaged by her experiences overseas as well, but mostly because of her disease. She's reckless and unreliable on one side, and he's unknowable on the other.

NL: Once you had the pilot written, did you map out the arc of the first twelve episodes?

AG: We did. Howard and I had a very clear idea of the first twelve and what they were going to look like. We knew that Brody was going to perpetrate some terrorist action against America. But we didn't, for example, know that he was going to put on a suicide vest. We went through a litany of other options: Were there other targets? Was a drone center a target? Was there a particular drone pilot who was responsible? We didn't know. Was it something bigger? Was it a State of the Union thing? Was he going to kill [Vice President William] Walden [Jamey Sheridan]? We just didn't know, and ultimately, the vest became very iconic. But, we all shied away from it at the beginning because it's such a signature of a terrorist. We were always a little unsure if a United States marine would go to those lengths.

NL: And, what about Carrie ending up with electroconvulsive therapy (ECT)?

AG: That was less clear when we arced the episode. In fact, every episode after the pilot, we were asking ourselves: "Is this the episode where Carrie has her manic breakdown?" And, we pushed it every single episode. So, by the time we got to episodes 10 and 11, we thought, "Well, this is perfect." Because here we are at the end of the season, just when the event is going to happen, and that's the time to make Carrie as unreliable and as reckless and as crazy as you could have her because her fellow intelligence officers were going to dismiss her. But yet she's carrying the truth.

NL: In terms of point of view and relationships, because you came from network television, did you map out A, B, C, or D stories? You have Carrie and Saul (Mandy Patinkin), who are such an anchor to the story. Brody and Dana (Morgan Saylor) also became very central. Do you arc things individually character by character? Do you focus on exploring this relationship in a multi-episode arc? What is the process of breaking story on the show?

AG: It's a combination of all the things you've said. A lot of it is done episode-by-episode. And, a lot of it comes out of the character. For example, if you look at Saul and his relationship with his wife. That was born out of the fact that we didn't have a role for Saul to play over a couple of episodes. So, we thought here we have an opportunity to tell a little bit about Saul and thought the audience might be interested. But, when we pitched that story originally, people were like, "Well, who fucking cares about Saul? We don't care about this guy and we don't care about his wife." So, there was a lot of investigation at the beginning of the series about what kinds of stories it could hold and what was going to be compelling. In fact, after the pilot was shot, Howard and I had a lot of disagreement about whether anyone would be interested in Brody's family at all. Would anybody care about his relationship with his wife? Or, his kids? There was a terrorist attack up and running—would anyone even pay attention? Were the episodes going to feel unbalanced? What became interesting and evident in the first couple of episodes was that you were almost more interested in what was going on in Brody's house than what was going on in the more traditional bad guy part of the story.

I believe it was Joseph Conrad who said: "Writing is like mining coal with your hands." And we're in the mines, trying to find the veins of stories to uncover. Sometimes they're evident at the beginning of the season. We knew where the Brody/Carrie relationship was going to go. That was something that we knew we had to plot out at the beginning. We knew, for example, that Dana was going to be the character that talked Brody off the ledge at the end. So, if you watch the pilot and you see when they meet for the first time in the waiting room after Brody comes off that plane, you'll see that the hug with his wife is awkward, tentative, and hesitant. But, his hug with Dana is heartfelt. And, that's when you start to see his emotion come through. So, that relationship, we always knew was going to be central. We basically knew the Carrie/Brody arc. I'm not quite sure if we knew she was going to wind up being in electroshock therapy at the end. But we knew she was going to have a breakdown.

NL: Did you know from the beginning that Marine sniper Tom Walker (Chris Chalk) was the POW who had been turned?

AG: The whole relationship between the soldiers we really took wholesale from *Hatufim*. One of the soldiers was carrying around this dark secret that he beat his fellow prisoner of war to death. We thought that would be a great psychological underpinning of Brody's captivity.

NL: Are there any story rules when you're breaking story in terms of pacing and doling out what and when you're revealing from episode to episode? In other words, we seem to get one major new piece of information in each episode, and they each end in a cliffhanger. Is that a very conscious approach when you're breaking story that you need to have one of those big revelations each time?

AG: I think that was very much the strategy of our first season. And, it was a legacy of working on *24*.

NL: It works very well. It's addictive.

AG: Because we were so uncertain and so unsure whether anyone was going to be interested in the family stories or the story of Saul's dissolving marriage. We always wanted to make sure, especially during that first series of episodes, that we would end on something that genuinely wanted to make the audience come back. It was definitely a narrative strategy and something we worked for in the room—sometimes effectively and sometimes not so effectively, in my opinion. Because thriller tropes are so universal and people have seen them so often, we knew that there were certain muscular action moves that were going to take place over the course of the season. And, what we did narratively was to have them happen before the audience was expecting them to happen. Everybody knew that Brody and Carrie were going to have some kind of an emotional/physical relationship, but the fact that it happened in episode 4, just blew everyone's minds. Because they thought: "Wait a minute, how the fuck is that possible?" So, I think we were able to deliver the audience's expectations before they were expecting them, which made them feel fresher than if we had dragged them out.

NL: In the episode called "The Weekend," the scene where they go to the cabin and have tea in the kitchen is an apt example of that. I thought, "No way—he's not going to figure this out this soon." And then, next thing I know, Brody's got the gun in his hand aimed at Carrie.

AG: At the beginning of the season, we were following the blogs a little bit. And, after every episode, there would be these whole lines of debate like, "They've painted themselves into a corner. How the fuck are they going to get out of this?" We definitely compressed the story and energized the entire season by doing that. Also, when you're starting a series, you have no idea whether it's going to be successful or not. So, all of us who have been around for a long time, all the writers in here—we're all middle-aged at best—and we want it to succeed or fail on our own terms. So, we pushed the envelope, we didn't take the safe route, we got Brody and Carrie together way before anyone saw it coming, so we had some interesting building blocks in place.

NL: How are you mapping out the next season? Is it going to pick up right where you left off? Are you going to jump ahead?

AG: We're definitely going to jump at least six months.

NL: Will there be a main or central question? A new mystery to explore?

AG: There will be. Although it will not have the same purity of the first season's questions. It's the curse of a second season. You're able to float a lot of questions in the first season, but you have to answer more of those questions in the second season. I think you have to dig deeper to create a compelling story again. You're catching us right in the middle of breaking stories for the second season and that's the struggle we're engaged in.

NL: I would imagine that one of the biggest challenges from the get-go would be how to get Carrie back into the CIA again.

AG: It's interesting—everybody says that, but that has been the least of our problems. (*Laughs.*)

NL: When Carrie has her mini epiphany in episode 8 ("Achilles' Heel") with Saul, it's such a memorable moment for me. She tells Saul that she's come to the realization that: "I'm going to spend the rest of my life alone"— just like Saul. It seems like that's another thing you can explore in season 2, Carrie's personal/romantic life which was left in a state of total chaos.

AG: The real trick at the center of the show is Carrie and Brody. That's what we have to accomplish in the second season: to bring them together in a way that feels believable and dramatically pregnant—to ultimately push their doomed romance forward for another season.

10

GET TO THE HEART OF YOUR STORY

Television, unlike films, lets us live with a group of characters over many seasons. That's part of the attraction. We invite these same people into our living rooms every week for years and years. And, the best shows can have a hundred or more hours of story to tell. Great television writing is, therefore, all about the characters.

Certainly, the best television writing has an external dimension. In other words, we have to know what a character wants in a series, a season, a story, a subplot, and a scene. But we also need to understand who they are, what they fear, what they hope for—the subtext, the emotional challenge, the dimension of their internal struggles. *We need to care.*

This is what great dramatic television is *really about*. We tune in to *feel* something as we go on a journey with someone we care about.

To help you see how this all plays out, this chapter deals with the seemingly "small" example of amazing scenes from the pilot episodes of great shows. Great scenes are examples of story in a microcosm. They have a beginning, middle, and an end. They have depth and nuance and are typically organized around a character's attempt toward a goal, i.e., the external event and the more layered internal nuances of subtext, arc, emotional change and thematic relevance. However, unlike most big-budget films, the "event" of many dramatic shows is often fairly small, particularly once we move outside the procedural arenas of police, medical, and legal series.

Pilot episodes are the blueprints for a series and, as the first episode (the prototype), they are vital for getting a show green-lit, attracting talent and drawing in both critics and a loyal, dedicated audience. The storylines must therefore get to that core combination of both premise and characters rich enough to keep exploring for years.

Now, let's look at some examples.

CASE STUDY 1: *Parenthood*

Lesson: Make a lead character, group, or family face their greatest fears head-on.

Parenthood is a critically acclaimed drama-comedy based on a feature film written by Lowell Ganz and Babaloo Mandel and directed by Ron Howard. This multi-award-winning TV series was developed and adapted by its showrunner, Jason Katims, and revolves around the Bravermans: a big, loud family of colorful and imperfect people dealing with modern life in all its messiness.

In the pilot, we see a number of the themes that will engage us as an audience for the first season and beyond. In one of the major storylines, Adam (Peter Krause) and his wife, Kristina (Monica Potter), learn that their young son Max (Max Burkholder) has Asperger's—a disorder that impacts his emotional functioning. Adam initially refuses to accept and believe this fact about his son. Then, in the climactic scene for this storyline, Adam waits with Max outside a family event while the rest of the family watches Max's little cousin Sydney (Savannah Paige Rae) play an angel in a recital inside. The scene begins just after Adam's father, Zeek (Craig T. Nelson), realizes that Adam and Max are missing and goes to find them.

Zeek is a brash, tough veteran and a man's man. His first line to his son is, "What the hell are you doing out here?" The external stakes of the scene are very simple. Will Zeek bully Adam into bringing Max inside to watch Sydney's recital? That's it. But, if that was all there was, we would not really care. What's at stake is Max and Adam and their family's future. Will Adam accept his son's condition?

We care about these people already at this point. Adam doesn't want to accept that his son Max has an issue. He has been fighting this. So, when Adam tells Zeek they can't go in because there are candles inside and Max can't walk past them—we know what he's wrestling with. Zeek then wants to force the issue, thinking they are just babying Max. He tells Adam that he raised four kids. He knows what he's doing. This is the "traditional" male character. Just fight through it. This is where Adam learned his model of masculinity.

Adam finally admits to Zeek, and to himself, that his son is different and they're both going to need his dad's help. This is all Adam can do. He's been physically trapped by Zeek into admitting that there's a real issue and he can't pretend that there isn't anymore. His son can't walk past candles. The show's writers backed him into a corner, where he has to face up to the challenges his son presents.

Zeek finally sees the truth, his son is hurting and needs his help, and he acknowledges the reality with a single word, "Sonny." And he goes to him. They love each other.

Let's review. In this simple, single scene, Adam has finally acknowledged that his son has a problem. He's asked his dad for help. Both of these are very hard for Adam to do. They are all in uncharted territory. This single issue chosen for the Adam storyline will be something that the Bravermans will wrestle with and come to understand more fully over the life of the show. It will exist in nearly every episode. That's what great television does: explores the emotional and moral complexities of life as they evolve over time. And the writers explore these issues with nuance, subtext, and the specificity that grows out of each distinctive character. TV is all about the accumulation of these little moments. If you're only gunning for plot, you're going to be whizzing past the real drama of all stories: the emotional impact and its accompanying ripple effects. Take your time and allow each significant incident to breathe and resonate—that's the lifeblood of all great TV series.

CASE STUDY 2: *Shameless*

Lesson: Make characters live and confront socially combustible issues in interesting ways that fit who they are.

Tonally, *Shameless* is a harder-edged series than *Parenthood*. Whereas *Parenthood* is a series parents can watch with their kids on NBC, *Shameless* airs on the premium cable Showtime network, which enables its showrunners to push the boundaries of nudity and coarse language. *Parenthood* is evocative. *Shameless* is a provocative, one-hour *dramedy* developed and adapted by Paul Abbott and John Wells, based upon an award-winning series created by Paul Abbott for the BBC. *Shameless* is about a family of six kids and an alcoholic, drug-addicted, absentee, and exploitative dad, Frank (William H. Macy). These are the Gallaghers. And on most days, all they have is their love for each other as they struggle to make it through life in a tough section of below-working-class Chicago.

In the pilot episode, we have a number of storylines, but let's examine the one that revolves around two of the brothers, Lip (Jeremy Allen White), age seventeen, has just learned that his younger brother, Ian (Cameron Monaghan), is gay. Despite the fact that the two brothers share a room, Lip never had a clue. They've fought badly over this earlier in the episode. It was at least a draw. Now we need to know, what happens next? Does being gay cost you your family if you are a Gallagher?

Ian is outside, smoking in a van. Lip arrives with a magazine of gay porn. He slaps it down in front of Ian. "How can that be good for you?" Is the fight gonna continue? Is this new fact gonna drive these two apart permanently? That's the question of this scene. That's real stakes. And, it's in the "how it plays out" that everything about these two characters, both as individuals and as brothers is revealed.

Lip begins to ask questions. "Was Kash your first?" Kash (Pej Vahdat) is a grown man, and Ian's boss. Lip learned Ian was having sex with him, earlier. He's asking about his brother's love life. His brother doesn't want to talk. He's angry. But, then Lip asks the question that turns the scene, and gets to the emotional heart of these two: "When have I ever let you down?" With Ian's response we have our answer—Lip has never let him down.

Lip teases him about it, but the hard edge is gone. They share a smoke. Make jokes. It's going to be OK. It's not going to be easy for Ian in this neighborhood. But his brother's got his back. This reality is a central conflict and source of support in his storyline for the next several years. Bottom line, no scene is just a scene. Not in a pilot or over the course of a great series. And no scene is just about "an external objective" if we want the audience coming back and caring.

CASE STUDY 3: *THE West Wing*

Lesson: Never make it too easy for your main character; keep the pressure on, and the complications and reveals coming.

The West Wing was created for network television by Aaron Sorkin, a prolific and highly decorated writer in both film and television. The show ran for seven seasons and won two Golden Globes and twenty-six Emmy awards.

Let's examine a single, small scene from the series pilot. This scene occurs at the beginning of act 4, which is the final act of the pilot. Sam Seaborn (Rob Lowe) is the White House deputy communications director. The show was initially intended to focus on him with his co-workers being the secondary stories. In this scene, Sam is having a really bad day. Politically. Personally. All around. His best friend might get fired over something he said on *Meet the Press*. Something Sam thinks is true. There are Cuban refugees off the coast of Florida, with a giant storm coming and the Governor of Florida is refusing to let them land. And Sam unknowingly slept with a prostitute.

Now, he's been asked by his boss, Chief of Staff Leo McGarry (John Spencer) to show his daughter's fourth-grade elementary class around the White House. And he really needs this to go well. So what happens? Sam knows nothing about the history of this building. He begins to talk about himself, but the Teacher calls him out and pulls him aside. This brings us to our scene.

The scene opens in a hallway. And the teacher immediately blasts him: "I'm sorry to be rude, but are you a moron?" How's that for a scene opening?!

She's not going to make this easy for him. Why should she? Conflict is the heart of drama. The teacher goes on to list the extensive number of historical facts he just got glaringly wrong. This brings us to the heart of the scene for Sam. He asks her if she could just point out his boss's daughter. If she could, it would really make his life easier. She tells him the kids worked hard. They wrote essays. She's not inclined to make his life easier.

He then goes on to explain how bad his day has been. Including the prostitute. At which point, she informs him that *she's* his boss's daughter, Mallory (Allison Smith). Ouch. This, like the entire pilot, is a terrific scene.

Look how little of it is about the "external motivation." On the outside, Sam just wants to figure out which fourth grade elementary school girl he needs to impress to get back in good graces with his boss. He's dealing with macro-level fires, but is not up high enough to avoid these micro-issues. Because he has assumed that the daughter is one of the students, he makes a series of blunders. These anger and upset the teacher. He then confesses things he absolutely doesn't want his boss to know, and it unexpectedly turns out he's confessing them to his boss's daughter. That's great writing. Internal complications. Faulty assumptions. Real emotions of frustration, anger, etc. We believe and feel for Sam—even as he digs himself that much deeper.

CASE STUDY 4: *Game of Thrones*

Lesson: Your characters don't all need to be invincible at the outset. Major character traits evolve, and can, and often should, be hinted at, and rolled out slowly over time. Draw your characters in extremes early in the series to give them somewhere to go.

Game of Thrones is an epic fantasy airing on HBO and created for television by David Benioff and D. B. Weiss, adapted from a series of novels by George R. R. Martin. In it, seven noble families fight for control of a mythical feudal land.

In this scene from late in the pilot, we are at the wedding of a seemingly weak and frightened girl, Daenerys "Dany" Targaryen (Emilia Clarke). Despite not speaking the language, or having ever met her soon-to-be husband, she is marrying Khal Drogo (Jason Momoa), the fierce leader of a tribe of nomadic warriors called the Dothraki. Dany is being forced to marry Khal Drogo by her older brother, Viserys (Harry Lloyd), who needs the Dothraki to be his army and help him take back the throne which his family lost fifteen years ago.

From an external plot development standpoint, the scene is really about delivering a few key pieces of information: showing us how weak Dany appears and that the Dothraki are very fierce warriors, reminding us how and why Viserys wants them on his side, and introducing the dragons' eggs that she is given as a gift.

However, this scene is rich in layers. Over the next several seasons, the dragons' eggs hatch, allowing Dany to become the "Mother of Dragons" by growing into a compassionate, strong, and smart Dothraki leader. The seeds of all that are in this one scene.

The scene opens with Viserys being told by his advisor that Khal has promised him a crown and will go to war when the omens favor it. We then see the Dothraki women doing sensual dances and the men sexually taking them. Dany is not in her little sheltered world anymore. Two men want the same woman and fight to the death for her. Everyone cheers. Dany looks scared and uncertain. As the advisor speaks to Viserys, we get exposition—a Dothraki wedding is considered dull without at least three deaths. Who are these people? We feel sympathy and compassion. Dany is the weak, frightened innocent beauty being forced to marry a man who is seemingly a barbarian. She cries on her wedding night like a lost little girl. We fear that this will not end well. It is not until a few episodes later that we begin to see her act like the queen she is meant to be.

CASE STUDY 5: *The Good Wife*

Lesson: There is no such thing as a small or unimportant scene. Every scene gets better with layers and strong visuals pointing to deeper emotional subtext.

Police, medical, and legal procedurals have been the go-to shows of networks for decades. *The Good Wife* is a legal drama that first aired in 2009 and was created by Robert and Michelle King. The show has been nominated for more than twenty Emmy awards during its first three seasons.

The pilot features a terrific, but atypically lengthy, sixteen-page teaser. The first five pages of this opening introduce us to our lead character, Alicia Florrick (Julianna Margulies), a former lawyer turned stay-at-home mom. She stands beside her husband, Peter Florrick (Chris Noth), a former state attorney, as he faces the cameras and a swarm of reporters regarding corruption charges, including sex with prostitutes and conspiring to cover it up. But our eyes are magnetically drawn to Alicia's face: a stoic mask belying her pain and humiliation. She's trying to "stand by her man," but this is *hard*. He chose a public life of scrutiny; she didn't. She did nothing wrong, and yet now she's ensnared in his scandal. She wants to bolt out of there, but needs to keep up appearances for the sake of their kids. She can't even think about what the future may hold for her family. And that's when she sees it: a tiny loose thread on his suit jacket. She is the woman who cleans up his messes. Keeps him going. In this moment, her inner world collides with her outer circumstances. In slow motion, she reaches her hand out to remove the stray thread. But before she can grasp it, time speeds up again, the press conference is over, and she and her husband are ushered out of the pressroom. Once alone, she can't even look at him. All he can muster is a feeble, "Are you all right?" And she hauls off and slaps him across the face, turns on her heels and walks away—down the hall toward the waiting throng of reporters and flashbulbs. Then we cut to *six months later*, and the series is off and running.

She's trying to reboot her life, and re-enter the workforce after more than a decade as a stay-at-home mom. Only she's waiting for her very first meeting on the wrong floor. Perfect. But, what I want to look at is the very last scene. Just over a page. On its surface, a simple scene. The major thrust of the pilot and its storyline threads have been all wrapped up. The template for the show has been set. Alicia will have her case most weeks. She'll work to solve it, leading to a courtroom verdict. She'll usually win. That will be the A story. But she will also have all of the personal issues she is dealing with. That's what sets this procedural apart.

In this final scene of the pilot, Alicia has just finished her first new case. She won. And, as she walks back to her office, late at night—she is on her cell phone with her mother-in-law, Jackie (Mary Beth Peil). The external action is as simple as it gets. The mother-in-law wants to know what time Alicia's coming home because she cooked. That's the external event: "When are you coming home?"

But Alicia doesn't answer right away. She laughs. Not at her. At herself. At life. And tells Jackie that she's laughing because that's the call she always used to make. She was the one always asking her husband when he'd be home. She's self-aware. And, we are getting a sense, a reminder of how far she's come in this single network hour. What she's enduring. She's moved from loyal wife standing beside her husband, to this take-charge attorney. But she's only beginning. She's still going to have to try to make it all work—and will need to rely on her judgmental mother-in-law to do it.

Eventually, Alicia tells Jackie that she'll be home "in about an hour." However, the scene doesn't end. Even though the *external event* has been answered. Alicia has a new desk in a new office. Her office is in order, for the first time in the episode. Files put away. She is starting to feel like she belongs. We get all of this in the visuals, how she looks around. What she sees, the neatly ordered shelves. The nice, new chair. The pictures on the wall. We had a scene earlier to set up the office—everything in boxes and disarray. This demonstrates her change through visuals.

And she tells Jackie "thanks for stepping up." She has been her. She gets it. She will keep needing her. And Jackie tells her, "of course she would."

And says "she'll see her at nine." They are in this together. Two women who understand each other. Future stories—what I like to call *story tentacles*—are suggested with this scene.

Then, Alicia's new boss, Will Gardner (Josh Charles) shows up. Her one-time boyfriend from way back. The guy who got her this job. And he tells her that she's made second chair on his case and has to be in court early tomorrow morning. She is in the mix of things. With her new love interest active and present. Tomorrow's another day. We are left knowing and wanting more. That's great writing. That's a great page.

Great television scenes:

1. Reveal and deepen character dimensions by allowing us to see their major dominant traits, and then by challenging them.
2. Explore, complicate, and challenge relationships between main characters.
3. Present an "event" or "question" of the scene that moves the plot forward in some meaningful way.
4. Entertain; surprise; withhold information and play it out in ways that are both unexpected and inevitable.
5. Follow structure; great scenes have an arc; they start with a bang and end with a button, with complications and twists in the middle.

INTERVIEW: Jason Katims

Jason Katims Credits

Best known for:

Parenthood (Executive Producer/Writer) 2010–2012
Friday Night Lights (Executive Producer/Writer) 2006–2011
   Emmy Award Winner (Writing) 2011
   Emmy Nominated (Drama Series) 2011
   Humanitas Prize 2009, 2011
   WGA Nominated 2007–2011
   Peabody Award 2006
Boston Public (Executive Producer/Writer) 2003–2004
Roswell (Executive Producer/Writer) 1999–2002
My So-Called Life (Writer) 1994

NL: I'd like to begin with your approach to developing characters particularly on *Friday Night Lights* and *Parenthood*. I think a lot of people can create plot lines and stay on the outside, but you're able to continually dig deep into your characters and surprise. Do you start off with a sense of all this complexity or do you discover it along the way?

JK: My first job in television was on *My So-Called Life*, which was created by Winnie Holzman with Marshall Herskovitz and Edward Zwick as executive producers. I had been writing plays before that and had never written for television at all. In fact, I never thought I would be writing for television, but if I did, I thought it would be for a half-hour sitcom. It was a surprise to end up on a drama, but *My So-Called Life* was essentially my graduate school, and their approach to storytelling, has had a huge influence over how I have approached writing since then. One of the things that they tried to do was to set out to tell as little story as possible, so that you could focus on the nuance and have time to develop and get underneath the story. I remember there was one episode of *My So-Called Life* called "The Zit," which made me think, "We're going to do an episode about a pimple?" Angela [Claire Danes] wakes up with a zit, and that's the inciting incident for the story, but it became a story about beauty and what our idea of beauty is. We expanded it to include Angela and her mom [Bess Armstrong] by coming up with this idea of a mother–daughter fashion show as a way in to talk about all of these ideas. It was fascinating as a beginning television writer to see how they developed story. It became the foundation for me—and that's what we try to do in the writers' room which is where all of these ideas are developed into stories.

To me, it's always about, "What is the story about? What are we saying?" When we're struggling with a plot, I always stop and say plots aren't that hard. Particularly for us, we're doing ensemble shows with four or five storylines, so we're talking six beats—which is not a lot to do. So, if we're struggling with a plot, maybe it's because we don't know what we're trying to say or accomplish with the story. When something feels both real and intimate and gets underneath the skin, that's what I'm always focused on as I'm telling the story.

NL: Some of this, as in "The Zit," example speaks to theme. Is that an approach you take? Are you thinking about a thematic for A, B, C, and D stories?

JK: Theme is important of course, but I also try not to let it get in the way. Everyone has different ideas about this, and sometimes I wish I did more episodes where every storyline was thematically tied to the others. But, I'm much more interested in the evolution of character and the evolution of these individual storylines over time. Sometimes thematically people are in different places, so I try not to force them together too much. The joy of a show like *Friday Night Lights* is that the episodes seem like continuing chapters to me. I think of the way Dickens used to write novels where each chapter would be a weekly installment in the newspaper. *Friday Night Lights* has a similar feel. What I'm most interested in is how the character is evolving over time, week to week, season to season. When a unifying theme emerges in an episode, I think of that as icing on the cake. Certainly there are themes within each storyline, but for an episode, I don't feel that story needs to connect into one theme.

NL: How many episodes do you tend to arc at one time? Do you map out the full season in terms of: I know I'm going to start this character here and this is where I want to end up? Or, do you do it six or seven episodes at a time?

JK: *Parenthood* and *Friday Night Lights* are the two shows I've done most recently. And, although they look like two completely different shows, to me, they're very similar. They're large ensemble dramas that are ultimately about family. In *Friday Night Lights*, it's largely about surrogate families and *Parenthood* is about extended family, but they're both about family. I approach them in a similar way. Basically what we do at the beginning of the season is that we spend a little time talking about our characters in broad strokes. Talking about where they are—where they left off from last year and what's going to happen to them this year. We map out in very vague terms—and by the way nothing is written down—whatever their journey is going to be. Of course, you have your fulcrum characters like Coach [Eric Taylor as played by Kyle Chandler] and Tami [Connie Britton], and that family is certainly at the core of it, but all the characters are important. When we do that, it starts to suggest story, and we start to put up some cards. Again, it's still very vague, but we're starting to think about tent poles of where something is going to start and where something might end up by the end of the season. I hesitate to get too specific. It's nice to have a roadmap, but you don't want to have it tied up too much or put you too far ahead. Some stories suggest all the twists and turns even from the beginning and some don't—and that's okay. As long as you feel like your characters are on the road, and you have a vague idea of where it might lead, I think that's good.

Then, from that point, it gets real. We break them usually into movements by groups of episodes. And, they're usually four or five or even six episodes where something big is happening over the course of those episodes. For example, during the first season of *Friday Night Lights*, in the pilot episode, the star quarterback gets injured badly—and the big question that this incident suggested to me was: "Will the town of Dillon survive the loss of Jason Street [Scott Porter]?" In a way, you can look at that as a question for the whole season, but, I really looked at it as the question for that first movement. Because you have this coach who came in with an expectation from the town and the crazy boosters that he was going to bring home a championship, but then the guy that he had to do that with is now gone.

So, how is this coach going to pull it together? Then, there was the question about this second string quarterback, Matt Saracen [Zach Gilford], who is now this deer-in-the-headlights kid: Is Saracen going to be able to step up? Then, there's the question of what is going to happen to Jason Street? Is he going to be able to come back to the team? You don't know. It's TV after all—and three episodes later, he could be playing again. So, when you find out that he is paralyzed, the question gets even more interesting then because now you're wondering what's going to happen to this guy? This kid who was expecting to go to the NFL. Is this kid going to be okay? And, that led to the triangle between him and Riggins [Taylor Kitsch] and Lyla [Minka Kelly]. The question of Matt Saracen also led to the introduction of this quarterback that Buddy Garrity [Brad Leland] was trying to recruit from New Orleans named "Voodoo" [Aldis Hodge]. It became a question of who was going to be the quarterback, and then ultimately, as I recall, I think that movement ended in the rivalry game in the fifth episode. You resolve who's going to be their quarterback and what's going to happen with this team. You get to a certain point of resolution and then you start to raise new questions—which begins the next movement. That's the way it works for us.

NL: So, you might have some vague ideas in those early discussions about where the end of the season is going to lead you, but you're open to where it might take you?

JK: The beautiful thing about a show like *Friday Night Lights* is while you don't have closed-ended stories, since you don't have a mystery to solve, you do have a season of football, so you can break your season of television around your season of football. You know there's going to be a certain point where playoffs start. Do they make it to the playoffs? How far do they get in the season? On a good year, there's also State. It's a nice way to help you with structure. On *Parenthood*, we don't have football, so what we try to do is come up with bigger storylines that will give you movement over a whole season. For example, building a business one season or planning a wedding. In the first season, you have this incident where Max [Max Burkholder] is diagnosed with Asperger's Syndrome which grounded you in the show and gave you something to go along with for the season—and even the entire series. These bigger ideas help you get from place to place. Basically, I try to break the arcs down in terms of movements, I try to know where I'm going and be flexible. Again, this is something that dates back to when I worked with Ed and Marshall, you want to be able to let what you're doing evolve. It's a very collaborative form, and my feeling about that is to embrace the collaborative nature of it—instead of just saying, "Well, I'm dictating every single thing." Because what will happen is that you'll put a script out and suddenly the directors and actors have ideas that I never would have thought of, and it makes me learn things about the characters I never knew. That's the exciting part. And sometimes, things that you pictured as interesting ideas, aren't as exciting as you thought, so that maybe that movement will just be three episodes instead of seven. And, then there are other things, where you're like, "Wow, we want to explore that." My feeling is that I want to leave room to let myself be influenced by what the actors are doing, how the directors are directing scenes—all these things are exciting. It makes it fun to do TV. The single greatest thing about doing television is that the show evolves and gets better over time. With movies, you've got a hero . . .

NL: It's finite.

JK: And, there's usually only a few characters that you can genuinely tell stories about. But, in television, the person who's eleven on your call sheet could wind up being number one on your call sheet for an episode. You end up getting to know so much about all of these people. This is the beauty and the fun of doing TV.

NL: In your ensemble shows, are there any rules like the A story always has to be Eric and Tami or is it more fluid than that?

JK: It's way more fluid than that. We definitely didn't have the feeling that the A story was always Eric and Tami, and it certainly wasn't, if you look at it. As much as they were the core of the show, it just wasn't natural that they would have all the A stories because you're dealing with a bunch of teenagers. Teenagers are going to have the crazy A stories. They're going to have the stuff going on in their lives all the time. The married couple has the bigger story because it's about their lives and their marriage, but they don't literally have the stuff that's the engine for the stories each week.

NL: In *Friday Night Lights*, they anchor the story, but in *Parenthood*, the siblings primarily anchor the show. It seems that the A story is always going to be about one of the brothers and sisters in that show.

JK: Typically. I felt like when I started *Parenthood*, I just needed a way to think about it because it was such a big cast with so many possibilities. I basically decided that I was coming at it from the point of view of these four siblings. When I started breaking stories, it was always from them. As a show evolves, you're able to do stories that are still about that, but able to shift point of view—it's more of Kristina's [Monica Potter] point of view than Adam's [Peter Krause]. You're telling a story that's more Zeek [Craig T. Nelson] and Camille's [Bonnie Bedelia] story than the kids or you tell stories from Max's point of view. It's always good to have a place to start from just so you don't confuse yourself too much, but then you can expand that as time goes on. You're always balancing what's expanding with what's just not in keeping with the show. And, that's a decision that is really left for the showrunner. Writers will pitch a lot of different ideas which are very good, but the showrunner has to be the one to say, "Yes, that's a good idea, but it's not this show."

NL: When I watch *Parenthood*, there's always at least one moment where I get teary-eyed. There was one particularly heartrending scene in the first season where Kristina and Adam must come to terms with their son's Asperger's. Here is their energetic, curious, sweet, innocent little boy—and they're confronted with the reality that he's struggling with impairment. It breaks their hearts because they know it's going to be a road difficult for him (and them) to navigate. And Kristina and Adam are so emotionally raw as they move from denial to acceptance of Max's condition. My question for you: when breaking stories, is your barometer that a worthy plotline must be capable of pushing your characters to become vulnerable?

JK: Absolutely. Both when I'm thinking of story and I'm in the room talking about it. I'm always looking for when am I feeling something. And, again that's personal to me—the stories that I'm attracted to. I feel like when you know the core of what the story is about emotionally than you're better able to more easily break that story. And, also, by the way, to find the humor in it. To me, the humor comes after you figure out what you're getting to emotionally. It's easier then to find what's funny because you're talking about working through some sort of conflict. And, out of conflict, comes humor.

The example that you brought up became an issue when I was developing the pilot of *Parenthood*. The idea of having a kid with Asperger's was a debate within myself. I have a son with Asperger's and I didn't know if I wanted to go there. Whether it was a violation of privacy for my son and my family, number one, and number two, whether I wanted to talk about it every day when it was already such a big part of my home life. But, what I felt ultimately is that

> *If I'm going to do a show about parenting called Parenthood, I should probably look for stories that I'm going to be able to tap into myself and that are going to scare me a little to tell.*

And, ultimately I did that—not knowing if I could find an actor who could pull that off. How we would be able to tell this story in a way that felt real. When neither of the actors doing it knew the particulars of what this situation was like. It would be terrible to me—the idea of doing it and having it look fake and stupid. I went into it not knowing how well we'd be able to pull it off. It became one of the most profound experiences of my career in telling that story. We were lucky enough to get Max Burkholder to play this kid, and he's just done such a great job, but also watching how Monica Potter and Peter Krause have grown. They've just so invested themselves in that storyline. It's just amazing and then to see the response that people have to it has been great. Sometimes you want a storyline that's a little scary to you—it's a good thing. It means you're pushing yourself and you're getting out of your own comfort zone. Especially in television now, where drama is written at such a high level. The audience's expectations are so high. They have so many choices. It's endless amounts at their fingertips—anytime they want to watch stuff. It's a requirement for people doing television to dig deep and find those stories that are ambitious.

NL: That's another thing about your work—it's surprising. I can't get ahead of you—which I so appreciate. I want to be surprised more than anything. I like not knowing where things are going.

JK: That brings up a good point too which is that I get excited about a story when we're in the room, and you've got eight people with eight different passionate opinions. And, when some of them say, "Oh, I would never do that . . ."—that's when I always feel like we're on to something. I know this is an issue where you don't know what the ending is going to be. If there's eight people in the room and they're all arguing about the answer, then the people watching will feel the same—that they're not sure where it's going to go. The way to tell stories where you don't know where it's going to lead is by coming up with things that are genuinely the stuff of life. Sometimes we have to stop ourselves from having too many twists and turns in the story because when plot gets too big—sometimes it gets in the way of what's real.

I'm very lucky to have shows like *Friday Night Lights* and *Parenthood*, where the cast is so good and so strong. A little bit goes a long way with them. You don't have to have these huge turning points within a scene for them to find stuff. It just needs to be real as opposed to feeling fake, so we try as best we can as writers to give the actors material where they are not hitting false notes as they are doing it. The actors help a lot with that too— making sure this is grounded and true to their characters. It truly is a collaboration. When you all feel you're after the same thing on the same show, that's when you have a possibility of succeeding. It's very hard to do television. You're telling lots of stories in a short amount of time and you make those episodes very fast. I feel like where TV goes off the rails a lot of the time is when the network thinks the show is one thing and the writer thinks it's something else and the actors think it's a third thing. And the result is that the audience is not being served. What's important as a showrunner is to make sure you're doing everything that you can so that everybody feels that they're doing the same show. Everybody is excited about it and there's ownership in that. They feel like they are invested in it. To this day, one of the things I love so much about *Parenthood* is when I'll talk to the actors after they've gotten the script, and they'll say how much they love another character's story. They're into the show. They're not just going through and looking at their pages. They are into the show as a whole. And, that's what keeps the show feeling real and fresh.

11

KNOW WHO AND WHAT THEY'RE UP AGAINST

Creating stakes: Give your protagonist(s) something to gain and something to lose. The antagonistic forces on a series will serve to escalate the stakes and intensify the urgency to solve a given problem. Think about the role of *time* in your series. Notice how characters in all genres are always rushing somewhere—they must hurry and do something *or else.*

In *The Killing*, detective Sarah Linden (Mireille Enos) is all set to move to California with her fiancé and her teenage son when she gets assigned a murder case. Sarah plans to wrap the case up quickly so she can move on with her life, but the case gradually turns into a sprawling conspiracy that drags on for weeks. The case ruins her relationship with her fiancé, jeopardizes the custody of her son, and puts her life at risk. And those are just the stakes for one of the characters. This case destroys many lives and careers as it changes the political climate of the city.

In *Homeland*, the stakes intensify for Carrie (Claire Danes) as her feelings for Brody (Damian Lewis) complicate her mission to protect America from a developing terrorist plot. Carrie's affection for Brody turns into love, which compromises her judgment and puts her career and reputation at risk. The stakes are heightened for Brody as well, who finds himself at odds with his new celebrity status as an American hero, his conflicted allegiance to terrorist Abu Nazir (Navid Negahban), and the disconnect with his family who learned to live without him.

Weeds raises the stakes for protagonist Nancy Botwin (Mary-Louise Parker) with each passing season. Recently widowed Nancy operates a modestly successful marijuana business in the upscale suburban-gated community of Agrestic, and as her business literally grows, so do her problems.

Among other challenges, Nancy faces off against rival dealers, a shrewd DEA agent (whom Nancy eventually marries, complicating matters), and the leader of a drug cartel (whom Nancy also marries and bears his child, further complicating matters). Also at stake is the welfare of her two sons. The dysfunction caused by the drug trade ropes her eldest son Silas (Hunter Parrish) into the business, and leads her youngest son Shane (Alexander Gould) to sociopathic behavior and, ultimately, murder.

In sitcoms, the stakes aren't "life or death," but they should feel like it. In the season 4 finale of *Friends*, Ross (David Schwimmer) calls his bride Rachel at the altar, but her name is Emily! It's a gut-wrenching moment that dooms his marriage and further muddles his complicated relationship with Rachel (Jennifer Aniston).

In *How I Met Your Mother*, Ted (Josh Radnor) learns that his fiancée has never seen *Star Wars*, his all-time favorite movie. Ted says to his friend Marshall (Jason Segel), "If Stella doesn't like this movie, I can't marry her." Ted anxiously observes his fiancée as she watches the film, hoping they're compatible. This is a trivial problem linked to a much larger, deeper fear of intimacy—and the stakes of a lifelong commitment could not be higher for Ted.

Man against man. The most common obstacle comes in the form of a person—the antagonist. The goals of the protagonist and antagonist come into direct conflict with each other. In *24*, the antagonist is almost always a terrorist with a specific anti-American agenda. Jack Bauer (Kiefer Sutherland) must foil a series of escalating attacks carried out by the antagonist and his henchmen.

Sometimes the identity and motivation of the antagonist are unknown. In *Person of Interest*, a complex machine predicts murders before they happen, but the machine only delivers the identity of a person. The protagonists are tasked with discerning if that person is the potential victim or the antagonist.

The antagonist could also have supernatural abilities. In the fantasy series *Once Upon a Time*, protagonist Emma Swan (Jennifer Morrison) struggles to break the curse that the Evil Queen (Lana Parrilla) has cast on the town of Storybrooke.

Sometimes the antagonist might be someone that the protagonist is trying to help. In the pilot for *Scandal*, political fixer Olivia Pope (Kerry Washington) must prove that a decorated war hero didn't commit a murder. Olivia discovers the veteran's alibi, but revealing the alibi would out him as being gay. In order to complete her mission, Olivia must convince the reluctant war hero to tell the truth.

Man against society. Characters often have the burden of facing a social construct far beyond their control. In *The Wire*, the drug trade systemically corrupts the city of Baltimore. In season 3, disaffected policeman Major Bunny Colvin (Robert Wisdom) secretly legalizes drugs in the most abject areas of West Baltimore in a desperate attempt to curtail the growing drug violence. Even though his plan works, the societal pressure requiring a hard-line stance on drugs ultimately destroys his experiment as well as his career.

In *House of Cards*, the social construct standing in the way of protagonist Frank Underwood (Kevin Spacey) is Beltway politics. After failing to receive his promised appointment to secretary of state, Frank schemes to get more power. However, he can't simply take the president's job. Instead, he must orchestrate a byzantine plot to become vice president in order to position himself to win the presidency in eight years.

In *Game of Thrones*, the political barriers are medieval. Ned Stark (Sean Bean) agrees to become Hand of the King, the king's trusted adviser. Ned eventually learns the king's heir, Joffrey (Jack Gleeson), is illegitimate. He was the product of an incestuous affair between the queen and her brother. As the king's health fades, Ned honorably tries to find a righteous succession plan, but he's betrayed by his allies and sentenced to death by Joffrey after he's dubiously crowned king.

In *The Walking Dead*, the zombie apocalypse creates a society completely devoid of laws. It's purely survival of the fittest. In the season 2 episode "Nebraska," protagonist Rick Grimes (Andrew Lincoln) and two of his cohorts encounter a pair of survivors in the bar of an abandoned town. The survivors implore Rick to allow them to join his group, but Rick refuses. As their anger swells, Rick shoots them dead before they have the chance to shoot him.

Man against self. Sometimes the main character is his own worst enemy. In *Mad Men*, Don Draper (Jon Hamm) fights to conceal his checkered past, a far cry from his urbane advertising executive persona. Don also grapples with his serial philandering, which comes into conflict with his role as husband and father.

In *Breaking Bad*, Walter White (Bryan Cranston) constantly battles his own hubris. Instead of taking money from his former colleague for cancer treatment, Walter embarks on the reckless journey of becoming a meth kingpin. Presented with several opportunities to walk away, Walter forges ahead. He doesn't quit until his wife finally gets through to him and shows him that he's accumulated too much money to count—far more than his initial goal of $737,000.

In *Nashville*, Juliette Barnes (Hayden Panettiere) is the young country superstar who wants to be taken more seriously, but is plagued in both the past and the present by her drug addict mother. She is both independent yet vulnerable which causes her to be reckless and angry all the time. Her inability to admit she needs help and wants love may just keep her in the one place she doesn't want to be—alone.

In *Revenge*, Emily Thorne (Emily VanCamp) is similarly trapped by her anger at both the death of her innocent father and her terrible memories of an abusive childhood full of foster homes and juvenile prison. But where

Nashville's Juliette lashes out, Emily is cool and reserved. Her intense focus on revenge has made her numb and is also blinding her from seeing that it's coming at the cost of other people she cares about—including her long-lost love, Jack Porter (Nick Wechsler). In the season 2 finale, Emily finally admits who she really is to Jack, so we'll have to see what they'll do. Will he feel betrayed and turn against her, or will they join forces and align against their mutual adversaries?

Man against nature. Mother Nature can serve as a powerful adversary to the main characters. In *Lost*, the survivors battle mysterious forces, but they also encounter the pitfalls of being stranded on an island: scarce resources, rough terrain, and dangerous wildlife.

In medical dramas such as *House, M.D.*, doctors continually face an array of deadly organic pathogens moving through the atmosphere invisibly.

Mother nature can also be an ironic adversary, incidental to the main obstacle. In *Breaking Bad*, Walter and Jesse (Aaron Paul) cook meth in an RV in the middle of the New Mexico desert for the purposes of privacy. However, in the season 2 episode "4 Days Out," Walter and Jesse almost die of heat exhaustion as a result of being accidentally stranded in the solitary desert.

Man against fate. The main character may find himself against an inevitable outcome. In *Boss*, unscrupulous mayor of Chicago Tom Kane (Kelsey Grammer) receives a diagnosis of Lewy body dementia, an incurable disease that causes hallucinations and loss of motor skills. Tom battles uncontrollable delusions, which affect his perception, judgment, and memory.

Characters often suffer the consequences of random fateful events. In *Friday Night Lights*, star quarterback Jason Street (Scott Porter) gets paralyzed from the waist down after a brutal hit on the football field. The harrowing injury causes a ripple effect in the football-crazed town of Dillon, Texas. Jason's promising football career is over, ill-prepared backup quarterback Matt Saracen (Zach Gilford) is thrust into the starting role and searing spotlight, and head coach Eric Taylor (Kyle Chandler) suddenly finds his job in jeopardy, which could mean uprooting his family yet again.

In sitcoms, the characters are often ill-fated by the construct of the show. The passengers of the S.S. *Minnow* are not going to get off *Gilligan's Island*.

In *Married . . . with Children*, Al Bundy is fated to be a sad-sack loser, predestined by the "Bundy Curse." In the season 8 episode "Luck of the Bundys," everything suddenly goes Al's way, much to his skepticism. Once Al finally embraces his good fortune and declares, "Al Bundy is a winner!" everything immediately falls apart.

In *My Name Is Earl*, petty thief Earl Hickey (Jason Lee) attempts to avoid a grim fate by embracing karma and making amends for all the wrongs he's committed in his lifetime. Earl reaches this epiphany after losing a $100,000-dollar lottery ticket—and only finding it after selflessly picking up trash to atone for years of littering.

Man against multiple forces. As evidenced by some of the preceding examples, antagonistic forces can intersect. The more obstacles, the better, so long as they're organic to the story.

Intersecting antagonistic forces are most effective when they're thematically linked. In *The Sopranos*, Tony Soprano (James Gandolfini) is constantly at odds with law enforcement and rival families, but he's also at war with himself. The constant threat of losing his family is the source of his panic attacks, which is what causes him to find a therapist.

> As obstacles intensify for your characters, so should the *stakes* or *consequences for inaction and/or failure*. Determine what they value most and put it at risk. Without the potential for loss, there is no substantive conflict, and without conflict, there is no dramatic tension (which is essential in comedy, too). If dramatic tension is M.I.A., there will be no suspense, and a series with no suspense will be D.O.A.

INTERVIEW: Tim Kring

Tim Kring Credits

Best known for:

Touch (Executive Producer/Writer) 2012–2013
Heroes (Executive Producer/Writer) 2006–2010
Crossing Jordan (Executive Producer/Writer) 2001–2007
Providence (Co-Executive Producer/Writer) 1999–2001
Chicago Hope (Producer/Writer) 1996–1997

NL: This chapter is all about stakes—physical, emotional, and spiritual consequences for characters—and will also encompass sources of antagonism. I'd like to begin by discussing *Touch*. Are you in production yet for season 2?

TK: We're in preproduction. We've written the first couple of episodes and have broken a few others.

NL: You wrote the pilot, did you reverse engineer? Did you start knowing how the season would end?

TK: I knew that I wanted the first season to center around this child custody issue that Keifer Sutherland [as Martin Bohm] and his son [Jake played by David Mazouz] have. His son is in a board and care facility. And, in this board and care facility, we start to feel that something is not right—that there are other secrets there. We were asked by the network to not introduce any serialized element for the first six episodes to give the audience a chance to sample. A lot of statistics have found that there would be large groups of new viewers who would come in to watch a show within the first six weeks. To not alienate them, you would have a stand-alone episode. So, we didn't introduce a serialized element until we killed off Danny Glover's character [Arthur Teller]. There were little questions in the first six episodes in that there were strange things happening in the basement of this place behind room number six. But there was very little you would have to know in order to watch those first few episodes. Once that serialized engine started, we slowly ramped it up until the final three episodes until it is very clear that there is something up in the board and care and that people are interested in Jake. There's a mysterious corporation called AsterCorp who clearly have some designs on Jake. This all ramps up to an exciting season finale where Martin takes Jake and runs. We are able to end the season with them landing in California. We introduced also late in the season the idea of Maria Bello's character [Lucy Robbins] as a satellite story that you didn't know how to connect at all. Only to find out that she is the mother of Amelia [Saxon Sharbino] who was the girl in mysterious room six and those two stories collide in the last thirty seconds of the finale. That will hopefully propel you into the second season that takes place in Los Angeles. The first season was all about this board and care and the introduction of these antagonistic forces. The second season is all about finding Amelia.

NL: Do you already know if she's alive? Or who has her?

TK: Yes, we introduce all of that into the season premiere of the second season. We tell you where she is and we tell you who the major antagonists of the second season are. We put a face to the AsterCorp villains. It turns out to be more complicated than that because it turns out to not be necessarily AsterCorp, but one person inside the company who is a younger genius who has made AsterCorp a fortune by producing these algorithms that have predictive qualities for customers and various shipping routes that are shortened. So we introduce that character whose name is Calvin Norburg [Lukas Haas] who had sold his algorithm company to AsterCorp for quite a bit of money a few years ago. He's the one who's been interested in Amelia and Jake. We've also introduced the idea, in a spiritual way, of the idea of "The Thirty-six." That there are thirty-six chosen people which comes from the Kaballah, the lamedvov tzadikim [spelling from Wikipedia], which are the thirty-six righteous ones. It says that at any time are on the planet there are thirty-six people who keep the world from spinning into evil. They are righteous people unaware of their own position and power in the world. Humble usually. It's not necessarily heads of state. It's the butcher down the street who doesn't gyp you for two cents a pound on ground chuck. We introduced this through the character of Avram [Bodhi Elfman], a Hasidic Jew. It turns out that there is something to that and something that Calvin is interested in. He has Amelia and is using brain mapping to figure out these algorithms. He's twisted, but he starts off with some very altruistic motives thinking that he's going to make the world a better place by taking these abilities that people like Jake have and make it a better, more connected place.

There are two antagonistic forces: one represented through the corporate idea of Calvin with resources and money and the other is a fallen version of one of these thirty-six who is a former priest and has decided in a twisted way that there will be no other idols before God. So he is trying, one-by-one, to kill them. So that is a tangential force that is going to be a threat.

NL: So you have a central mystery from the past that is always running through, but you also have central questions regarding the present.

TK: One of the truths about working in television—especially when you introduce a serialized engine that depends on you having things mapped out many, many episodes ahead—the truth is that things change for any number of reasons. And sometimes it's for reasons you never saw coming.

NL: Like you have to write an actor out.

TK: Exactly. Or someone you've hired that you thought was going to be great is terrible or difficult. The relationship you were going to hinge a tremendous amount of story on—you get the actors together and they have no chemistry. You're a heat-seeking missile. You go where the heat is. You want the show to speak to you as much as you speak to it. And it will tell you what it wants to be. It's a very organic process that is a river that's taking turns that you're not fully in control of. That's part of the excitement, but part of the challenge as well.

NL: Like writing yourself into a corner and not knowing how to get out?

TK: You try not to write yourself into a corner, but sometimes there are some shows that turn on that idea. There are some shows where you want the audience to go, "How are they going to get out of this one?" And the audience has almost a gladiatorial relationship with that show. They want to see it get to the brink of jumping the shark and then somehow pull itself out of it. There's a thrill ride quality to that. As much as you hope that you can avoid those things, you really can't.

NL: I had that feeling when I thought: "How is Martin going to get Jake out of the facility?" You always had Clea [Gugu Mbatha-Raw] in the gray area of wanting to be loyal to Martin and yet also trying to do her job. It was totally organic. Almost all of your stories have to hinge on what is considered a bad word for screenwriters: *coincidence*. And yet the whole theme of the show is that synchronicity exists that these are not really coincidences that we are all connected by this thread. Do you have certain rules for writing this way? For example, I believe that coincidence can work best in fiction if it makes things worse for the protagonist; but if it helps or makes things easier for the protagonist than it can feel forced. Your thoughts?

TK: I actually wish that I could be more articulate about it. It's one of those things that we looked at so hard that it stopped having rules. It's like when you stare at something too long; it loses its essence. We did so much talking about whether this is coincidence or synchronicity. Is this senti-mental or sappy? I've never worked on such a show that had such a thin rail that you ride on. One degree to the left sentimental becomes sappy and one degree to the right and magic becomes coincidence. It was a very hard thing. It was really just a gut reaction in the editing room and a pull-ing back. It's a very nebulous thing that happens in the editing room. You get the right piece of music and the right shot and the right performance with the right take. You cut it the right way and you do a digital push-in at the right moment, and it somehow works. Take one of those elements out and it falls apart. This was one of those shows where there were not a lot of rules. You just had to go into the editing room and see whether it landed or didn't. I think there were times on this show when it worked really well. That moment of coincidence felt less convenient and more magical. And those were the ones that worked for us. One of the things about the show is, as you said, it boldly states from the outset that this is what the show is about. Then you get a little bit of license when it happens in the fifth act. Part of the fun of the show is that it is like a procedural in that way. When I did *Crossing Jordan*, you had a dead body that you rolled into the show in the teaser and somebody did that body wrong and you had to figure out who. So you would introduce three suspects. In the end, you hoped that you would have that moment when the audience says, "I never saw that coming. I thought it was the brother-in-law." And, in a way, Touch does very much the same thing. It introduces threads of stories, and you don't have any idea how they are going to come together. Everything hinges on that moment where you say, "I didn't see that coming." That sense of never seeing it coming hopefully trumps the coincidence factor because in reality it's a show about how coincidences are real. And if you know how to look at them, then metaphorically they start to become a valuable tool in your life. Hopefully, if the show has said anything, it's that the smallness of your own life, or what you think is insignificant, actually has great significance. That everything matters, and if that's the case, then maybe you'll live your life in a more conscious way.

NL: There's a great sentiment in one of Jake's voice-overs where he says, "We'll send three billion e-mails and 19 billion text messages and yet we will still feel alone." So on the one hand, we're all seeking connection, and on the other hand, we all feel separate.

TK: Yes, and I think that's a sentiment that the audience is feeling very much right now. They feel very connected, but that communication doesn't give them a sense of community. The technology that's allowing us to be that connected has the dual effect of making us feel more isolated. We can retreat into Facebook, but we don't go out to eat with our friends any more.

NL: *Crossing Jordan* was very localized and Heroes was very global. Is Touch going to continue to be global?

TK: Yes. One of the issues we did have production-wise is doing the number of worlds we did. While that's fun and exciting for the audience, it's very hard to produce. We're going to try in the second season to do one less story each week. But it will continue to still have these satellite stories that give you a sense that these things are connected. In many ways, the show taught the audience very slowly how to watch it. It crept up on people; ramping up to a very serialized finale. The second season will start with that same serialized energy. We've earned this new engine.

NL: If it's going to be more serialized, is it going to be contiguous? Where you start up exactly where you left off?

TK: At times. The first season was only over a few week period. I think the second season will follow that same model. I think what happens when you inject too much time into a story is that the audience starts to feel that. They start to feel the pressure deflate. The shortening and compressing of time really does help to put tension on things.

NL: Will the voice-overs continue?

TK: Yes.

NL: It's so great because you have a character who doesn't speak on screen, who only speaks in voice-over to us. And his words are so poetic and wise. When you constructed the pilot in terms of stakes, Martin's antagonistic forces were his son who he's not quite sure how to handle; you also have Child Protective Services who wants to take him away; and Martin is trying to keep his job, and then you bring in the corporation.

He's a very put upon character from the very beginning. He's having trouble making ends meet. He's having trouble keeping his kid in school and loses custody because of it. His resources are cut off. And you're right, that's an antagonistic force in itself—just the sheer weight of pressure on him.

Having a child who you can't communicate with becomes the central goal of the show. It's a quest for communication. Little by little, he begins to read these small signs that his son has. Actually in the pilot, he learns a very big one that his son is actually trying to communicate with him through these numbers. It's that revelation that is the big engine of the show: "My son is trying to tell me something, I therefore must be his eyes and ears in the world and go out and do what he is trying to tell me to do."

NL: Martin mentions that "bad things will happen if he ignores the numbers and Jake will suffer," which adds another element of stakes.

TK: We introduce this idea that he was in a type of psychic pain, if these numbers were not remedied. The premise is basically that Jake can see the patterns in the universe and when all is status quo, the numbers all line up, and when they're not, there's an anomaly. The anomaly presents itself as a number and you must go out into the world and try and find out why that particular number is anomalous in that episode. Until that number is righted and rectified, Jake is feeling some kind of psychic pain for the world. That's the spiritual essence of the show. He is clearly a mystical connector that has some greater purpose in the world. Housed in this frail, seemingly insignificant, disenfranchised person, is someone who holds many of the secrets of the universe.

NL: What attracts you to characters with extraordinary abilities? It seems like that in itself creates this conflict between the thin line of what is a blessing and a curse.

TK: That's it, actually. I had a long freelance career before I did series television. I did any number of genres from horror to teen comedies to thriller, so I didn't move into this superhero thing until Heroes. So I haven't always had this fascination, but I have to admit when I did think about people with extraordinary abilities, it wasn't about the genre, it was about the struggle it presents for a character. The conflict that it presents. If you are someone who has a job which you are struggling in or a woman you are trying to get to fall in love with you or a dying parent that you are dealing with or a brother you have to take care of because he won't grow up—and you think you can fly. That to me was what was interesting. You take this world with problems that we can all relate to and you add a layer of an extraordinary calling and it is in that conflict of how to live your life while having a calling is, I think, the stuff of great drama. The whole idea of Heroes was based on that idea of how you take ordinary people—the guy you went to high school with or the person you see at the laundromat when you take your shirts in to be cleaned—how do you take those people and layer on top of it a kind of mystical calling to do something great. Inside of that is also a postmodern view that we are not going to find the answers to the big questions of our world in the normal institutions that we've always put our faith in—it's going to come from a grass roots, ground up solution—from an ordinary person who has something extraordinary to say. When you look at the way technology is working now, it's coming from two guys in a garage who come up with something or it's an Arab Spring—it's people taking to the streets or the Occupy movement. As for Jake, I was much less interested in where he placed on the level of Autism, but in the idea that someone who has this extraordinary ability is one of the most disenfranchised people on the planet. He's small, he's meek, he can't speak. He's perceived as being severely on the spectrum of Autism. He is the least likely candidate and the most disenfranchised person on the planet. And yet, inside this person is this most extraordinary human being . . .

NL: . . . who just might end up saving the world.

12

MINE THE MYSTERY

A s recounted in TV critic and author Alan Sepinwall's exceptional book *The Revolution Was Televised*, AMC was very interested in *Mad Men* after HBO ostensibly passed on it. AMC was getting into the original scripted one-hour drama business, and being a period piece, *Mad Men* seemed like a good companion to AMC's slate of classic movies programming. AMC executive Rob Sorcher read the pilot script, penned by *Soprano*'s alumnus Matthew Weiner, and wanted to make it.

According to Sepinwall, Sorcher liked the script so much that he only gave Weiner one significant note:

"Don Draper Needs to Have a Secret"

The rationale behind this note—which one of my UCLA colleagues refers to as "the note beneath the note"—was that Don Draper, like Tony Soprano, needed a vulnerability.

As a mafia kingpin, Tony Soprano routinely commits terrible acts—and yet we were compelled to care about him because he suffers from clinical depression. We aren't asked to *forgive* Tony for his trespasses, but we are asked to relate to his struggles (panic attacks) and empathize with his secret shame that comes in the form of a pill (Prozac) and a shrink (Dr. Melfi).

Like Tony Soprano, Don Draper is an adulterer, a manipulator, a liar, and a self-centered narcissist. Don may have cold blood running through his veins, but he's not (as far as we know) a cold-blooded killer. In fact, Don is a total charmer: dashing, irreverent, rebellious, debonair, handsome, whip smart, a romantic—not to mention a brilliant ad exec. In the *Mad Men* pilot, we first meet Don on a train bound for the city, and we follow him on his daily routine—which includes a visit to his sexy, bohemian girlfriend's artist's apartment. We're impressed and envious of Don's seemingly perfect life—the guy seems to walk on air. It's not until the end of the pilot episode—when Don returns home to the suburbs and we discover that he's actually married to a gorgeous blonde and has two young children who worship him—that our perception of him completely changes.

Now we think he's a cad. An adulterer. Despite his good looks and charm, the ease with which Don perpetrates his lies makes him all the more slimy. And he's the lead character of the series. How are we going to root for him every week? And why should we care about him?

The answer that's gradually revealed in the central mystery of season 1 is that Don Draper is not really Don Draper. He's an imposter. His real name is Dick Whitman. Don may be slick and successful now, but Don/Dick came from dire poverty. His father was a hobo, and we'll find out later that his mother was a prostitute (which explains a lot about Don's erratic relationships with women). Dick had assumed the identity of a dead soldier, Don Draper, in his effort to leave his past behind. Don/Dick's secret is rooted in *shame*. His vulnerability is his desperate need to reinvent—or re-brand—himself. He gave his image a makeover and then set out to sell this newly packaged version of himself to the American public. It worked, and Don rose to the top of his game. The King Midas of Madison Avenue. But his secret was his Achilles' heel and, deep down, Don was/is terrified of being found out, lest he topple from the heights of a skyscraper like the cardboard cutout in the iconic opening credits.

His secret past was a strong "story engine" for the first season. *Mad Men* is serialized, but is not structured contiguously; in other words, each episode does not pick up directly after the previous one. After the infamous lawnmower episode in which a Sterling Cooper employee tragically lost a foot, the following episode picked up about a month later—and no one even mentioned the incident. We don't follow the lives of the *Mad Men* characters according to real time, a la *24*. Instead, we are dropped into their lives and quickly get up to speed on their current woes. Each character has a plotline that extends for the entire (relatively short) season.

Character arcs on *Mad Men* are all in service of a specific *central question* for each character: Will the fortunes of Sterling Cooper rise or fall? What will happen to Peggy's baby? Will Joan stay with her unstable, controlling fiancé/ husband? Will Betty stay with Don? Etc.

All TV series have several central questions to pique the audience's curiosity to find out *what happens next*. The central question usually leads to some answers—that lead to even more questions (see Chapter 19, on cliffhangers).

In addition to central questions that concern the future, many TV series also include a central mystery that concerns the past. With a central mystery, the question isn't what's going to happen; the question is *what happened— and why?*

On *Mad Men*, Don's wife, Betty (January Jones) discovers his secret and throws him out of the house. Betty divorces Don and gets remarried. But Don can't divorce his past. It continues to shadow and plague him, fueling his self-destructive behaviors, even after he gets remarried and attempts once again to reinvent himself. *Mad Men* continues to put forth secrets and lies and scandals, but there has not been another significant central mystery to match this one—until the recent introduction of Bob Benson (James Wolk). And the blogosphere has been all a-Twitter.

In the original pilot for *Desperate Housewives*, writer/creator/showrunner Marc Cherry establishes the main POV of the series with an omnipotent narrator, Mary Alice Young (Brenda Strong). We learn in the pilot episode that Mary Alice committed suicide. It's her voice-over narration at the beginning of each episode that sets the theme and tells us how her death impacted each of the housewives residing on Wisteria Lane. This long-running, ratings juggernaut explored the sudsy, scandalous and often very funny sisterhood, family, and love lives of four disparate women, each desperate in her own way. Given Marc Cherry's solid comedy résumé, I'm told that ABC decided to recruit soap opera veteran, Charles Pratt (*Melrose Place, General Hospital*), as a consulting producer—and season 1's central mystery was hatched.

As Mary Alice's close friends, Susan Mayer (Teri Hatcher), Lynette Scavo (Felicity Huffman), Bree Van de Kamp (Marcia Cross), and Gabrielle Solis (Eva Longoria), struggle to come to terms with the tragic suicide news, Mary Alice's husband, Paul (Mark Moses), asks Susan, Lynette, Bree, and Gabrielle to sort through Mary Alice's belongings, as he's too overcome with grief. In a box of Mary Alice's clothes, the women discover a blackmail note reading, "I know what you did. It makes me sick. I'm going to tell." The postmark indicates that Mary Alice received it the day she took her own life. At the end of the pilot, Mary Alice's son, Zach (Cody Kasch), awakens in the middle of the night to find his father unearthing a mysterious chest from the drained swimming pool in their backyard. And now, in addition to the central questions facing the present and future for each housewife, we also have the central mystery of who had blackmailed Mary Alice—and why.

On *The Mentalist*, we track the central mystery of who murdered former TV "psychic" Patrick Jane's (Simon Baker) wife and daughter. We know it's a serial killer (so-called Red John) who had a vendetta against Patrick, but the killer remains at large and continues to vex Patrick who can solve every mystery that comes before him—but not that one. Patrick is compelled to give up his "practice" and join the California Bureau of Investigation as a consultant, using his acute observational abilities to "read" suspects and uncover the truth. While there are new cases in virtually every episode, the central mystery case of Red John is the horizontal line that runs through the entire season.

On *Bates Motel* (creator/showrunners Carlton Cuse and Kerry Ehrin), several mysteries are introduced in the first two episodes. Primary mystery number 1 is who killed Norman Bates' (Freddie Highmore) father (who Norman finds in a pool of blood on the ground in the garage)? The possible suspects are Norman's mother, Norma (Vera Farmiga), and her estranged first child, Norman's elder half-brother/reprobate Dylan Massett (Max Thieriot). Even though Norman seems genuinely shocked when he discovers his father's freshly dead body, the chief suspect is Norman himself; it's not the evidence that clues us in—but rather the Norman we remember from the classic 1960 horror film *Psycho*. And so, we enter this *Bates Motel* with our own baggage.

Sure, this is a much younger, more innocent-seeming Norman in 2013, but he's still creepy and there is the subtext of Oedipus which hangs over every mother-son scene, like a thick Oregonian fog (the show's new setting is the fictional White Pine Bay). In this updated iteration, Norman's mom is very much alive, a sultry Hitchcock Blonde, in vivid color. Recently widowed, she takes Norman away from their California suburb to begin a new life as the proprietress of the Fairview Motel that she bought out of foreclosure. But even before the new Bates Motel sign goes up, one of the previous motel owner's kin, Keith Summers (W. Earl Brown), comes by in a drunken rage to scare them away. Undaunted, Norma warns the drunkard to get off *her* property or she'll kill him. Later, Summers returns for revenge and tries to rape her—but he gets clobbered over the head by Norman and stabbed to death by Norma. Determined for a fresh start and desperate to avoid bad press at her new motel, Norma and Norman dispose of Summers' corpse—setting up (open) mystery number 2: will they get found out by the town sheriff Alex Romero (Nestor Carbonell) who's already suspicious of the pretty yet jittery Norma?

Another mystery is set up when Norman picks up the old carpeting (blood-stained via Summers) and discovers a small sketchbook hidden under the carpet in one of the motel rooms. The sketches are Manga-style and depict a naked young female junkie, bound and gagged, a syringe going into her arm and multiple track marks. The drawings indicate that she's a hostage in a shack in the forest—setting up closed mystery number 3. Norman's new high school friend, Emma Decody (Olivia Cooke) a quirky outcast who lugs around an oxygen tank due to cystic fibrosis, borrows the journal and calls Norma with news that she knows where the shack might be.

Mystery number 4 involves a car that careens out of control and crashes near the motel. Norman and his new school friends race over and discover the driver is burned almost beyond recognition; it turns out he's the father of one of the girls, Bradley Martin (Nicola Peltz), and he's still alive but in a coma.

In mystery number 5 (and this is all in the first *two* episodes!), Norma befriends "good cop" Sheriff Deputy Zach Shelby (Mike Vogel) to win him over to her side. Deputy Shelby confides to Norma that White Pine Bay has its own secrets and illicit wealth, and that these denizens are likely to take justice into their own hands with "an eye for an eye." By the end of episode 2, Norman and Emma have discovered a marijuana field and are chased out of the forest and away from the mysterious shack by shotgun-wielding mountain men.

Last, Norma sees Deputy Shelby diverting drivers and pedestrians away from an unrecognizable man burned to death and hanging upside down in the town square. Is this burning man Bradley's father? Or yet another burn victim? This could be linked to mystery number 4, or maybe it's a whole new mystery number 6—or even a serial killer/arsonist? If the new Bates Motel sign that buzzes like a bug zapper is any indication, the carnage has only just begun.

On Many Series, Each New Season Brings Forth a New Central Mystery

On *Scandal,* the short (seven-episode) first season focuses on the mystery surrounding Amanda Tanner (Liza Weil) who claims she had an affair with the President and was now pregnant with his baby. After it's discovered that Amanda made up the story to help a political rival, she's found murdered. But that story arc doesn't end the central mystery of season 1. The larger mystery involves Olivia's new hire, Quinn Perkins (Katie Lowes), who's revealed in the season 2 premiere to be Lindsay Dwyer, on trial for murder for allegedly killing her ex-boyfriend and six other people. As it turns out, Olivia has pulled some high-level strings in order to get Lindsey acquitted of all charges, which only deepens the mystery as we discover that Olivia has something to do with Quinn/Lindsey's past. The season 2 central mystery orbits around election fraud and Olivia's secret role in getting President Fitzgerald Grant into the Oval Office. The fun of this series is that Olivia not only fixes political scandals for her clients, but she *is* the scandal, too.

On *Lost,* the central mystery is synonymous with the series' intricate mythology (see Chapter 18, "Establish the Mythology"). Season 1 of *Lost* teases and taunts us with supernatural happenings on the remote tropical island, including a polar bear (?!), an unseen viciously carnivorous creature (referred to as the "Smoke Monster"), and the elusive, mostly unseen inhabitants on the island ("The Others"). There is also the mysterious French women, Danielle Rousseau (Mira Furlan), who was shipwrecked on the island sixteen years before Jack Shephard (Matthew Fox) and the other survivors crash-landed on the island. And then there's "the hatch" which is later revealed to be a door down into a research station built by the Dharma Initiative (basically a series of science experiments that had been conducted on the island decades before). While the overarching central question of *Lost* never veers off course (will they ever get off the island?), the central mysteries vary from season to season. As one part of the mystery is solved, it only leads our ensemble of survivors to seek more answers—until the series finale when we finally discover the meaning of the island. SPOILER ALERT: In the flash sideways version, they all died instantly in the plane crash and the island was really limbo.

> While not essential, a little mystery in a pilot can go a very long way. The wisdom behind this adage is this: audiences are more compelled by what they *don't* know than by what they *do* know.

INTERVIEW: Damon Lindelof

Damon Lindelof Credits

Best known for:

Star Trek Into Darkness (feature) (Producer/Writer) 2013
Prometheus (feature) (Executive Producer/Writer) 2012
Cowboys & Aliens (feature) (Writer) 2011
Lost (Executive Producer/Writer/Co-Creator) 2004–2010
    Emmy Award Winner (Outstanding Drama Series) 2005
    Emmy Nominated (Outstanding Drama Series) 2008–2010
    Emmy Nominated (Outstanding Writing for a Drama Series) 2005–2007, 2009–2010
    WGA Award Winner (Dramatic Series) 2006
    WGA Nominated (Dramatic Series) 2007, 2009–2010
    WGA Nominated (Episodic Drama) 2008, 2011
Star Trek (Producer) 2009
Crossing Jordan (Co-Producer/Supervising Producer/Writer) 2002–2004
Nash Bridges (Writer) 2000–2001

NL: My first question has to do with the Mystery Box Ted Talk that J. J. Abrams [Creator, Executive Producer of *Lost*] did—it seems like his message was a governing principle for the series. The title graphic speaks to that. It's blurry, but as it gets closer and into focus, it disappears, so that it is just out of our grasp. Was that the storytelling strategy? Keeping things slightly blurred—always instilling in the audience the need to know more and then carefully doling it out?

DL: I think to ascribe a specific strategy into the overall design of the show would be doing retroactive rewriting of history. I think the reality was that we had a very specific issue that we were dealing with when Lloyd Braun first came to J.J. and J.J. came to me. I was certainly involved in the same question, which was, "How is this a TV series?" We all know what an hour-long TV series looks like, so what is the thing that we're going to present in the pilot of the show that gives people a sense of how the show is going to work? Because while it can be an enormously exciting idea of like, "Wow, I don't know what's going to happen next," that can also backfire when, "I don't know what's going to happen next," leads you down so many roads that it has no structure whatsoever.

I think mystery was a word which appeared many, many times in my first meeting with J.J. I was clearly a huge fan of *Alias* which, although I really liked *Felicity*, *Alias* was a show that I was much more dialed into. At the time that I met with J.J., it was about halfway through its third season. I had all these questions about the deep and involved mythology of *Alias* which I wanted to ask him and the idea of that being his brand.

*A*lthough he wasn't openly talking about mystery boxes at the time, I think that we both were engaged by the idea that not only was *Lost* going to be a show set on an island that was incredibly mysterious and very unwilling to give up its mysteries but that every single character on the show had to be surrounded by mystery.

They didn't want to talk about themselves. They were deeply conflicted and troubled people. One of the most compelling mysteries that first season was just finding out who they were. Many of the characters would be unreliable narrators, who didn't necessarily tell the truth, and we could dramatize this by revealing to the audience, "You're now in on the joke. You're behind the curtain. You got through the velvet rope." We're going to tell you that Locke [Terry O'Quinn] was in a wheelchair, but no one else is going to know on the show—just you and Locke. We adapted the format of a mystery show. *Twin Peaks* was a show that we mentioned a lot in our early planning sessions because it was huge on both my and J.J.'s pop culture radar in terms of shows we loved and were dialed into. It was a crowdsource show before the Internet even existed. The idea behind it was that you would watch an episode and when it ended you would need to go find someone else who had seen it, so that you could talk about it and theorize in an attempt to understand what the hell was going on there. And more important, it transcended, "Who killed Laura Palmer?" Laura Palmer was an interesting question, but much less interesting than, "What the hell is this place, Twin Peaks, and why are people acting so weird?"

NL: Like *Blue Velvet*, also.

DL: Right, exactly. We felt if we could ground the show—and all credit to David Lynch, who is a genius, there's something about his voice that's very ethereal or strange or weird that makes him less of a mainstream jeopardized case. So if we went to ABC and said, "We need you to give us millions of dollars to produce this show," we couldn't sell them on weirdness. But we thought that *Twin Peaks* was a good thing. So when we submitted the outline to Lloyd, he loved it, but there were a couple things that concerned him like the polar bear and the monster in the jungle—which, for us, were the cornerstones of what the show was going to be, but were the only really strange things that happened in the pilot that we had written. Lloyd said to me and J. J., "We don't want to pull a *Twin Peaks*." J. J. just looked at him, and this is the way that I remember it, and said, "You're using *Twin Peaks* as a cautionary tale fifteen years after it was actually cancelled. Don't we want to aspire to be like that?" The idea that although it's ultimately a cautionary tale in that they only made thirty episodes, it completely and totally peaked and valleyed within a two-year period. They obviously tapped into something. We wanted to tap into that same thing, and find a way to not burn out on it. By not having a central mystery, but lots of mysteries, we're ultimately going to engage the audience with the characters. I don't think it was just the political thing to say or a way of deflecting focus from the mystery because the mystery was a huge part of the show. It's what people were talking about. It's the way that we ended almost every episode before we went to the *Lost* card. It was our bread and butter in terms of building audience investment. It was just a delivery mechanism for the real pill that we wanted people to swallow, which was an emotional investment in the people on the island.

NL: How much of the mythology was worked out from the beginning? For example, was Charles Widmore [Alan Dale] always intended to be the super villain? Were "the others" always part of your plan? Was time travel and the hatch created from the beginning or did those things evolve?

DL: When you say the beginning, I'm assuming that you're talking about the pilot, and let's just say that I met J. J. the last week of January in the year 2004. We then wrote the next episode, "Tabula Rasa," in mid-June of that same year. From February to mid-June, there was a period within which we actually wrote the pilot, produced the pilot, edited the pilot, and then the show got picked up and ordered to series. During that period, February to June, there were many, many conversations not just between J. J. and myself, but we also hired a staff of writers whose job was to make fundamental island mythology and pitch story ideas. In that period of time, many ideas were discussed, but not necessarily committed to. For example, the idea that they would find a hatch—that was in the very first meeting that J. J. and I had together. He pitched that idea. The fact that there were other people on the island—and they were not necessarily the people responsible for building this hatch, but a different group of people, that was discussed in the first meeting with J. J. What the monster might be versus what it actually looked like was discussed in the first couple weeks because there was a lot of interest from the network and studio in terms of what the monster was. What's that noise in the jungle? When are we going to see that thing? And what is it? So we had an answer for that which ended up being very close to what we ultimately revealed on the show minus, I think, the Man in Black/Jacob implication.

There is a certain level of figuring things out, we have ideas, we have stuff that we're working toward, but sometimes (1) it doesn't work and (2) sometimes you change your mind because you have something better. I think we always had it in the back of our minds and were always talking about what the fundamental end game of the show was going to look like. Although some things changed along the way, I would say the lion share of the real mythological work got done between season 1 and season 2 because there was just no time to do it before then. We were off and running, we produced twenty-five hours of the show in a ten-month period. We had basically a month before we had to start writing the first episode of the second season, which, because we were going into the hatch, required a tremendous amount of thought being put into the Dharma Initiative and the idea of the "Others." The hatch represented Dharma, and the "Others" were represented by Mr. Friendly [M. C. Gainey], who basically abducted Walt (Malcolm David Kelley) in the season 1 finale. So although we had the idea for those guys, that's when we started having larger, more involved conversations about who these groups were and how they came to be on the island.

And then we did it again between the second and the third season of the show. That was a dark time for particularly Carlton and myself because we were pretty certain that we would be leaving the show after the third season because we were lobbying unsuccessfully for an end date for the show. We let our contracts lapse because they had us locked down for two years, and then between seasons 2 and 3, we realized that quitting the show at that point would basically leave the show with no fundamental leadership. So season 3 was about putting together a succession plan. We inherited Jeff Pinkner (Executive Producer) from *Alias,* which had ended, with the idea that he was basically going to run *Lost* once we left. So between seasons 2 and 3, we were fairly despondent. There was still some stuff that we wanted to do. We had this idea about several of the castaways leaving the island—the "Oceanic Six." But we knew that we couldn't pull the trigger on it because that would be the first step in moving toward the end game. The end game was always designed as a three-phase idea for the show. Phase 1 is they crash on the island, we learn who they are, they learn about each other, they start to understand what the island is and at the end of Phase 1, several of them are able to leave the island. And then we were into Phase 2, which was those who were left behind on the island were finding themselves in peril because, as a result of the first group leaving the island, the island was now in flux and moving through time. Phase 2 basically ends with the people who made the decision to return being reunited with everyone else and then that begins the denouement or Phase 3, which was the final battle as it were. That was always the idea.

We just couldn't end Phase 1 because they wouldn't give us an end date. They were very reluctant to do so, but halfway through the third season, ABC changed their mind because either they realized that Carlton and I weren't bluffing, or the audience was starting to echo our sentiment, which was, "We're just doing middle. We can't move forward. We're only moving backward. The show is getting boring. We're just introducing new mysteries without resolving old ones." Once they instituted the end game, the season 3 finale, and the introduction of the flash-forward, we basically put our stake down and said, "We're not only telling you that people are getting off the island, we're telling you that Jack (Matthew Fox) and Kate (Evangeline Lilly) are two of those people, and we're committed to that now because we've just showed you the scene." Once we started doing flash-forwards, we had to have a very specific mythology and plan worked out because every single episode we did was showing the audience scenes from the future.

NL: Do you think this was ABC's comfort level with *Gilligan's Island* where they just stayed put, and they were afraid that once you got them off the island that it would "jump the shark"? Do you think they were just afraid that the show would fall apart or that it was going to change into a different show? What do you think their hesitation was?

DL: I think that a large part of it just boiled down to television is about repetition—that's the way that they understand it. And I can't blame them because if you look at all the successful Top 10 network television shows, including reality shows, there's nothing new about *American Idol*, CSI, or NCIS. Not to take anything away from those shows, but the shows that perform very well are deeply formulaic, and I think that the network looked at *Lost* and said the formula is working because lots of people were watching it. Every week, we tell a story that takes place on the island and then we have a flashback story that is about one of these castaways off the island. Like a *New Yorker* short story. And that's working really well, so why change it? Why do you guys need to push it forward? At the time that we were doing *Lost*, serialized TV or the word "serialized" was still an ugly word. Obviously, *Desperate Housewives* and *Grey's Anatomy* which both premiered the same year, were both serialized shows, but they had a certain Tom and Jerry-like ability to kind of reset. The character relationships were constantly evolving and heavily serialized, but at the end of the day, with *Grey's Anatomy*, there was always a new medical case that would come up.

NL: Exactly—they had the franchise.

DL: And although *Desperate Housewives* resolved the Mary Alice murder at the end of its first season, it was able to introduce new overarching mysteries into that show. But ultimately, it became a very effective nighttime soap opera with a particularly mischievous and fun, tongue-in-cheek voice to it. But because *Lost* was mystery based, you could only have someone's attention for so long until they started to get extremely frustrated. While we could resolve the character mysteries fairly easily and often, the fundamental mystery that began to dominate us was, "What's the purpose behind all this?" Locke keeps talking about this being their destiny—that they've been brought there for a reason. Okay, tell us what it is. What's the reason? What is this place? What is this island? Why is it able to do the things that it does? Why do people see the ghost of their dead fathers or visions from their own past? Why is there some type of healing property in this place? The big fundamental mysteries that we couldn't answer, because they were end game reveals, began to piss people off—and who can blame them? We were pissed and frustrated as writers.

NL: Very interesting. I never heard anyone say that before from that perspective. Did you know when you were going to introduce the "Oceanic Six" that there would inevitably be a second plane crash that would allow you to reset things? And then that shifted you into this whole other time travel element with the island disappearing. What I loved about the show was that once the island vanished I thought, "OK, now anything can happen." Is predictability for you the worst demon of storytelling? I felt whenever I was watching that I thought I knew where it was going, but then it didn't go there which I liked because it was always surprising to me.

DL: To answer your question, what I preach is that the perfect twist is the one that half the audience might have guessed—and it doesn't mean that half the audience does guess it and the other half doesn't. You have to lay enough track for them to anticipate it. If you do something and you haven't established any precedent for it at all, it'll feel arbitrary and unfair or it's just a twist for twist's sake. So you need to have that *Sixth Sense* moment when Bruce Willis puts his hand on the doorknob, and you go through the entire movie and say, "Oh my god, this is fair. They totally set up this idea all the way through." The idea of time travel—we knew we were going to do it from early on, but we also knew that if we did it too early on, we would alienate that part of the audience who thinks they don't like science fiction. We had to invest the audience in the characters before we started taking them down that road, but there were moments as early as the end of season 1 and season 2 where Sayid [Naveen Andrews] finds a radio and he hears like a Glenn Miller broadcast or we were talking about electromagnetic disturbances all along. As soon as we introduced Candle's [Dr. Marvin Candle played by François Chau] first film, embedded in the idea of what the Dharma Initiative was doing there was time space experimentation, and clearly by the premiere of the third season when Desmond [Henry Ian Cusick] was basically running through the jungle naked. He then had the ability to see and predict Charlie's imminent death. Our first time travel episode was a Desmond flashback episode early in season 3. Season 4 was much more committed to the idea. We were laying track for the idea that this was where the show was going to go. And when it went there and we did time travel, it was going to be non-paradoxical time travel where you couldn't change the past or the present or the future. Everything was fixed. This is all the way that it happened before. So we felt that by the time you started seeing craziness like the island disappearing, that the show, as unpredictable as it might be, had prepared you for the possibility that such a thing might happen.

NL: I agree.

DL: Not everybody does, but I'm glad you do.

NL: I did. It was like a ride which I always wanted to stay on. I felt that the storytelling was so confident. I was fully invested in the characters, but there were also motifs that kept bringing me back like the extreme close-up of the eyeball which was how the show started and how it ended. I always felt like there was going to be this cosmic, psychological, metaphysical connection to everything which kept pulling me through. Did you invent the flash-sideways? I'd never seen that before.

DL: Invent is a bold word. I think that everything we've ever done has been done before in some sense. We had known for a couple years that the audience was very interested in this idea of purgatory. And the reason they were so interested in it was because the whole show was a metaphor for purgatory. In fact, the characters were openly talking through the pilot, and in the first couple of episodes after the pilot, in that language. So Jack would say, sitting down with Kate, "We all died in that plane crash. Everything about who we were has died and now we have this chance to basically reinvent ourselves. Let's take it." He wasn't speaking literally, he didn't think that he was dead, but the audience took that ball and ran with it. We always felt that the end game of the show had to be a meditation on the afterlife and since this island is a metaphysical, metaspiritual place, we wanted to examine that. We also knew that per the Lynchian concept of "let's not get too weird" or "lose people," because the show was already ambiguous enough as is, that we had to offer a Trojan horse by which to present that mechanism. If we're going to do fifteen minutes of story every episode in the final season that takes place in a projected afterlife, depending upon what your interpretation of that is, we have to couch it as something else.

So the fifth season became an exercise in setting up that Trojan horse. What if they were able to avert this incident? That basically created the hatch in the first place, and if they were able to avert that incident then they never would have crashed on the island, so we're going to show you what their lives would be like if they had never crashed. Then, very quickly in the final season, we began to establish that the idea transcended, "what if they didn't crash land on the island?" because quite obviously their lives were different in small, but noticeable ways. Jack had a son, for example, which he never did before. Or Locke was married to Helen [Katey Sagal] or Ben Linus [Michael Emerson] was a school teacher. The audience began to go, "Well, this feels like it's much more far-reaching than just 'what if they never crashed on the island?'" How do we account for these other differences? And the answer for that was not a scientific answer; it was a metaphysical/spiritual answer which, as you know, created a significant amount of controversy surrounding the show. But that's what we wanted to do, and we were committed to that idea for quite some time. I can't tell you exactly when we first had that idea, but we'd known from very early on that we wanted to present what the audience was calling purgatory in a very real way in the final season of the show. We knew that Jack was going to die and that he would be the primary conduit by which we showed that. I think that we had basically burned all the flashback stories and flash-forward stories that we wanted to do, so that created one final and ultimately very exciting option for us.

NL: How did you keep track of all of this? The audience of this book is going to be storytellers and aspiring screenwriters. It became so complex with the different timelines and characters' stories. Beyond a whiteboard, I'm sure there were lines and different color cards. How did you keep track of it in your mind and for the team?

DL: The answer is that I didn't nor did Carlton. I think that the writers were so busy just making the show and constructing the scripts that the actual organizational principle of the show had to be maintained by someone else and that was a guy by the name of Gregg Nations. He had this Rainman-like ability to completely and totally keep all of this straight. So that anytime we asked him a question, he would have the answer based on the precedent that the show had already spoken or it was already in canon. Or he would say, "Well, you said this back in season 3, and it would be pretty hard to undo that and get out from under that." He had to keep all of these timelines and vast character crosses straight because we constantly kept going back to the well. Greg managed the bible as it were.

NL: Are there any things that you learned from doing six seasons of sustaining an overarching mystery? Is there anything you learned that you might take into your next episodic series project? Anything you might have done differently?

DL: That's always such a loaded question, and I think it's a fair question to be asking. I think the more appropriate question is the way that you phrased it moving forward: "Is there anything I would do differently on the next one based on knowledge that I learned about *Lost*?" I don't feel like I can lay out any specific lesson because what I would say is on one side—and it would be: "Just know exactly where you are going at all times. Know exactly what the ending is going to be and how many episodes it's going to take for you to get there, so that you can meticulously plan." But when you say that, you're not allowing for the plan to go wrong. It always does—that's just the nature of life. You wake up in the morning and you get out of bed and you say, "This is what I'm going to do today," but your plan doesn't take into account anybody else's plan conflicting with it or just random happenstance or your car not starting or there being an accident on the freeway or you getting sick. There are just too many wild cards. I think it's finding that balance and that level of confidence in yourself to say, "This is what I want to do, this is what my gut is telling me is right. It's probably not going to work out exactly the way I want it to, but I'm going to stick to this as much as humanly possible." At the end of the day, I do think that the experience I gained on the show is much more valuable than any lesson that I gained from it. Every time we made a mistake, there was a significant amount of back and forth before we made it, in terms of whether or not we should do this: "I'm not sure this feels right. Should we do this? You know what? We're going to do it anyway." I would feel much more trusting of that instinct in the future.

13

BLUEPRINT YOUR STRUCTURE

Television scripts vary in numbers of acts depending upon the type of show—sitcom, one-hour drama, single-camera dramedy, MOWs ("movies of the week" made for television), and so on. Broadcast networks (ABC, CBS, NBC, and FOX) and basic cable networks (such as AMC, A&E, FX, TNT, and USA) are supported by advertising, with commercial breaks interrupting the drama or comedy. Premium cable networks (HBO, Showtime, and Starz) are subscriber supported and have no commercial breaks.

Up until about ten years ago, virtually all sitcoms were two acts and all one-hour drama series were structured with four acts. In 2013, these basic templates have changed in order to satisfy network programming, advertisers, and viewers' shorter attention spans.

It's not difficult to predict where this is all going as more viewers are watching their favorite shows online—via computer, iPad, smart phone—thus enabling them to skip over commercials. "Binge viewing" is also becoming more prevalent. *House of Cards* premiered and made available its entire first season simultaneously. Over the next few years, we'll start seeing fewer commercials and more product placement or embedded advertising (as part of the content of a show). And eventually, you'll be able to "like" an item of clothing or accessory, "click" on that item while the series is playing, and immediately be linked to a website to purchase the items—all with a stored credit card and another click on your mouse or remote. Before you know it, a TV set will become as obsolete as a typewriter or VCR. Your computer will be your window to all entertainment. Stay tuned.

Structural Formats

Each show fits into a particular format that allows it to be easily identified. Dramas are generally classified as either procedurals or serials. Procedurals, such as *Law & Order*, *CSI*, *The Mentalist*, and *House, M.D.*, deal with a new case each week. At the end of the episode, the cops will catch the bad guy, the lawyers will win their case (or not), or the doctors will save their patient (or not). Even though procedurals are much more plot-driven, sometimes they break format and deal with more personal stories. In the season 6 finale of *Law & Order* titled "Aftershock," the entire episode showed how the cops and lawyers spent a personal day after witnessing an execution, a big departure from the follow-the-string, investigatory backbone of the series.

Serials contain more complex storylines that span multiple episodes or even seasons. Most serials use a *direct pickup* (or DPU) in which each new episode starts *exactly* where the previous episode ended (examples: *Weeds*, *House of Cards*, and the latter part of season 2 of *Scandal*).

Other serials, such as *Breaking Bad*, *Mad Men*, and *Homeland*, are looser and begin new episodes in what might be the next day or week or month. *Mad Men* jumped ahead a year between seasons. Season 5 of *Desperate Housewives* made a quantum leap five years after the previous season and used flashbacks to bring the audience up to speed.

In the first season of *The Wire*, the cops' mission is to arrest drug kingpin Avon Barksdale (Wood Harris), but they don't even know what he looks like! It's not until the third episode that the police are able to locate an old photo of him. In a procedural where plots move much quicker, Avon would have likely been captured in one or two episodes.

Comedies are generally classified as either multi-camera or single-camera sitcoms. Multi-cam sitcoms, the more traditional format, are filmed (but usually videotaped) with four cameras running simultaneously on a stage in front of a studio audience, for example, *The Big Bang Theory*, *2 Broke Girls*, *Friends*, and *Two and a Half Men*. (*I Love Lucy* was one of the pioneers of this format, with Desi and Lucy shooting each episode in chronological order for a live, in-studio audience to enjoy each episode like theater.) Many classic sitcoms (*Taxi*, *Cheers*, *Happy Days*) were shot on 35 mm film for a rich, movie look, but that's a rarity in 2013 due to efficiency and expense.

Single-cam sitcoms such as *The Office*, *Modern Family*, and *30 Rock*, employ one camera and tend to shoot more characters, scenes, and locations. Single-cam shows are more prevalent today.

To wrap your brain around the difference between multi-camera and single camera sitcoms, here's an example I like to use.

On a multi-camera sitcom, we're generally *inside* one of two or three main locations: the hangout/workplace, the apartment/house, and one "swing set" (optional interior location) depending on the story. If a character on a multi-camera gets mugged in the park, he will rush into a room out of breath, very distraught with ripped clothing, and explain to whoever's present what just happened.

On a single-camera sitcom or dramedy, we would probably get to go outside to the park and see the mugging take place, along with the chase, and maybe even the race back to the apartment where he would *then* recount the story but with far less detail because we would have already seen it—unless it's revisionist history for comedic effect.

Multi-camera sitcoms are more contained and primarily shot indoors on the same sets week after week. We come to view these places as familiar and iconic. The bar in *Cheers* was *our* bar, too. In fact, for the first two seasons of *Cheers*, we never left the bar. We went into the backroom, Sam Malone's (Ted Danson) office, and maybe a bathroom or alcove. There were stairs leading up to a restaurant above the bar, but we didn't actually go there for many seasons.

Single-camera comedies and dramedies (*Modern Family, Louie, Parks & Recreation, Weeds, Girls*) take us everywhere: inside, outside, up in the air, in the ocean—wherever the story needs to go, we get to go there as well. Animated comedy series (*The Simpsons, Archer, Family Guy*) can take us anywhere the writers can imagine without limitation; if it can be drawn, it can be done. There is also the hybrid sitcom, which blends multi-cam and single-cam characteristics, such as *How I Met Your Mother*.

The ABCs of Episodic Structure

The A Story

Primarily services the central concept of the series—known as the *franchise*. This dominant plotline concerns the principal character(s) and contains the most scenes (or "beats") within the episode. The franchise also serves as the signature—or "sweet spot"—of the series, and offers the most possible evolving plotlines (known as *story engines*) from episode to episode.

In *The Mentalist*, the A story revolves around Patrick Jane (Simon Baker) using his exceptional powers of perception and persuasion to help the California Bureau of Investigation solve a case.

In *Dexter*, the franchise usually deals with vigilante serial killer Dexter Morgan (Michael C. Hall) hunting a vile criminal who eluded justice.

In the sitcom *Arrested Development*, the A story typically consisted of Michael Bluth (Jason Bateman) attempting to keep his eccentric family afloat after his father plunges the family into financial ruin by committing fraud.

The B Story

If the A story services the case and higher external stakes, the B story is usually a personal story, with more internalized, emotional stakes. The B story serves to make the main character relatable and vulnerable.

In *Castle*, Richard Castle (Nathan Fillion) is a multi-millionaire playboy crime novelist who shadows NYPD detectives to get research for his next book. These A stories involve mystery, suspense, and danger. However, he's also a devoted family man, providing for his mother and teenage daughter who both live with him. The B story concerns Castle's interactions with them.

In *Sons of Anarchy*, Jax Teller (Charlie Hunnam) is one of the leaders of the felonious Sons of Anarchy motorcycle club. While the franchise deals with club business (murder, trafficking, etc.), the B story follows Jax's relationship with his girlfriend/wife Tara (Maggie Siff) and his two young sons.

Runners. Shows may also contain less significant C and even D storylines called runners. They might consist of a semi-trivial conflict that's secondary to the franchise, a personal story involving the supporting characters, or a running gag. In a recent episode of *Mad Men*, Peggy Olsen's (Elisabeth Moss) apartment is invaded by a big rat. She struggles throughout the episode to get rid of it. But when the pesky rodent gets caught in a trap and leaves a bloody trail, Peggy desperately calls coworker Stan (Jay R. Ferguson) in the middle of the night for help—even offering him sexual favors in return, but Stan is in bed with another woman and declines. By the end of the episode, the rat problem is solved when Peggy gets a cat. Actually, we don't see her acquire the cat; it's just sitting beside a much calmer Peggy on the sofa at the end of the episode—a good example of *elliptical storytelling* (telling the story "in the cut"). Other *Mad Men* runners include Don and Betty's daughter Sally's (Kiernan Shipka) crush on a teenaged neighbor boy; Don's new actress wife Megan's (Jessica Paré) blossoming soap opera career; Pete's (Vincent Kartheiser) brazenly senile mother. And what about mysterious new colleague Bob Benson (James Wolk)—who may or may not have a crush on Pete—or is he just a passive-aggressive opportunist?

Serials often have several runners because there are more characters to service. In the pilot for *The Sopranos*, Tony (James Gandolfini) passes out from a panic attack during a backyard barbecue, and soon thereafter begins therapy with his psychiatrist, Dr. Jennifer Melfi (Lorraine Braco). Meanwhile, Tony's wife Carmela (Edie Falco) and their daughter Meadow (Jamie-Lynn Sigler) grow further apart; Tony tours an assisted living community with his overbearing mother, Livia (Nancy Marchand); and Tony has a tryst with his mistress. On *The Sopranos,* the A story is usually a mafia crime story that begins and ends with Tony; the B story is usually a personal domestic Sopranos story; and the C and D runners might involve Tony's nephew Christopher Moltisanti (Michael Imperioli), or sister Janice (Aida Turturro), or Uncle Junior (Dominic Chianese) or a more *personal* story about one of his other relatives.

In a subsequent episode, Dr. Melfi's personal life becomes more prominent as she starts seeing her own therapist. In a powerful memorable story arc, Dr. Melfi is raped in a parking garage, and even though she would like nothing more than to tell her client, Tony, about her ordeal so he could hunt down the rapist and exact revenge, she maintains her professional distance and keeps her secret. This is also a good example of how the path of characters from different spheres can intersect in surprising or even shocking ways—which leads us to. . .

Crossover. A, B, and C stories are clearly delineated, but sometimes they intersect. In the two-part season 5 finale of *CSI* (co-written and directed by Quentin Tarantino), the "case of the week" becomes personal when Nick (George Eads), one of the crime scene investigators, gets kidnapped and buried alive. In *The X-Files*, sometimes the paranormal "case of the week" deals directly with Fox Mulder (David Duchovny) and his personal journey to find out what happened to his sister whom he believes was abducted by aliens. In *The Mentalist*, some of the cases lead Patrick one step closer to finding "Red John," the notorious serial killer who murdered his wife and daughter years earlier.

Sometimes B stories or runners become bigger stories. In *Burn Notice*, Michael Westen (Jeffrey Donovan) is a former CIA agent who was framed as a rogue spy. The franchise deals with Michael and his friends (an ex-Navy SEAL and a former IRA member) utilizing their training to help people get out of dangerous situations. The B story tracks Michael's quest to find out who framed him and why. However, there are a few episodes which deal primarily with the overarching mystery of who "burned" Michael.

In *Terriers*, private investigator Hank Dolworth (Donal Logue) tells his partner Britt (Michael Raymond-James) that he thinks he's losing his mind because sometimes things are randomly out of place in his house. It's a runner that begins as passing dialogue, but then escalates when the audience learns someone is sneaking around his house at night. The runner grows again when the mysterious person is revealed to be Hank's schizophrenic sister Stephanie (Karina Logue) who's been secretly living in his attic. The runner grows yet again when the audience discovers that Stephanie is a brilliant MIT graduate who helps Hank solve the big mystery of the show.

In *Breaking Bad*, DEA agent Hank Schrader (Dean Norris) tirelessly searches for the mysterious meth dealer Heisenberg, who is actually his brother-in-law Walter. The storyline of Hank and Walt's ironic relationship has its peaks and valleys. . .until [SPOILER ALERT] mid-season 5 when Hank gets wise to Walt's alter-ego.

Storyline intersections work best when they occur with thematic links. In *Burn Notice*, Michael helps people who've been wronged while he attempts to rectify the injustice done to him. Family is always a strong thematic link. In *The Sopranos*, Tony must balance his mob family and his actual family. In *Sons of Anarchy*, Jax must balance his biker gang family with his actually family. In *Modern Family*, different portraits of nuclear families deal with similar issues.

Tentpoles. Within these format and pilot guidelines exist various structural models. Each model has a different number of tentpoles, which are teasers, act breaks, and tags (a very brief scene/sequence at the end of the episode). Dramas can be four acts, five acts, six acts or even longer (sometimes pilots are extended to properly set up the show), with or without a teaser and a tag. Comedies can be two acts, three acts, or four acts, with or without a teaser and a tag.

The teaser sets up the hook. The first act establishes the problem that the main characters will face. In the middle acts, the problem complicates, the stakes intensify, and the solution seems impossible. In the final act, the story reaches its climax and resolves. The tag is as an epilogue that puts a button on the episode. It may be a runner that pays off, or it could be a *cliffhanger* that services the franchise or the B story.

Each act generally has four or five beats, and ideally ends on the A story about the main character's dilemma. The franchise (A story) tracks throughout every act, while the B story and runners can be sparse. Occasionally, you might elect to end an act on a potent B story. It's extremely rare to end an act on a C story. If the story is worthy of an act break, then it's not your C story—it's probably more of your A or B story.

In the pilot for *Breaking Bad*, {**the teaser**} opens with Walter White's madcap dash through the desert in an RV-turned-meth lab. Amid the growing sound of sirens, Walter prepares himself for a police confrontation {**the hook**}. Act 1 jumps back three weeks earlier to orient the audience in Walter's normal world. He's turned fifty years old, he has a pregnant wife, a teenage son with cerebral palsy, and he needs money {**the problem**}. He supplements his high school chemistry teacher salary by working at a carwash. His problems complicate when he's diagnosed with terminal cancer {**problems and stakes intensify**}. Now Walter needs money for his family before he dies. After watching news footage of a DEA meth lab drug bust worth $700,000, Walter asks his brother-in-law Hank if he can go on a ride-along so he can surreptitiously learn how a drug operation works. During the ride-along, Walter encounters Jesse Pinkman (Aaron Paul), a former student of his who narrowly escapes a DEA raid. Walter convinces Jesse to team up. "You know the business, and I know the chemistry." Walter and Jesse cook meth, but they have no distribution in place. Jesse goes to former partners in crime to sell the product, but the former partners think Jesse double-crossed them, so they intend to kill Jesse and Walter {**impossible solution**}. Walter improvises and kills the former partners in the RV with a chemical mixture. A fire begins to rage in nearby shrubbery because one of Jesse's former partners had tossed his cigarette out the window. Walter drives the RV as far away from the fire as possible, which brings the episode full circle back to the teaser. As the sirens approach, Walter discovers the sirens were from fire trucks racing toward the blaze created by the cigarette, not police cars {**climax**}. Jesse and he are off the hook—for now {**resolution**}. The pilot wraps up with Walter withholding information from his wife about his new business as well as his cancer. This sets up the rift that slowly grows in his marriage {**the epilogue**[1]}.

The franchise is Walter building his drug business. The B story is Walter's struggle to balance family life with his secret enterprise. Some of the runners include Walter dealing with his cancer, gleaning (and hiding) information from Hank, and working with his impetuous new partner Jesse.

Some showrunners of premium cable series still use act breaks in their scripts—even though there will be no commercials. Why? Because writing in act breaks can be highly beneficial to telling a story that's at once riveting on the plot level *and* fits in the allotted time slot. Pick up a script from the HBO series *Deadwood* (created/written/showrun by David Milch) and you'll see four clearly delineated acts. On the other hand, examine a script for the Showtime series *Homeland* and lo and behold: no act breaks.

Here's a quick, random sampling of different structural breakdowns.

One-Hour Dramas

Breaking Bad: teaser + 4 acts
CSI: teaser + 4 acts
The Good Wife: long teaser + 4 acts
Grey's Anatomy: no teaser. 6 acts.
Justified: teaser + 5 acts + tag
The Mentalist: teaser + 4 acts
Once Upon a Time: no teaser. 6 acts.
Parenthood: teaser + 5 acts
Royal Pains: 7 acts
Scandal: 6 acts. Short first act functions as teaser, followed by title card.

Sitcoms

The Big Bang Theory: cold opening + 2 acts + tag
Modern Family: 4 acts (short act one functions as a teaser)
Two and a Half Men: cold opening + 2 acts + tag

---

[1] In a sitcom, the epilogue is known as the "tag."

The Teleplay: Basic Guidelines

Most half-hour, multi-camera sitcoms are written in double-spaced sitcom format and run around fifty pages.

Most half-hour, single-camera comedies and dramedies are written in single-spaced screenplay format and run approximately thirty pages.

Most one-hour drama series teleplays run between forty-eight and sixty-three pages. However, many pilot episodes run longer and then get cut down during the production process, especially in post-production. Teleplays for *Moonlighting, The West Wing,* and *E.R.* could run eighty-five pages or more due to their fast pacing and rapid-fire dialogue. But even at that higher page count, the produced show would fit into its one-hour time slot.

It's not always easy to gauge the actual length of an episode until it's shot. The rhythm of the actors' deliveries, the pacing of scenes, editing styles, and musical interludes (such as on *Glee*) can impact actual length versus page length. For this reason, once a show is up and running and becomes a well-oiled machine, a series' script supervisor will read the script and do a "timing" or estimate of the actual length of the episode. For a writer who's trying to sell an original pilot script, it's usually best to work within the basic page length guidelines (see "basic guidelines"). Aaron Sorkin gets to break the rules and do his own thing because he's won Emmys and Oscars and is a genius.

When writing a pilot for a sitcom or one-hour drama, I advise you to study current, successful series that have the same tone, rhythm, and pacing that you'd like your series to have—and study the structure. Does it use a "teaser"? How many act breaks? How many scenes per act? Is there a "tag" or epilogue?

For *script* formatting—that is, how the words need to look on the page, line spacing, indentation, pagination, please read as many teleplays as you can and emulate the script format. I also recommend an excellent book that delves into this area with specific examples: *Write to TV* by Martie Cook.

Writing a teleplay without an outline is like going on a road trip without a map. But, in the TV biz, the schedule necessitates the most direct, expeditious route. If you're hoping to succeed as a TV writer, learn to embrace the outlining process; it's not only a valuable GPS to keep your script on track, but it's also compulsory (for the studio and network to sign off on the script). No outline, no paycheck. Never bite the hand that feeds you.

INTERVIEW: Glen Mazzara

Glen Mazzara Credits

Best known for:

The Walking Dead (Executive Producer/Writer) 2010–2012
    WGA Nominated (New Series) 2011
Hawthorne (Executive Producer/Writer) 2009–2011
Criminal Minds: Suspect Behavior (Consulting Producer/Writer) 2011
Crash (Executive Producer/Consulting Producer/Writer) 2008–2009
Life (Co-Executive Producer/Writer) 2007
The Shield (Executive Producer/Supervising Producer/Co-executive Producer/Writer) 2002–2007
Nash Bridges (Writer) 1998–2000

NL: *The Walking Dead* is based upon comic books. In plotting your series, how much are you basing on the source material, and how much are you inventing?

GM: We invent most of the story we have here whole cloth. We crib major characters and plot points or settings from the comic books. So, for example, in the upcoming season, we introduce two major settings: one is the prison that Rick (Andrew Lincoln) and the core group of survivors we're following discover and decide to take over and set up shop there. There are two major characters that are being introduced. One is Michonne (Danai Gurira) who is an African American woman. We consider her a soldier. She carries a Katana sword and she's a fan favorite. So we've now worked her into the show.

We also have The Governor (David Morrissey), who is an arch villain in the comic book and he is the leader of a walled community called Woodbury. Our version of The Governor is very different. Our version of Michonne is very different. The way our characters are introduced. What they say. That's all original to the show. We are doing our takes on these characters because we feel the fans want to see those characters dramatized, but we really make that material our own.

NL: In season 1, the first six episodes move very quickly. It seems like each one was almost like a feature film, and as much as I liked it, I thought it might be difficult to sustain that. So my next question is about pacing. How do you gauge the pace of the storytelling?

GM: That's a great question because I think when the show first came out I was only a freelance writer that first season. I think there was a need to tell as much and to grab the audience because they only had a six-episode order. When we went to thirteen for the next year, we decided to slow down the pace and push in to examine some of the characters' lives. This show developed into a character-driven cable drama that fit nicely into that paradigm. However, there's a larger audience wanting to watch the show and those are horror fans and comic book fans. It's a lot of youth. We have a much more eclectic audience than the typical cable drama audience. So when I became showrunner in the middle of season 2, my natural tendency was to put more story in. This is something that I really learned on *The Shield* and the first show I started on, *Nash Bridges*, where I was writing partners with Shawn Ryan. And *Nash Bridges* became a great training ground for other showrunners: Shawn and Damon Lindelof. So I wanted to move up the story and pack it in. At the time we started doing that in the second half of the season, we were airing the first half of the season, while we were already shooting the second half. And the feedback from the audience came in that it was very frustrating, frustratingly slow. That pacing was not something that the audience was responding to.

So when the second half of the season came out and I was responsible for all of those scripts, it seemed to answer an audience need, but we were already ahead of the audience. I believe we were responding to something we felt slowed the brakes on a little too much. I think we had to define what is the story we're telling. We're talking about an apocalypse. We're talking about a civilization. We're talking about desperate survivors. So the stakes are higher than a living room drama, and we were doing a little bit too much of a living room drama. So we started increasing the pace, and by the end of the season, it was pretty much where I wanted it to be. Moving forward, it's interesting because I do want to pack a lot of story in and the risk is that you reach a tipping point where it's too unrealistic or too fantastic or too shocking for the audience. It's my job as a showrunner to say what is too much. I have to go with my gut. We do have episodes that I describe as a pool in a rainstorm, it's just about at that level, but it's not spilling over yet. I feel that it's my job to both push the material and to make it exciting and surprising and satisfying the horror element which is unique to this show. This is the first show that I've worked on with a horror element. And yet, you want it to stay grounded and for it to feel real. This is really a debate that I have every day with our cast, our directors, our producers, and our network and studio, AMC. I would say that is one of the biggest challenges of my job right now.

NL: It's a balancing act.

GM: Right. And the way I approach that is that I do have an overall arc for the season. But I focus on each individual episode and there are elements that I want to have associated with the show or incorporated into the show, but I can't fit every thing in every episode. So instead I have sixteen episodes where some episodes can be a little more character focused and others could be a little more horror focused or action focused. Some could have some comedy. By the end of the season, I think the total experience will be satisfying.

NL: How vital to you is an overarching central mystery? Because in season 2, you had a few mysteries going. You had "What happened to Sophia (Madison Lintz)?" You had "What did Dr. Jenner (Noah Emmerich) whisper to Rick?" Etc.

GM: In a genre show like this that has a horror and science fiction element, the fans in the audience are very, very interested in mysteries. They want to know the rules of the game. They want to be convinced that this is a worthwhile ride. That the end of this experience will be satisfying. And there have been other genre shows that have not necessarily delivered a satisfying experience and that is disappointing to a very, very dedicated fan base. I'm aware of that. However, I am not that type of a writer. I don't feel that the mysteries are why people watch TV. Because my bottom line rule of TV is that it's cool people doing cool shit every week. That's it. Let's break down that sentence. Cool people doing—doing—cool stuff every week. Not learning cool stuff every week. They need to be active. To have their backs against the wall. To be in dire straits. They need to made desperate choices. David Mamet says that drama is basically a decision between two horrible choices. That is certainly something that we use on this show. I've worked on a number of other TV shows in which writing staffs try to go for the big payoff and revelation. That only works sometimes. I actually think there's too much emphasis on revealing the answer to a mystery as being satisfying to an audience. We didn't do it on *The Shield*, I'm not really interested in doing it here. For example, "What caused the outbreak?" is a question that people ask a lot. Who cares? That's not part of the original comic book. So, what do you do with the information that you have? If you look at the episodes in the back half of season 2, I think that that's important. That's the type of storytelling that I'm very interested in.

Let's look at the major revelation of season 2 that Sophia's in the barn. Sophia steps out of the barn. We could have stopped the show there. Instead everyone is paralyzed by the horror that she was right under their noses and Rick, who doesn't know what to do, steps forward into a leadership position and does what no one else is able to do. This revelation led to character action and then the show ended. So to me, that was a scene of character action, not revelation.

NL: What about the role of theme? The first six episodes seemed to very much be about the theme of survival.

GM: Yes.

NL: In season 2 what emerged for me were the themes of hope and faith. There's a whole episode where they go to a church. Then there's thematics where the A, B, and C stories connect. How aware and deliberate are you about thematic links between the stories?

GM: When we are trying to achieve something artistic, you let some type of energy or spirit flow through you. You have to be able to listen and you let the work reveal itself to you. And the minute you try to inject your ego into that, it actually screws things up. *The Walking Dead* is the first show for me where theme is important as we're developing it. On other shows, particularly *The Shield*, the theme became apparent very, very late in the game. When we sat down to break season 3, we had some ideas and I had some larger themes that I wanted to examine. When I pitched it out to all of the other, non-writing producers and then to AMC, I did approach it thematically and usually when I've done that, it usually feels like horseshit. It feels like something I'm just telling an executive so that get what box the show is in. But it turned out to be true and there were certain themes on season 3 that we keep coming back to. It just works. What we try to do is focus on the story, and then when we step back, we see that the theme is there. And now we have confidence in the story. We do not try to construct the story to fit the theme.

We broke this season in detail for eight episodes and then we went off and wrote them. And then when we came back in to fill in those next episodes, the theme still applied and was still connecting. We've had two themes for this season, and they've both been very necessary lifelines to get through all the confusion of the daily making of the show.

NL: Are Rick stories always going to be your A stories?

GM: There are different forms to tell a TV story. And in an ensemble piece like this, you'd usually have the Rick character as the A story, someone else would be the B story, and someone else would be the C story and then you would intertwine those stories. That doesn't always equal a theme. It just pushes the ball further on each one. That is the case with *Game of Thrones*. When you watch an episode, you watch an installment where all of your characters advance, but that episode may or may not be a total story within itself. We do have elements of that A, B, C story here, but I think for the most part we reject it. I think we look at each episode as having a beginning, middle, and an end—and whatever fits to that theme for that episode. For instance, the episode when the girl steps out of the barn and when the herd overruns the farm at the end. Each character has a place in that larger story. This is the first time I've ever worked on a show that's rejected the traditional A, B, and C story format—and gone for more of just "What is this episode about?" What gets lost in that is perhaps the opportunity to examine particular characters. Sometimes minor characters just stay minor characters. That's a risk, but I feel the story drive of the engine is strong enough that it will be satisfying to the audience.

NL: In season 2, you started to introduce some flashback elements.

GM: When I joined the writing staff, there was a tendency to try to embrace those flashbacks. I have rejected those flashbacks, so in the episodes where I've been a showrunner—and I'm open to doing flashbacks—but I've rejected them here because I don't believe that flashbacks are an element of horror films. They're an element of science fiction films. When you introduce flashback, you start playing with the space-time continuum. I think it takes you away from the visceral and immediate horror. At the end of the day, I feel that *The Walking Dead* has to be a horror show—that's what's unique about it. I don't find flashbacks scary. They were just giving more information or explaining the rules. Part of the difference between the first half of the season and the second half is that I focused on the horror elements.

NL: If you're not identifying things as A, B, and C stories, what's the process of doing outlines and beat sheets?

GM: I don't use outlines. I've been taught to react or follow my gut from reviewing a written script. An outline is an interesting tool, but I can't shoot an outline. It's really about the script and the execution of the script. I really feel like outlines take up a lot of valuable writing time and that they are used to engage TV and studio executives. So that they can cover their asses and know what's being written. None of their notes are applicable to script. So we write a two- to three-page story document and send it over to the network. It's written in paragraph form. It's what we're going for in the episode and what the major set pieces are. I leave it to the individual writer to write it. What I do is work off of the beat sheet, I can work off of two or three words per beat. For example, "Rick kills Shane." I don't need to flesh that out. All script problems, for me on *The Walking Dead*, come down to structure problems. But if the structure is right and you start in a linear fashion, I have confidence in the writing staff that we can execute it. There was one scene I wasn't happy with and I went back in to re-beat it and discovered that it was a structure problem. And a beat sheet for me is a piece of scrap paper with ten words.

NL: In the pilot episode, there weren't any act breaks. It was regular screenplay format. But now you're using four acts, correct?

GM: We use five acts actually. They split us into a teaser and five acts. There were four acts—good catch. AMC wanted an additional commercial break. Let me say this though, I absolutely love TV. I'm a student of TV. I loved TV when I was a kid. I'm more of a TV guy than a film guy. So when I first joined the show, those act breaks were not important, and I feel that those act breaks are an important part of the viewing process. What do you go off of?

I learned this from Nash Bridges and The Shield, which had very, very good act breaks. It forces you to make choices. It's about compression. We pack in a tremendous amount of story into forty-two minutes. People have that expectation, and yet you don't want to do it in a way that it feels like an assault—you need breathing room.

Look at our season finale last year [in 2011], there was a huge zombie attack in the first half, and yet in the second half, there was very little zombie stuff except for Andrea (Laurie Holden) in the woods. That's very different, so you really have to make all those act breaks count.

I do find that TV shows that embrace the TV form embrace the act break. There are some people who say, "Our TV show is not really TV. It's like making a film every week." Which I find disparaging to the art of TV, and I could certainly say if you look at all the great TV shows on TV today, *Mad Men, Breaking Bad, Game of Thrones, Homeland,* hopefully, *The Walking Dead,* and you count the total number of hours that those shows produce, you'll probably come up with seventy or eighty hours. In turn, name fifty feature films this year. So the action is all in TV right now, it's all in TV. And yet, there's this snooty attitude in TV that when it's good, it's rejecting itself as TV. "It's not TV, it's HBO." No, it's TV and it's very well done.

People really, really care about this show. They feel emotionally invested. So much so that they cry when our characters die. But name a horror film when you cried when a character died. That doesn't happen. You never cry in a horror film.

NL: What are the biggest challenges of running a show?

GM: I'm sure a lot of people tell you time management. I don't think that's necessarily true. I think one of the biggest challenges for me is to not settle. There are a lot of people, including myself, I have fifteen producers on this show. They're all talented. They're all smart. Some write, some don't. They all have strong opinions. It's hard for me to get fifteen people to agree. It's hard to listen to all of their notes. I have a very open door policy, in which I invite everyone's notes, from the cast, from the director, and hopefully, I get a lot of input while the script is being written and I can then use the best ideas. It's hard to (1) not take a barrage of criticism and feedback personally and (2) to make sure that everyone feels heard and yet not lose my vision as the showrunner by trying to make everyone else happy. I still have to realize that I have to be the singular vision for the show—that's my job and that's how the show will hopefully be successful. The rule that I've been following is that I only do something if I love it. If I absolutely love it, I believe it will work, and right now, I'm in that position. I think in the past on other shows, I tried to be too amenable to other people, too accommodating, and perhaps I didn't stick to my guns. But you never want to be a tyrant or a dictator or shut down someone else's creative voice.

The other challenge is to keep the show grounded—to keep it real. And yet, to deliver something that has a horror element. Part of horror and science fiction is that there's a sense of high adventure. You want action, but you never want it to tip over into something unreal or ludicrous. If you have a clear direction, all the other stuff works itself out. And you go for a vacation at the end. Showrunners don't sleep.

NL: Do you do a polish or a final pass of each script?

GM: I do an extensive polish on every script, if needed. There are many times that I will say I write a lot of each script. I don't put my name on it. I have several scripts this year that I've written every word of and have not put my name on them. I have an executive producer credit on all of those. It's my job as the showrunner. When I first became a showrunner on *Crash*, I didn't rewrite some of the writers because I liked them. But then, I realized that part of my responsibilities as a showrunner is to be the voice of the show. So if a show comes out and it's not necessarily my voice, the producers, the cast, and the crew might feel that it's off. So no matter how well written—we do have a very, very talented writing staff. I'm very proud of them. But I also have a very specific thing in mind. I also try to push the material. I very often write stuff that people don't think is going to play because I have a very stripped down writing style. So when people read it, it feels sparse and a little awkward and yet what I'm doing is writing directly for camera. I write the way I know the scene is going to be edited. So when you read my writing, you say, "Wow, I saw that." You see everything there—including the silences and the looks from the actors. I'm writing less and less dialogue. I'm just letting the picture tell the story. I've gotten better at suppressing my ego and letting the story reveal itself through the writing.

One of the scenes I was really happy with is when Rick finds Carl (Chandler Riggs) sitting in a hayloft and he gives him a gun. He says, "I wish I had more to say, my dad was good like that." You just get a whole sense of who this man's father was. We know that Carl has lost his grandfather and that Rick is an inarticulate hero. And he gives him a gun which ends up being the gun that will kill Shane (Jon Bernthal). It's a very underwritten scene, and if you look at how it's filmed, we just set up a camera. Man enters frame and sits next to his son. Push in for a little coverage and get out. It's very simple. On the page, when you read it, it might read a little flat, but then when it comes together, it plays, it's right. I'm very careful not to overwrite, particularly on this show where things can get overwritten.

NL: What's the best thing about being a showrunner?

GM: I have two answers. One, I realize how lucky I am and that I have a great gift in the sense that I get to do what I want and tell stories and work with talented writers and directors and that some studio puts up millions of dollars to make each episode. There are so many filmmakers and artists around the world trying to figure out how to do their art. I can't take that for granted. I get to come to work every day and whatever I am passionate about will get made right now. And that's very, very exciting. So I see being a showrunner as a gift. Last week, I went to Atlanta and I screened our season premiere for the cast and crew. Everybody cares so much about this show. Every part of the organization just loves *The Walking Dead*. And I'm the one person in the entire organization that gets to see everybody else do their best work. So I get to see the writer who's excited about the fact that they found a great scene or they've got a great pitch. I get to see the casting agents excited because we got the perfect person. I get to see the director excited and the cameraman excited because he's going to get the best take. And it goes all the way through special effects and the music. The composer, Bear McCreary, is fantastic. It goes all the way to this little studio at Warner Bros.—this little sound mixing room— and you walk in there and there are three guys and they say, "We just love this episode. It's the best show we've worked on." And they're so excited. I'm the only person who gets to go through the whole process from inception to completion. That's really special. That's what's unique about being a showrunner.

Top Television Series by Structure

Series	Year	Format	Network	Structure	Pilot	Showrunner
2 Broke Girls	2011	multi-cam	CBS	cold open + 2 acts + tag	premise	Michael Patrick King, Whitney Cummings
24	2001	serial	FOX	5 acts	premise	Joel Surnow, Robert Cochran
American Horror Story	2011	serial/anthology	FX	teaser + 4 acts	premise	Ryan Murphy, Brad Falchuk
Big Bang Theory, The	2007	multi-cam	CBS	cold open + 2 acts + tag	premise	Bill Prady
Boardwalk Empire	2010	serial	HBO	no act breaks	premise	Terence Winter
Bones	2005	procedural/serial	FOX	teaser + 4 acts	premise	Hart Hanson, Stephen Nathan
Breaking Bad	2008	serial	AMC	teaser + 4 acts	premise	Vince Gilligan
CSI: Crime Scene Investigation	2002	procedural	CBS	teaser + 4 acts	non-premise	Anthony Zuiker, Carol Mendelsohn, Ann Donohue
Dallas	2012	serial	TNT	teaser + 4 acts + tag	premise	Cynthia Cidre
Damages	2007	serial	FX	teaser + 4 acts	hybrid	Todd A. Kessler, Glenn Kessler, Daniel Zelman
Deadwood	2004	serial	HBO	no act breaks	premise	David Milch,
Dexter	2006	procedural/serial	Showtime	no act breaks	non-premise	Scott Buck, Chip Johannessen
Downton Abbey	2011	serial	PBS	no act breaks	non-premise	Julian Fellowes
Entourage	2004	single-cam (serial)	HBO	no act breaks	non-premise	Doug Ellin

E.R.	1994	procedural/serial	NBC	teaser + 4 acts	non-premise	John Wells
Friday Night Lights	2006	serial	NBC/The 101	teaser + 5 acts	premise	Jason Katims
Game of Thrones	2011	serial	HBO	no act breaks	non-premise	David Benioff, D.B. Weiss
Girls	2012	single-cam (serial)	HBO	no act breaks	premise	Lena Dunham
Good Wife, The	2009	procedural/serial	CBS	long teaser + 4 acts	hybrid	Robert King, Michelle King
Gossip Girl	2007	serial	The CW	teaser + 5 acts	premise	Josh Schwartz, Stephanie Savage
Grey's Anatomy	2005	procedural/serial	ABC	6 acts	premise	Shonda Rhimes
Homeland	2011	serial	Showtime	no act breaks	premise	Howard Gordon, Alex Gansa
House of Cards	2013	serial	Netflix	no act breaks	premise	Beau Willimon
House, M.D.	2004	procedural/serial	FOX	teaser + 4 acts	non-premise	David Shore
Justified	2010	serial	FX	teaser + 5 acts + tag	premise	Graham Yost
Killing, The	2011	serial	AMC	teaser + 5 acts	premise	Veena Sud, Dawn Prestwich, Nicole Yorkin
Law & Order	1990	procedural	NBC	teaser + 4 acts	non-premise	Dick Wolf, René Balcer, Peter Jankowski
Lost	2004	serial	ABC	teaser + 5 acts	premise	Damon Lindelof, Carlton Cuse
Mad Men	2007	serial	AMC	no act breaks	non-premise	Matt Weiner
Mentalist, The	2008	procedural/serial	CBS	teaser + 4 acts	non-premise	Bruno Heller
Modern Family	2009	single-cam	ABC	4 acts (short first act)	non-premise	Steven Levitan, Christopher Lloyd
NCIS	2003	procedural	CBS	teaser + 4 acts	non-premise	Shane Brenna
Nurse Jackie	2009	single-cam (serial)	Showtime	no act breaks	non-premise	Liz Brixius, Linda Wallem

(Continued)

Series	Year	Format	Network	Structure	Pilot	Showrunner
Office, The	2005	single-cam	NBC	cold open + 2 acts	non-premise	Greg Daniels
Once Upon a Time	2011	serial	ABC	6 acts	premise	Edward Kitsis, Adam Horowitz
Parenthood	2010	serial	NBC	teaser + 5 acts	non-premise	Jason Katims
Revenge	2011	serial	ABC	6 acts	premise	Mike Kelley
Rizzoli & Isles	2010	procedural/serial	TNT	6 acts	non-premise	Janet Tamaro
Royal Pains	2009	procedural/serial	USA	7 acts	premise	Paul Frank, Rich Frank, Michael Rauch
Scandal	2012	procedural/serial	ABC	6 acts (short first act)	non-premise	Shonda Rhimes
Sopranos, The	1999	serial	HBO	no act breaks	premise	David Chase
Touch	2012	procedural/serial	FOX	teaser + 5 acts	premise	Tim Kring
Two and a Half Men	2003	multi-cam	CBS	cold open + 2 acts + tag	premise	Chuck Lorre, Lee Aronsohn
Walking Dead, The	2010	serial	AMC	teaser + 4 acts	hybrid	Frank Darabont, Glen Mazzara
Weeds	2005	single-cam (serial)	Showtime	no act breaks	non-premise	Jenji Kohan
West Wing, The	1999	procedural/serial	NBC	teaser + 4 acts	non-premise	Aaron Sorkin, John Wells
X-Files, The	1993	procedural	FOX	teaser + 4 acts	premise	Chris Carter

14

UNIFY STORYLINES (VIA THEME)

Theme is a central idea expressed through action. It can add dimension and resonance. In episodic television, theme is the glue that holds multiple, and sometimes divergent, storylines together.

Theme is what the story is *really* about. Not just a series of events, but some kind of underlying universal truth about life.

Themes are always related to power—and sometimes that's the power of the human spirit. Such themes include the following: can good triumph over evil? Can one person make a difference? Love conquers all; no man is an island; crime doesn't pay. The list goes on . . .

On a TV series, theme can be articulated by a character—through dialogue or V.O. or some other narrative device (such as Carrie Bradshaw's magazine column). But, for me, theme works best as subtext on a subliminal level for the audience.

I've been an avid TV watcher since I was a kid, but most shows just sort of washed over me; I didn't watch TV analytically. I tuned in to escape my humdrum existence. I had many favorite shows, but if you asked me why one show was better than another, I couldn't put my finger on it. The actors were always key. Like most people, I took the writing for granted, as if the actors were making up their own dialogue as they went along.

The whole notion of a *unifying theme* didn't really make sense for me until 1998, while I was watching an episode of *E.R.* The episode was titled "Stuck on You"—which was my clue as to how the disparate A, B, C, and D stories were going to coalesce.

In the episode, Dr. Mark Greene (Anthony Edwards) rides with EMTs and treats a beating victim who turns out to be a sixteen-year-old gay male prostitute. He then helps the boy evade the police who have a warrant for his arrest; Lucy (Kellie Martin) has a crush on Dr. Carter (Noah Wylie), even though he's harsh with her; two brothers come into the hospital glued together after a carpet cement accident and end up getting some of the E.R. staff stuck with them; and an elderly patient (played by Harvey Korman) comes in for his blood pressure appointment but doesn't want to leave the nursing care of Nurse Carol Hathaway (Julianna Margulies) or the E.R. personnel because he's so desperately lonely.

So how do these strands of stories weave together into a cohesive theme? The title is the first clue: *stuck on you*. The male prostitute is lucky to discover he's HIV negative, but goes back to his former self-destructive behavior. He's stuck, even though he knows he's putting himself in danger; Lucy is "stuck" on Carter even if he is dismissive of her; Nurse Hathaway is "stuck" with a patient who doesn't want to leave; and the brothers are literally stuck together. Expanding on this idea is the larger truth that we are all stuck with each other, so we'd better take care of each other.

In the episode "The Other Woman" from *Mad Men,* Pete Campbell (Vincent Kartheiser) asks Joan (Christina Hendricks) to sleep with a man in order to land an important account; Don Draper (John Hamm) doesn't like the impact Megan's (Jessica Paré) acting career will have on his life; and Peggy (Elisabeth Moss) is offered a job at a rival company as chief copywriter.

Don lays out the theme as he pitches for the Jaguar account: "Oh, this car. This thing, gentlemen. What price would we pay? What behavior would we forgive?" There is a price for the things we want to attain. For Joan to become partner, she has to become a sexual bargaining chip; for Peggy to move on and up, she needs to leave the safe haven of Sterling Cooper Draper Pryce. For Don, Megan is no Betty (January Jones). Megan has her own dreams and is willing to pursue them.

A subtheme could be the price that women pay in the workplace. Megan is stuck having to deal with success but only on Don's terms. The final part of Don's pitch is literally "At last: something beautiful you can truly own." Men dominate women in this prefeminist society.

Finally, how far will you go to get what you want? Which moral boundaries will you cross in the name of success?

In the *Homeland* episode "Achilles' Heel," Brody (Damian Lewis) comes back to his wife Jessica (Morena Baccarin) after a week of having sex with Carrie (Claire Danes); Saul's (Mandy Patinkin) relationship with his wife Mira (Sarita Choudhury) is crumbling; and Carrie looks to exploit a weakness in order to capture rogue former soldier and "turned" POW, Tom Walker (Chris Chalk).

Once again, the theme of the show is hinted at in the title: everyone has an Achilles' heel, a weakness, and it's only a matter of figuring out what it is. For Saul, it's his dedication to work. In the throes of losing his marriage, he still goes to the Agency when called. For Carrie, she realizes she may be lonely her whole life and her job will probably consume her. For Tom Walker, it's his love of family that puts him at risk for getting caught; he phones his wife, not realizing the CIA is listening in and tracing the call. A minor theme is the theme of marriage, and how marriages last, or don't based upon the weak spots in the relationship: failing to communicate, holding grudges, taking one another for granted, and having unrealistic expectations.

In the penultimate episode of season 1 of *The Americans* entitled "The Oath," duplicitous D.C. Russian Embassy worker Nina (Annet Mahendru) pledges her oath to the Motherland, but then has a crisis of faith and confesses her double-dealings to her Russian boss. Nina admits her affair with FBI agent Stan Beeman (Noah Emmerich)—ready to accept the harshest punishment for treason. She broke her oath and is prepared to accept the consequences. But she's also smart and resourceful and offers her boss an enticing compromise: he can either kill her or allow her to continue her illicit relationship with Stan—but now she'll be working *against* Stan to atone for her sins.

Meanwhile, at FBI counterterrorism headquarters, executive assistant Martha (Alison Wright) agrees to plant a recording device (bug) in her boss Gaad's (Richard Thomas) office, but only after her lover "Clark" [alias of Phillip (Matthew Rhys)] agrees to tie the knot. Sure, Martha is suspicious of "Clark's" motives, but she's willing to do *anything* for the man she loves—as long as he's willing to stand up in front of her parents and God and marry her. To make his side of the aisle look convincing, "Clark" invites his "mother" (actually his U.S. KGB contact playing the part) and "sister" (played by Philip's current fake wife, Elizabeth [Keri Russell] to attend the small ceremony.

Elizabeth has to watch her fake husband get into *another* fake marriage with a woman who thinks it's real in order to forward the KGB espionage mission. It's a funny, layered sequence of subtext because Martha has no idea what's really happening, while Elizabeth realizes that she and Philip never had a wedding, real or otherwise—which leaves her feeling melancholy. And Martha marries "Clark" without knowing very much about him or his top-secret government work. Of course she assumes that "Clark" is working for the U.S. government and agrees to keep their marriage a secret indefinitely. Ironically, KGB spies Philip and Elizabeth were never officially married, but their effectiveness as sleeper agents is dependent upon everyone believing that they *are* married.

But though Elizabeth suggests to Philip, in a conciliatory tone, that things might have gone very differently for them if they had said their wedding vows, "The Oath" reinforces the thematic that commitment without follow-through is meaningless, as actions speak louder than words.

In the same episode, Viola (Tonye Patano), the Weinberger's God-fearing maid, comes clean to the FBI that she planted a bug in the clock of their office.

Sure enough, the title of "The Oath" played a large part in the theme, as the episode was bookended by characters literally reciting oaths. The theme is clearly about loyalty—about how loyalties to country, religion and marriage play out over time, especially when they intersect and conflict with each other—and, in those cases, which loyalty is more important?

Sitcoms are not exempt from using theme. In the episode "The Kiss" of mockumentary/sitcom *Modern Family*, we follow three storylines that, you guessed it, deal with kisses and showing affection. Cameron (Eric Stonestreet) is upset that Mitchell (Jesse Tyler Ferguson) isn't into public displays of affection; Claire (Julie Bowen) becomes overbearing when she finds out her daughter Alex (Ariel Winter) likes a boy. Haley (Sarah Hyland) pressures Alex to get her first kiss. While the Gloria (Sofia Vergara) and Jay (Ed O'Neill) storyline is more about Gloria's Colombian heritage, and ends with Jay, known for withholding affection, bestowing a kiss on his son, Mitchell. Also, akin to *Sex in the City*, the voice-over at the end, in this case from Gloria, reinforces the theme.

However, just as there are shows that use theme, there are shows that do not work according to one unifying theme. *Breaking Bad* doesn't. *Parenthood* and *Friday Night Lights* have themes and motifs, but they don't all line up symmetrically because not all the story lines match up so neatly.

Revenge uses season-long themes identified by a subheading at the beginning of the season. The first season was from Confucius: "Before you embark on a journey of revenge, dig two graves." The series follows Emily Thorne (Emily VanCamp) in her quest for revenge against the Grayson clan, headed by Victoria (Madeleine Stowe) and Conrad (Henry Czerny). The theme is quite clear that while you may get revenge, you will harm yourself, too. And sure enough, throughout the series' first season we watched as Emily whittled away her sense of morality—not caring about the collateral damage around her.

The second season's theme revolves around destiny, as shown by the subheading from Henri-Frédéric Amiel: "Destiny has two ways of crushing us . . . by refusing our wishes . . . and by fulfilling them." It teases the question of whether Emily will be destroyed by the very knowledge she wants to gain.

Great TV pilots tend to support a strong central theme—either explicitly or tacitly, articulated or inferred. Sometimes theme is deliberate on the part of the scriptwriter. And sometimes it's not. Or maybe there are *several* themes at play within the same episode and it's open to interpretation by the audience.

Mad Men, in particular, is a series that often requires more than one viewing to fully extrapolate its rich subtext and complex themes. For me, the first viewing is to see where the characters and evolving plotlines are heading; the second viewing is a much closer reading of details and nuance, leading toward deeper meaning and discussion.

> After all is said and done, theme is a Rorschach test for each viewer, as our unique life experiences influence everything we see.

INTERVIEW: Chip Johannessen

Chip Johannessen Credits

Best known for:

Homeland (Executive Producer/Co-Executive Producer/Writer) 2011–2012
    Emmy Award Winner (Outstanding Drama Series) 2012
    WGA Award Winner (New Series) 2012
    WGA Award Nominated (Drama Series) 2012
    Golden Globe Winner (Best Drama) 2012
Dexter (Executive Producer/Writer) 2010
    Emmy Nominated (Outstanding Drama Series) 2011
WGA Award Nominated (Drama Series) 2011
24 (Executive Producer/Co-Executive Producer/Consulting Producer/
    Writer) 2009–2010
Dark Angel (Consulting Producer/Writer) 2000–2002
Millennium (Executive Producer/Consulting Producer/Writer) 1996–1999
Beverly Hills, 90210 (Co-Producer/Writer) 1992–1995

NL: How do you approach constructing story? Do you start with plot, character, theme . . . how do you come at it?

  CJ: It depends a lot on the series. I came out of the Chris Carter [*The X-Files*] camp. That's where I learned how to write and produce. And where I really learned the discipline of putting stories together. We did something there that a lot of shows say they do, but no one really does: which is that we made little movies every week. In that case, what we needed was an idea that was enough to sustain forty-four minutes of television. But the really good episodes had ideas big enough to sustain a feature-length film. They obviously tended to be sci-fi kinds of stories, which meant that they were already a little writerly. They were pushing an idea.

  In terms of having thematic structures, those stories were a lot more open to it. For example, I did a story with *Millennium* that had to do with gifts. There was this sort of karmic cycling, and it had a theme of gifts in it. There's this book by Marcel Mauss about gifts, and how gifts flow through society . . . and that theme showed up in a lot of the construction of the story. But those episodes were all stand-alone.

And since then, with *Homeland* and *Dexter*, we've been doing stuff that's serialized, so it's a whole different ballgame the way you construct stories. One thing we're trying to do on *Homeland*—which is different than what we did on *24*—is to construct stories that, even though they're serialized, have a slight stand-alone component. Each episode looks and feels different, so you really don't know what you're going to get week to week. We're doing that in a way to distance ourselves from *24* a little, which became a pretty homogenous wash of stuff. In both of these shows, what we're looking for is some kind of character-driven story that also fits the flow of the whole season. At Homeland, we're trying to do all this while also maintaining a high degree of verisimilitude, a general feeling that it's actually real. One way to do this, and this comes out of *24,* is to embrace a lack of writerly devices. A lack, for example, of putting themes into things. If you want something that looks and feels real, throw out the writerly devices.

NL: And yet, in one of your excellent episodes of *Homeland,* titled "Achilles' Heel," theme is so prevalent. Was that subconscious or the exception to the rule for you?

CJ: Actually, I struggled with that when writing that episode because we do not ascribe to themes in episodes. In *24*, we had a mantra about that: "We don't do themes." We just don't do the kind of stuff that is the writer injecting his opinion into things. That's not to say that we don't have ideas that we push, but we try very much to have things feel real, especially on *Homeland*. So we shoot it that way, we write it that way, and we think about dialogue like that. We just don't put these writerly constructions in.

NL: Although I have to say in that "Achilles' Heel" episode, each character was struggling with a specific weakness, which seemed to track through the whole episode thematically—and beautifully, in my humble opinion.

CJ: Thanks. And you're right. And that theme even made it into text. Saul [Mandy Patinkin] actually says in dialogue that his work, his willingness to sacrifice everything else for it, that that's his Achilles' heel. But I really don't tend to like to do that sort of thing. It's too writerly. It feels phony to me. On these serialized shows it's like "what is the story?" It's all about that.

NL: So for you, it's first and foremost about figuring out the basic arcs of the stories and the relationships?

CJ: Yes. There was a big thing in Chris Carter Land about the science of storytelling, and endlessly just looking at all your cards and talking it through with everybody, and making sure it really hung together. Much more than an artsy exploration of human behavior and you alone in a room. It's really not like that. I'm more interested in human behavior set against a bigger event.

NL: Okay, but that's more on an episode-by-episode basis, what about over the course of a whole season? Isn't there always some sort of thematic question to be explored over the course of a given season? For example, in

Dexter, there's the big umbrella or macro theme of, Is he a human being or a monster?

CJ: Right.

NL: And then more micro themes within in each season, such as, Can he be a husband? Can he be a father? And in *Homeland*, has Brody (Damian Lewis) been turned, and if so, is he going to commit a large-scale terrorist act in the United States? And then the central theme of sanity versus paranoia—for Carrie (Claire Danes)—and will she be vindicated or crushed . . .

CJ: . . . as she was at the end of season 1.

NL: Maybe those aren't exactly thematic questions, but they were central questions that sustained the whole season. Is that something that you're thinking about when you talk about the science of story—more than theme?

CJ: Yeah. I don't think you need any thematic stuff at all. You have a very operational question there. You have an attack on the United States and then you have these two extremely unreliable narrators; one is Brody and he's sort of a mystery, you don't really know which side he's on. And then you have Carrie—who's a little crazy. And that's an interesting situation. You can just kind of lay it out. We don't just play it forward the way we did in *24*. We try to construct slightly stand-alone episodes, and in that sense they're about something. We chose where to direct our focus for a particular week. But we don't put these writerly devices onto it and say, "Oh, this one will be about the theme of gift giving in the world." We just don't do that.

NL: I suppose there are different ways of thinking about theme. At its most basic, theme is a universal truth about life. But another way, I think, to look at theme is this: there's the story, and then there's what the story is *really* about. So when you said that each episode is stand-alone and about something, to me, that means theme. So, for example, in the season finale of *Homeland*, that you co-wrote (titled "Marine One"), there seems to be the theme of loyalty. Brody is caught between his allegiance to Abu Nazir (David Negahban) and his loyalty and responsibility to his family at home, and particularly to his daughter, Dana (Morgan Saylor), with whom he shares a special bond. And, ultimately, Dana talks Brody down and prevents him from detonating the suicide vest when he's in the bunker with the Vice President and other top government officials. Or, is this something I'm imposing on your storytelling as a viewer and not something that you ever fully intended?

CJ: I did write a lot of that episode, and there was never the veneer of a thematic in it for me. What we go for though—and I think this is important—is that we go for a kind of recognizable emotional life. We try to construct that. We're not just playing out some CIA operation, we're very character based in terms of how that affects the people, the characters, the relationships. But we're never trying to push our ideas. We just don't do it.

In fact, I had a problem with the staff that I inherited when I took over as showrunner in season 5 of *Dexter* because to them it was all about the ideas, and I kept saying, "You know what? Your ideas are not that interesting to me. They're just not that fucking interesting." I would hear a lot about themes, and at one point I got so frustrated that I actually instituted a no metaphors rule in the writers' room. Because everyone came up with metaphors and nobody came up with an actual story.

And that's an issue. I've come to the place where I really value verisimilitude, a kind of naturalism. I picked up a lot of this from Josh Pate who created a series called *Surface*. It was a weird, sprawling sci-fi thing, but we tried to root everything in reality. It was a good lesson in this naturalistic thing. We did naturalistic dialogue, shot it pretty naturalistically, and tried to have naturalistic situations. There was always this tension because it looked like real life but it wasn't because, in that case, there were these sea monsters. And we try to do the same thing on *Homeland*.

NL: It sounds like it kind of freed you up as a writer, not to be shackled to the "rules" of a unifying theme and these higher story ideals—well, maybe not *ideals* but—

CJ: It's not an ideal. To me, imposing theme is just a bunch of bullshit.

NL: (Laughs) You're actually perfect for this chapter because you go against convention—and your impressive body of work demonstrates that it's working extremely well for you.

*A*nything that feels written, I just don't believe in anymore. What I do believe in is interesting, complicated characters, and then seeing what they do.

NL: Okay, so in telling a great story, can we talk about what makes a worthy, effective A story? It seems to me, a good story will have what I like to call "story tentacles" meaning it leads to more story. For example, in the season 5 opener of *Dexter* that you wrote (titled "My Bad"), Dexter (Michael C. Hall) discovered that his wife, Rita (Julie Benz), was murdered and he felt responsible, which led to a whole lot more story because he didn't know how to grieve. He lacked empathy. And we got to see how Dexter dispassionately studied how the people around him—Rita's family—all grieved for her, but Dexter just had this bemused void.

CJ: You know what. I have to take back everything I said. (*Laughs.*) In breaking season 5 of *Dexter,* we were going around and around and everyone was getting frustrated and I finally realized I was the new showrunner, I had to come up with something, and I woke up in the middle of the night and wrote down the word "Atonement." I realized I had the arc for the entire season. Dexter would cross a line that he'd never crossed before. He'd actively decide to help someone as a means to atone for not being able to save his wife. He wouldn't do it consciously; he'd kind of stumble into it. But eventually it would become clear that that was what the season was about.

NL: And that's what led to the Lumen (Julia Stiles) story? That entire season 5 arc?

CJ: Exactly. There was a, I hate to say it, a kind of theme that emerged. And in atoning for Rita's death, Dexter found a kindred spirit, Lumen, who'd been sexually abused and victimized and wanted to get back at the people who did that to her, and Dexter could align and help her carry out her cause. And he could fall in love with her because they shared the same passion— but then he'd lose her as a result of it.

NL: Yes, because once they're able to kill the serial abusers, Lumen is ready to let the past go, to move on . . . and Dexter isn't going to be part of her future?

CJ: Right.

NL: Your episodes are always so nuanced. There's a degree of detail and subtext that lets you mine the emotions of each character. I'm reminded of those Mickey Mouse hats in the "My Bad" episode of "Dexter." Rita's parents had taken her kids to Disneyworld, and Dexter discovers Rita's dead body in the bathtub while her kids are on vacation. He's freaking out, and then they call from Disneyworld . . . and he just can't bring himself to tell them what's happened.

CJ: Right, which is so real. How do you tell a kid something like that over the phone?

NL: And then they return from Disneyworld with these funny Mickey Mouse hats that have their names stitched on them. They give one to Dexter.

CJ: Yeah, my wife, Virginia, came up with those Mickey Mouse hats. Actually she comes up with a lot of stuff.

NL: Props to your wife. Such an ironic detail.

CJ: Yeah, Dexter puts it on, he's actually wearing it when he breaks the bad news to the kids . . . and he just looks ridiculous . . . until his stepdaughter knocks the thing off his head and runs out. Then Dexter follows her out to the car and they have a more genuine exchange.

NL: She accuses him of not caring about her mom because he's not crying, and she wishes it had been Dexter who'd been killed.

CJ: And he doesn't react.

NL: You know, it just occurs to me now that Dexter's lack of being able to feel any empathy allows the audience to empathize with him in a significant way. We know he's hurting but unable to express it. We feel his emotional pain and grief even more than if he'd just been able to bawl his eyes out.

CJ: But he is able to grieve for Rita in his sort of random, unpremeditated murder of the stranger.

NL: Yes, in the bathroom at that dilapidated marina store when he beats the crap of out some redneck asshole?

CJ: Right. Dexter goes ballistic, just rails on him, and then just leaves him there, all the blood, all the mess—not really his M.O. He just loses it. He crosses a line.

NL: "My Bad" was such a memorable episode for me because Dexter is pushed so far to the edge that he feels his only alternative is to escape. So he gets on his boat and takes off, but then he decides to return for Rita's funeral after he beats and kills the redneck stranger in the bathroom. It's as if he's now ready to start grieving for Rita in a more conventional way.

CJ: Yeah, he's had his release.

NL: When I hear "release," I think about Aristotle and catharsis—which I know is very artsy, but still . . .

CJ: He has his release and then wants to be around people who loved Rita. The final moment of the episode is when he also realizes that maybe he wasn't as able to grieve for her, but he did love her. He is capable of love.

NL: So instead of theme, would it be fair to say that your approach to storytelling is to push your characters to the edge? To make them as vulnerable as possible in each episode?

CJ: Maybe not in every episode, but I am interested in how people cross lines they haven't crossed before and what motivates them to do it. That's what draws me in.

15

PIQUE OUR INTEREST WITH
A POTENT TEASER

A teaser is the opening segment of a television episode. Most shows open with the teaser, then cut to the main title sequence. On the page, the teaser is approximately five pages long, but can run longer (the pilot teaser for *The Good Wife* was sixteen pages). A good teaser does exactly what it suggests: it "teases" viewers with a compelling opening that leaves them wanting to find out what happens next so they don't change the channel. Pilot teasers often have to work harder because viewers are experiencing the show cold, whereas teasers for established shows don't have the burden of introducing dynamic characters, or grounding the audience in an unfamiliar world.

The hook. Effective teasers will hook the audience immediately. In *The X-Files* pilot, the episode begins with superimposed text over black: "The following story is inspired by actual documented accounts." The first image is of a young woman in a nightgown frantically running through the woods at night. Suddenly a blinding white light emanates from the distance, and a shadowy figure approaches the woman as the wind swirls. The screen fades to white. In the next scene, the woman is found dead in the forest with no obvious cause of death, only two odd marks on her back. One of the crime scene analysts says, "It's happening again, isn't it?" The teaser not only poses a paranormal mystery, but it also hooks the audience with the suggestion that it could have actually happened.

Orient the audience. Good teasers also establish the world and tone of the show, and often give defining actions for the main character. In the pilot for *House of Cards*, the show opens with the sound of a car accident over black. A dog is critically wounded by a hit-and-run perpetrator. Frank Underwood (Kevin Spacey), the show's main character, puts the dog out of its misery by choking it to death and says to the audience, "I have no patience for useless things." By the end of the teaser, the audience learns Frank is the House Majority Whip, and he expects a reward for being instrumental in the President-elect's victory. The teaser establishes how the show deals with the seedy underbelly of D.C. politics, the Machiavellian code of the main character, and the recurring narrative device of breaking the fourth wall.

In the pilot for *Lost*, the show begins with an *eyeball* in extreme close-up. And then the camera pulls back revealing a man, Jack (Matthew Fox) lying on the ground in a tropical forest, staring up at the sky, disoriented. It starts with his eyeball because he's our POV, our way into the series. Jack wanders onto the beach and sees the chaotic aftermath of a catastrophic plane crash. This may look like paradise, but it's a form of hell. Jack's adrenaline kicks in and he races from injured passenger to passenger, giving them aid, establishing himself as a doctor and natural leader. (This indelible shot of Jack's eyeball was also the final image of the series when it ended its run.)

The crux of the show. Teasers can also establish the central conflict of the show. In the pilot for *The Shield*, the teaser intercuts a scene of Vic Mackey (Michael Chiklis) and his morally gray Strike Team chasing down a drug suspect along with a scene of newly minted, straight-arrow police Captain David Aceveda (Benito Martinez) giving a press conference about how he's going to clean up the streets of Los Angeles. Aceveda's crusade to destroy Vic and his law-breaking team runs through all seven seasons of the show.

In *Doogie Howser, M.D.*, the pilot opens with sixteen-year-old Doogie (Neil Patrick Harris) taking his driver's test with his mother in the backseat. The driving instructor tells Doogie to turn around because there's an accident up ahead, but Doogie speeds toward the scene. The boy genius springs from the car and offers medical assistance, winning over skeptical police officers in the process. The core of the show deals with Doogie balancing adolescence with his medical career as well as his struggle to garner respect from adults.

The bookend. Other teasers can hook the audience by playing with the chronology of the episode. *Breaking Bad* frequently places its characters in a precarious situation, and then shows how they got there throughout the course of the episode. In the pilot, Walter White (Bryan Cranston) careens through the New Mexico desert in an RV with dead bodies rolling around on the floor. He steps out of the RV in a rumpled green dress shirt and underwear, records a tearful goodbye to his family on a camcorder, and then wields a gun as the wail of sirens grows louder. The episode comes full circle and shows the aftermath of what transpired in the teaser. But the genius of this teaser is that its payoff is not as we had anticipated: turns out the sirens were not the police but the fire department—who then *zoom past* Walt to go put out a brush fire. He's in the clear—and ready to bury the camcorder confession to begin his new secret life as a meth cooker and drug dealer. This setup and pay off style of teaser and epilogue is what's referred to as *bookends*.

The (seemingly) innocuous teaser. This kind of teaser presents us with a detail that seems random and innocuous at the outset, but by the end of the episode, we actively discover its real meaning. And it turns out to be a crucial plot point or game changer for one or more of the characters. Take for example the season 5 episode of *Breaking Bad* entitled "Dead Freight." The episode opens with a kid riding his motorcycle in an isolated stretch of desert, then stopping, catching a tarantula and trapping it in a Mason jar. As the kid examines the captive spider, we get a bit of foreshadowing: a train whistle in the distance. That's all. But this out-of-context setup will lead to a tragic payoff. The audience learns at the end of the episode that the kid was a witness to what Walt and his cohorts had assumed was a successful train robbery (they stole mega amounts of methylamine from the freight train). But now they've got a loose thread to contend with: the kid on the dirt bike. Before they can formulate a plan, one of Walt's underlings shoots the kid point blank and kills him. The kid drops the jar and the camera lingers on the spider trapped inside, an apt metaphor for Walt, Jesse, and Mike's predicament. An innocent child was gunned down, making them all accomplices, and pushing their criminal operation into uncharted, more dangerous territory. The stakes of the series have been exponentially ratcheted up, and it all stemmed from the spider in the teaser.

The case. Crime procedurals like *Law & Order* or *CSI* almost invariably open with the crime, and then end the teaser with a wisecrack or one-liner from one of the lead characters. These shows are built on the promise of an unusual crime in the opening that will be solved by the end of the episode. This also extends to medical procedurals such as *House, M.D.* Dr. Gregory House (Huge Laurie) will be presented with an intriguing medical case that one of his colleagues or he will solve at the eleventh hour.

No teaser. Cable shows like *Game of Thrones*, *The Sopranos*, *Homeland*, and *Mad Men* simply open the show with their credit sequences and jump into act 1. These shows are heavily serialized, serving almost as mini-movies each week. It's not as common in network television to see a show without a teaser. However, *Castle* is an example of a show that begins with act 1. The structure of the show is six acts with no teaser. The show's title sequence is displayed at the end of act one. Different networks have different structure preferences. It's not unusual for ABC shows to have six acts with no teaser.

The cold open. Comedy teasers are called "cold openings." They function the same, although they always end with a punch line or a gag. In addition to being funny, good cold opens introduce the main issue and thematic throughline of the episode. In the season 4 episode of *Modern Family* titled "Fulgencio," the cold open deals with Jay Pritchett's (Ed O'Neill) mother-in-law wanting to name his newborn son Fulgencio, much to his chagrin, but he doesn't have the nerve to stand up to her. Despite Jay's best efforts, he can't get his mother-in-law to like him, which he soon realizes mirrors the relationship he has with his son-in-law Phil (Ty Burrell). By the end of the episode, Jay finally tells off his mother-in-law, and they reach an understanding. He agrees to name his son Fulgencio Joseph Pritchett.

Direct pickup. Some serialized shows pick up exactly where they left off in the previous episode. A direct pickup is referred to in the TV biz with the abbreviation DPU. At the end of the *True Blood* pilot, waitress Sookie Stackhouse (Anna Paquin) is being brutally attacked in the parking lot by a pair of sinister restaurant patrons late at night. The second episode teaser begins in the same spot with Sookie being beaten. Suddenly, the attackers are whisked away into the darkness, and vampire Bill Compton (Stephen Moyer) helps Sookie to her feet. The direct pickup model gives episodes a cliffhanger feel and also shows how compressed time is in the universe of the program. See also *Weeds*. (FYI: In daytime soap operas, DPUs are used at the start of each new episode. Given that daytime soaps tend to move, by design, at a snail's pace, many daytime soaps also utilize "frozen time" between storylines, so that when we cut away from a scene and then cut back to the same scene, it's as if those characters were frozen in their exact same positions. Frozen time is to be avoided in primetime. When we cut away from and later return to the same scene, best to show some movement or progress in the scene or else there is an artificial stasis in the storytelling.)

The wildcard. Some shows employ teasers that don't always fit into an established pattern of the series. In season 1 of the anthology show, *American Horror Story*, some of the teasers consist of past grisly murders that took place in the creepy house that serves as the main setting of the show, while other teasers give backstory on key characters.

In *The Walking Dead*, many teasers deal with the survival horror aspect of the show, while others touch on poignant character moments. In the season 1 episode "Vatos," the teaser opens with sisters Andrea (Laurie Holden) and Amy (Emma Bell) reminiscing about their father while fishing on a serene lake, and ends with another character, Jim (Andrew Rothenberg), curiously digging ditches. This is in stark contrast to the gory, suspenseful teasers that routinely place the characters in dangerous situations.

A kickass teaser is like an irresistible appetizer before the main course of a meal. It needs to whet the audience's appetite and leave them hungry for more. If there's a "tag" (epilogue) at the end of the episode, think of that as dessert.

See interview with **Dawn Prestwich and Nicole Yorkin** *on the companion website:* http://www.focalpress.com/cw/landau

16

HIT THE SWEET SPOT

TV pilots are always creative experiments. There is no guarantee that the series is going to work based on the first prototypical episode. And even if the pilot is totally brilliant, there is no guarantee that the series will be able to sustain that level of writing week after week.

The fact is, despite best efforts and good intentions by smart, talented showrunners, the vast majority of new series get cancelled. The networks don't know why—and if they did—they'd course correct and fix the maddeningly inefficient, hyper-expensive process called *pilot season*. Extenuating circumstances, disclaimers, and excuses abound when a new series fails to connect. Was it:

1. right series/wrong time slot?
2. weak lead-in show?
3. too much competition at other networks?
4. premise too risky/groundbreaking/provocative?
5. too gimmicky?
6. stale premise/too derivative?
7. fatally flawed casting—with lack of chemistry between leading characters?
8. lackluster advertising campaign?
9. all of the above?

In tennis jargon, the *sweet spot* is the center of the racquet; when the ball connects at the core, it's the source of its greatest power. The same holds true for a TV series.

Identifying Sweet Spot by Genre

Unlike Forrest Gump's box of chocolates, when a viewer tunes in to a sitcom, they know what they're going to get: the sweet spot.

The sweet spot of most sitcoms occurs when the characters are placed in variations on the same situation—they are put to the test. The insular Leonard (Johnny Galecki) and Sheldon (Jim Parsons) in *The Big Bang Theory* routinely clash with the "normalcy" of the outside world. Larry David on *Curb Your Enthusiasm* finds himself in a cringe-worthy situation at odds with his skewed ideals. Phil (Ty Burrell) and Claire (Julie Bowen) on *Modern Family* continue to embarrass their kids and themselves in their quest to be ideal parents. *Married . . . with Children* milks laughs by treating marriage and parenthood as the ultimate punishment. The two men in *Two and a Half Men* are a modern day variation on Neil Simon's *The Odd Couple*.

One-hour drama series can also greatly benefit from clarifying and adhering to the sweet spot. I'm not suggesting a rigid formula for each series. I *am* suggesting that a series must deliver the promise of its premise every week. Hopefully, there will be unexpected character development that's organic and *earned* from previous episodes. Hopefully, there will be twists and turns in the plot. But, at the core, the series sweet spot remains the same. This is the tacit contract the showrunner is making with the audience. Keep tuning in—and we'll keep giving you new iterations on the same premise.

The sweet spot of a procedural series is the fresh, innovative element of the medical/legal/criminal case—and the surprising/unpredictability of the resolution. These shows are all puzzles, and the sweet spot is how the missing pieces fit into place toward the inevitable solution, but the challenge for writers it to avoid being too formulaic and predictable. Medical, legal, and police procedural series are all, essentially, murder mysteries. We tune in each week to witness the experts solve the cases; the killer might be a person or a disease. And as technology evolves, the issue has become less whodunit and more *howdunnit*.

Identifying Sweet Spot by Series

In *The Walking Dead*, the sweet spot is survival of the fittest in a post-apocalyptic world. The sweet spot of this series isn't simply man versus zombie—that would get old and repetitive fast. Instead, the zombie-slaying is the backdrop for a disparate group of renegade survivors attempting to form a new society. They actually form an extended family and watch each other's backs. The sweet spot of *The Walking Dead* straddles the fence between the genres of horror and family drama. The emotional core of the series stems from the relationships. The creepy, gory, chills, and thrills emerge organically from the constant threat of the living dead (who are also survivalists in need of fresh flesh). Remove the blood and guts and the show collapses. But if there were only gore, the show would also falter. And so this phenomenally successful cable series gives us both every week. It knows its sweet spot and finds the right balance. The central question of the series remains constant: Who will survive and how? The central mystery—what happened to cause this zombie apocalypse?—has never, and probably will never, be answered.

The sweet spot of *Breaking Bad* is how the formerly meek Walter White (Bryan Cranston) becomes a ruthless drug kingpin story set against a dysfunctional family drama with gallows humor, twisted alliances, devious minds, and self-delusion. Greed and power, corruption and cover-ups. The sweet spot is a group of novices playing in the big leagues and, against all odds, succeeding on their own terms. It's a show that's evolved from underdog to top dog. The central question remains constant: Will Walter get caught—and at what consequence?

The sweet spot of *Mad Men* is the disparity between superficial appearances and the truth—an apt metaphor for the advertising trade. But the metaphor extends to power dynamics at home and in the workplace. It's less of a show about who's loyal and who cheats—and more a show about why. The tone of the series is slick, ironic, funny, and dark. *Mad Men* flourishes by digging deep into its cast of characters to help us understand their wholly self-destructive patterns; indeed, the more they each get ahead, the more likely they are to self-sabotage. Ads tend to show us a "perfect" version of reality, a life to which we all aspire. And the ultimate irony of *Mad Men* is how that lifestyle is unattainable.

The sweet spot of *Homeland* is duality. Brody (Damian Lewis) is both a war hero and a terrorist; Carrie (Claire Danes) is both a hyper-vigilant CIA operative and a traitor. Against this backdrop, how does one remain faithful to one's ideals in a morally complex, dangerous world? It's not a show about black and white. It's a show about shades of gray. As characters' perceptions and beliefs shift, we find ourselves asking more questions—and there are no easy answers.

The sweet spot of *The Americans* is half dysfunctional family drama and half Cold War espionage thriller. The best episodes operate on both of these levels simultaneously; dialogue is layered with delicious, duplicitous subtext. In the series, undercover KGB agent Elizabeth Jennings (Keri Russell) is posing as a suburban hockey mom but no one has a clue (yet). And we get fun exchanges of dialogue laced with double entendre, such as when Elizabeth's neighbor, Sandra (Susan Misner), mentions that she saw Elizabeth doing something innocuous from her kitchen window, then innocently adding: "I mean, not that I was spying on you or anything." The sweet spot of this series was epitomized when Elizabeth's husband and fellow KGB operative, Phillip (Mathew Rhys), posing in disguise as "Clark," has no choice but to marry Martha (Alison Wright), the secretary to a high-level FBI agent so that he can use her to bug her boss's office. In a small, civil ceremony, Clark and

Martha say their vows before the Justice of the Peace, and standing beside him are Clark's "family members": incognito Elizabeth and their KGB supervisor Granny (Margo Martindale). As Clark says "I do" to Martha, Elizabeth is unexpectedly moved and saddened because she and Phillip never had a proper wedding ceremony; their marriage was arranged based upon politics and espionage—not love. And we realize that the steely, calculating spy Elizabeth might truly love Phillip after all. It's the perfect intersection of premise and franchise, and the sweet spot of the series is typified by its smart tagline: All is fair in love and cold war.

> The sweet spot of a series is where the show lives every week. It's the intersection between the show's genre, tone, theme, central conflict, franchise, and central question/mystery.

INTERVIEW: Hart Hanson

Hart Hanson Credits

Best known for:

Bones (Executive Producer/Writer) 2005–2013
The Finder (Executive Producer/Writer) 2012
Joan of Arcadia (Consulting Producer/Writer) 2003–2004
Judging Amy (Executive Producer/Co-executive Producer/Consulting Producer/Writer) 1999–2003
Snoops (Co-Executive Producer/Writer) 1999–2000
Cupid (Supervising Producer/Consulting Producer/Writer) 1998–1999
Stargate SG-1 (Writer) 1997–1999
Traders (Creator/Supervising Producer) 1996–2000
Avonlea (Writer) 1992–1996

NL: I'd like to discuss the "sweet spot" (to use a tennis racquet metaphor) of your remarkably long-running series, *Bones*. As the creator and showrunner, you seem to both honor and transcend the expectations of your series' fans, season after season. So let's start with your myriad of A story cases of the week. What makes a worthy A story for you?

HH: A stories come from a number of places. Every once in a while we will rip them from the headlines, but not much—especially not as much as in the last couple of years. Most of our A stories spring first out of finding an arena—a world that Booth [David Boreanaz] and Brennan [Emily Deschanel] can go into that maybe the audience hasn't seen or thinks they know, but ours has a twist in it. A typical homicide where a husband kills his wife—the characters and the twists and turns would have to be absolutely fascinating to fill six acts. By the way, we went to a six-act structure in season 3 at the behest of the FOX network. We used to be a teaser and five acts. The teaser was in fact a teaser—a minute or two. With the addition of the sixth act, we needed one more plot twist. *Bones* is a procedural hybrid with characters and humor. There's always a very personal storyline around the romance or lack of romance between Booth and Brennan. With six acts, we were pushed into this idea that we needed interesting arenas. It was not a conscious decision—we got shoved there by the network. Generally, a good arena will give you one or two plot twists that you don't have to invent out of air. For example, we did our homage to *The X-Files* with the world of UFOs. And given the speed with which we have to push out twenty-two episodes, that's a big gift.

It was very early in the first season that we realized that we were killing [overtaxing, burning out] our lead actors, and I knew we needed to figure out which scenes could we do without them. You can do a few with the *squinterns* (what we call secondary characters). But another way to do it was with the body find. The first scene is almost always an innocent person finding our [dead] body. What we want is to make people barf before five minutes into the scene and say, "What the hell—how did that happen?" And then that will generally lead into the arena.

NL: And the arena can also suggest possible red herrings? Like the episode with Bill, the reality TV personality who busts people for having affairs. You have the TV producer and various people on the show, which gives you at least one or two twists or turns.

HH: We've made an unspoken deal with our audience that the killer is not going to be someone we spring out of nowhere—we are going to meet them. That is a tough balance to do. If you go on the message boards, people have theories like, "It's always the third person you meet." The interwebs don't really have a lot of effect on us, but it did make me think we have to make sure that that doesn't happen accidentally. So we pay attention to that. We also need an arena which provides a wealth of suspects because you know you're going to meet them probably before the end of act three and definitely before the end of act four. And we definitely don't want people getting ahead of us.

NL: In the early seasons of the show, it seemed like by the end of act four, you'd have the climax of the show. You'd have the revelation of the suspect and then act five was very short—like an epilogue. Has that shifted? Because structurally, that's actually a question that comes up in class at UCLA a lot now. It used to be that every one hour was four acts—a teaser and four acts.

Now, most shows are five or six acts. Some because of the influence of TiVo. So the question becomes then, "Where does the climax happen?" I tell them it depends on the show. What about for you?

HH: It hasn't been as interesting for us in a six-act structure to figure out who the killer is by the end of act 5 and then catch them in act 6. It's generally that, once we know who that person is, we wrap it up. This is basically due to my boredom. For example, we have a serial killer now and we will know who it is by the end of act one—maybe even by the end of the teaser—because of the four or five episodes he'll be in for the season. Then it's the cat and mouse game. Most murderers are not coming back at our people. We're chasing them. It's a whodunit. The mandate that the writers' room has is that the climax is probably going to be when Brennan realizes something forensically that the body gives a clue that he's perhaps left-handed, not right-handed. The climax to the show is when she turns to Booth and says, "That's the guy." That's the climax of the case.

NL: Then you have your B story to track and resolve—or advance—for the season?

HH: Yes, and our B story is very often more important to a chunk of the audience. They are watching the murder to get to the gushy stuff. And the other chunk is putting up with the gushy stuff to get to the murder. We try and have them resonate and join together in axis with our climax which is halfway through act six in the big exciting "who did it" scene when our puzzle is solved.

NL: For me, what I've noticed is that the A story impacts the B story or vice versa in terms of a thematic that is running through. Like the episode when Brennan and Booth were trying to decide whose apartment they were going to live in. So her lack of memory in the A story case triggered their fears of moving in together because of his father and because of her foster childhood. Do you consciously strive to have a unifying theme between A, B, and C stories?

HH: Our best shows are when something in the case resonates for them in their personal life. Our second best shows are where something happens in their personal life and they go, "Oh, that applies to this case." That's always a bit clumsier and seems more coincidental. My personal feeling about life is that the universe speaks to you. If you have something in your head, something that speaks to you, then the universe seems to provide a lot of examples of it occurring out there in the world. I don't believe there is a mystic force speaking to us, but I do believe the universe is telling us something all the time. And when the two stories are not connected at all, they're not our best episodes. They can be our best case and they can even be our best romantic episode, but if the two don't hook into each other—it's just not as good.

NL: I like when A, B, and C stories resonate on some type of level—even where there's the DNA of theme in each story.

HH: I'm doing a pilot right now for CBS. That's what I'm obsessed with—creating a universe. Storytelling is a way of ordering a chaotic universe and that is satisfying to us—that is why we like stories.

NL: What's the internal story document process? Do you go from writers' room to beat sheet to outline? What's the timeline?

HH: Everything is as fast as humanly possible. The writers upstairs know that their best chance to get their words said by the actors are to do as many drafts as they can with notes from me and my right-hand man, Stephen Nathan, because I'm a big rewriter. It's easier for me to do a rewrite than to spend time with a writer giving them notes. It's one of my weaknesses as a showrunner. Every once in a while, some poor writer out there gets to do one draft of a script—and after all the revisions, nothing they wrote, no dialogue, will be said. And that's tough on a writer to watch something with your name on it.

NL: Does it threaten their job security if that keeps happening?

HH: No, it doesn't in any way threaten their job security because they've done their part. If the train of production catches up and you've got to take this script, it's not their fault. You've got to pay a lot of attention to what people do for other writers. Because there are a lot of writers who will help other writers. You do your due diligence at the end of the year when you're thinking about who to bring back and you have to take into account who helped other writers with their scripts. It takes a village. We don't have a cut-throat situation. The room is very nice. They are supportive of each other. It's not like we would get rid of the person who put the least amount of words on the page.

At CBS when I was doing *Joan of Arcadia* and *Judging Amy*, the network was comfortable with no outlines. I would call and pitch the stories to them. It would take five to ten minutes. I would say here are the beats while I was looking at a beat sheet. They would say fine, and the writer would go off. FOX wants to see the outlines and it's their call. Here's what generally happens. The guy who runs the room right now is Jon Collier, co-executive producer, who is just awesome at it. I don't spend a ton of time in the room. I get pitched arenas, and then we discuss with Jon what the personal B stories might be in that arena. Then we go upstairs and the writer pitches six acts with the act endings. Stephen and I respond and give notes. That takes maybe an hour and a half to two hours. Then they turn that into an outline. I don't look at outlines, neither does Stephen, but Jon and another co-executive producer, Kim Clements, produce the outline and send it to the network. Sometimes it comes back with questions, and then we beef it up. Then the writer goes off to write the script. And the faster they write the script, the faster they will get notes. Every once in a while, we will hand over a script from a junior writer to a co-executive producer to do a pass with our notes, so that the rewrite doesn't have to be as big.

NL: Is the outline about ten pages?

HH: It's twelve pages long.

NL: One of the things that was tough for me when I was first on staff on Aaron Spelling's shows was that they required fifteen- to twenty-page single-spaced outlines which included everything. Then, what I learned when I went to other shows is that if the draft would come following the outline, the co-executive producer would say, "It's the outline"—and that was not a compliment. Because the script needs to transcend and elevate.

HH: Elevate is the word. It needs to get better.

NL: I think a lot of writers starting out don't understand that and that's the danger. If you spend all your time on the outline, you're not going to make those discoveries later in the script.

HH: Because once you have people talking and interacting, what looked right in the outline can and should change in the script. Doing a procedural, certain things tend to stick like when you discover stuff, but how and who's there can change radically. New writers should also know that if I give notes on a script and all that writer does is insert the notes—that's not useful. It's also not a good script. The notes should change everything. You can give three little notes, but it often means that every line of dialogue needs to change. To me, a real writer is someone I give a note to like: "You know, this scene should be a funnier take on this—not so melodramatic. And up here, I don't know does she hate her mother or not?" and he or she goes ahead and changes the whole script to adopt those notes. The better a writer is, the more that that happens. And it takes courage because the outline's been approved.

NL: There's been some evolution with your characters with Temperance softening and getting into a relationship and having a baby. Do you have any comments on that and do you know instinctually when that evolution is supposed to happen?

HH: The changing of characters is the trickiest element to a network show. Twenty-two episodes a year, and if you're lucky, five years—that's 110 episodes. You have to keep the thing that makes the audience watch. I refer a lot to taking care of your story engine. If you knew that a show was going to last three seasons, and the question was, "Will they or won't they?" you'd know where to parse it. We didn't think we would last until Christmas the first year. We were always on the bubble,[1] so it was, "How do we keep two young, healthy, unattached people in a free society from going to bed?" I'm okay with the audience screaming and yelling and being unhappy, as long as they keep watching. I've said that out loud a few times and gotten into trouble for it. They hear, "You don't like us. You don't mind us being unhappy." I don't

---

[1] When the series is on the cusp between renewal and cancellation by the network.

mind the audience being unhappy if I'm doing it on purpose and they're still watching. What I really mind is the audience being bored or going away. The story engine on our show was the chemistry. First and foremost, it's a procedural. We have to have good cases. There's another question with network shows which is, "Do you try to get new audiences or do you try to hang on to the audience you have?" In the case of *Bones*, I was trying to hang on to our loyal, loyal audience, and it was a function of real life because we were bouncing around the schedule. For me, to turn my efforts into getting a new audience each night, I think we would have been dead. It appears that that was a good plan.

NL: Yeah—seven years on the air.

HH: We're still bouncing around the schedule. FOX has never felt the desire to turn us into a hit. We mostly survived. They put us on after *American Idol*, and we could talk a lot as to whether that was a hit-making position or not. But we had to keep the story engine between those two to keep our loyal audience coming back week after week. I went as slowly as possible. At the end of season 5, I just thought, "Okay, they will take one more year. We are going to have them together by the end of season 6." I knew how it was going to happen. I knew that a beloved character would die and that they would go to bed. The little gift from heaven was that Emily came to me and said, "I'm pregnant." And I said, "Okay, we know what to do." The horrible uncertainty went away. I don't know exactly how we would have gone into season 7 if she wasn't pregnant. I just knew they would have slept together. I had about five or eight things written out for what that arc could be, but none of them delighted me. My favorite one was not too far off from what we did—which is that they were going to try to get together.

> *A nd by the way, I think the real story engine to* Bones *is a very simple, time-honored one, which is the rational versus the spiritual, the empirical versus the humanist in just those two people. That's our sweet spot.*

No matter what they are doing—ours happen to be solving murders and raising a child now—they're going to give you two different views of the universe.

NL: You also have your ensemble, and they get to weigh in with their points of view.

HH: I've ranked them on a line for rationality—the mystic over here and the rational over there. So oddly enough, her best friend, Angela [Michaela Conlin], was the farthest over to the mystical, humanist side of things. Booth is probably next to her. When we started, there was even someone more rational than Brennan, but that didn't work out. But it was so that everyone would have a stance on everything they were going through.

NL: When you created the pilot for *Bones,* I know that you started with the books by Kathy Reichs and her experience and background as a forensic anthropologist. You hear a lot with pilot development about whether it's a premise pilot, a non-premise pilot, or a hybrid. It feels like with *Bones* that it was not a premise pilot because they had already known each other when he picked her up at the airport. How did you make some of those choices and why?

HH: Some of it's out of your hands. At that point, I think it was both studio and network—and certainly network—did not want a premise pilot. They just didn't. I never understood this by the way. I love premise pilots. It was a thing for years.

NL: They were afraid that if the audience missed the first show, you would never get them hooked.

HH: I always thought that was faulty logic because then you're starting as if it's the second episode or the tenth. The math didn't make sense to me, but I accepted it. I got as close to a premise pilot as I could. They knew each other and they hated each other from something in the past. It was a year later from the last time they had a disastrous outing as partners. I also had to explain why a scientist would be out in the world with a cop because in real life that wouldn't happen. It had to be her insistence for some reason. We had all sorts of rationalizations: "I need to make sure the evidence isn't . . . I'm a cultural anthropologist." We just needed them to be together.

NL: Given the real science and verisimilitude, where does the show rest?

HH: I am delighted and surprised that either *Popular Mechanics* or *Popular Science* did a ranking of the procedural shows in terms of reality, and we won. *Bones* won. I think it's because I don't know enough to lie. We do lie. Angela's machine did exist. There were seven of them when *Bones* started, but they were not being used for forensic things. They were doing things like climate mapping. It's a multi-gazillion-dollar machine, and you can't program it in five minutes. The rest of the forensic stuff is rooted in reality. We take out a million steps and we compress the time. You can get DNA evidence in an hour, but it takes two months in real life. The monstrous expense of what our team would actually do—you can't do that. But our science is good. If we have a legitimate criticism in the writers' room or from us [the executive producers] on a plot point or on the science, we say, "That's not true. I call bullshit." Anyone can say that and say why they don't believe it. We all have to feel like it could really happen.

NL: Bones has been a great training ground for showrunners: Josh Berman, Noah Hawley, and Janet Tamaro. I know Josh had a lot of experience when he came here, but now he's running two shows.

HH: He just had another one picked up. Josh is a force of nature and so is Janet.

NL: Besides "quality scripts on time," what else would you say are the most important skills for a showrunner to have to be effective?

HH: There's a few things I'm a fanatic about. One is that the director of the episode have a prep-able script the first day of prep [preproduction]. They are not wasting two or three days trying to work off an outline that might change. I think that's the first responsibility. We have some kind of responsibility to our actors as well—to respect them. They are the face of the show. They have to go out there and say this stuff and make it work. They have to make it work. They have to feel listened to. You have to get trust with your actors over time. I put that right up there amongst the things you have to do. I think the toughest thing about showrunning is that, if you are doing your job well, everybody is a little bit annoyed at you, but doesn't hate your guts. So if you're someone like I am who likes to be liked, it's not a perfect job because it's very high pressure. Janet Tamaro, Josh Berman, and Noah Hawley—these are very, very good writers. Any number of the people I work with—Stephen Nathan, Jonathan Collier, Karen Usher—can be show-runners, but this is my job. Any one of them may be more right at any time than I am or have another way to do it, but it's my job to be the showrunner. I could easily go work for any of these people and then they would have that job. And I'm telling you that the best job in the world is second in command on a show. Noah Hawley said a great thing to me when he came back after *The Unusuals*, which I think, aired on ABC about four times, but was critically acclaimed. He said to me that he had stood there right beside me when I was running *Bones*. And he used to think, "I wouldn't do it that way. Oh, what an asshole." He said that the shock of all of a sudden being that guy is like a tornado coming at you. I remember being this guy by the way, being second in command, and thinking I would do it way better and what an asshole my showrunner was. And then you step into the job, and everything is noisier and there's yelling and a huge amount of chaos. It's just so noisy all the time. Constant decisions. If you take the money and the credit, you have to do the job. It's better to be second in command, it's a little quieter. You can hear yourself think.

NL: Well, what's the best part of being a showrunner then?

HH: Last year, I ran a new show called *The Finder* and we were getting there . . . we were getting there.

NL: I loved how irreverent everything was.

HH: That guy's [Geoff Stults] a star. He deserved it. By the season finale, I said, "Give us one more. I'm telling you we know this show. We know how to use these actors." I was very tired, and when it finally went down, I literally said to my wife, "We can go somewhere." The most time I've had off since *Bones* started was nine days. And now there was three weeks that we could go somewhere. So we went to Europe and when we came back, I was immediately pitching another show. I don't know why. I need to go to therapy and find out why. It's so much work. You don't get all that much more money for doing two shows instead of one. I have enough money. When *The Finder* went down, I felt terrible for my hardworking crew, but they're all working now.

NL: So what drives you—do you know?

HH: Here's what it is: I'm all excited about the next world. When I think about doing the series, I go, "Oh, my god." When I think about the creative part of this character, it's called *Backstrom* for CBS, I get all excited. I think about who might get cast in that role—and I have three or four people in mind. Each one of them changes the series in a way that's very exciting to me. You get to create a world.

NL: And then run it. What could be sweeter than that?

17

PAY OFF THE SETUPS

I'm a pilot junkie. I love reading the teleplays and later watching the premiere episodes to see how they've translated from page to screen. It's like unwrapping a gift and finding either a wonderful surprise or a well-intentioned disappointment.

I'm always filled with anticipation as to how the pilot will open: will it be an origins "premise" pilot or of the drop-me-into-the-world-already-in-progress variety? How will the voluminous exposition be doled out? Where is it going to be set? Who's in the cast? What's the X-factor that makes it fresh and exciting? How is it structured, at what pace and style? Will there be voice-over? Flashbacks? Flash-forwards? Will it be genre bending, innovative and break the mold, or will it follow a well-established formula for other shows of its kind? With each new show, there are so many variables to behold.

The "Aha" Moment

When I think about all the pilots I've read/viewed over the years, there seems to be a common denominator between the pilots that transcend my expectations and those that underwhelm. To me, the most satisfying pilots deliver an unexpected "*aha moment*" by the end—and provide me with a sense of discovery and wonder. It's that final trump card that I should have seen coming—but didn't.

Several years ago I was fortunate enough to see the great mystery author Walter Mosley speak at a writers' conference. Mr. Mosley is a charismatic orator and his talk was peppered with lots of valuable guidance and wisdom for writers. But the three words that remained indelibly etched in my brain are these:

Plot Is Revelation

This was such a revelation to me because it so succinctly articulated what all writers are mining for: unexpected but earned discoveries about their characters. Mosley was mainly addressing novelists in his talk, but his words resonated deeply with me as a screenwriter. My interpretation of plot is revelation is that as the story progresses, we're learning more and more about what makes a character tick. We're also actively finding new information that changes our perception about the characters as they get into and out of trouble.

Think of a Pilot Story as a Puzzle to Be Solved

Remember, audiences are usually more compelled by what they *don't* know than by what they do know. So don't tell us everything in the pilot. Create intrigue and suspense (even in a comedy) by withholding crucial information—until the final card is dealt. The audience may presume that they understand exactly what's going to happen next, so switch things up with a well-earned plot reversal to keep them on their toes and surprise them.

A Subtly Foreshadowed Plot Twist Can Be a Potent Game Changer

Ideally, the viewer has patiently waited for *something* unexpected to happen that brings the whole pilot full circle, so give them what they want—but then leave them dangling, so that they're impatiently waiting to discover more in the next episode and the next and the next . . .

There are myriad strategies for writing a pilot, but the ending is usually the clincher. It's the last impression that the agent/producer/studio/network executive is left with—and it needs to deliver. There are three basic strategies to wrapping up a pilot.

Launching the Franchise

This pilot ending shows us how the protagonist's role in a new setting is solidified toward future episodes—and in service of the show's (week-to-week) franchise—and the central question/mystery/conflict/relationship/premise of the series comes into focus for the viewer.

In the pilot for *Cheers*, Diane Chambers (Shelley Long) snaps out of denial that her professor/fiancé is coming back for her, and she woefully accepts a waitressing job at the bar despite her love/hate feelings for proprietor Sam Malone (Ted Danson).

At the end of the pilot for *Girls*, struggling twenty-four-year-old, self-absorbed, aspiring writer Hannah Horvath's (Lena Dunham) parents have financially cut her off. Hannah is devastated, forlorn, and a little bit terrified. But she dusts herself off and goes back to her tenuous existence in Brooklyn—and as she crosses the street, the spring in her step lets us know that she's (probably) going to make it after all.

By the end of the *Once Upon a Time* pilot, outsider Emma Snow (Jennifer Morrison) decides to stay put in Storybrooke and the second hand on the town square clock starts moving again—as if by magic. Change is in the air and fantasy and reality are on a collision course.

By the end of the pilot for *The Killing*, the police locate a stolen car believed to contain the body of the disappeared girl. And seasoned Seattle homicide detective Sarah Linden (Mireille Enos) delays her early retirement and an impending move with her son to Northern California to start their new life with her fiancé, because she is compelled to solve the mystery of "Who Killed Rosie Larsen?" In the pilot script, Sarah instructs the uniformed officers to open the trunk of the car. As Sarah looks into the deadened eyes of Rosie Larsen, we can see that from her POV it's as if the girl is imploring her to stay on the case. The last two words of the pilot script read: "Find him."

The Final Montage

This type of pilot ending gives us a snapshot of the main characters in the series. It's often accompanied by music and indicates where each character might venture in his/her life in future episodes. It's primarily visual, but sometimes contains voice-over and/or economical dialogue. It gives the viewer a lay of the land in a poetic, lyrical way. Sometimes the camera cranes up to give us a global view of the characters in their respective worlds. Sometimes the camera is like a bee buzzing from flower to flower—and then settling down on one main flower: the main protagonist on the show. For examples of this type of ending, check out the pilots for *Parenthood*, *Friday Night Lights*, and *Sons of Anarchy*.

At the end of the pilot for *Boardwalk Empire*, we get a montage that demonstrates Enoch "Nucky" Thompson's (Steve Buscemi) ascension to power: from corrupt county treasurer to notorious crime kingpin of Atlantic City during the Prohibition Era. The climactic montage sequence shows how Nucky's brother, Sheriff Eli (Shea Whigham) kidnaps and murders Hans Schroeder (Joseph Sikora) as retribution for Hans beating his wife Margaret (Kelly Macdonald) so severely that she miscarries. When Hans' body is found in a fishing net, along with today's catch, Nucky frames Hans for the massacre of gangster Arnold Rothstein's (Michael Stuhlbarg) men that occurred during an earlier botched bootleg heist. The revelation that Nucky ordered the hit on Hans is made clear when he innocently brings Margaret flowers in the hospital. We know from the first scene of the pilot that Nucky is a morally bankrupt opportunist, but by the pilot's end, we discover his dark side, his true ruthlessness. Atlantic City is *his* town, and he'll destroy anyone who tries to challenge him.

Earlier in the pilot, there are two particularly potent, revelatory moments that foretell Nucky's transformation. In the first, as Nucky walks past a storefront nursery along the Boardwalk, he looks in the window and sees a nurse cradling a newborn baby. He is mesmerized by the infant's purity and innocence. Then later in the pilot, Nucky walks past a storefront fortune-teller as she reads a customer's palm to predict the future. She glances up and meets Nucky's eyes, as if to say, What will be *your* future? Near the end of the pilot, Nucky's driver, Jimmy Darmody (Michael Pitt) presents Nucky with the spoils from the botched bootleg heist, saying, "It's your cut of the proceeds." When Nucky tells Jimmy that he never asked for the loot, Jimmy responds with, "You can't be half a gangster anymore." As a result, when Nucky accepts the blood money, his fate as a full-blown gangster is sealed.

The Final Discovery

The other type of pilot ending packs a stronger punch by essentially pulling the rug out from under us (which in a TV pilot is a good thing).

Here are more examples of pilot endings that succeed in pulling us into the deep end of the series in surprising ways:

- *Alias*: Sydney (Jennifer Garner) learns that she doesn't work for a sector of the CIA (she works for the enemy), *and* so does her father. He's not the mild-mannered guy she thought he was.
- *The Shield*: In the final montage, as Kid Rock's "Bawitdaba" thumps on the sound track, Detective Vic Mackey (Michael Chiklis) and Detective Shane Vendrell (Walton Goggins) kill a drug dealer rival to their boy, Rondell Robinson (Walter Jones), in self-defense, and then Vic shoots fellow Detective Terry Crowley (Reed Diamond) in the face with the drug dealer's gun. If we didn't already realize Vic Mackey was a dirty cop, this is a major game changer.
- *The Newsroom*: The audience learns MacKenzie (Emily Mortimer) was actually present for Will's (Jeff Daniels) rant against America (not a hallucination); she was holding up the signs that prompted him.
- *Homeland*: Carrie (Claire Danes) finally convinces Saul (Mandy Patinkin) something is amiss with returned POW soldier Nicholas Brody (Damian Lewis) when she points out that Brody is seemingly sending a signal with his fingers whenever he's being interviewed by the media.
- *Scandal*: The audience learns Olivia had an affair with the president, and perhaps he isn't telling the truth about the woman who claimed to have had a relationship with him (the phrase "sweet baby" arouses Olivia's suspicion).

- *The West Wing*: Near the end, the audience learns that Chief of Staff Leo McGarry (John Spencer) was instructed by the president to fire Josh Lyman (Bradley Whitford) for his comments on a talk show, and Leo was working behind the scenes to resolve the conflict and save Josh's job.
- *Mad Men* plays its final trump card when Don Draper (Jon Hamm), who we'd assumed was a womanizing bachelor, goes home to his wife and kids in the suburbs.
- *Damages* reveals that Patty Hewes (Glenn Close) is the devil (more or less) when we see her tossing a studded dog collar into the Long Island Sound beside her beach house. Earlier, we'd witnessed the horrific murder of the dog as a fear and coercion tactic. And now we know it was Patty who ordered the hit.
- *Lost* builds to the reveal that they're not on an ordinary tropical island because there are otherworldly creatures. They're in a version of *The Twilight Zone*.
- By the end of the *Modern Family* pilot, we realize that Jay Pritchett (Ed O'Neill) is Claire (Julie Bowen) and Mitchell's (Jessie Tyler Ferguson) dad. And as "The Circle of Life" from *The Lion King* plays in the end scene, it's Jay who is the vital link between this disparate but loving family.
- At the end of the pilot for *The Following*, former FBI agent Ryan Hardy (Kevin Bacon) manages to apprehend an escaped convicted serial killer Joe Carroll (James Purefoy) and lock him up—but then we discover that Carroll's followers are still at large and are actively continuing to carry out his nefarious mission.

Bottom line: give us something to discover by the end.

INTERVIEW: Veena Sud

Veena Sud Credits

Best known for:

The Killing (Executive Producer/Writer) 2011–2012
Emmy Nominated (Outstanding Writing for a Drama Series) 2011
WGA Award Nominated (New Series) 2012
Cold Case (Executive Producer/Producer/Writer) 2005–2008

NL: My first question is about the murder mystery that played over the two seasons. Did you reverse engineer the plot? In other words, did you start out knowing what you needed to reveal and then structure and back into it?

VS: That's a great question because we didn't. All we knew was that at the end of two seasons, we would reveal the killer of Rosie Larson [Katie Findlay]. But, as far as creating enough material and journeys for each of the characters, over the course of twenty-six episodes, we started from the beginning and from a very character-based place, which was, who is this person? What is their backstory? What is their secret? How do worlds collide? How do secrets become unearthed? And partnerships, and friendships, and family—and a political campaign. We spent a lot of time walking in each character's shoes before we decided that this was how it would all lay down—the macro plot of the conspiracy and how Rosie Larson walked into the middle of this plan—the final twist of who her killer was. Ultimately, it's interesting because on Cold Case, we did the very opposite, or at least I did as a writer, which was fleshing out the beginning: Where do you find the body? How does this murder become unveiled and discovered? And then what are the final true moments of this person's life before they were killed? And then filling in the middle. I knew the beginning, I knew the end, and it was my job at that point to put flesh on that skeleton. Inevitably the end would shift: place would shift, time would shift, things would shift, but for the most part the murder itself would stay intact with the murderer (who would be revealed by the end of each episode). But The Killing was a different type of animal. It was a longer form story. It took, obviously, more time to reveal the truth of the story, and in order to service that we had to be able to go on a very long voyage with these people who, overtime, we identified with and cared about.

NL: You definitely had a lot of plates to get up in the air, just in terms of getting us invested in each person and what they had to lose or what they had to gain from it—both in the political campaign, within the family, and with Sarah Linden (Mireille Enos). You're saying though that you didn't know that Terry (Jamie Anne Allman) would ultimately be the one who pushed the car in—and put the car in gear—that it was something that evolved? That Jamie (Eric Ladin) was the one who accidentally beat her up?

VS: We knew that in the original Danish series, Forbrydelsen, that the character of Ulrik Strange was the killer. And Søren [Sviestrup], who created the Danish series, wanted everything to circle back to something very personal and close to the family. And I loved that idea and having done a lot of research for the last fifteen years with cops—that is the great tragedy of the vast majority of homicides—it's love and money. It's the people you know and the people you love—and those are the people you kill. And that's what was so resonant to me about the tragedy of homicide. I knew I wanted to elicit that feeling—that I wanted it to be a similar place for us. We got to it pretty quickly. Because it's character based, there's a ton of time we spend with these people. We wanted to make sure that we weren't just connecting the dots plot-wise. There were almost two tasks at the beginning: one was to create the macro plot and we knew we would get to the place that was resonant with this particular killer, but what we had to do was say, "OK, let's just not talk about plot, let's talk about these people. And, from the characters, let's start talking about all the different routes and the different roads and the red herrings. And all the different ways that the story could play out." We knew that as we went along in the first two weeks of meeting in the writers' room at the beginning of season 1, it was very clear that the world would get bigger and bigger and bigger. Because I loved the idea too that this seventeen-year-old girl from the wrong side of the tracks, crossed paths with this macro-world of powerful men and power brokers in a major American city and how that happened. Everything either had to build on or create a view for the audience into what Rosie was doing that night, who she was, and/or the bigger machinations that were going on in the city of Seattle.

NL: Was the Danish series one hour for each day of the investigation? Was it twenty-six days also?

VS: The Danish series' seasons were shorter. They had a total of eleven episodes per season. But every episode of their story was one day—that was the DNA of the show which we brought to the American version.

NL: What's so fascinating about the show for me is its profound exploration of grief. Because grieving is something that gets glossed over in just about every American story. We either want to shy away from it, or with how fast the news cycles go—what is a tragedy on Monday is not even in the news anymore by Wednesday. Everything just passes, when the reality with grief is that it's an extremely arduous and up and down process. For me, I commend you and your team on letting us know how that feels on so many levels—and also making the body count—count. Every death resonates and has a ripple effect throughout each story and all of the relationships are impacted. To me, that's one of the great triumphs of the show. When it comes to delving deeper into your characters in every episode and not just a new piece of information for the plot, but going deeper into character—do you have strategies for that? Because it tends to be the weakness that a lot of students struggle with—just digging deeper, finding the nuance, finding the subtext—and the unexpected. Do you create backstory biographies? Sarah is such a complex character. How did you conceive her complicated backstory?

VS: Research is extremely important to me because I think real life has all these nuggets of incredible scenes and incredible stories and characters—and we can't beat it. It's there out in the world, and we just have to pick off these specific moments. When I was writing the pilot and when the writers convened for season 1, we spent time—and I had spent time—with families who had lost their children. There's a national organization (with a branch in Los Angeles) that was so generous with their time. They were such open books about what they went through. I am a cop writer, so

I spend a lot of time with cops. In particular, Sarah was a compendium of four different women I had met over the years. Two of them were homicide cops and one of them was homicide and sex crimes on the east coast and one of them was an undercover detective in narcotics in Los Angeles. She actually introduced me to the person who became the basis for the Holder (Joel Kinnaman) character prior to writing the pilot. Hiding out with these undercover cops—I think that's so important—you have to actually go; you can't just look it up online. You have to actually go and meet the people and hang out with them or drink coffee with them. Just sit there and shoot the shit and see all those interesting things that they do and who they are and why they do what they do—which is the fascinating thing to me. I did that a lot with the political campaign, prior to writing the pilot, I went up to Seattle and met with various city council members in Seattle. That was my beginning point, before I committed pen to paper. I needed to go out into the world and see what's there first before I rushed to any judgment about who these people are. Of course, the driving thing for any storyteller is that there's an element of yourself or a thing that you feel this character can speak to. What we did with all our characters in the writers' room in season 1 and prior to writing the pilot was just, "Who are they?" Don't rush the plot because sometimes I do that, and I totally get why students do that because you want to see the action of the character. But I think you have to know who that person is, and then they'll start instructing you in what they do—and it's surprising.

In season 1, Holder smoked pot with the girls, and it was a surprising moment. We had spent weeks and weeks and weeks talking about this guy. The writers met the undercover cop he was based on as well as two other undercovers. We talked about them; we mused on them. We talked about Holder—where did he come from? Where did he grow up? What did his family look like? Who is he? It's in these moments that scenes come out. It's surprising—I didn't even expect that that would happen. I was breaking the story and all of a sudden I was like, "Shit—what if Holder did this?" And, that actually was not even based on any of the research.

> *When you infuse yourself and marinate yourself in the real world of these characters, they will start telling you things and leading you down these roads that are happily surprising and interesting and cool.*

NL: Both Linden and Holder are very flawed and they're both damaged. In season 2, we will find out how extremely damaged she is when she gets placed in seventy-two-hour hold. It creates a lot of empathy for her and deepens the stakes in terms of why she's so driven. And for Holder, he's a rookie trying to prove himself. Do you consciously think about likability and empathy and who we are rooting for? Because she's kind of a bad mother, negligent from time to time. She's very unconventional and very flawed—and yet doing something heroic and noble. Does it matter to you when you're creating a flawed protagonist that she's inherently likable and positive?

VS: It's a good question because I think it's one of the hardest things to do, but it's essential, at least for me it is, that what the world thinks about your character stays irrelevant to you as you're writing it. If you can see their humanity—and not by providing a litmus test that the world approves of, but that *you* approve of—that's all that matters. In terms of Sarah and the bad mother question, it was essential to make her like many, many mothers that I know who are struggling and are torn and are wracked with guilt. I think a lot of people recognize that aspect of the character and that made her human. She's not a TV mom who somehow juggles it all with a big smile on her face. We all come from places where we wish we could have done more. We wish we could be better—especially with motherhood—it's such a sacred cow. That was very important for me in terms of all the characters—making them human. Ultimately, we're all flawed and we have secrets and we've done things we feel horrible about—and we'll do them again. But, those are the type of characters that I find interesting and I'm not even concerned with whether they are likable or not. If I see their humanity, that's what matters.

NL: It's a great answer because most broadcast network TV shows tend to idealize and sugarcoat stuff, and I like that she's struggling. There were places where you really challenged me as a parental viewer, like when Linden's son has the flu and she's stuck at the precinct. I'll admit that I judged her for that, but I could also see how heavily it weighed on her responsibility to crack the case. Mitch Larsen (Michelle Forbes) is also a flawed mom who chooses to leave her family to grieve, but in doing so (temporarily) abandons her sons and husband when they needed her the most. There are a lot of interesting parallels between Mitch and Sarah in terms of our empathy and how it shifts like a pendulum. The same holds true for Darren Richmond (Billy Campbell); in season 1, he's slimy and I didn't trust or like him at all. I thought, of course, he was the murderer early on and Gwen (Kristen Lehman) and Jamie also. But once Darren gets shot, our empathy shifts, and he swiftly earns our compassion. It was a great way to raise his political fortune, but he also genuinely seems to find redemption.

VS: Yes, that's what we were hoping. I'm glad you felt that way about him.

NL: Regarding point of view—when you wrote the pilot and when you were conceiving the show, were there different points of view? There are times where we have an omniscient point of view, and times when it feels very subjective—where we're in Linden's head and we're seeing things through her eyes. Did you ever wonder what the point of view in terms of telling the story should be? Did you have any rules in the writing room in terms of what you're limited in showing or not showing? Or was it more organic?

VS: We, for the most part, used the device of three worlds—and all three worlds had their own point of view. So that created somewhat of a sense of omniscient point of view. If there was a rule, it was that we had to stay within the world of those characters. It was like the characters in that world were the only points of reference. But when a character got more and more important in the story and more of a player, then we could drift over and see them. Like in season 2, we saw Roberta [Patti Kim] and Nicole Jackson [Claudia Ferri] in the security room when they discovered that Sarah had . . .

NL: Right—when she smashes her hand in the door?

VS: Right, but it was tied to the security cam footage. There was always the delicate balance of how much we could show within the world. With any of the main characters in the world, we clearly could use them as reference points, to see what they experienced, but then when the secondary characters were introduced later, they had to earn weight in the story in order to be a part of it. The other thing you said in reference to the omniscient [POV]—it's a good question in the beginning because Patty Jenkins directed the pilot and the finale. She had this brilliant visual conceit which was that *the camera had a point of view*, so the camera wasn't just sitting there, flaccidly, recording and documenting. There was a very subtle point of view that the camera had—and I loved that. I loved it because it influenced all of her moves in the pilot. It influenced the freneticness of the camera, the slowness of the camera, the longing—she really infused the camera and us with these emotions as we took in scenes. And even the aerials, we spent hours talking about them.

NL: I actually noticed them in a particularly vulnerable scene. For example, there were shots that at the top of a high-rise building where it was just precarious. They weren't just neutral interstitials. I felt like they did have that commentary.

VS: We shot the aerials after we shot the pilot. I realized that I wanted the aerials to be something, but I couldn't articulate what that was. There's something very evocative about seeing the city from a plane. Patty and I got to this place where those aerials were almost the point of view of Rosie—almost the point of view of a dead girl. They had emotion. It's as subtle as coming out of a scene; you'd feel the sadness of that scene or you'd feel how askew things were in the scene. That's how she went and shot the aerials.

NL: I hadn't even thought of it in *The Lovely Bones* kind of way—as if looking down from heaven. Did you have tone meetings with subsequent directors where you would say to them, for example, "I want it to look like this character's guilty in this episode"? Like in the "Donnie or Marie" episode, where it starts with it very much looking like Gwen is guilty, but then it shifts—and I've noticed this in reality shows sometimes where you think they're subtly hinting who's going to get voted off. The way that they're showing a little bit more of that character or less of another character. Were those discussions ever conscious in terms of the way it was shot?

VS: Yes, absolutely. It always began with the script. Especially the "Donnie or Marie" episode, because we were very conscious of bopping between them, so in breaking the story in the writers' room: How do you create the sense that "this is the one" or "no, this is the one." Tone is really important to me. I think it's probably really important to a lot of showrunners that we spend a lot of time with directors. Because you're analyzing the script, you're going over your hopes, page by page, visually for the episode both emotionally and thematically—and about the subtle turn at the end of the scene—what you're supposed to think at the end of it.

NL: Was there a difference in breaking story on *Cold Case* and on *The Killing*? Obviously, I know they are completely different—they're almost polar opposites. In terms of *Cold Case*, it's one case which gets solved by the end. But did you break A, B, and C stories and structure the story in the same way or was it a very different process with *The Killing*?

VS: The mechanics of the documents that were created were very similar. I learned that from Meredith Steihm, the creator of *Cold Case*, and that process was hugely helpful. There are many documents generated before someone goes to script. You're kicking the tires constantly without again robbing the story of its magic because you can overwrite—you can overanalyze something. So the mechanics of *Cold Case* and *The Killing* were very similar. The difference I guess was that besides having to spend so much time with these characters over twenty-six episodes that we had to have so much material and know them in such an intimate way—the cops included. The A story in *Cold Case* was the big story—that was the hardiest part of every episode and where we had to devote most of our time. With *Cold Case*, we knew season-wise what the B and the C stories were for our cops. This is what personally they were going through—and these were the scenes that we would pepper in throughout the season to show this arc in their character, but because 90 percent of the episode was about the killing—the investigation was its own mini-arc. That's where the majority of the time was spent. Whereas with *The Killing*, what we had to do is take three big worlds and over the course of each season map out where each world was going. We had this gigantic board in the writers' room with every character, every episode, and our touch points of each character's development—what was going on with them over the course of a season. And, then there's obviously the investigation—how the investigation is tied into Sarah's backstory and Holder's secret. It was this incredibly intense juggling session.

NL: In the season finale, the footage that Rosie shot on the video camera—it's the closing valentine for the Larson family. It's used in a totally different way than we're anticipating. Because it seems like it's going to be incriminating evidence, and it's going to completely tie into everything. It's bittersweet, but it leaves us with a kind of happy resolution. Where did this idea come from? Any final thoughts on the end of the season?

VS: We were in the room first season when we were talking about the big arc and how things would ultimately end, and we started to talk about this film camera because the film plays a part early on in season 1. Through the teacher and this revelation that she's running around the city with this camera. We watched this young artist from Seattle, this fifteen-year-old girl, Olivia B. We were just looking at how young girls shoot things because we didn't want it to look professional—what she was shooting at the beginning of season 1. There was this incredible beauty and voice of this girl, and we were all so moved by it. It was ultimately about this girl [Rosie] who you just think of as a victim, and in a way, has never been present. We don't flash back to her. We are like people left behind in a real-life murder. You don't get anything. You just get what's left in her bedroom—in the album. And to have this graceful moment of just this gift to us, the audience and the family, but the audience mostly, we've never seen Rosie alive except when she was running in terror. We saw her on film for a split second at that dance.

NL: And there's the very brief moment where Mitch is packing for the camping trip and you get to see the last moment when she was at the house alive.

VS: That was the biggest discussion: Should we have flashbacks of the victim? Should we see her? How do we make her a presence in the story and not just a body? But then the tension is that you don't have anything except for the memories that she left behind. It's heartbreaking. It's eerie too and a little bit interesting to see. One of the homicide detectives I was telling you about on the East Coast, I think she fell in love with this guy who had been murdered because she just saw these things in his house. Well, not "fell in love," but it was just interesting this relationship she had with the dead. This is not just about body counts, and not just about exciting plot and getting the bad guy—this is about the price of a life. And this is who this girl is and this is the tragedy of her loss and this is the hope of her life. And losing this is losing the world. Our final touch that we wanted to put on the story is that we get to see Rosie alive—that finally after twenty-five hours, we get to see what's lost.

NL: It was a very beautiful, graceful endnote.

18

ESTABLISH THE MYTHOLOGY

All series contain some inherent mythology. At a minimum, this will include the backstories for each main character—which may or may not be completely true. As this book is all about *scripted* television series, all characters and plotlines are fictional. And fiction is always open to interpretation. In other words, every character has his/her own agenda and perspective on past events. "If memory serves . . ." is about as reliable as it gets, even for the most honest among us. Other characters present the version of themselves they'd like others to see versus the full truth. Watching a TV series is interactive in that viewers tune in to discover and learn more about what makes these people tick on the inside, and how ongoing external challenges might force them to embrace change, ignore it (aka denial), or actively resist it.

Whereas central mysteries concern something lost or obscured in the past, and central questions concern the future outcome of problems, a *series' mythology concerns the rules of the game.*

Creating a Credible, Alternative Reality

In science fiction, we're presented with a world that bears *some* resemblance to our own. But how does this sci-fi world differ from ours? Here are some basic questions for you to consider as you develop your series' mythology:

- Are we in present day or in the near or distant future?
- Is it a post-apocalyptic, dystopian world?
- Is it a space colony?
- Is it overpopulated or are there very few survivors?

- Is the environment sustainable?
- Is the air toxic?
- Is the Earth burning up or flooding or arid and arctic?
- Do animals and/or other anomalous creatures live among us?
- Are humans the dominant species?
- Are food and supplies in abundance or is there poverty and famine?
- Is your version of the future or this alternative world light or dark?
- Who governs?
- What kinds of laws keep the order?
- Is it a militant state? Anarchy? Somewhere in between?
- Who enforces the laws?
- What kinds of weapons exist?
- What kind of special abilities do the police and citizens have?
- Is there a class or caste system or equality?
- Does artificial intelligence exist?
- Is the world on the verge of singularity theory?

Humans versus Cylons

In *Battlestar Galactica*, a human civilization has migrated from their homeland of Kobol to a group of distant planets known as the Twelve Colonies. For decades, the Twelve Colonies have battled against a cybernetic race—the Cylons—whose mission is the annihilation of the human race. The Cylons wage war against the Twelve Colonies and the Colonial Fleet of starships that protect them. These attacks devastate the Colonial Fleet, destroy the Colonies, and virtually all of their populations. Of the entire Colonial battle fleet, only the Battlestar Galactica, an enormous battleship and "spacecraft carrier," manages to survive the Cylon attack. Under the leadership of Commander Adama (Edward James Olmos), the *Galactica* and the pilots of "Viper" fighters lead a fugitive fleet of survivors in search of the fabled thirteenth colony—planet Earth.

What was most revolutionary about *Battlestar* is its showrunner Ronald D. Moore's resistance to old school science fiction mythology. In his manifesto, "Naturalistic Science Fiction, or Taking the Opera out of Space Opera," Moore makes a provocative pronouncement: "Our goal is nothing less than the reinvention of the science fiction television series . . . [and to jettison] the stock characters, techno-double-talk, bumpy-headed aliens, thespian histrionics, and empty heroics." Moore set out *not* to make another *Star Trek* or *Star Wars*; rather, he's after something much more nuanced, with the character complexity and contradictions of *The West Wing* or *The Sopranos*. Moore's manifesto goes on to proclaim: "We want the audience to connect with the characters of *Galactica* as people. Our characters are not super-heroes. They are not an elite. They are everyday people caught up in an enormous cataclysm and trying to survive it as best they can. They are you and me."

Perhaps the best way to sum up *Battlestar Galactica's* approach to mythology is *less is more*. Rather than a strict adherence to the tropes of the sci-fi genre or even the laws of time and space, Moore and his writing staff were cognizant that the audience actually connects to the people—not the mythology and technology. You can create the biggest, most mind-blowing, climactic battle sequences ever, but nothing trumps those small moments of character emotion.

Welcome to Doomsday

In *The Walking Dead* pilot, we enter the arena after some sort of zombie apocalypse. We're not sure if the cause was biological, chemical, nuclear, or environmental. All we know is that virtually everyone is dead—but then resurrected as a zombie in constant need of living human flesh in order to survive. In season 1, the small group of survivors makes their way to the Center for Disease Control (CDC) in Atlanta. The episode teases us with an explanation of the apocalypse, but provides no clear-cut answers to this cataclysmic mystery. But we do get one horrific piece of news via the Director of the CDC (Noah Emmerich) who whispers something cryptic into Rick's (Andrew Lincoln) ear before they both depart (Rick leaves with his fellow badass survivors; the CDC Director kills himself). SPOILER ALERT: By the end of season 2, Rick tells his comrades the ominous news: all survivors are already infected with the virus—and it's only a matter of time before each one of them is going to turn into a zombie—whether they're bitten or not. In other words, inside each one of them is a ticking time bomb. How's that to ruin your whole day? At this point, we have also become well versed in the Rules of the Zombies:

- They have very low intelligence and live only to eat living human flesh.
- They do not talk or communicate with one another or use technology.
- They congregate in flocks and each new prey causes a feeding frenzy.
- They're not smart enough to scale walls or climb over fences.
- They can't deliberately strategize, set fires, or use weapons or explosives.
- They can't pick locks or operate cars and other machinery.
- They don't eat each other, but will feed on animals.
- They can't procreate.
- They can be killed by non-zombies, but only by crushing their skulls, thereby destroying their brains.
- If an uninfected human is bitten, there is no antidote; it's just a matter of time before he or she will transform into a snarling, vicious cannibal.

At press time, these rules have remained constant. The series is based on a series of comic books of the same title, but I haven't looked ahead to find out what's going to happen next because the TV series doesn't always follow that roadmap. I can only prognosticate and hope for zombie evolution over time. For example:

- What if the zombies can start to *learn* and aren't simply the Walking Stupid?
- What if a zombie accidentally fires a gun or gets behind the wheel of a truck?
- What if they start to be able to communicate in some sort of zombie language (à la the book and movie *Warm Bodies*)?
- What if all that rotting flesh and septic wounds cause bacterial and viral infections and those viruses started to mutate?

So many possibilities—or maybe the show's creators and showrunner plan to keep all the rules constant?

When I interviewed the now former showrunner of *The Walking Dead*, Glen Mazzara, I asked him if the viewers were ever going to find out what caused the zombie apocalypse and why? Glen's response was a definitive no. In his view, it didn't matter. To him, the show was all about survival of the fittest and how to build a new civilization amid chills and thrills. To him, this was/is a horror show, so he preferred to keep the scientific gobbledy-gook to a minimum. Our motley crew of survivors are all on the endangered species list, overwhelmingly outnumbered, and there is no escape. See also *Revolution*.

Blood Is Thicker Than Water

In the science fiction/fantasy series *True Blood*, created and produced by Alan Ball and based upon *The Southern Vampire Mysteries* novels by Charlaine Harris, we're indoctrinated into a fresh, new twist on the classic vampire genre: they feast on synthetic blood (brand name: Tru Blood) that's readily available in all convenience stores, like six packs of beer or bottles of ketchup. The show's mythology is that vampires have been living among us for centuries, and it's only recently that Japanese scientists have created synthetic blood to enable vampires to "come out of the coffin" now that they no longer need to feed on humans to survive. But as with every revolution, there are inherent politics. Some vampires desire to join and integrate with the human race. But hardcore vampires are resistant and feel it's against their violent nature.

Set in the small town of Bon Temps, Louisiana, the series' main protagonist is Sookie Stackhouse (Anna Paquin), a "Halfling," who is later revealed to be a human–fairy hybrid with telepathic abilities. Sookie works as a waitress at Merlotte's Bar & Grill, owned by Sam Merlotte (Sam Trammell). Unbeknownst to most of the townsfolk, Sam is a shapeshifter. Sookie meets and falls in love with Bill Compton (Stephen Moyer), a sexy 173-year-old vampire who looks about 30. Also in this phantasmagoria are: Sookie's sex-crazed brother Jason (Ryan Kwanten); the Sheriff of Area 5, Eric Northman (Alexander Skarsgård)—who also happens to be a thousand-year-old vampire; and then there's Lafayette Reynolds (Nelsan Ellis), a flamboyantly gay, black, fry cook, drug dealer, and *medium*. In this show's universe, mythological beings (and Tru Blood) are, more or less, the norm.

In contrast to the well-defined, narrow parameters of, say, *The Walking Dead*, we get the sense that virtually *anything* can happen in Bon Temps. And so, in addition to the proper care and feeding of vampires, the show also explores the humanity of fairies, werewolves, witches, and a Dionysian cult. The "sweet spot" of this series is how its authors skillfully correlate these fantastic, esoteric, sexy supernatural plotlines to relatable contemporary issues, such as racism, homophobia, drug addiction, faith and religion, pervasive media, and the quest for identity. At the core, this is a show about "family" values, and the blood ties that bind us together and rip us apart

On a supernatural series, the mythology deals with the rules of magic. Here are some basic questions for you to ponder as you conjure:

- Who has special powers?
- How do they work?
- What is their limitation?
- How are they activated?
- Can they be neutralized or reversed?
- Is there a totem or book of spells or amulet or material device needed to invoke the magic?

In the pilot episode of *Once Upon a Time*, we learn that the sleepy town of Storybrooke, Maine has stopped and that every resident is a fairy-tale character with no memory of that life. Henry (Jared S. Gilmore), a young resident of Storybrooke convinced that he knows the truth, runs away to Boston and persuades bounty hunter Emma Swan (Jennifer Morrison) to come back home with him. Once Emma enters the town, time starts moving again, telling us that Emma is an important cog in Storybrooke's clockwork.

When Setting Up the Rules for an Unfamiliar World, Bring an Outsider into the World to Help the Audience Get Up to Speed

In the *Once Upon a Time* pilot, we cross-cut between the fairy-tale world and Storybrooke and learn that the Evil Queen (Lana Parrilla) has placed a curse on Snow White (Ginnifer Goodwin) and Prince Charming (Josh Dallas) and relegated them to Storybrooke where there would be no more happily ever afters (which is the Evil Queen's own happy ending). Emma's arrival upsets the balance and overrules the curse. We also get to witness how each character in Storybrooke has a double (or *doppelganger*) counterpoint in the fairy-tale world. The creators and showrunners (Edward Kitsis and Adam Horowitz) were careful to ensure that the rules of their Storybrooke world were clear, simple, and easy to understand. And they provided us with Emma as our guide to navigate it. As an outsider trying to make sense of the place and her role in it, Emma got to ask questions that the audience would ask and investigate for us.

The Ethos of Westeros and Essos

On *Game of Thrones*, created for HBO by David Benioff and D. B. Weiss, adapted from a series of fantasy novels by George R. R. Martin, seven noble families (the houses of Stark, Lannister, Baratheon, Greyjoy, Tully, Arryn, and Tyrell) fight for control of the mythical land of Westeros. The political tensions between houses build to an epic "modern" war. On the continents of Westeros and Essos, summer has lasted a decade, and the impending winter is foreboding as the lore of its mythical monsters (or "White Walkers") foretells.

Showrunner David Benioff tagged the series "*The Sopranos* in Middle Earth," referring to the ruthless rivalries among powerful families; killing sprees, steely coercion, murder, and a self-serving code of ethics within its medieval Europe–inspired, fantasy setting.

The series also offers allusions to Hadrian's Wall, the decline of the Roman Empire, the legend of Atlantis, Icelandic Vikings, and the Mongols (known on the series as the Dothraki), along with elements of the Hundred Years' War and the Italian Renaissance. Author George R. R. Martin and series creators/showrunners, Benioff and Weiss, brilliantly succeed at weaving these contrasting elements into their own alternative history, replete with balls of fire, White Walkers (reminiscent of a zombie apocalypse), and flying dragons.

With its enormous cast of hundreds (the largest of *any* TV series, ever), it can sometimes be difficult to keep track of every character and subplot without a crib sheet. Nevertheless, the series succeeds by tapping into mythic structure that's hardwired into our DNA. Its legions of fans across the globe aren't daunted by backstory, and can recite the show's complex mythology, chapter and verse, as if it's a badge of honor.

What's truly amazing about *Game of Thrones* is how all the rules of the world relate to each other and the theme of "fire and ice." By creating rules around these opposing forces, it fuels constant conflict. And who is to say which is stronger:

fire or ice? There is speculation that the final battle will come down to Jon Snow (Kit Harington), representing ice, and Daenerys Targaryen (Emilia Clarke), representing fire. The main quest is to take the Iron Throne (although Jon Snow isn't after the throne), so it seems for each character that the main obstacle will either be fire or ice. If you wanted to get obsessive you could probably link each of the main contenders to either of those elements. For example, Tyrion Lannister (Peter Dinklage) used wildfire to win the battle at Blackwater Bay. Stannis Baratheon (Stephen Dillane) worships the Lord of Light (fire). Robb Stark (Richard Madden) is from the North (ice).

In terms of *Game of Thrones'* mythology, here are the lists of rules for the dragons, White Walkers, and Lord of Light.

Rules for the Dragons:

- They were thought to have died out 150 years ago.
- They hatch from eggs exposed to extreme heat (fire).
- Humans can have some dragon traits (extreme heat doesn't affect Daenerys), but it's not clear how she can be a descendent of dragons.
- They are extremely loyal.
- They can be trained. Can learn to respond to a vocal command. (Daenerys can command them to breathe fire.)

Rules for White Walkers:

- They have not been seen for eight thousand years.
- The wall was erected to keep them out.
- If you are killed by a White Walker, you can also be reanimated by them in order to become one of their servants.
- White Walkers have scaly white skin and blue eyes. Servants have pale skin and blue eyes.
- Both fire and a special artifact can kill them. (Interesting tie-in with the fire and dragons.)
- Considered by most to be legend. (I consider this to be a rule about them because it sets up how people react to them or any mention of them.)

Rules for Lord of Light:

- Centered on one, all-knowing god—the Lord of Light. (What does that sound like?)
- Lord of Light is represented by fire. (More fire tie-ins.)
- Priests/priestesses have the ability to bring people back from the dead.
- Shadows can be manipulated by practitioners to do their bidding. (Shadows are created by Light.)

Taking Dramatic License

There is also historical mythology. These series, such as *The Tudors, The Borgias, Vikings, Hatfields & McCoys,* and *Spartacus,* are loosely based upon (and in some cases merely "inspired by") "true" historical events. But they all take dramatic license to serve the needs of drama, suspense, and overall marketability. They are historical series, not documentaries, so the audience is willing to suspend their disbelief to come along on the journey. Henry VIII was an unattractive, corpulent, sickly, petulant bully. And yet on *The Tudors,* Henry was portrayed by the virile, handsome movie star Jonathan Rhys Meyers. Don't get too bogged down by meticulously adhering to historical details.

Do your research, avoid anachronisms, and aim for verisimilitude. As long as the time period and setting *feel* right, the audience will allow themselves to get swept away in the dramatic action. Of course, there will always be history scholars that cry foul. You can't please everyone. Off with their heads!

INTERVIEW: Adam Horowitz and Edward Kitsis

Horowitz and Kitsis Credits

Best known for:

Once Upon a Time (Creators/Executive Producers/Writers) 2011–2012
TRON: Legacy (Film) (Writers) 2010
Lost (Executive Producers/Supervising Producers/Producers/Writers) 2005–2010
    Emmy Nominated (Outstanding Drama Series) 2008–2010
    WGA Award Winner (Dramatic Series) 2006
    WGA Award Nominated (Dramatic Series) 2006–2007, 2009–2010
Felicity (Producers/Writers) 2001–2002
Popular (Writers) 1999–2001

NL: The question for this chapter is "What's the mythology?" I read that you had this idea for awhile—even before you were on *Lost.* Where did the idea come from and why did this interest you?

AH: The idea came from almost ten years ago now. We had been writing on *Felicity* on the WB. That show ended its run. We were sitting around talking about what's the kind of show that we would want to do.

EK: Because our agent was like, "Why don't you guys think about a pilot?"

AH: Yeah, which led us to talk about things that we loved, stories that were formative to us, that got us going which led to a discussion of fairy tales. I had just read this book called, *The Uses of Enchantment* by Bruno Bettelheim, which was about fairy tales and their influence on kids.

EK: At the time *Smallville* was out, but no one had really done fairy tales. We realized what we loved about them was the open canvas. What was great about *Lost* was that one week you were writing a show about a guy who won the lottery and the next week it was about a con man. You never just wrote only cops or only lawyers. So when Adam read this book, he started talking about fairy tales and about how much it would suck to be the Evil Queen [Lana Parrilla] because you were literally in a place where everything had a happy ending, but everything you do, fails. You get a working oven inside a gingerbread house and that stupid blind witch can't kill two kids? So that was our genesis of: "Where would she go to win?" And that was our world. That was our premise.

AH: And what we had cooked up almost ten years ago is pretty similar to what it is now. In terms of there was this woman [Emma played by Jennifer Morrison] who came to this town who is the daughter of Snow White [Ginnifer Goodwin] and Prince Charming [Josh Dallas]. And there was a curse and a kid. But there were various incarnations.

EK: In one she had two kids and in one she had no kids. In one, she didn't know she had a kid which was a weird one.

AH: We played with a version where she didn't know she had a kid. She didn't know she was pregnant. She was in a coma and the kid was delivered, but she never knew. We thought it was a cool idea, but we could never figure out how to make that work as a series. I think the problem was that in 2002 or 2003 that we just weren't ready to concoct such a big canvas. But I think what we did know that if we wanted to do our own show, we wanted to do something that would allow us the freedom to do many types of stories but finding an umbrella under which they all could exist.

EK: It wasn't until we got to *Lost* that we thought, "Oh, this is how you could do it." That was our learning experience. I remember going into the last season we were having dinner with Damon Lindelof [Executive Producer/Creator, *Lost*] and he asked us what we were thinking of doing after this, so we pitched him our show. He said, "That's a good idea." And then once the show ended, we said this is what we wanted to do.

NL: Did you go in and pitch it to ABC?

EK: Yeah. We had a general meeting with ABC Studios with Barry Jossen and Patrick Moran. They had a couple of books and properties in mind, but they asked, "Do you have anything?" And we pitched our idea. And they said, "This one." What happened was that Adam and I went to Damon about going to pitch Paul Lee at the network.

AH: We pitched them what the broad strokes of the pilot would be. Paul Lee said to go ahead and write the pilot. Everybody seemed very enthused and excited. All these ideas from all these years that had been swirling around. It was a huge, massive challenge to figure out how to turn that into a fifty-page script.

EK: We literally had four outlines that we threw out. We just couldn't figure out the way in. Plus, we had a movie coming out called *Tron*. It was our first experience having a movie coming out which was very stressful and distracting. We came back after Christmas and ABC said, "You understand you have two weeks before you're out of the cycle." So we were like, "Fuck, this can't be done. We have a good idea that we can't figure out." Damon came down and the three of us were talking and we were just going to tell them that we couldn't do it. And then it turned into, "Well, there's really no show unless you do this." And then someone said, "And then you do that." And then all of a sudden, we found it.

AH: I think one of the breakthroughs for us was that we always in the many incarnations of the outline had talked about opening it with the birth of Emma and the dwarfs seeing the curse come in. Then it hit us, "Wait. That shouldn't be the opening of the pilot—that's the story running concurrently." Because we had so much backstory for all these characters and once we realized that we shouldn't just shove it all into the pilot and be done with it. Let's take all that mythology and all that backstory and make it part of the show.

EK: We were so late in the process that we went in and pitched the outline. We literally pitched the pilot beat by beat.

AH: We literally spent an hour with the network.

EK: Scene 1, scene 2, scene 3 . . . and when we were done, they said, "Okay, go write it." We had ten days to write it before it was the final deadline. They had already started picking things up.

AH: This was late January of 2011.

EK: We handed it in on a Friday and it got picked up on a Monday. Of course, there were still notes and things to be done, but that's how late we were in the process. It was like we started six weeks behind.

NL: Sometimes writing with that kind of pressure and terror, you don't have a lot of time to second guess yourself.

AH: I also think what was helpful was years of thinking about it. It wasn't just a case of writing a pilot in ten days. Once we found the way we could see it and execute it, then all of those pieces fell into place with that script and we wrote it relatively quickly.

NL: Where did the rules of the world come from? One of the things that's so tricky about this show is that I watch it and think, "How did all of these elements come together?" It's so impressive and seems so seamless—now that it's come together.

EK: I think one of the hardest things to do is to be simple. Figuring out the way to make rules for your world that are seamless that when you're watching you don't have to think about them. If you have a lot of scenes where you have characters always explaining what is going on and then your audience has to take notes on it, it just doesn't work. If you can come up with rules that feel intuitive, then you've won.

AH: And for us, we knew there would be a mythology, but we never wanted it to overwhelm the character. We were much more interested in why Grumpy was grumpy, why the Evil Queen is evil, why the Mad Hatter is mad. We may not have planned out the whole season, but for questions like, "Why does the Evil Queen hate Snow White?" We knew what her story was. Once we had those stories in place, then we were able to tie them together. The key was always what does the character want, and you build your mythology around that. We knew from the start of the pilot process that the Queen was casting this curse. We had come up with the story that she had lost her love and blamed Snow. Basing the curse around a queen who had lost her love, that became the cornerstone behind the first mythology that we unfurled in season 1. That's how we make a mythology. Just thinking about what the character wants and what their issues are with the other characters. And then all the other stuff about the magic and curses just needed to be tailored to fit that. We feel that if an audience is invested in why a character wants her revenge then they'll go with all the other stuff.

EK: Damon and Carlton [Cuse, Executive Producer/Creator, *Lost*] gave us a great note when we were on *Lost* which helped our writing a lot. It was, "What am I supposed to be feeling in this scene?" It was this weird note that should have just seemed obvious. The thing about *Lost* is sometimes it would be two scenes about people trying to find water, but there was such manufactured intensity to it because of the emotions behind it. So what is the Queen feeling at this wedding? She's feeling pain because she is staring at everything she wanted and never got.

NL: Because you have two different sets of rules for the forest and the magical realm and for Storybrooke. It seems that right around the halfway point was a benchmark because it was the first place it's been revealed that Belle (Emilie de Ravin) is being kept . . . it seems as though you have central questions running through both worlds. One is that Emma doesn't believe what Henry (Jared Gilmore) is telling her and then by the end of the season, she finally believes. And then she is transported to the other world. It's the first major crossover for Emma. Did you have some of these benchmarks mapped out structurally?

EK: It was one of those things when we started to break story for season 1 that we knew that it was going to be about Emma believing. We had to figure out where that would happen.

AH: We actually thought we would never get away with it past eleven—that people would be horrified and annoyed. And then we got to episode 7 because the death of Sheriff Graham [Jamie Dornan] is going to hold her back. Then we started to realize that her believing was something important which was why we introduced Pinocchio [Eion Bailey]. We didn't want to just put it in a middle episode. We wanted to try to earn it. Because the realness of it would help it sell better and, for us, she could not believe unless it was her son who got her to believe. Look, we thought we'd be cancelled after two episodes.

EK: And, by the way, every critic in town predicted us to be the first cancelled. We were opening against the World Series and the Super Bowl and by the fifth critic I read who predicted us to be DOA, I was then like, "OK, fuck it Adam, let's just do six great episodes."

AH: You just cannot predict what an audience will watch. We just tried to balance big ideas from where the series could go with the big ideas of where a season could go. We tried to set up things that hopefully we'd have a chance to do in season 1. Then we started to construct our tent poles around that. [Episode] 109 was when we introduced the Stranger [Eion Bailey] and there was no way we were going to wrap up that story in three episodes. We knew we wanted to do this bigger thing. By the time we were in the back half of the season, we were able to ramp things up and build to a finale with the curse breaking.

NL: And Emma and Regina aligning against a common enemy.

AH: What was cool about that for us was finding this idea that your protagonist and antagonist both want the same thing which is this kid. In many ways, their motivations are both laudable, but it's how they are going about earning Henry's trust that creates conflict between Emma and Regina. Then it's fun to find situations where the two of them do have to work together for the common good.

NL: It's interesting that you said that Henry was not part of the original concept because his book and his role in the show is so significant in terms of explaining things and getting us up to speed.

EK: Yeah, that was the breakthrough when we realized that we needed to write a ten-year-old version of ourselves coming to get our mom. Henry is the heart and soul of the show. He's the true believer. Our show is for believers. We wanted to make this show about hope and not be cynical—which is tough in today's world when usually anything that is cool is cynical. We wanted people once a week to feel the way I felt when I watched *Charlie and the Chocolate Factory* and the boy got the golden ticket. For me that personally was important. I like that feeling and it's important. Henry embodies that.

NL: When you conceived of Storybrooke, this weird combination between a 2012 beach town and something stuck in the 1950s where there are rotary phones, but are there also cell phones. How did you make that decision?

EK: We felt that these stories were timeless, so Storybrooke had to be timeless. Originally, when we set it, we said that the fairy tales would be the Spielberg side and that the town would be our [legendary film director] Hal Ashby side. But then we realized that Storybrooke became our childhood. A lot of it is little things from our youth that we may remember or that stuck out at us. We just love the metaphor that Storybrooke is timeless because these stories are timeless. We loved the aesthetic of both a rotary phone and that someone could still check their e-mail. We called it faded glory. There was this Reagan documentary that the two of us and Mark Worthington, our production designer, saw. They went back to Reagan's town where he grew up and there was a bandstand—it was the way downtown Disney is. And now, it's abandoned like a ghost town. For us, it was the way you would go see a band in an old theatre. In the 1920s, it was beautiful, but now it's been shit on with stickers. That was Storybrooke. So Emma's car coming in was the first bit of color—and that's why we had the yellow bug coming in.

AH: One of the challenges was, how do you make a cursed town a place people want to spend time in?

EK: Yeah, it was cursed, but not so cursed that you wouldn't want to be there.

AH: For us, the answer was making it reminiscent of places we love, but not quite able to get back to. Emma becomes the catalyst for revitalization.

NL: Theme has been the most polarizing topic for both this book and my last book on film. Where do you stand on theme?

AH: We're theme guys. There's this balancing act, too, between theme and story. For us, if you get them to all coincide, that's the greatest thing for us. And some work better than others. Ultimately, you want the audience to be engaged to care about the story. For us, theme is a means to that end.

EK: It's a unifier. We don't sit down and say, "What's the theme about?" We actually talk about the character. What does the character want? "Well, this week, Regina needs to do _____." And then you start talking about what she wants. And then you say, "What's the theme? What is she learning?"

AH: We've done it many different ways. Sometimes the theme reveals itself clearly.

EK: Beauty and the Beast is the easiest example because Rumple [Robert Carlyle] couldn't love himself.

AH: Sometimes we have an idea that we think is really cool for a story with these characters and then we try to figure out what's the theme. Once we do that, then sometimes the story changes and molds to it. Ultimately, we like to land on a theme which can unify things which helps guide us into making each scene feel like it fits into the show and feels necessary.

NL: It seems like in the Hansel and Gretel episode that you start off with the children planting the candy bars in the backpack, and then you have the kids in the other realm who are told they have to go into the house made of candy. So sometimes the stories between the realms feel very parallel and sometimes they're not.

EK: Some of my favorite ones are when they are not parallel, but the Hansel & Gretel one, we felt that these kids were homeless and they needed their dad, so it had to carry through.

AH: Sometimes you can do it, but sometimes it's too matchy. You can have the connective tissue be more of an emotional issue that both characters are going through in each world or even a thematic question that they're both dealing with. It doesn't have to be so literal.

EK: In the Dreamy episode in the past, all he wanted to do was run away with the Blue Fairy and everyone was telling him not to do it. And in the present day, it was a festival where he had to sell candles. And people were like, "What?" But we said it would work because you're seeing the dream right now. And one of my favorite moments was when we were at the Paley Festival and we were showing that episode. One of the act outs was when Grumpy [Lee Arenberg] smashes all the lights in the town and Mary Margaret [Ginnifer Goodwin] says, "What are you doing?" And he says, "I'm selling candles, sister." And the whole audience started to cheer as if Spider-man had just saved the bus. I looked at Adam and I said, "I can't believe it worked." Because really the story was he's selling candles.

AH: That was a case of us trying to attach it to something emotional. He was in love with this woman. And he didn't think that he could be with her, so he was trying to find a way. It was also that he and Mary Margaret were trying to redeem themselves in the eyes of the town, so that was also the connective tissue.

NL: Once you have an arc and you know where this is going, how do you make the decisions of breaking them down? Are you trying to get them all to dovetail at a certain point?

EK: I feel that oftentimes the episode dictates it. It's an organic process where you want to reveal why the Queen hates Snow White. You plan to do it in episode 15, but then you start to tell the stories and you go, "Oh, there's a little piece before that happens that you want to get to, so then it gets pushed." As you're telling the story, the story starts to reveal itself with what is necessary to be told. You have to be flexible about your plans with what the needs of the stories are.

NL: What I love about your series is that you don't rush things. When you're a kid having a story read to you, you don't want it to end.

EK: That was something we learned on *Lost*. It's funny because in today's world of the Internet, there's a more impatient public. For us, we had a plan for the season and we wanted to give each story its due. People come along for the ride. They are not watching your show for answers because once they do that, then they don't care about anything but the answers. We never want mythology to overwhelm character. We always felt that at the end of season 1 we were going to break the curse because we didn't want every episode to be, "When are they going to break it?" We want people to enjoy Grumpy and enjoy Ruby.

> *O*ne of the greatest lessons that we took from Lost was that the most engaging mysteries are character mysteries. Why people do the things they do? Whether an audience knows it or not, that's what I think they find most engaging. All the other mythological questions are cool and fun, but if they're not attached to engaging character mysteries, then they're not nearly as satisfying.

EK: Exactly, so for me, one of my favorite scenes is when Emma wakes her son up—now she believes. Yes, it broke the curse, but that's secondary to the fact that she saved her son's life. To me, that is the perfect blend of character and mythology.

NL: How much do you trust that your audience is going to be able to keep track of the mythology? Do you put little reminders in?

EK: Sure. You try to build in little reminders, but ultimately, I feel like if you can create within the episode, an engaging story for that character in that episode, the audience will go along for the roller coaster ride—even if they don't remember every detail. For the audience who wants to go closer, then you reward them by saying, "Look, this is how it fits into the larger tapestry."

NL: Audiences are really smart.

EK: Yes, *Lost* was intricate, but go look on the blogs. Everyone got everything. Everything. People loved that the show wasn't dumbing down for them. As long as you do what Adam said and give them something engaging, then they can enjoy it.

AH: Audiences crave meaning. They want things to matter. They want there to be something more to everyone. I think it's that questioning nature that makes people like stories. If you can dig a little deeper and find something behind the story, I think that's very rewarding and makes an audience want to see more.

EK: It's funny because one of the greatest lessons we learned on *Lost* was what Damon and Carlton said when we joined, "This is a character show. Mythology cannot overrun character." We've taken that to heart on this. And when you think about *Lost* and your favorite moments, at least for me personally, it's the character moments.

AH: Or the episode where Sun [Yunjin Kim] goes to the Medical Hatch and sees the ultrasound that says she is pregnant which is super emotional, but then we're also in a Dharma Hatch and there's all this other stuff that's unfolding about the larger mythology, but it's attached to a story of a woman who didn't think she would be pregnant and then realizing it is Jin's [Daniel Dae Kim]. It was based on what a character wanted—and yes, in that episode, you may have gotten a download about the Dharma Initiative, but it was always tied to a character mystery. For us, that's how we try to approach this show with thematic character-based storytelling.

19

PUSH THEM OFF A CLIFF

A cliffhanger is a plot device that leaves a character or characters facing either a dangerous situation or a shocking revelation. As all drama is essentially manipulation (and not reality), a cliffhanger leaves the audience asking, what's going to happen next? Or a version of "holy crap!"

Broadcast networks also try to use their strongest cliffhangers during sweeps periods (February, May, July, and November) when advertisers calculate ad rates. "Sweeps" is calculated using Nielsen ratings. The better the ratings, the more networks can charge.

So let's start with this basic question: *what are the ingredients of an amazing cliffhanger?*

Character in peril. Think of the timeworn image of the damsel in distress tied to the railroad tracks, with the train barreling toward her as the hero rushes to the rescue. It's the classic "ticking clock," and the serial ends with the woman in danger. This tried-and-true device is a mainstay of TV show endings.

Probably the ultimate cliffhanger was "Who shot J. R.?" from the original *Dallas* nighttime soap. In the final scene of the 1979–1980 season, J. R. Ewing (Larry Hagman) was shot twice by an unseen assailant. Audiences had to wait until the next season premiere to learn whether J. R. would survive and who was responsible. The cliffhanger made an indelible cultural impact.

An oldie but a goodie was "The Best of Both Worlds," the third season finale of *Star Trek: The Next Generation*, in which Captain Jean-Luc Picard (Patrick Stewart) was captured by the Borg and assimilated.

Ticking bomb. There is no easier and more effective way to create a cliffhanger than to have a ticking time bomb.

In the season 1 finale of *Homeland* (titled "Marine One"), after a sniper attempts and fails to assassinate the vice president during a press conference, the scene turns into chaos. Emergency protocol measures are initiated. The V.P. and other top-level government officials, including military "hero" and congressional candidate, Nicholas Brody (Damian Lewis), are immediately ushered to safety inside a basement bunker. They hunker down until they can be given the "all-clear" signal. The perceived threat is from a terrorist outside the bunker. But what they don't realize is that Brody is wearing a vest laden with explosives. The enemy is among them—and he's on a suicide mission to kill not only the V.P. but also to destabilize the U.S. government.

In this excruciatingly suspenseful sequence, Brody tries to detonate his vest, but it doesn't work. The activation switch malfunctions. Sweating profusely, Brody surreptitiously goes into the bunker's bathroom to repair the switch. Meanwhile, discredited former CIA agent Carrie Mathison (Claire Danes) frantically tries to alert the government to Brody's real mission—only no one believes her. Desperate, Carrie drives to Brody's house and appeals to his daughter Dana (Morgan Saylor). Dana doesn't believe Carrie either, but Carrie's intense warning motivates Dana to call her father on his cell phone, begging him to come home—now. In this cliffhanger moment, Brody is torn between his loyalty to his jihad mission and his duty as a father. Brody's bond with his daughter is strong, and he promises her he'll come home. As he ends the call, sweat and tears run down his face—just as the personnel in the bunker get the "all-clear" signal. Brody will go home to his estranged wife and concerned daughter and son. He'll make good to her on his promise. Meanwhile, Carrie will be arrested for harassing Brody's family.

Outside the police station after her sister bails her out, Carrie is humiliated by her erratic paranoia and apologizes to Brody for her behavior. He once loved her, and probably still does. But she got too close to his true agenda for comfort. Now it's Brody's turn to issue a warning: stay away from me and my family. And now Carrie feels that she has no other choice but to admit herself into the hospital for E.C.T. (electroconvulsive therapy).

The ultimate cliffhanger of this first season finale occurs when [SPOILER ALERT] the audience realizes that although Carrie was right about Brody's terrorist mission, she's now convinced that she was wrong. Just as she realizes that Brody had met terrorist Abu Nazir's (Navid Negahban) son, her memory is being erased. She was the only one who could thwart Brody, but now she's being neutralized. Like all great cliffhangers, the season ends on the highest level of conflict imaginable. The cliffhanger is literally shocking.

Love is in the balance. Like the saying "all's fair in love and war," love makes for good drama, and when star-crossed lovers finally realize their true feelings, it can make for a good cliffhanger.

In the season 4 finale of *Friends*, "The One with Ross's Wedding," Rachel (Jennifer Aniston) finally realizes she's in love with Ross (David Schwimmer) and rushes to London to tell him before he gets married to Emily (Helen Baxendale), but she's too late. The wedding goes as planned until Ross utters Rachel's name instead of Emily. It's a Freudian slip because he truly still loves Rachel, and this is certainly a deal breaker "I don't" moment for Emily.

Surprise/twist. A surprise or twist, seeded correctly, provides a jolt to the audience, leaving us saying, "I didn't see that coming!"

Many Spoilers to Follow

In the season finale of the first season of *24*, we see that Nina Myers (Sarah Clarke), an employee at CTU (Counter Terrorism Unit) is actually the mole. Trusted throughout the season, Nina ends up killing Jack Bauer's wife, Teri (Leslie Hope).

In *Downton Abbey*, Lady Sybil (Jessica Brown Findlay) dies in childbirth halfway through season 3, a death that took the audience completely by surprise.

At the end of season 1 on *Mad Men*, Peggy Olson (Elisabeth Moss) heads to the hospital thinking it's due to bad office food, only to realize she's pregnant and gives birth to a healthy baby boy. The pregnancy was not only a surprise to the audience; it was a surprise to the character, as well.

Death of a character. Sometimes the death of a character provides an emotional cliffhanger at the end of a show, figuratively resetting chess pieces and altering relationships. Ultimately, the lives of the remaining characters will never be the same.

In *NYPD Blue*, Detective Bobby Simone (Jimmy Smits) dies after a heart transplant, and his partner, Andy Sipowicz (Dennis Franz) will never be the same until his own demise.

In *Lost*, Charlie Pace (Dominic Monaghan) died so that his fellow survivors might be rescued.

In *E.R.*, Dr. Mark Greene (Anthony Edwards), a main character, dies of brain cancer while in Hawaii. The emotional send-off reverberated throughout the next season.

In *Breaking Bad*, Mike Ehrmantraut (Jonathan Banks) is shot and killed by Walter White (Bryan Cranston). It's less about him dying and more about the unexpected execution: after a life of murder and mayhem, Mike dies almost Buddha-like sitting in the reeds.

Discovery of a secret. Characters with secrets make good dramatic fodder because so much is at stake if the secret is revealed. Series that correctly use this device tease the audience with the tension of will-they-find-out-or-not anxiety. Examples include cop shows where someone is undercover, or character dramas where a secret affair or the object of affection becomes clear.

A good rule of thumb is that a strong, viable cliffhanger should grow out of character jeopardy, risk, or fear. A bad cliffhanger is just a plot point that comes out of nowhere solely for shock value. So even a "surprise" cliffhanger needs to be (subtly) set up so that the audience feels they should have seen it coming—but didn't. Or, at the very least, the surprise is credible within the rules and tone established for the series. Soap operas, in particular, have a tendency to overuse cliffhangers in every episode, sometimes multiple times, which leads to a lack of storytelling credibility.

For most of its seasons, Dexter Morgan (Michael C. Hall) keeps his life as a serial killer a secret. At the end of season 6, however, his sister Debra Morgan (Jennifer Carpenter) discovers his Dark Passenger, forever altering their relationship.

In *Breaking Bad*, [SPOILER ALERT] when Walt's brother-in-law, Hank Schrader (Dean Norris), realizes that Walt is actually the notorious drug king-pin "Heisenberg"—discovered via a gifted book with a revelatory inscription—it's Hank's "Eureka!" moment. But instead of it being in the bathtub, it's when Hank's on the toilet. We're left to ponder—at midseason—what it portends for Walt now that Hank knows his secret, but Walt has no idea he knows.

In *Mad Men*, Betty Draper (January Jones) discovers her husband's true identity as Dick Whitman after she unearths evidence from a locked drawer in his desk. The secret ends their once "happy" marriage.

Lack of closure. Many shows end their series with closure: a finale that answers every question and provides viewers with a sense of well being. Star-crossed lovers usually get married, and the show ends on an upbeat note. There is an opposite choice, however, but it's difficult to pull off.

The series finale of *The Sopranos* literally cut to black after Meadow Soprano (Jamie-Lynn Sigler) enters a restaurant and Tony Soprano (James Gandolfini) looks up. Seconds before, a man had been staring at Tony. The audience is left hanging: what is Tony's fate? Was the man an assassin or just someone who recognized Tony? Did Tony live or die?

However, if a cliffhanger feels too ambiguous or information is withheld, there can be viewer backlash: *The Sopranos* series finale felt too enigmatic for most audience members. But at least it wasn't predictable, and we're still studying it and writing about it, so showrunner David Chase's groundbreak-ing series started and finished with the same level of controversy. Win-win.

The season 1 cliffhanger of *The Killing* was anti-climactic and alienated many loyal viewers because the identity of Rosie's killer was not revealed, leaving many fans frustrated by the pace of the storytelling. This series was "officially" cancelled by cable network AMC at the end of season 2—when the killer was finally revealed. Fortunately, AMC decided to grant this series a pardon. At press time, season 3 has begun with a whole new murder mystery, and showrunner Veena Sud has vowed to reveal its killer by the end of the same season. Lessons learned.

Life events. Many cliffhangers in character dramas employ various life events: marriages, affairs, divorces, engagements, break-ups, pregnancies and births to pit characters against forces in life not in their control.

In the second season of *The Walking Dead*, in a world of chaos due to a zombie apocalypse, Lori Grimes (Sarah Wayne Callies) discovers she is pregnant. She is torn as to whether to bring a baby into such a terrible world or to abort it.

Mini-cliffhangers. No drama would be complete without "act breaks" or mini-cliffhangers, originally designed so that when commercials aired, viewers would not change the channel. Mini-cliffhangers are important plot beats, such as a detective finding a clue that pushes the story forward.

While there aren't any official act breaks in the cable series *Homeland*, we can deduce where the act breaks would be. For example, in the episode "The Vest," the Teaser ends after the audience sees a bomb maker creating an explosive vest. The end of act 1 is Saul (Mandy Patinkin) discovering the secret that Carrie (Claire Danes) has been suffering from mania due to her bipolar disorder, which threatens her security clearance, as well as the veracity of her theories. The end of act 2 is Saul protecting Carrie's secret from David (David Harewood). The end of act 3 is Brody (Damian Lewis) picking up the suicide vest in Gettysburg. The end of act 4 is Saul piecing together Carrie's mish-mash of information and realizing that she was on to something: a timeline. The end of act 5 is Carrie calling Brody to tell him the CIA knows an attack is coming and she needs his help. The final cliffhanger/climax is Carrie preparing for what she thinks is a romantic visit from Brody, only to find he betrayed her: her timeline is torn down. On the cusp of solving the attack, she's out of the CIA. Each act out raises questions, raises tension, and propels the viewer forward to find out what happens next.

Comedy cliffhangers. In a two-act sitcom, the break between acts 1 and 2 is crucial. Something has upset the balance in the world of the series and act 2 will be an effort to restore harmony (because all sitcoms have happy endings).

For a three-act sitcom, there are two act breaks and thus two mini-cliffhangers. In the pilot for *Big Bang Theory*, at the end of the cold open, Sheldon (Jim Parsons) and Leonard (Johnny Galecki) meet their new adorable neighbor, Penny (Kaley Cuoco). It's central to the series, as her introduction will change their relationships forever. By the end of act 1, Leonard's friend, Wolowitz (Simon Helberg), meets Penny and is smitten with her, too. This creates competition between Leonard and Wolowitz, which leaves us asking "who will get Penny?" The end of act 2 is a resolution of the drama, where Leonard helps Penny get "closure" after a breakup by retrieving *her* TV set from her ex-boyfriend's apartment. She is now officially single, and Leonard is still smitten, setting up a long-running yearning of "will-they-or-won't-they-get-together?"

> Cliffhangers are most effective when the moment grows out of character and feels inevitable without feeling too out of the blue or unearned.

INTERVIEW: Michael Kelley

Michael Kelley Credits

Best known for:

Revenge (Executive Producer/Writer) 2011–2012
Swingtown (Executive Producer/Writer) 2008
Jericho (Supervising Producer/Writer) 2006–2007
The O.C. (Consulting Producer/Producer/Writer) 2005–2006
One Tree Hill (Co-Producer/Writer) 2003–2004
Providence (Writer) 1999–2002

NL: Chapter 19 is all about cliffhangers, so my first question for you is about the *Revenge* pilot. It's so layered and intricate. What was your process in constructing that puzzle? For example, did you start with Amanda's (Emily VanCamp) story in the past and then construct the present story for alias Emily (also Emily VanCamp) and the Graysons? What was your way in to the show?

MK: I did construct Amanda's story to start. I needed to know exactly what the inciting incident was and I needed to know emotionally my entry into the story. Because if you aren't behind your protagonist as an audience, you won't understand what she's there to do—especially in a story as dark as revenge. Then you've lost them out of the gate. The imagining began with what happened to this little girl and her family and her father. Then, you start branching off from there. Well, if this happened to her father, how did he fall in with this woman and what was his part in what happened to this family? I had a terrific assistant at the time who now writes on my show, and he and I very quickly sat down and started talking about it and calling it "The Countess of Monte Cristo." So we just called it "The Countess" before we called it "The Revenge of Emily Thorne," then it just became *Revenge*. Since we were taking this from Dumas' *The Count of Monte Cristo*, we knew we had a twenty-year linear story of Amanda coming back to haunt the people that messed them over. So, to answer your question, you have to begin with the mythology.

NL: And, besides having the rooting value for Amanda/Emily because she was wronged, it seems like in each of the stories, at least in season 1, there are present stakes as well. Most of these people are continuing to perpetrate these sins against current people. Like the financial guy she ruined—all these people are bad people, essentially. So, you're righting the wrongs from the past, but there's also a corrective force in present scenes.

MK: Yeah, that was something that I also wanted to be clear about with this character. She's evolving into a Batman-style character where she's righting the wrongs—the bigger wrongs—not just the wrongs done to her. And that's, to me, a big part of season 2. I always said that the rule of thumb that the audience needs to understand is that the punishment is always going to fit the crime. So, for example, the guy you were talking about—the crooked investor—gets his comeuppance and loses everything. But, she's not going to throw somebody off a cliff or scratch their car.

NL: That's right—the show is about karma. You reap what you sow.

MK: The show is also about the cliffhanger. It's all the same thing because I need where we're building to. I need a theme for each season, and so organically, you want the cliffhanger to be rooted in the kind of story you're telling.

NL: So, there's a theme for the whole season that you are doing over twenty-two episodes, and then also a thematic within each episode. There's obviously the franchise element in season 1: where she crosses off someone on her revenge list by drawing an "X" over their photo at the end of each episode. Is that going to continue in season 2?

MK: You have a game plan when you set out to tell these stories—especially these deep serial types of stories. I liken it to a trip across the country where you know where you're headed and you have the destination all mapped out. You know that you're going from New York to California, but you're allowed to go wherever you want across the country. I just want to make sure that I'm always very clear about where I'm headed and the themes that I choose help me with that. I started the first episode of season 1 with a Confucius quote.

NL: Yes—"Before you embark on a journey of revenge, dig two graves."

MK: I wanted that to carry through to the season finale. We're blowing up a plane with Victoria [Madeline Stowe] on it. These events were set in motion, and you can argue that they were set in motion by the people who did the evil things all the way back then. But, also Emily has a hand in it. And all the evidence that could exonerate her father is gone. Her raison d'être is no more. So, these two things, these two deaths have occurred, and I wanted to honor that. I just chose a quote for season 2's opener by Henri-Frederic Amiel: "Destiny has two ways of crushing us: by refusing our wishes and by fulfilling them."

NL: So, it's always a double-edged sword.

MK: That's right. That's the fun of telling these stories. A reaction—some you can predict and some you cannot.

NL: I want to talk to you about some of the narrative devices that you built in to the story. You have the box that she finds with her father's journal. You have the double infinity symbol. You have voice-over and flashback. Were these things all in place from the beginning? Did you always intend to use voice-over? She calls the box and the journals a "roadmap for revenge," but it doesn't ever quite turn out the way she's expecting.

MK: We did have all those devices in place. Serial drama can be difficult for people in this day and age to engage with right out of the gate. Especially in network television because so often people get burned and show's get cancelled. But, when you're embarking on a journey of a cable series, you have faith that they won't cancel it—that you can dole out the story a little slower. That you'll be granted a second season. Fans of that genre are usually more rewarded in cable than in broadcast where they could feel more burned. So, I wanted to make sure there were elements of the show that you could come into as a viewer that weren't completely enwrapped in the serial nature of the story. Plus, now that we have so many formats, you can catch up. I wanted to make each show feel like it had a containment. At least in the beginning. So, when I start with Emily's voice-over, it's her telling us what happened as a little girl and that this is not a story about forgiveness. She's telling a story that's already happened; she is the narrator. Voice-over is one of the hardest things to write. It always takes the most time and is the most frustrating, and I'm usually rewriting it all the way up until air. Sometimes it doesn't fit the picture that you wanted it to fit. A great example of that is the episode where the dog Sammy died (that episode is called "Grief"), and I didn't land on the voice-over until the final mix which is really cutting it close. As far as the rest of the conventions, the double infinity symbol, that's just an immediate emotional connection to what she has lost. I think if you don't remind your audience of what has been lost, then you just might think that this girl is a psychotic bitch that can't be controlled. This is why we take the viewer back to foster care and all the adults who lied to her and show just how kind and pure the relationship with her father was—and the fact that she's missing a mother as well—which we will obviously get into in season 2.

NL: There's the mystery connected to the past with her father and Victoria, and then there's the central question of whether she is ever going to finish this and if she is going to get caught. The revelation about her mother was a big part of the cliffhanger for the first season.

MK: It is big. I think that you want to surprise the audience and yourself, but you want to make sure it's rooted in the larger story. With a single lead protagonist like Emily with a very clear agenda in every episode, you want her to be as prepared and driving story as possible—you don't want her to get caught up in it. You want her to be in the driver's seat, but you want her to get side swiped a handful of times. One of the hardest things for me to learn as a TV writer was how to keep your protagonist in an active place. I think it's a challenge for all of us. And, now I've got so many strong characters from Victoria to Conrad [Henry Czerny]. Everybody has their own very specific, strong agendas, and none of the actors (nor myself) want to give up their power and their ability to lay down their own agenda.

NL: Victoria exacts her revenge—every bit as much.

MK: She does, and that was a design as well. Victoria has such a rich, untapped backstory that we haven't even really gotten into yet, but we will. Just what built that woman. How she became what she is. When we begin season 2, you find out what happened with the plane exploding and . . . I don't want to ruin it for you.

NL: So, she was on the plane, but obviously, doesn't die.

MK: She was on the plane. The audience saw her get on that plane, but what you'll find in season 2 that there was a larger plan for her to do a quite similar thing to what Emily did—which is to throw her old life away and start another one. And, of course, she didn't count on her daughter Charlotte [Christa B. Allen] overdosing and needing her. But, I will tell you when you come back to season 2, Victoria's been dead for eight weeks and nobody knows.

NL: I wanted to talk to you about pacing in relation to cliffhangers in terms of how much plot you dole out at a time. How do you make those judgment calls not to burn through story too quickly?

MK: I made a decision to burn through story very early on. I've worked in serial drama for most of my career and I'm a big fan of daytime soap operas. I actually hired a guy who was on *One Life to Live* for a long time. I think that I'm slowing things down emotionally for this season. It's not as plot intensive because you only have so many major cards to turn over before it starts getting ridiculous.

I feel like the show lives in an emotional place when it's firing at its highest.

I burned through a shit ton of story last year on purpose, and there's a lot of surprises coming up in the first several episodes that for me feel like hangovers from season 1 that we need to wrap up. For me, I feel like a giant wave is about to come and wash the sand clean and we have to start rebuilding. But, we definitely made a choice and literally jumped off that cliffhanger. I've seen people do that, and it's splat on the ground. We were lucky to have enough safety measures in place on the show that a lot of shows don't have which is the strength of our villain and of our protagonist. The strengths of those two characters: they are neither all good or all evil and the characters that surround them, they all have at least two sides to their personalities. We were able to create stakes for the audience for each character. Each major discovery did not have to be about our lead character. It could be about Victoria and her daughter or Nolan [Ross as played by Gabriel Mann], so we were finding that we got very lucky with some genuinely compelling characters, so it didn't get ridiculous.

NL: It's so smart and yet emotional at the same time. The Nolan Ross character—at what point did he enter the process? Because I would imagine she needed a confidant, someone to talk to, and someone who knew her secret. Someone with power as an insider in the Hamptons' social scene who she could also think of as an ally. Tell me more about the genesis of Nolan.

MK: I thought of him first as what was missing emotionally, as you said, from the story and that's where I like to start. I think of them as siblings in many ways. They shared at least a father figure in David Clarke [James Tupper]. I was thinking how do you ask the audience to emotionally connect to this girl if no one else is willing or able to bond with her. In spite of her barbs and thorns, Nolan just sprouted out of that need for someone to be our emotional guide to why we care about Emily Thorne. You can only get so much material from a girl reading from a diary about her father or looking longingly at his picture. Her frustration and her real emotions—we needed someone to be able to see that. The truth of her rage and her betrayal, and someone who also is an outsider who feels those same things. He quickly became Robin to her Batman at least in their shenanigans, but emotionally he's like her brother and I felt that that's what we needed to pull in the audience.

NL: Is *Revenge* a five-act or six-act show?

MK: We're six. I always treat the first act as a teaser as something that will just set up the episode. I still am a little old school. I'll still call it a teaser, plus five. We're being asked to come up with five or six cliffhangers an episode. Five cliffhangers to get you back from the commercial breaks and one to bring you back next week. It's a tall order on a show like this.

NL: So, you're going to have at least an A, B, and C story because you've got three basic families to service. You've got the blue-collar story, you've got the Graysons, and you have Emily.

MK: We have nine characters we owe story to every week.

NL: But, what's so great in the pilot, is it's all so clear, even though there are so many characters introduced. I know how hard that is to do. Within your A, B, C, maybe even D story, you've got your thematic title for the story. Do you try to track that through?

MK: Always. It's hard sometimes to pull all your stories through and sometimes we do it to better success than others. The finale being called, "Reckoning," makes a lot of sense for everybody. I feel like we're returning with an episode called, "Bound," and it's very cool for me to be able to start with that word which I was thinking about over hiatus. How they're all bound together. I'm stuck with them too. You can choose your friends or your husband and wife—the people that you bind yourself to, but you can't choose your father and your mother. And, you're still bound to them. So, for me, starting with a theme is very helpful. We don't always start with theme.

Sometimes it eludes us, you realize what it is when you're breaking story and then you have to retrofit a lot of things. Of course, even with the best laid plans, I reserve the right to change my mind. And often do.

NL: In terms of cliffhangers, you've got your A, B, C stories on theme—are there any rules about cliffhangers on *Revenge*? For example, do they always need to end on an A story or on Emily?

MK: Generally, you want Emily to be the A story, but sometimes we throw in those surprising moments that you didn't realize were coming—those are the sideswipes I was talking about. If you're earning each mini-cliffhanger, then generally they're on the A or the B story. But, at the end of the finale of season 1, the mother being alive was not something that was germane to anything we were doing in season 1. We weren't leading up to that moment in a way that anybody could say, "Well, this is all logical, and we knew we were getting to the mother here." So, that cliffhanger was in the sideswipe category.

NL: It was the one thing that was not never discussed. What about in terms of cliffhangers for each episode: revealing a new nugget of information and trying to take us to a new emotional or vulnerable place within each one? Is that something where you're saying consciously, "We have to reveal another piece to the puzzle in each episode"?

MK: I'm not a big fan of spinning wheels and I don't like retread or withholding because you don't want to repeat yourself. I think that for me I like to throw down the answers to questions a lot quicker than probably most networks and writers are comfortable doing because it's scary and traditionally you want to draw that out. Twenty-two episodes—that's a real challenge—I feel like we've already told two giant seasons. The end of season 1 should have been Victoria whispering into Daniel's [Joshua Bowman] ear, "Don't say a word," after there's a murder on the beach—that would have been the logical [way to end it]. Then, we told another season after that, and now we're on to seasons 3 and 4.

But, it's fun and challenging, and I've got some smart people around me— from the actors to the writers to the directors—it's a group effort. I'm not afraid anymore. I think I would have been. That was the cool thing coming into this season because now that I've done it, I know that it's possible— and I know that we can do it again. So, I'm not coming from a place of fear anymore—maybe that will end up hurting me more than helping, but for now, I think just taking that leap of faith and knowing that you can't know every answer. You have to be open to things you weren't expecting. Sometimes the characters surprise you or the writers' room surprises you— and things that you wanted to do turn out to be things that you don't do which unravels something down the road that you wanted to do. So you have to find a new avenue to get there, but for me that's exciting and that's the process that keeps me coming back. That's my cliffhanger.

20

DESIGNATE AN EXPERTISE

All series feature a variety of characters with different personalities and skill-sets. This is done to create conflict, illustrate multiple points of view, and help the audience differentiate characters. This dynamic is probably most prevalent in series involving cops, feds, spies, antihero criminals, doctors, and lawyers.[1] Let's examine these specialists in various genres.

Law Enforcement

In *Person of Interest*, Harold Finch (Michael Emerson) is a computer genius who invents an incredible surveillance machine that can predict acts of violence. He recruits former CIA field operative John Reese (Jim Caviezel) to help him stop the violent acts before they happen.

Castle works in a similar vein. Richard Castle (Nathan Fillion) is a famous crime novelist with a vivid imagination, while his partner Kate Beckett (Stana Katic) is an experienced New York City detective who believes in the simplest explanation. Even though the show is grounded in reality, Castle's insane theories and outside-the-box thinking help the team solve their weekly mystery.

---

[1] On shows involving supernatural characters and magical realism, their specialization usually comes in the form of a power. On *True Blood*, Sookie Stackhouse (Anna Paquin) has mental telepathy and photokinesis (the ability to manipulate light). On *Medium*, Allison Dubois (Patricia Arquette) is a clairvoyant who works with the police as a psychic. In *Ghost Whisperer*, Melinda Gordon (Jennifer Love Hewitt) can see and talk to dead people. See Chapter 18 for more on series mythology.

Law enforcement shows often have main characters whose ethics clash. In the season 8 episode of *Law & Order* titled "Stalker," police partners Lennie Briscoe (Jerry Orbach) and Rey Curtis (Benjamin Bratt) come out on opposite sides of the law while investigating a murder. Lennie commits perjury to ensure the killer will get justice, while good Catholic Rey is unwilling to back his partner up in court. Due to their conflict in morality, the killer almost goes free.

In *The Shield*, Vic Mackey (Michael Chiklis) leads the corruptible Strike Team, and Captain David Aceveda (Benito Martinez) desperately wants to take down the renegade cops. However, more often than not, their interest is the same: catch the bad guy. In the pilot episode, the police frantically search for a missing girl whose junkie father sold her to a pedophile. And even though they have the pedophile in custody, he's unwilling to talk. As the girl's life hangs in the balance, Aceveda reluctantly unleashes Vic who mercilessly beats a confession out of the pedophile. As a result, the police find the little girl before she dies.

Law enforcement shows invariably have a scientific/technological geek as a sidekick who helps the main characters solve a case or complete a mission. In *NCIS*, there are actually two of these characters: Abby Sciuto (Pauley Perrette) is a gothic forensics specialist, and Timothy McGee (Sean Murray) is an MIT and Johns Hopkins grad who serves as tech specialist. However, some shows place this "geeky" character in one of the lead roles. In *Bones*, Dr. Temperance Brennan (Emily Deschanel) is a brilliant forensic anthropologist who lacks social grace, and she's partnered with savvy FBI agent Seeley Booth (David Boreanaz).

The X-Files uses the common "skeptic versus believer" dynamic. FBI agent Fox Mulder (David Duchovny) believes in aliens and the paranormal, while his partner Dana Scully (Gillian Anderson) is a doctor who believes in what can be empirically proven. Their opposing viewpoints help them solve their bizarre slate of cases.

In *Elementary*, "geeks" comprise both lead roles. Sherlock Holmes (Jonny Lee Miller) is an aloof police consultant with unparalleled deductive reasoning skills, and former surgeon and current "sober companion," Dr. Joan Watson (Lucy Liu), assists him with her medical expertise. The police detectives on the show simply help *them*.

Criminals and Antiheroes

Shows that deal with illegal enterprises also have characters who specialize in certain areas. In *Sons of Anarchy*, motorcycle club president Clay Morrow (Ron Perlman) is valuable because of his relationship with the IRA, which supplies the club with guns. Bobby Munson (Mark Boone Junior) is a level-headed member of the club who handles the books. Tara Knowles (Maggie Siff), wife of main character Jax Teller (Charlie Hunnam), is a doctor who provides clandestine medical assistance to members of the club. Happy

(David Labrava) and Tig (Kim Coates) are two of the more savage members of the club, willing to handle the jobs that are particularly despicable.

In *Breaking Bad*, Walter White (Bryan Cranston) is the expert meth cooker due to his chemistry background and Jesse Pinkman (Aaron Paul), an experienced but petty drug dealer, handles distribution. Saul Goodman (Bob Odenkirk), a low-rent attorney, serves as the "drug lawyer," helping his clients launder money and evade capture. As the enterprise grows, Mike Ehrmantraut (Jonathan Banks), a former Philly police officer and corporate security expert, switches allegiances and joins Walt's side as "cleaner" and hit man— after Mike's former crime kingpin boss, Gustavo "Gus" Fring (Giancarlo Esposito) is literally blown away. Walter's wife Skyler (Anna Gunn), an experienced bookkeeper, handles the accounting. As the operation expands, cold and calculating corporate executive, Lydia Rodarte-Quayle (Laura Fraser), helps the team expand into a global operation—but only to save her own hide.

Doctors

Medical shows also have characters with various specialties. In *Grey's Anatomy*, the doctors each have different specialties: cardiothoracic surgery, neurosurgery, orthopedic surgery, plastic surgery, trauma, pediatrics, and other areas. The characters are defined by their specialty. For example, overachiever Cristina Yang (Sandra Oh) fights her cohorts for the privilege to work with the "cardio gods" on any and all interesting heart surgeries.

In *Royal Pains*, Hank Lawson (Mark Feuerstein) works as a concierge doctor in the Hamptons after being fired from a New York City hospital for tending to a poor patient in critical condition instead of a bigwig in stable condition who dies unexpectedly. In order for his new business to thrive, Hank needs the help of his business savvy younger brother Evan (Paul Costanzo) who serves as CFO and his highly competent physician's assistant Divya (Reshma Shetty).

In *Nip/Tuck*, Sean McNamara (Dylan Walsh) and Christian Troy (Julian McMahon) are best friends and partners in a successful plastic surgery business in Miami. Ranked at opposite ends of the spectrum in medical school at the University of Miami (Sean at the top and Christian at the bottom), Sean is the more skilled surgeon, while Christian is more adept at being charming and growing their client base. Nevertheless, they begin each new client consultation with the same question: "Tell me what you don't like about yourself?"

In *House, M.D.*, Dr. Gregory House (Hugh Laurie) purposely surrounds himself with doctors who disagree with him in order to come up with different ideas and approaches to solving their weekly medical mystery. In season 4, House is forced to assemble a new team from a pool of 40 applicants. He disqualifies the applicants for a host of reasons, but he cuts one doctor in particular because he's too similar in thought process and logic; House doesn't believe blanket agreement is conducive to helping patients. This is the method to his madness—and genius.

In *The Mindy Project*, Mindy Kaling portrays Dr. Mindy Lahiri who runs a small ob/gyn practice with her fellow doctors, Dr. Danny Castellano (Chris Messina) and Dr. Jeremy Reed (Ed Weeks). They are constantly at odds with the "quack" midwives who work upstairs and start to lure clients away from them. It's science versus naturopathy between the two practices until it reaches a personal level when the midwives steal Morgan (Ike Barinholtz), the hilarious and earnest, ex-convict nurse whom Dr. Mindy and her colleagues have come to depend on, but Dr. Danny fires for sending a letter to his ex-wife. They win him back by proving that he's part of their "family."

The Workplace: Execs, Lawyers, and Fixers

Teamwork and specialization applies to shows that center around an office. In *Mad Men*, each member of the Madison Avenue advertising firm has an important role to play. Don Draper (Jon Hamm) is the wizardly wordsmith who (almost) always manages to pull off a magical campaign to the clients. Roger Sterling (John Slattery) is the gregarious partner who placates the big clients with frivolous nights on the town. Pete Campbell (Vincent Kartheiser) and Ken Cosgrove (Aaron Staton) are the young account men who prove their worth by bringing in new business. Harry Crane (Rich Sommer) makes himself invaluable by becoming an expert in television before it became essential. Peggy Olson (Elisabeth Moss) begins her rise from Don's secretary to his protégé by providing a unique perspective on a lipstick product; and Joan Harris (Christina Hendricks) is the glue that holds the office together. She wrangles all of the secretaries, manages the books, and later leverages her feminine wiles into a full partnership at the firm.

In *Scandal*, political fixer Olivia Pope (Kerry Washington) runs a D.C. crisis management firm. Her team of "gladiators in suits" includes lawyers, investigators, and a former CIA agent who works as her technology expert. Each is beholden to Olivia for rescuing them from a disreputable past incident, and since she helped them reinvent themselves, they'll do anything for Olivia now. See also: *Ray Donovan*.

Legal shows often have firm employees who bring a special set of skills to the table. In *Suits*, Harvey Specter (Gabriel Macht) is a brash partner in a top-tier New York City law firm who has a knack for anticipating his opponent's move and coming up with a clever counterattack. Mike Ross (Patrick J. Adams), his young associate who secretly doesn't have a law degree, is indispensable because of his eidetic memory and nonlinear thinking. Louis Litt (Rick Hoffman), a surly partner in the firm, proves his worth with fastidiousness and skillful forensic accounting. In addition to the lawyers, the secretaries and paralegals play a vital role. Harvey's secretary Donna (Sarah Rafferty) is a trusted confidant who knows all of the firm's secrets, and Rachel (Meghan Markle), the firm's best paralegal, provides key research assistance.

In *The Good Wife*, Alicia Florrick (Julianna Margulies) is a junior associate who's fifteen years older than her competition at a Chicago law firm. However, her wisdom and motherly compassion give her an edge over the callous social-climbing young lawyers in the firm. Also, her husband Peter (Chris Noth), in prison for corruption while serving as state's attorney, is uniquely qualified to give her inside information on cases and police misconduct. The firm also has a valuable investigator, Kalinda Sharma (Archie Panjabi), known for her assertiveness and discretion.

In *The Office*, we meet the people we see at work everyday: Michael Scott (Steve Carell) as the Regional Manager of the Scranton office of the paper company Dunder-Mifflin. Over the years, we watch as salesmen Dwight Schrute (Rainn Wilson) and Jim Halpert (John Krasinski) compete to see who can sell the most paper, but also to see who's really Michael's right-hand man and later to be his replacement. Until poetically in the final season, Dwight is finally named Regional Manager of Scranton and Jim and Pam (Jenna Fischer) begin their new life in Austin at the sports marketing company that Jim's been working at part-time. In addition to sales, accounting, reception, and the warehouse are all represented in this funny, irreverent, mockumentary-style workplace satire.

Out of Their Element

Sometimes characters are forced out of their specialty, which often leads to near disaster. In *24*, Chloe O'Brian (Mary Lynn Rajskub) is a skilled computer analyst for the counter-terrorist agency, CTU. She routinely helps Jack Bauer (Kiefer Sutherland) thwart terrorist attacks with her unmatched computer expertise. However, when she's forced into the field out of desperation, the mission almost falls apart.

In *The West Wing*, each member of the president's staff has a role to play. C.J. Cregg (Allison Janney) is the press secretary who deftly handles the White House reporters. On one occasion, Deputy Chief of Staff Josh Lyman (Bradley Whitford) is needed to brief the press. The briefing goes terribly awry when Josh's sarcastic wit and cavalier answers causes a feeding frenzy amongst the reporters.

In *The Wire*, officer Roland "Prez" Pryzbylewski (Jim True-Frost) is an apathetic cop who's practically useless. However, he finds his calling within the police department as an in-house investigator while working on a sprawling drug case. In season 3, Prez randomly finds himself out in the field while picking up food and responds to a radio call. He draws on a suspect and kills him, but being unfamiliar with working in the field, he fails to identify himself as a police officer. Tragically, the suspect he shoots and kills is an undercover police officer.

According to Glen Mazzara, former showrunner of *The Walking Dead*, "Great TV shows are about cool people doing cool shit." Designating an expert is the very definition of this cool adage.

INTERVIEW: Janet Tamaro

Janet Tamaro Credits

Best known for:

Rizzoli & Isles (Creator/Executive Producer/Writer) 2010–2013
Trauma (Supervising Producer/Writer) 2009–2010
Bones (Supervising Producer/Writer) 2006–2008
Sleeper Cell (Producer/Writer) 2005
    Emmy Nominated (Outstanding Miniseries) 2006
Lost (Writer) 2005
    WGA Award Nominated (Dramatic Series) 2006
CSI: New York (Co-Producer/Writer) 2004
Line of Fire (Co-Producer/Writer) 2003–2004

NL: What were the most significant challenges you had in adapting the *Rizzoli & Isles* novels?

JT: This was massively challenging partly because of where my head was at the time: I didn't want to do (another) adaptation. I'd just had HBO pass on an adaptation I'd written of a memoir, so I was licking my wounds on a staff gig and in the middle of writing a spec pilot (coincidentally set in law enforcement). I probably said, "I'm *never* doing another adaptation," on the day the project that became *Rizzoli & Isles* walked in my door.

The long boring Hollywood story (trust me, I'm so un-Hollywood, I do my own laundry and vacuum when I'm anxious) is the following: I'd changed agents and I was a new client at CAA. My agent, Rob Kenneally, called (here's more un-Hollywood—Rob and I first met when I coached his kid and my kid on a soccer team. I'm sure he thought I was that loud soccer mom coach lady before somebody told him I was also a writer). He wanted to set up a meeting with a man named Bill Haber, who'd read a play I'd written and wanted to meet me. Haber is a legend in Hollywood—one of CAA's three original partners who started that beast. He's an eccentric, brilliant, kooky man. He'd optioned one of Tess Gerritsen's murder mysteries. Here's the part that is only getting funny four years later: he didn't know which of Tess' *seven* books he'd optioned. In fact, no one could tell me—not even my agent. Bill is busy and important and a jet-setter and a man with more energy than me, which is a fuck of a lot.

So I read *all seven* of them. (Yes. I overprepare. I did this when I was a reporter, too.) The hardest part of an adaptation is you feel like it isn't yours. Like from the beginning, you're wearing someone else's clothes to something important—think your wedding. And you have to ask permission to cut off the sleeves or take up the hem. Or tear the whole thing apart and make a new outfit. I have a lot of respect for other writers—plus the fans of any adapted book will inevitably be disappointed. I'm an avid reader—but I'm also a screenwriter. What you envision in your head when you're reading a book is different from what makes a good TV show. The biggest difference is probably that Tess' books aren't funny—they're dark mysteries. In fact, I do believe the original mandate was to write something tonally that was more like *The Silence of the Lambs*. Fortunately, Tess Gerritsen is an extremely nice person—and, lucky for me, she'd had her books optioned before (don't ask me which ones)—and nothing had ever even been developed past a pitch. She was so grateful that I was actually writing a pilot script that she gave me tacit permission to make it my own. Once I stopped worrying about the "other" writer, I made it mine.

NL: How does your conception of Jane Rizzoli (Angie Harmon) and Maura Isles (Sasha Alexander) differ from the books, and why did you choose to make those changes?

JT: Tess is a doctor—and she has a meticulous style—her books are dense and well-researched. They're also page-turning, layered mysteries. But the mysteries and the forensics, not the characters, take center stage. I wanted the women and the supporting characters to be the reason people tuned in. It was important to me that the two women—Jane and Maura—be very, very different. Drama is conflict. I wanted them to not only look different, but to be very unlikely allies. They're site-specific friends—they would never have become friends if they hadn't been thrown together in their work. It was important to me to mine the organic humor that emerges when you have a job like Jane has (homicide detective) and like Maura has (medical examiner/coroner). They see plenty of dark shit. But they're also people—and they take themselves and their lives with them to work every day. When I was a reporter, I covered some really terrible, sad dark stuff—I'm talking serial killers and school shootings on any given day. You're committed to what you do, but you also have to find a way to do it every day—and survive the darkness. Laughter in this context is a coping mechanism, a pressure-release valve, a bonding agent. You hear humor all the time in police stations—it doesn't mean they aren't deadly serious about their work.

NL: How much of your life experience as an ex-journalist, wife, mom, and woman informs your series—especially when it comes to family, love, loss, and justice? Can you provide any specific examples of a real life event that impacted your storytelling?

JT: I said my head was in a strange place because of a failed pilot, but there was personal trauma, too. My best friend had been killed [in a car accident] right before I started writing *Rizzoli & Isles*. I wasn't thinking about it at the time because so much of writing is your subconscious working things out, but what I was really doing by making a female buddy show was mourning the loss of my best friend. The loss of her was very raw. The unexpected piece of this show was their friendship—Jane's and Maura's. When you're a writer and you're grieving, you don't really know how it will manifest. We should know what we're writing, but we don't always know where it's coming from or why it's finding its way on to whatever page we're in the middle of writing. I spent ten years covering all sorts of crime stories and spent a lot of time around cops, FBI agents, and victims and their families. It was important to me that the people who populate the show feel real and are like the people that I came across all over the country. It was also important for me to come up with smart mysteries that could actually happen. If you talk to my husband or either of my daughters, they'd probably complain that's it's hell living with a writer . . . little bits and pieces of my life and their lives are all over this show. Steve and I were having one of those "we've been married forever" fights— and I went to the laundry room because that's what I do when I'm upset: I clean. I was trying to find mates to socks. And so many were missing their mates. I felt a sudden pang at the thought of losing Steve—and that "sock" moment turned into a beautiful scene with Angie Harmon after her lover leaves. And yes, props used my family's socks (which they complained about).

I steal their lines, too. Julia, my younger daughter, was in a really terrible "I hate middle school" mood one night. I tried to soothe her and said, "I'll make you something. What do you feel like eating?" She said, "People." Lorraine Bracco [as Angela Rizzoli] and Angie Harmon had this exchange in one of my favorite episodes.

It's a Herculean task to come up with fifteen mini-movies in a short amount of time. The show chews through material. They are very densely packed scripts—potentially too dense; I'm sometimes forced by the format to give short shrift to things. But the one thing that has always been front and center is Jane and Maura's friendship. It took me a year of producing the show before I realized how deeply the loss of my best friend had influenced this relationship on-screen. My friend and I had the kind of friendship that I've worked to build for Jane and Maura (another thing that really isn't in the books at all). She wasn't competitive. She didn't judge. She embraced my flaws. She knew me. There was a purity to the relationship. She celebrated everything that I did. That's a really hard thing to replace. I had also known her for seventeen years—I met her when I was pregnant with my first daughter. I knew there were things I didn't want to do with these two women. I didn't want them to be fighting over boys. I didn't want them desperate to be married. I didn't want them to be doing the "tick-tock my biological clock is ticking and the eggs are getting old" thing. I just thought that would be a big yawner for me. I've had really wonderful friendships with both men and women, but there's something that happens when you're with your own gender. You have that closeness even if you don't see each other often. You pick up where you left off and you drop the mask and you are who you are. So Jane could be tough and a tomboy, but she could also be awkward and insecure. Those are the types of things that people close to us allow us to see. I'm also very interested in the extremes of the human condition. When do people snap and why do they snap? I do believe that a lot of that research about the brain is spot on: in the right situation, people are capable of anything.

NL: It seems like there's a shift back to doing more serialized stories on broadcast network television, probably from the influence of cable series, like *Breaking Bad* and *Mad Men*. Did you ever consider serializing *Rizzoli & Isles* with ongoing cases versus closed-ended crime stories that start and resolve within each episode?

JT: I would *love* to serialize this show. Writers in general love to serialize. But those shows are harder to sell—and harder to get people to "sample." It's like showing up late to a play or a movie—you don't want to go at all if you feel like you've missed too much. Non-serialized shows also tend to sell better to foreign buyers because they then have the freedom to run the episodes out of order or even blend seasons. It's purely a business decision that gets made for you. This was always a "closed-ended procedural." And the fact is, it's not my money. I feel creatively like it's "my show," but it's not really "my" show. I work for people. Warner Horizon is the studio and TNT is the network. We're in a funny period where I do have to think about the mandate and the series' future resale value. Or I have to stop making this show.

So far, the total number of series that started on cable and made it to domestic syndication is zero. So we could make a hundred episodes and it may not syndicate. And the hope with *Rizzoli & Isles* is that the people who pay for it (and are essentially my clients) will eventually be able to syndicate it. Hart Hanson [creator of *Bones*] taught me how to find my way in and how to turn the car in the direction that I felt it needed to go while also infusing the characters with humor and life. Finding a way to keep both art and commerce in the same "car" isn't easy.

But you have to. If your "buyers" can't find a way to finance the show, then you can't make it. People love these characters, so I can't not serialize or "continue" their stories to some extent. How much that happens is part of the collegial push–pull process of making the series. My hope is to someday write a show that does not have five commercial breaks. It's a bit intrusive for me as a storyteller and for you as the viewer. It creates challenges because my goal is to maintain the natural flow of the narrative. An interruption breaks that flow. But I'm used to writing to act breaks.

NL: So you're a teaser and five acts or is it a teaser, four acts, and a tag?

JT: Cold open and five acts, yes. Our network execs like a very long first act. So that cold open can be anywhere from seven to ten minutes. The title sequence floats around, and I decide when I'm in post where it feels most appropriate. TNT is a wildly pleasant place to work, and I'm not just saying that because one of them may see this interview. They have given me a lot of autonomy in how I build the show within very general constraints—they have allowed me to make this show what it is.

NL: Are there rules on your show for when you're breaking story? Like the A story has to end the act?

JT: Not as such. If I made myself actually chart and dissect it, I would probably find there are certain structural elements that feel "right" in our show and others that don't—but there is no "set of rules" manual I hand out to prospective writers. But pretty strict "rules" have developed. I think my writers would tell you they're hard to get a handle on because a lot of them are in my head. I need freedom to dance on the page, but my brain finds a way to organize all of it.

The fact is when I did sit and analyze it so that I could get better at communicating what I needed from my writers, I discovered that every story has, on average, thirty-two beats. So is that a formula? Maybe. I figured out that I almost always have a fifty-fifty split in my act breaks: half are character act breaks, half are story act breaks. That stuff wasn't planned, but my guess is it's my training (working on other people's shows), my natural inclination, and my subconscious striking a balance between crime and character stories.

Now that the audience is engaged with these characters, I'm not afraid that they won't come back. The lovely thing is that people do care about what happens to these characters in a very real way. Of course they want our characters to solve the mystery, and it's our job to make the mysteries tight and complex, but as savvy viewers, they know the mystery of the crime will get solved at the end of the episode. It's the more personal stories where the real surprises are. That's true for me as a writer, too.

NL: Given your extensive background as a journalist, how is being a showrunner similar and how is it different than being a journalist and/or news editor?

JT: There are definitely similarities, but to answer the question you have to understand the disparate operational structures. I've worked in print for both newspapers and magazines. I've worked in broadcast news on weekly newsmagazine shows and daily live event coverage. I've worked on long-form narrative programming as a writer, a writer-producer, a producer-writer (essentially), and now as a showrunner. How much space do you have here?

Maybe the best way to explain it is that anyone who comes to be in a position of serious responsibility like this is only able to do it because of the specific set skills and experience they bring to it. I've done all the aspects one would imagine in journalism: thinking of the story, researching the story, setting up and conducting the interviews, the door kicks and ambush interviews, the backgrounders, shooting stills and/or video, acquiring other source material, understanding the equipment and all of the technical aspects, hiring and managing people, blah, blah, blah. But you are always thinking story. That's first in your brain. And along the way, you have to continually shake the themes and facts and emotional elements in your working bag while asking, "Is this the best it can be?" There was so little space—and so much to tell when I was a news reporter. I feel the same way when I'm writing a screenplay. Everything has to matter.

I've always done a ton of research. I'd generate a small mountain of material as a reporter, so that by the time I'd shot, written and edited my piece, it was a tightly formatted, cohesive finished product that hopefully engaged, informed and, when appropriate, entertained. I always think it's like an iceberg—you may just see the tip but you know there's a hell of a lot under it. It also feels so similar to what I do now because as was true when I was a reporter/producer, there are so many hats to wear as a show-runner.

Being in charge of a series from prep through production to post-production is a bigger version of my life as a broadcast journalist. It turned out to be great training, though I never (*never*) intended to leave news to do this. I value that experience and draw on it all the time whether in planning, actual production or seeing the show through the many stages of Post. Clearly, it's not the only path to becoming a showrunner, but it was mine. And none of those really valuable skills would matter if I couldn't write—studios and networks will only throw you the keys if you've demonstrated the ability to turn blank pages into truly compelling and shoot-able scripts that turn into shows people want to watch.

I could always write. Journalism taught me how to write quickly. It also taught me the near magical value of research. In the narrative world where there is generally more value placed on just "making stuff up," it's important to remind ourselves that writers need to experience what we're writing about. When I write *Rizzoli & Isles*, I don't think of Angie and Sasha on TV. I think of Jane and Maura at a murder scene, I will go to the fish warehouse to listen to the sounds or smell the smells. When Jane and Maura are in a mud bath or hanging from an inverter, I do that stuff myself. What does it feel like? What are you thinking when you do it? Verisimilitude is not just a goal, it's the foundation—and since we're deep in the world of crime-solving, I'm pretty anal about getting it right. The actors and the crew really, really appreciate it. They do their homework, too.

When I was writing the pilot, I reached out to friends from graduate school (Columbia University) and tapped a Boston Globe reporter. I said, "Give me a homicide detective who'll talk to me." He made the introduction, and four years later, this cop went from full-time tech advisor to a writer on my staff.

No line or prop or action is too small because everything contributes to how the show feels. "Would our bad guy toss or burn bloody clothes? Why did he use a gun? What kind of gun?"

These things mattered as a journalist covering crime stories; they matter as a writer creating crime stories. The devil is in the details, but you also can't let that run your life because as the showrunner, you've got a factory to run. I'm always thinking: "What's been shot? Can we change this or hide it?" It's about punting and being creative—as a writer and a producer—all day long. I love that. Reminds me of doing live news: you have to think on your feet or you'll look like an idiot in front of a lot of people.

I have a couple hundred very talented people, but we all work under very stringent time/money resource parameters. Showrunners have to make sure the assembly line keeps moving, and if any one of the hundreds of components breaks down, the whole thing grinds to a loud, painful, expensive and sometimes very public halt.

Our overall goal is that no matter what aspect of the production you examine, you'll see the money and time was spent wisely in service of the story, and that the end result is something that engages, entertains, and maybe even informs and inspires. So it's not all that different in qualitative terms. It's more a question of scale and the natural pressure that comes with having a lot more at stake.

NL: What gives a fictionalized crime story on *Rizzoli & Isles* the dramatic juice for you as showrunner/arbiter to have a eureka! moment in the writers' room? And what might cause you to kill a story for not meeting those specific needs?

JT: I see it in my head as the writer pitches it. And what I'm thinking is: "Is this the show? And how badly do I want to write this?" The question I ask myself is simple: "Am I *dying* to write this?" If the answer is yes, then it's something we'll pursue. There are stories that are perfectly good stories for other shows—that just don't excite me. Kind of like people at a cool gathering: some you're drawn to; some, not so much.

And then when you decide to proceed, it's a lot of time and thought and experimentation: go this way or this way? Trial and error. If you don't have a story turn or a line or a resolving moment that gives you the kind of resonant tingle every viewer rightly seeks, you keep at it until it comes. I think I'm like other writers in that I never really stop writing this show—even when I'm sleeping. So sometimes that story-saving idea comes very late at night, or while I'm working out at the gym or yeah, while I'm vacuuming. That messy creative process drives us all nuts—writers included. But I learned all about deadlines from my news career: if you don't meet the deadline, there's dead air or a blank page . . . and you don't work again.

I also really like to push it—myself, my writers and most especially the story. I don't want your first idea—or *my* first idea. I want the idea we haven't thought of yet. That's hard.

NL: It seems like it's a very thematically driven show. How important is theme to you?

JT: I think theme emerges. I think you find your way to things that when you're done make a whole lot of sense. As I said, I didn't realize until I was a year and a half into this project that my grief about my friend created a celebration of friendship between Jane and Maura. That to me is the writing process and why I want theme to emerge from the work—you don't go out trying to hit the beats of a pre-conceived "theme" (or at least I don't). Your writer's mind finds and makes all of those connections as the story forms.

NL: How are you at coming up with the crimes? Are they coming from the books?

JT: No, the crimes aren't coming from the books. We've used one story from one of the books in the pilot. But otherwise we've generated the stories ourselves largely because what works in a three hundred plus page book doesn't necessarily work in a TV show. As for technique, I have a couple ways that I'm sure can make being on my staff somewhat maddening. Sometimes an episode can start with just an idea for a scene. For example, I wanted to kill a guy in a car wash. That's how the episode began. Another one began because one of my daughter's is a dancer. We did a competitive dance episode. My other daughter is massively into art, so that's figured into several episodes and into Maura's mother's background. My brother is currently doing a tour in Afghanistan. Jane's lover, Lt. Col. Casey Jones, was in Afghanistan.

I read a lot, I eavesdrop, and I try to listen closely to my children's worlds because the world of teenagers is nearly impenetrable. I know something is worth pursuing when I hear it—and story just naturally starts to spin in my brain. What I tend to do at the beginning of every season with my writers is we sit in the room for a week or two and brainstorm. I ask everyone to read as much as they can about local politics and life and crime in Boston. I have my former tech advisor turned writer who is constantly digging up murder stories.

I grew up on the East Coast and lived outside of Boston in elementary school, so I've done Revolutionary War–themed episodes, Salem witches, and a marathon. I sometimes find myself wishing Angie, Sasha, and Angela had Boston accents. I've been dying to do *Strangers on a Train*, but every time we try it out, we're in the world of electronics and cell phones and computers. *That* is the single hardest piece of a procedural show to get around: there are a bazillion ways to track people now. How do you come up with a crime without an electronic footprint? It's very hard, so I'm now in the place where I'm trying to challenge myself to make the mysteries stronger and tighter. I think when you think of the show, you think of Jane and Maura and the relationships and the family. But the things that really hold the show together are those flexible walls and the floor, which is the crime. The show is grounded and begins with a good mystery—that crime has to be good and solid.

NL: So you start with the crime?

JT: I always start with the crime. That is a rule that I think I've always had from my first procedural staff writing job. This has made for some very crazy circumstances for my children. When I was on *CSI: New York*, I wanted to kill a woman with a redwood stake. I'm very tactile and I've already said I was a journalist who liked to do research. So I went to the nursery with my then seven-year-old and the guy came over to say, "Can I help you?" And my daughter piped up and said, "My mommy's looking for a redwood stake to kill somebody." The guy rushed off saying something about having to bring the manager. I get myself to think like the murderer and plan it to the point that I think if I'm going to kill somebody, I'm going to get away with it. So I tell my writers that the mandate is this: but for super sleuths, Jane and Maura, the killer would get away with it. It also has to feel like if the stakes [no pun intended] are that high, if I'm willing to commit murder, I'd better have a damn good reason. When you're trying to sustain this mystery, and you're trying to get all of your actors on board, it's got to make sense. Not "TV" sense, but real and true sense.

NL: What's one of your favorite mystery stories that you've told? And why was that specific crime story particularly powerful/memorable for you?

JT: I really love the season enders that I've done. Given how truly hard this is, it's easy to get into a not-so-fun place where you're just brain dead and you have near-panic: the season opener and season ender *always* throw me for a loop. I go into my "I'll never get it. I've done too many. How are we going to top that?" mode—and drive everyone in my life nuts.

NL: At what point do you have a sense of where you're going to end the season?

JT: I knew early on with season 1 and season 2. I knew in season 1 that I wanted to end on a cliffhanger with something very unexpected with Jane. I figured I'd probably be out of money and have to do a bottle show [a whole episode set primarily all in one location]—which would play into how it was constructed. In season 2, I knew from the very beginning that I wanted to see them in conflict—not knowing if they were going to continue being friends. So the challenge was coming up with the mechanics of how that would happen—and how to do it in a very unexpected but real way. It comes down to the last few seconds of the show after Jane shoots Maura's biological father, who's a bad guy, and Maura looks up and gasps and says, "Don't touch him. Don't you dare touch him," as Jane, who is conflicted and tormented, backs away from her best friend. I was really proud of that when it all finally came together. I figured out how I wanted to end last season, which was season 3, only as I started to beat out that final episode. I couldn't decide how to end it really until I wrote that final scene.

We've just started shooting season 4—and I, thankfully, already know how I want to end it. Not saying I won't panic—just saying I think I know where I'm headed . . .

NL: Talk about Paddy Doyle, the "Whitey Bulger"-like character you created who is Maura's biological father. When Jane shot him, Maura had incredibly complicated feelings. He's a bad guy—but she loves him.

JT: They both had incredibly complicated feelings—and they're both right. That's the best kind of conflict (in my opinion) that there is. Neither is wrong . . . my favorite kinds of arguments to write are ones in which both people feel that they are right.

When I don't know how to write a scene, I know I'm headed in the right direction. That's the piece of me that wants to eventually write novels. I think a lot of TV writers worry that viewers don't think of us as writers because they're not aware that everything they are seeing in a television show has been imagined, processed, thought-through repeatedly and then *written* and rewritten—from every action line to parenthetical to line of dialogue. To me, the two best compliments are when an executive says, "That was really fun to read," and then way down the line we hear from viewers who don't just think it was fun to watch, but they have the sense that they're having these experiences along with the characters—as if they're transported into this world we've created.

In moments of massive shock or trauma, we are both capable of being our truest selves and of completely surprising ourselves with what we do or say. These are unpredictable catalysts. In that finale with Paddy, what I wanted was Maura to react in a way that she couldn't have anticipated. That's a universally human experience. It's that moment when you wonder, "Why did I just laugh at the most hideous thing that has happened to me?" I wanted to drop these best friends into a situation that threatened to sever years of friendship in an instant. Can you a lifelong relationship go away with one interaction? I think we know it can. How do you dramatize that in one scene?

But then of course, I had to pick up the pieces of that shattered relationship in the next season opener. Jane and Maura were no longer "best friends." In fact, they weren't speaking to each other. Paddy Doyle, Maura's father, was dying. Jane was equally pissed: what else was she supposed to do? Doyle was one of the FBI's Most Wanted—and he pointed a gun at *her*. I thought, "How do I revive this and how do I put this friendship back together? How do I do it in a way that doesn't feel like television, but feels real?"

NL: That comes through in every episode because they're both equally intelligent and equally impassioned. One comes from intellect and science, and the other much more from instinct, guts, and street smarts.

JT: I had an executive tell me that I couldn't have women fighting, that no one would watch women fighting. It's possible that there was a part of me that thought, "I'll show you how women fight and how you can be invested and how you can learn something if you're male." One of my favorite scenes of them going at it in season 3 is in Maura's office and Pike [Ed Begley Jr.] comes in and calls it a catfight. Yet, there are all kinds of real things being talked about in a funny way.

If we do our jobs as writers and students of human beings, we can hopefully get to something that feels both complex and simple and, at the same time, both resolvable and unresolvable. That's friggin' life.

NL: When I'm talking to my students about their one-hour drama pilots, I tell them to think of every show as being about a family—whether they're related by blood or not. In your show, you have both. You have the work family and mainly Jane's family because of her brother being a cop and her mom who is now working at the café. Jane and Maura are like sisters. Her mentor character, Vince (Bruce McGill), is like a father. How important are family dynamics to you when you're plotting?

JT: Originally, FBI agent Gabriel Dean [Billy Burke] was going to play a much larger role, but I didn't want a love triangle with my two female leads fighting over a guy. Because these two women are so committed to what they do professionally, their familial relationships would happen at work. And yet, once I had the use of Lorraine Bracco, I had to find a way to integrate her into their world, so that we weren't constantly stepping out of the Boston police department or the medical examiner's office to go visit Ma. But did I sit down and think: "How do I make this family important?" No.

We all are dramatists, and even if you grow up as an orphan, you have some patchwork of a family. We're all familiar with the archetypes, so maybe we just all naturally go there—to "family" both by blood and by choice. I think the contrast between these two people is that Maura had a little benign neglect with plenty of books and lots of intellectual stimulation, but not that huggy, kissy mom throwing her arms around her. Angela is a huggy, kissy, in-your-business Ma, but Jane is not a hugger. Why? Because it feels like Jane: nature won out over nurture. That's why you love it so much when there is that contact because it breaks down that hard shell Jane has on, and hopefully, that it also feels real. One of my favorite scenes is when Maura is really in pain, yet won't let Angela hug her, and it breaks her heart.

NL: One of the conventions of television is that characters don't change because you want to tune in and see who they are, but in some shows like

Breaking Bad, Walter has changed enormously—that's the whole point of the show. Do you see your characters as evolving over time? Do you want them to? Or will they stay rooted?

JT: I think that since these women go through some grisly experiences, they can't help but be changed. So I do feel that they have to evolve. Like all human beings, we become more of who we are or more of who we want to be. I wish in some ways that I could figure out a way to do five or ten seasons where they do stay the same. It's also about your thoughts of who you want to be—but paying attention to what the world is telling you about who you are—or at least which face you're showing.

I also think they are naturally affected by the friendship that's deepened as they go through experiences that we see them having. Truthfully, I miss some of the wonkiness of Maura from season 1. In some ways, it was easier. But to keep the actors interested, I have to keep them alive as creative people and as artists so that they're allowed to pick up a different colored pen—and flex different muscles.

Seeing Maura angry tonally is something we don't get to see as much. There's a scene at the end of season 3 where she's rude to her biological mother. She says stuff she wouldn't normally say. I struggled mightily with that scene because we'd never seen Maura do that. Was it consistent with who she was? Hell, yeah. She'd never been in that particular set of circumstances before. I do think that viewers don't always love that, particularly viewers who drop in and out. They want the same meal every time. But here's the thing: real people are full of contradictions. They don't always say what they mean. They don't always tell the truth. I love discovering something new about someone you're certain can't surprise you.

NL: You've gone to *CSI* camp. You've gone to *Bones* camp. What are the most important skills of being a showrunner to you?

JT: This is my second profession. My news skills have been absolutely invaluable. My ability to write very quickly when there are no second chances has also been invaluable. I also have a ton of production and postproduction experience. I was very lucky that way because writers don't always get exposed to that. When I walked into the *Rizzoli & Isles* edit bungalow, I already had ten thousand hours under my belt and that was a huge bonus. I think that many screenwriters don't understand the need to really go and learn post, and the only way to do that is to sit there and watch for a long time. There is so much story crafting that goes on (or should go on) in post, it's a terminal mistake for a writer to think of it as "some guy pushing buttons" or that it's someone else's department—it's often where you will rescue a show that's about to tank.

I am also one of those people who is very pragmatic. I know what my budget is and what I can and can't do. I prefer to only write stuff that I know we can do. It's a team sport. Production is not my adversary. They are my allies and the more they know, the earlier they know it, the better the "wedding" we're planning is going to be. You have to be able to handle criticism and problems and bounce back with great ideas and solutions quickly. I think I'm well suited for the sort of ADHD environment of showrunning because you don't have the luxury of days and days or even sometimes an hour to think through a problem and solve it through writing. You also have to be able to switch gears very quickly. So I think that my first profession and my news training was invaluable. I would say that writers who have come up through the TV drama system or have only been somebody's assistant are missing out. I'm very interested in writers who have had another career. I was interviewing a writer today who was a professor of philosophy. Those people are immensely, enormously valuable to me because they come at it from very different places. Their work tends to be less derivative. I find that some television writers' whole frame of reference is television. I don't want a writer copying me. I want them to go out and do what I did by seeing it for themselves: experiencing and smelling and touching in order to bring me something I don't see anywhere else. I'm not saying I'm able to do that in every story beat, but that's always the goal. Every time I write something, my goal is to give viewers some new experience. Even if it's just an interaction with someone they would never, ever run across in life. That's the part I miss the most about being a journalist: I went everywhere and talked to anyone. It was like an all-access pass to life.

NL: Production-wise are you a seven-day?

JT: Seven and a half.

NL: And do you have rules about how many days in or how many days out?

JT: I try to be flexible. Some episodes beg for three days out. It just depends on how well you've planned your season or how ahead you are. We generally go out one to two days an episode. The purse strings are very tight. There's no room for error. Everybody matters. When you're not doing your job, somebody else really feels it. The point is to get people who embrace the challenge. I can't imagine what we'd do with a shitload of money and time. How fabulous that would be, but there's also something exciting about knowing that even though you couldn't afford this, you made it work by collaborating and coming up with a solve. My brain loves puzzles—and I'm picky. Which means I have to figure out a way to get what I want. If we can't afford an idea, we'll find a way to make something else—or even something different but just as good—work. And when you're surrounded by people who rev up at a challenge, that's creativity at its finest.

21

MAKE US LAUGH

There are no rules in comedy except that it needs to be funny—which can be highly subjective. Not everyone is going to find the same material hysterical. Dark, edgy, subversive and/or "gross out" comedy is laugh-out-loud funny to some, and an offensive turn off to others. Dry, droll, sophisticated "British" humor is the bomb to some, but for others: not their cup of tea. If a joke is told badly, no matter how good the joke, it'll fall flat. The opposite can be true as well. If a bad joke is well told, it could be funny.

I believe that screenwriters can be taught structure and how to deepen a scene with heart and subtext. I even believe that some writers can learn to improve their dialogue. However, to me, comedy writing and performance is a gift: you either have it or you don't. Sure, you can master the comedic tropes of the rule of three, fish-out-of-water, role reversal, and odd coupling. But, seriously: *no one can teach you how to be funny.*

Nevertheless, I decided to ask the experts. This chapter contains words of wisdom from several of today's top comedy showrunners from *2 Broke Girls* (Michael Patrick King), *The Mindy Project* (Mindy Kaling), and *Parks and Recreation* (Mike Schur and Dan Goor). I also interviewed three showrunners from three very different kinds of half-hour comedy series:

- *Modern Family*: A single-camera broadcast network (ABC) sitcom with a large ensemble and no laugh track. Creators/showrunners: Steven Levitan and Christopher Lloyd.
- *How I Met Your Mother*: A multi-camera broadcast network (CBS) sitcom that also uses a single-camera style for some flashbacks and exterior sequences. Creator/showrunners: Craig Thomas and Carter Bays.

- *Web Therapy*: a low-budget, single-camera premium cable (Showtime) comedy that originated as a web series sponsored by Lexus. There are very minimal sets as the camera is primarily "fixed" with the limited POV of a web camera through which psychotherapist Fiona Wallice (Lisa Kudrow) dispenses advice to her online clients. *Web Therapy* is a groundbreaking comedy series offering a unique mode of storytelling based on a new business model. Each episode often features a big name guest star (Meryl Streep, Lily Tomlin, Conan O'Brien, David Schwimmer, Minnie Driver, and Julia Louis-Dreyfus have all made appearances). While *Web Therapy* is an unusual series with its own format, you'll note in my interview with creator/showrunners Don Roos and Dan Bucatinsky[1] (Kudrow is also a co-creator and co-writer; Roos also directs each episode) that this series adheres to the basic "rules" of the sitcom game.

The following is a very basic primer for aspiring sitcom writers and creators. For a more intensive crash course, there are some excellent books[2] solely devoted to the art and craft of situation comedies. But even more valuable is your total immersion into classic sitcoms from the past and present. In addition to the above esteemed sitcoms, some of my all-time favorites (in no particular order) are *All in the Family*, *M*A*S*H*, *Maude*, *The Mary Tyler Moore Show*, *Taxi*, *Seinfeld*, *Cheers*, *Rhoda*, *Barney Miller*, *The Office* (U.K. and U.S.), *I Love Lucy*, *Roseanne*, *Murphy Brown*, *Everybody Loves Raymond*, *Family Ties*, *Soap*, *The Bob Newhart Show*, *The Days and Nights of Molly Dodd*, and *Get Smart*.

Basic Sitcom Formats

There are two types of sitcoms: *multiple-camera* format and *single-camera* format.

Multiple-camera started with shows like *I Love Lucy* and continue today with *Two and a Half Men*, *2 Broke Girls*, and *Big Bang Theory*.

Single-camera shows are shot and formatted like films. Examples: *Modern Family*, *Parks and Recreation*, *Curb Your Enthusiasm*, and *Veep*

Some shows have teasers and tags, some have two acts (multiple-camera format) and some have three acts (some, but not all, single-camera shows). If you're planning to write a sample script for one of your favorite sitcoms, find an actual script from that show via one of the script websites and copy their format. Don't try to reinvent the wheel or break the mold. A spec episode needs to match the standards of the show. If you are writing a sitcom pilot, study various types of sitcoms and decide which is the best style and format for yours. There isn't one way to do it. Do your research!

---

[1] See the companion website for interview: http://www.focalpress.com/cw/landau
[2] I recommend *Writing Television Sitcoms* by Evan S. Smith (Perigree Trade).

Multiple-Camera Sitcoms

- *FADE IN*: ALL CAPS and underlined
- *SCENE X*: "numbered" using CAPS and underlined.
- *SLUGLINES*: location in ALL CAPS; DAY or NIGHT, and underlined.
- (CHARACTER LIST): should appear directly below the slug line and indicate which characters are needed for the scene. Also enclosed in parentheses.
- ACTIONS/DESCRIPTIONS: in ALL CAPS
- *CHARACTER INTRO*: ALL CAPS and underlined
- *SOUND EFFECTS/SPECIAL EFFECTS*: ALL CAPS and underlined
- *CHARACTER NAMES*: ALL CAPS before dialogue
- DIALOGUE: sentence case and DOUBLE-SPACED
- (PARENTHETICALS): to clarify how dialogue is to be said, such as (SARCASTIC)—appears within dialogue—on the same line—in ALL CAPS and enclosed in parentheses.
- The script is divided into acts and each new act begins on a new page.

As for time breakdown, the following applies to *multi-camera* sitcoms:

Teaser:	**1–2 pages**
Act One:	**17–20 pages**
Act Two:	**17–20 pages**
Tag:	**1–3 pages**
Total:	**40–48 pages in length**

Single-Camera Sitcoms:

- Formatted like screenplays and similar to the one-hour drama.
- Dramedies, such as *Girls, Weeds,* and *Nurse Jackie,* also use this format.
- May or may not have formal act breaks written on the page (this depends on whether or not the show has commercial breaks). Premium cable series (on HBO and Showtime, etc.) have no commercial breaks.
- Dialogue and stage direction are single-spaced.
- The characters are described in ALL CAPS the first time they are introduced.
- Scripts average at least thirty pages in length.

Basic Sitcom Structures

Multiple-Camera Sitcoms

The plots for these types of shows tend to be broad and simple. The show may have a major plot line (A story) and a minor plot line (B story), and may or may not have a runner.

Each act tends to be between three to five scenes. A single camera sitcom can jump around much more, with shorter fragmented scenes that get cut together in post-production to make a coherent, thematic whole. A multi-camera sitcom is usually shot in front of a live audience, in chronological order, more like a stage play. A single-camera comedy is like a little feature film every week.

The locations in a multi-camera sitcom are more basic and constant. According to 2 Broke Girls showrunner Michael Patrick King, who's worked on both multi-camera and single-camera series, multi-camera sitcoms are harder because of the limitations of locations. On 2 Broke Girls, they always need to figure out character entrances and exits within scenes, whereas on a single-camera series, like his Sex and the City, you could just CUT TO: the next scene.

On 2 Broke Girls, Michael Patrick King and his writing staff map out the full season (twenty-four episodes) arcs at the beginning of the preproduction cycle. "We dream up three basic plotlines for the season: broke stories, girl stories, and diner stories," King said. Then they break down those larger arcs into individual episodes that are assigned to individual members of the writing staff (unless it's a writing team duo). And there's a lot of story packed into what will be a twenty-one-minute episode "with a top, middle, and underneath [which I interpret to mean theme and subtext]," says King.

The writers' room at 2 Broke Girls is utilized to figure out larger story arcs for the characters, but King prefers for the actual script writing to be done by each writer outside of the writers' room to honor the individual voices of each talented writer.

Single-Camera Sitcoms

Single-camera sitcoms generally have more freedom to visit multiple locations, with a couple of regular sets. There are fewer locations and longer scenes on a multi-camera sitcom, necessitating more jokes on every page of the script. In a multi-camera sitcom, the live audience is expecting a joke or something shocking to come out of the mouths of your characters with virtually every line of dialogue—silence on a multi-camera sitcom is just dead air, whereas silence on a single-camera sitcom could make us cringe—but in a good way. On a single-camera sitcom, the audience has a different expectation and the rhythms of the comedy are more nuanced, with less emphasis placed on "jokes" and more reliance on visual gags and intercutting between scenes.

On Parks and Recreation, showrunners Mike Schur and Dan Goor break stories as a group, but then each writer peels off to go write their individual episode. Schur (an alum from The Office writing staff) feels that group writing an entire episode doesn't make the best use of each writer on staff. "After a while, it becomes the law of diminished returns," Schur said.

Showrunner Mindy Kaling from *The Mindy Project* (and also an alum from *The Office* writing staff) feels that having the first drafts of each episode crafted by individual writers (outside the collective writers' room) makes for a "wonderful patchwork of voices." Kaling runs her writing room in a similar fashion to the way her former boss, showrunner Greg Daniels, ran *The Office*. They use good old-fashioned index cards and a white board. At the beginning of their pre-production cycle, they'll pitch three to four episode ideas at a time to the network for approval, and then assign each script to a member (or two) of the writing staff. After the first draft gets turned in by the writer(s), "then the script becomes [the] communal property of the whole room."

Parks and Recreation also works according to this model. The first draft of the script will be dissected and new lines of dialogue and jokes will be pitched—these new lines are referred to as "alts" in the writers' room. According to Schur, they'll throw everything in at once, so that the teleplay will often balloon to fifty to sixty pages with alts, and then they'll cull the draft down to the requisite thirty pages.

Greg Daniels also did this and coined the phrase "the candy bag" for all the discarded jokes and bits that would then be saved for possible inclusion in future episodes. Michael Patrick King calls his version of the candy bag "the whipped cream." At the same time though, you don't want to save the juiciest plot lines, funniest lines and situations for later because, as Mike Schur points out: "Loyal audience members are a precious commodity. You need to make *every* episode strong or risk losing people." Or as Greg Daniels would tell his writing staff: "Pack the sausage [the episode]; put it all in."

Basic Formula Overview

Most broadcast network sitcoms adhere to a basic formula and utilize the same narrative storytelling models as feature films and one-hour dramas—so you can readily apply the first twenty chapters of this book to your sitcom pilot.

As for basic sitcom formulas, here's a quick overview:

- *Set up the ordinary world*: show the main characters in a bit of their daily routine, and then disrupt this relative normalcy with a problem (which provides the initial catalyst to the main plotline known as the A story). The A story is a problem that the central character of this episode has to overcome. It's typically called the "cold open" or "tease" and is followed by the opening credits. The stakes of this problem don't need to be super high on the life and death scale, but they should *feel* vitally important to the character. I've heard this referred to in the sitcom biz as a "tremendous trifle."

- *Act 1* in a sitcom begins after the opening credits. Now the character is looking for a solution to the problem. In the early stages of the act, the problems for the B and C stories also arise for the supporting characters. And then your main protagonist must decide on a game plan in order to deal with the problem.
- Link A, B, and C stories by a *unifying common theme* (there is often a moral at the end of the story).
- *Midpoint plot reversal with escalating stakes*: in a feature, this occurs in the middle of act two. In a two-act sitcom, this occurs at the end of act 1; in three-act structure, at the end of act 2. This is when the bigger problem comes up that takes the action into a sudden and unexpected direction. The goal may change. A new goal may be added, but your character is now on the horns of a major dilemma. Basically, in trying to fix the smaller problem, a bigger problem was (inadvertently) created. The best metaphor I've heard for this is that in act one your protagonist is being chased by a vicious dog and forced to climb a tree to escape, and then in subsequent act(s), bystanders throw rocks up at your protagonist in the tree.
- When the show comes back from the mid-point break, the central character works to solve the bigger problem, but things go awry, and they will reach a point where it looks like they will never be able to succeed. That's the low point of the story where failure seems imminent. In a sitcom, this *low point/all is (seemingly) lost moment* comes near the end of the second half of the story.
- By the end of the *second* (*or third*) *act* your character(s) overcome(s) the problem—usually through honest communication and/or making amends. In movies, the climax = the truth. I think this rule applies in sitcoms, too. After the climax, there's usually a commercial break.
- After the break, there is sometimes a very short "*tag*" to resolve any lingering conflicts. No matter how unruly the problem was, the viewers want to see that the main characters are safe and content in their ordinary world. There's usually one last laugh, and then the credits.

But, please note that with the prevalence of You Tube video shorts, websites like Funny or Die, sketch comedy shows like *Portlandia*,[3] and innovative comedy series such as *It's Always Sunny in Philadelphia, Community, Louie, Veep,* and *Girls,* the reliance on the tried-and-true sitcom formulas are

---

[3] Comedy series with a sketch comedy format, such as *Saturday Night Live, Portlandia,* and *Inside Amy Schumer,* follow an entirely different format than sitcoms and are categorized as "alternative programming" (not addressed within the scope of this book—sorry). Most animated series are structured similarly to single-camera sitcoms—minus the cameras and live audience.

becoming less essential for some viewers. Outrageous characters and envelope-pushing, surreal situations are becoming more accepted and desirable to this niche, but rapidly expanding audience.

> Having given you all these rules, the truth is that if it's funny every week, you can toss all the rules out and laugh yourself all the way to the bank.

INTERVIEW: Christopher Lloyd

Christopher Lloyd Credits

Best known for:

Modern Family (Executive Producer and Writer) 2009–2012
    Emmy Award Winner (Outstanding Comedy Series) 2010–2012
    Emmy Award Winner (Outstanding Writing for a
    Comedy Series) 2010
WGA Award Winner (Comedy Series) 2011–2012
WGA Award Winner (Episodic Comedy) 2010
WGA Award Winner (New Series) 2010
WGA Nominated (Comedy Series) 2010
Back to You (Executive Producer and Writer) 2007–2008
Frasier (Executive Producer, Co-Executive Producer,
    and Writer) 1993–2004
    Emmy Award Winner (Outstanding Comedy Series) 1994–1998
    Emmy Award Winner (Outstanding Individual
    Achievement in Writing for a Comedy Series) 1996
    Emmy Nominated (Outstanding Writing for a
    Comedy Series) 2000, 2004
    Emmy Nominated (Outstanding Comedy Series) 1999–2000
WGA Nominated (Episodic Comedy) 2001
Wings (Supervising Producer, Producer, and Writer) 1991–1993
The Golden Girls (Writer) 1986–1989

NL: I'm very interested in how you constructed the show from the beginning, particularly the use of voice-over and intercutting from family to family with the documentary style built into the more traditional structure of the sitcom. Once you decided you wanted to tell these stories about the new untraditional family, when did you decide and/or how did you decide that you wanted to have this direct address to the camera—documentary style?

CL: It was early on. We wanted to do a family show, but as you say, how are we going to do a family show that's different from the thousands that have been on television already? The first thing we thought was, "Okay, we haven't seen the documentary version of the family show—that will make it different, that will give the audience a way in that you may not have had in previous family shows. The direct address to the audience and the interviews give it a little bit more of a voyeuristic feel. It feels a little bit more captured than say in a traditional sitcom where you're laying it all right out there in front of the audience. It was an early decision, but even so, the question was, "If that's the way in, who is this one family we're looking at? How are we going to pick one family that's going to encapsulate the American family today?" So then we thought, maybe we'll do three different families and hope to catch the essence of the American family by triangulating one traditional family with two less traditional families. Then, we thought, "Well, that seems a little bit disparate. If we're just going to be looking at one family for two minutes here and then another and another, it's going to feel like we're telling three shows all in one." We tried to find a clever way to unite them, so that we felt like we really had a series, which led us to having them all be related which was the surprise revealed at the end of the pilot. We're telling a story about one extended family, but within it very different forms of the American family, which was a little bit different, and we also happened to use a different stylistic technique—documentary style. All of that added together made us feel like it was a different way to do a family sitcom. We can be somewhat traditional in the storytelling and in the jokes, but there's enough that is different that will intrigue people.

NL: Do you map out season arcs in advance? In other words, do you have an overall plan of where you want to take these characters each season?

CL: We have a loose plan. We've never mapped out anything close to a whole season at the beginning. If we're lucky, we map out half of them. That's our goal in pre-production. If we can have twelve of our twenty-four stories figured out in some detail before we start shooting them, then we feel like we're in good shape. We maybe had eleven this year. We don't do tight story arcs because there's not a particular romance that we're following or any of those stories that lend themselves to a serialized approach. But, for example, Gloria [Sofia Vergara] is pregnant. We know that she's going to give birth right around episode 11 or 12, so if we're going to do a baby shower episode or her family comes to see her before the birth, we know that we have to pop those in around episodes 3, 6, and 9 and be ready to have her give birth at episode 12. When we had Claire [Julie Bowen] involved in running for city council, we had to think about the big moments and where we wanted them to fall. Do we want the election to happen somewhere around episode 20? Then, let's have a debate prep episode right around 15. These are far from fully figured out stories, but it just gives us points to aim toward that we'll have to hit when we get to them.

NL: Will your characters ever change? I always felt that it was the Golden Rule of Sitcoms that characters don't change, but their situations do. Or am I wrong about that?

CL: There are aspects of the characters that audiences love and don't want to see change. That is on our show and many other shows. There are dynamics that work for us. You want to be rooting to see Phil [Ty Burrell] finally gain Jay's [Ed O'Neill] acceptance. You want to see a loosening of the tension between Claire and Gloria. At the same time, those conflicts are sources of a lot of humor for us, so we don't want to have them go away all together, but you can't have the same story week in and week out. We want to see some movement. It's a difficulty in doing a long-running series. You want to be showing some progress, but you also don't want to completely undo the thing that made people fall in love with your show in the first place. In terms of personal growth, sure we would like to see Claire, for example, be a little bit less uptight and find some outlet for her creativity. We've explored that from time to time by having her go out and get drunk with the gay guys and winding up with the straight guy that she took to be gay and letting her hair down a bit. We've seen her at a shooting range. These are things that you probably wouldn't have expected from Claire early on. Same with Phil. We've established him as this goofy dad, but there are many moments where we've seen a very sensitive side to him. Same with Jay. We have Jay this year, for example, letting us know that he's going to a psychiatrist. I don't think that's stuff that you would have anticipated from the Jay of season 1. It's a matter of expanding the characters, giving new dimensions to them, that you may find interesting, but don't stand in too much contrast to what we know of the character's traits. So that you don't say, "This just doesn't make sense. How could he be both A and B?" It's a challenge.

NL: Do you think of different plot lines as A, B, and C stories—or does each family just have their own letter to represent them in each episode? Any in-house rules to breaking story?

CL: It shifts. In some episodes, it might be one family who has more of a dominant story.

NL: Is theme important to you when you're coming up with stories in terms of how to unify and connect with three stories?

CL: The big theme is not to become predictable and formulaic, so we do occasionally say, "Let's tell an entire episode that's about jealousy or about forgetting things or the road not traveled." We couldn't do that every week because people would start to say, "This is going to be the one about X." We don't want to do that. We want to do a show that's about completely different stories that the three families are engaged in that have nothing to do with one another or a show that brings all the families together for the larger part of the entire episode, but has a different feel from the other two parts of the episode.

As far as A, B, and C stories, we tend not to because we're trying to service all of our characters. In order to do that, we usually apportion them about the same amount for each episode. The distinction we're more likely to make is: which will be our more emotional story with more of a heart aspect to it and what might be our sillier story within the episode? We try to keep a balance there too.

If we're doing something that's a little more farcical with Mitch and Cameron [Jesse Tyler Ferguson and Eric Stonestreet], we might want to do something for Phil and Claire that has a little bit more emotion to it so that the audience comes away feeling that they've gotten both things.

The number of pages we give a story is almost always dictated by what's the best way to tell the story. If we say, "Wow, we told a story here with Phil and Claire that's very economical and has reached a nice moving place, but it's going to take fourteen pages to do it. Now, we've also got this really funny farcical Mitch and Cam story that's also seeming like it's going to be fourteen pages, which doesn't leave us much for Jay and Gloria. We would probably just take one of those stories out and put it in a different episode rather than give some of our other characters short shrift.

NL: I want to talk about the way your writers' room works. Do you break stories and pitch jokes as a group, and then does one person go off and work on that episode individually or do you assign different story lines to different people?

CL: It's always done by one person or a couple of people. We sit together and we very thoroughly break a story, and my rule of thumb is that it takes us three days to do that. That's six or seven or eight writers in a room—sometimes even more—pitching away at something. It may start with an amusing thing that happened to one of us, and we try to build around that. Or it may start with a theme. It may start with a holiday that we want to do or with one of the markers of the season. We need to do the show where Gloria gives birth. What's a funny way to do that? Whatever the starting place is we pitch on that for a solid two to three days until we have a lot of notes accumulated and a pretty good idea of what our lead story is going to look like. We have cards that we put up on the board, so that we can see every step of it all the way through. Once we're convinced we've got a whole episode that works—stories with beginnings, middles, and ends with lots of opportunities for fun with this component of heart as well—we say, "Okay, it's ready to be written."

At which point, one person or a team of writers from that group will go out and write an outline. After a few days with the outline, which is just an expanded version of what we talked about with sentences, sample dialogue and some jokes, then we all come back and read it again. In the interim, we've been off on other episodes and figuring out other stories. It's usually a week or two later by the time we come back to the outline and we have a fresher perspective on things. You look at it and you say, "Alright, I like this part or maybe we can work on this part or maybe we can put a better joke here or maybe we can move the act break up in the story." And maybe take about a half a day or less giving notes to the writer. Then that writer (or writers) goes off and writes the script. He comes back two to three weeks later—at which point the staff sits with it and does a rewrite on it. It usually takes a day or two—and that should be just for refining jokes. You shouldn't be changing story at that point because that should have happened at an earlier stage. It should just be a matter of finding some better jokes, sharpening up some speeches, maybe giving a little contour to the scenes. Then we have our script that's ready to be read at the table which is the actors coming in for its first performance out loud which, of course, gives a whole new life to the script because you're actually hearing the characters' voices and you're able to say: "That speech, that line is great for that actor," or "That didn't sound quite right, or "That scene felt a little slow," or "That moment seemed a little bit rushed." With the new information from the table read, we go back and do another rewrite, which is a day or two, and then we have our final script which is what we shoot.

NL: Given that you're a single camera show and don't shoot in front of a live studio audience—providing an immediate reaction—what's your personal barometer to know if something's funny?

CL: The table reading gives you a certain measure because, in addition to the writers and actors, there's the department heads and other invited guests. We have a room of about a hundred people to listen to it, so we have a pretty good gauge right there. When you're on stage and you're shooting it, then you're trusting your own instincts. There are again people on stage while we're rehearsing—lighting people, hair people, makeup people, electricians—who do watch. They laugh or they don't. You get a little bit of feedback right there, but at that point, you're trusting your own instincts. The nice thing about doing single camera is you can stop and you can say, "We need a better joke here or a little bit more going on between these two actors. Let's take a minute and see if we can polish up this speech." And you sit down for fifteen to twenty minutes and you can change it and get it the way you want. That's not a luxury you have in front of a live audience because you're taxing their patience. The benefit in a multi-cam is you've gone to rehearsals all week—you've seen it performed at least three or four times in front of a big group of people laughing. All of these jokes have essentially been auditioned. Going into a multi-cam with an audience, you're almost always sure it's all going to work, but you can't stop. With a single cam, we take eight or ten hours to shoot four minutes worth of a show, so we can stop and refine it.

NL: I once heard Larry Gelbart talk about running the writers' room of *M*A*S*H*, and he said that his golden rule was, "Never be afraid to say something stupid," because it might spark something smart and valuable from someone else in the room. Do you and Steve have any governing rules of how to run a functional, successful writers' room?

CL: We have many different kinds of writers on our staff. Some are more extroverted, some more introverted. I wouldn't want to have a room where everyone was the same, where everyone was pitching jokes in the same way. So we try to encourage quieter, more thoughtful writers to come forward, and sometimes need to butterfly net the more aggressive ones.

NL: What are the best and worst aspects of being a showrunner on *Modern Family*? I would imagine all the Emmys and critical acclaim and high ratings must feel great. Everybody loves *Modern Family*. . .

CL: Well, I'm sure not everybody—

NL: Everybody I know, anyway. All ages. It must be incredibly gratifying for you.

CL: The best part of running this show is that, even though I've been in this business for a long time, this is my first hit as a series creator. I ran *Frasier*, but didn't create it. And I get to go to work with smart, funny people and laugh really hard every day. It's also rewarding to see how well the show is received by audiences. Back in the days of *Frasier*, the series would get reviewed at the beginning of the season, and maybe a paper would write something about it during or at the end of the season. But with *Modern Family*, we get immediate feedback from viewers from social media—hundreds of reviews sometimes even before a full episode has finished airing. We get a lot of feedback.

NL: Does that feedback influence you and your writing staff, or do you pretty much try to shut it out and write the stories you'd like to tell?

CL: We generally write what we want because even though there are hundreds blogging and posting, that's still a small fraction of our audience. So we try not to let those online views dictate what we're doing. On the other hand, if there is a big, loud consensus about a new character or plotline that people just don't like, then that might influence us going forward.

The most challenging part of running this show is that it's a grind. We have an incredibly talented group of writers on our show right now, and fortunately they're all staying put—so that helps a lot. But we do twenty-four episodes per season. That's a lot of pressure. And because the show is so successful, that sets the bar high; we don't want to repeat ourselves and be formulaic. But we also need to come up with many, many stories that are fresh, unpredictable, and hopefully generate a few laughs. And each story we tell means we can't tell that story again, so there's always the challenge of coming up with new material—new ways in to stories. But the positives far outweigh any negatives, and this is a great experience.

INTERVIEW: Carter Bays and Craig Thomas

Carter Bays and Craig Thomas Credits

Best known for:

The Goodwin Games (Creators, Executive Producers, Writers) 2013
How I Met Your Mother (Creators, Executive Producers,
    Writers) 2005–2013
    Emmy Nominated (Outstanding Original Music and Lyrics) 2010
    Emmy Nominated (Outstanding Comedy Series) 2009
American Dad! (Supervising Producers, Writers) 2005–2006
Oliver Beene (Co-Producers, Writers) 2003–2004
Late Show with David Letterman (Writers) 1997–2002
    Emmy Nominated (Outstanding Writing for a Variety,
    Music, or Comedy Program) 1998–2002
    WGA Nominated (Comedy/Variety—Including Talk—Series) 2000–2002

NL: How did you originally come up with the concept for *How I Met Your Mother* (*HIMYM*) in terms of its signature style: use of V.O., flashbacks, and intercutting between characters and time periods?

CB: I think initially we wanted to write a single-camera show, but the wisdom at the time was that single-camera comedy wasn't working (this is nine years ago, remember), so we took a lot of elements from that style—like more scenes, more edits, more cinematic camera work—and shot it with four cameras and added a laugh track. The style developed naturally out of that.

As far as flashbacks and intercutting and all that, our style is probably just a hodgepodge of the film and TV that inspired us enough for us to want to rip it off. I mean, *Annie Hall*, is the Tigris and Euphrates of modern romantic comedy. Turn to any page of that script and you'll find something that we and a hundred other people have co-opted over the years, wittingly or otherwise. The split-screen therapist sessions, the subtitled first date subtext, the story told out of sequence . . . the artistic message of that movie is that there are no rules. The audience is sophisticated enough to buy in on a little magical realism here and there, if they connect with the characters and the story you're trying to tell.

For what it's worth, my favorite part of *Annie Hall*'s nonlinear storytelling is the fact that you hear the end of the story right at the beginning: "Annie and I broke up." There's something beautiful about that, and looking back I think the ending of our first episode—"That's how I met your aunt Robin"—is an homage to that moment, and by homage I mean we totally stole it.

CT: Carter and I love packing as much story, as many ideas, into an episode as possible. (That's either ambition or poor attention span, depending on how you look at it.) We love twists and turns and reveals and mysteries and setups and payoffs, so our episodes can get pretty intricate. Traditional multi-cam shows often have fewer scenes per episode, and the scenes are longer. Some might have fifteen to twenty scenes in an episode. *HIMYM* sometimes has eighty scenes in an episode, and rarely fewer than forty to fifty. We wanted to take the multi-cam form and impose a single-cam (or even a feature film) editing style onto it, which meant shooting over the course of three days instead of the more conventional recipe of a live audience show with a few pre-tapes cut in. The fact that our entire series is a guy telling a story to his children informed this style—when you tell a story, you tend to stop, start, jump back, jump forward, digress (not to mention embellish a few details!). So that's built into the DNA code of the series.

NL: I love your show, but I'm wondering if you were worried about it being too limited as a construct (perhaps too much of a gimmick?) to sustain a series for so many seasons, or did you plan to break out of this style and reboot (such as revealing the mother sooner) as part of your original plan?

CB: Maybe it's me, but I love a good gimmick if it's well executed. The problem is, there's this feeling with TV where you can't enjoy a high concept show even from the first episode, because you're just sitting there thinking, "This is great, but how are they going to sustain this?"

I guess that's the difference with movies and TV. Movies are like dating to get laid, while TV is dating to get married.

But as far as our gimmick goes, it felt like it was incidental to the real meat of the story, which is the friendships of these five characters. For that reason, we always wanted to see if we could stick to our guns and take the concept as far as we could take it, and wait till the very end for Ted to meet the mother. Our feeling was, when it feels like the audience is going to start getting sick of what we do week to week, we'll have Ted meet the mother, end the series, and move on to another show. As it turned out, the audience didn't get sick of it. I mean, some did for sure, but the numbers continued to hold up, and we never felt like we were running out of story, so we kept going with a show about these five characters and their lives before Ted's wife showed up. We had eight very happy years like that. But once we started discussing the possibility of a ninth season—taking the show past its two hundredth episode—the conversation became, "What would we like to write? What would excite us?" And that's when the idea of meeting the mother before the series finale first took hold. So we kind of made a deal with our past selves: we're going to keep going with this rule that Ted can't meet the mother until the last episode . . . but in the meantime, we're gonna meet her first. And we're gonna play every variation we can think of around that idea without breaking the central rule.

CT: We pitched it as "a guy's hundred best stories about his crazy twenties." Ironically, we are now approaching our two hundredth episode and our characters are all in their thirties. So it went further than we ever imagined! And that's because the audience connects with and cares about the characters and the actors, not the title or the gimmick. The construct of the future narrator telling the story also provided a sort of safety net to do realer, darker, emotional stories—the tacit implication being that, by 2030, even if there was some turbulence along the way, things all worked out okay for Ted and by extension, his friends.

NL: Where did your core ensemble characters come from—based upon people you knew or purely from imagination or both?

CB: There was a lot of autobiographical stuff in the pilot. I was single and coming to that crossroads, and Craig was in his first few years of marriage and still figuring out how to be a grownup. And we were newly living in Los Angeles after five really fun years in New York. We were homesick. We had been hired to write for Letterman right out of college, so we were kind of cannonballed into this whirlwind of living in New York City, working and hanging out with a bunch of really entertaining folks, and drinking and running around and taking cabs and kissing unlikely people and making huge mistakes and being young enough to wake up the next day and not be all that hung over. It was a great time, much more fun than high school and college, and after a year or so in Los Angeles, we really missed it. It was the first time in my adult life that I understood what nostalgia was, and that newly discovered feeling went right into the pilot script.

CT: Our core characters are a mix—some are based on people we know, some are more original inventions. Marshall and Lily are based on my wife Rebecca and I—we've been together since the very beginning of college. When we wrote the *HIMYM* pilot, Carter was single and in his twenties and still searching for "The One," so that was the inspiration for Ted: A guy who really wants to find the right girl and whose two best friends have been an old married couple since they were eighteen years old. Barney is more of an original invention, although some aspects are inspired by dudes we used to hang out with in New York in our twenties. Robin was also not literally based on any one person, although certain traits of Robin are based on Cobie Smulders—her Canadian-ness, for example, or her independence. Over time, the characters—no matter how much you originally based them on known entities—become their own people, a collaborative construct between actors and writers. Still, it's important to us to hold on to what's fundamentally human and recognizable about each character. So we're always stealing from real life.

NL: Do you map out the season arcs in advance so you're building to "sweeps" episodes or cliffhangers—or do you generally break stories episode to episode?

CB: We always map out our seasons. It makes the writing easier, and while I also think there's some value in figuring it out as you go along—making an improv game out of it—in our case, we have a narrator who knows how this story ends. And everything he says is pertinent to that story, so we need to know where he's going with it. As far as "sweeps" goes, it's funny, we'll still reflexively say things like, "Oh, that's a big idea, we should do that in sweeps," even though, from what I can tell, nobody cares about sweeps anymore.

The big thing we try to do is to structure the storytelling around the gaps in the season. There are usually a few multi-week stretches in the late winter and spring when we're not airing new episodes. It's nice to have a good cliff-hanger going into one of those stretches, to entice the viewers to come back three weeks later.

CT: *HIMYM* is very arc-ed out each season, almost more like a drama. We like the show to have a memory of itself week to week—events have conse-quences, one thing leads to the next. Again, that's just how we like to write. Yes, we've done plenty of stand-alone episodes along the way, but we look at those as fun pieces of candy to be consumed between larger, more nutritious meals! And we like to write drama within the comedy. Each season we try to come in with an overall shape—what are the big emotional milestones we know we'll hit, what is this season about, what do we want the characters to go through, where do we want them to end up?—and remain as faithful as we can to that plan.

NL: From where do new episode ideas emerge?

CB: The best episodes always come from real stories. Like, 100 percent of the time, without fail. And conversely, the worst episodes are the ones that have never happened to anyone ever. We try not to make those episodes, but sometimes they slip past the goalie and get on the air.

But the good ones come from someplace real. The original "Naked Man" was actually one of our writers, who was bold enough to share that story with the room. A friend of mine named Justin Dickinson gave me the story that became "The Three Days Rule." Barney running a marathon without train-ing, getting to the finish line, then sitting down on the subway and discover-ing his legs no longer work and not being able to get up so he keeps riding it all day long? True story, or so I've been told.

CT: The best ones are usually from real life, and then you build on that kernel of truth (I can't not salute when I write "kernel of truth"—a joke sto-len, appropriately, from real life!). Carter and I encourage our writers' room to be as honest and therapeutic as possible—we want real life stories, dynam-ics, observations to ground the comedy. Even when something on *HIMYM* is insane, it usually originates from something recognizably human. That is to say, our best episodes usually do.

NL: What makes a worthy A story for you?

CB: Usually the thing that separates an A story from a B story is the emotional backbone. If it's a story that's dynamic enough to be more than just funny, and gives the actors somewhere to go other than comedy, it gets the headliner slot. If it's too silly or stupid or weird to carry any emotional weight, we make it a B story.

CT: We love it when all there is is an A story. We never approach an episode with, "What's the A, B and C story?" We love it when one idea can launch everyone's story in an episode, so that even if several characters diverge, they're all on one theme. Sometimes a story naturally takes an A-B-C theme, but we don't seek that out and sometimes we even try to avoid it.

CB: Honestly, we do try to avoid it. The best kind of story to me is one that's big and funny and variable enough to engage the whole cast. Since our show is a story being told by one guy, we like to structure it like a real story. And when you're casually telling someone a story, you don't break it up into A, B and C stories. You just tell one tale at a time. If I'm being honest, I think we were much better about doing that in our early seasons. "The Pineapple Incident," "Drumroll Please," and "The Naked Man" are all good examples.

NL: What is the comedy "sweet spot" of the series to you?

CB: I think we're one of those shows that's at its best when you relate to it as a viewer, and it illuminates something real in your own life. That's what was great about *Seinfeld*. As much as it was "a show about nothing," wasn't really about nothing. On a tangible level, it was more about something that most other shows. You know, you take a show that's "about something," like *The West Wing*. It's about the president. Have I ever met the president? No. Have I been put off by someone standing too close to me when they talk? Yes, absolutely. That's something.

CT: Our sweet spot—to me, *HIMYM* at its best—is when we can create a tone that is silly and funny and stupid that then turns into something poignant or even surprisingly dark/real/honest. One of the themes of the series is that everything in life is happening at once. We knew from the pilot that our season 1 finale would be Ted finally getting the girl (Robin) and then discovering Marshall sitting alone in the rain, holding a returned engagement ring on the stoop. To me, that is *HIMYM* at its best—a guy at his high point silently putting his arm around his best friend, who's at the worst moment in his life and wondering, where do we go from here?

NL: Do you work from beat sheets and outlines? If so, what's the basic length for your show's typical outline?

CB: There's usually an eight- to ten-page outline that serves as the basis for the script. Plus many, many pages of room notes. But the outline is a good way to whittle it down into what's important and fundamental about the episode. It's a good skeleton.

CT: After breaking the story in the room on dry-erase boards, we go to a detailed outline (usually seven to ten pages) and then write the script from there. We like the story to be as clear as possible, the structure the themes, the emotions—we're much more concerned about that than jokes. The jokes can come later.

NL: Do you group write episodes as a team, or assign and go write solo (unless a writing partnership) and then reconvene?

CB: No, we've never done the group-writing approach. There's always a first draft that someone has gone off and written independently. Room rewriting can be somewhat extensive, and often once we're done punching it up as a group, there's not much left from the original draft. But we always give people the opportunity to feel like writers, and go off and see what they can come up with on their own.

CT: We almost never group-write an entire script. Maybe once or twice in the entire series, and even then we were at least working off a rough draft. Carter and I both love being off on script—finding the quiet time to dig a little deeper and find an extra twist, an extra emotion, an inspired moment that could only be found by one person at a computer rather than ten people in a conference room. So we try not to rob our writers of that experience.

NL: How do you run your writing room? Do you and Carter each have a different leadership role on the show? How do you delegate and keep the room functional?

CB: It's funny, I have no idea what Craig's room-running style is! I assume he's pretty good at it, since he's been doing it for eight years and comes up with consistently amazing stuff. I'm not really sure what my style is either. It's a pretty safe, non-confrontational environment, and people are pretty unfiltered, but I try to keep it moving and focused on the task at hand. There's not a lot of delegation in the story-breaking department. From our perspective, that's the most important thing Craig and I can be doing at any given time. Everything else—punching jokes, shooting, editing—can be handed off. But story is job one, so one of us is usually leading that room. I think it's evolved into a thing where, from my perspective, I'm trying to figure out the story and these guys are helping me do it. That's how I approach it. It makes it easier than saying, "What do we as a hive mind think this story should be?" Craig and I have pretty specific tastes, so it's maybe not as democratic as it could be. But we have some great writers, so every voice is definitely heard and listened to.

CT: I don't know how anyone could ever run a show without a writing partner! Carter and I are best friends—in many ways like brothers—and having someone you trust that much to co-run the show seems so crucial. We almost always have two writers' rooms going, working off an overall plan/season shape that Carter and I come into the season with and keep refining as we go. We can be so much more efficient this way, as long as we can build in time to meet up, just the two of us, to talk about the overall story we're telling—sadly, that time can be hard to find! We each weigh in on the script or outline that the other one is working on—usually scribbles in red pen in the margins—so we each contribute to every story and script.

NL: So you're a hybrid sitcom—part multi-camera/part single-camera? Or . . . ?

CT: Yes, we are most certainly a hybrid. We shoot multi-cam, but we take three days to do so. And we often do more stylized, cinematic pieces where we are single-cam (or two camera). It's a bit odd, actually. A straight up single cam show with many location shoots is much more expensive and hard to produce than *HIMYM*, but a multi-cam audience show didn't fit the story we wanted to tell. So we found a weird middle ground that just sort of worked!

NL: You generally do not shoot in front of a live audience, so what's your barometer to know if something is funny?

CB: We have a pretty merciless crew. If they don't laugh, you know it's not funny. Plus we have a table read and a run-through, and there's network people and studio people and department heads watching those, so you can gauge their reactions as well. But mostly, the barometer for what's funny has to come from within. And I think that's a good thing. When you have a live audience, the funniest joke will always be the joke that has the word "poop" or "boobs" or "penis" in it. If you just go by that, you'll have a great tape night, but then you'll get into the edit room and it'll be "The Poop Boobs Penis Show," and . . . well actually, it'll probably go on to be a huge hit and make you very successful. So maybe we should get a live audience.

NL: How much rewriting comes from first draft to first table read and what's actually shot?

CB: A whole lot. I mean, it depends on how good the first draft is, but no matter what, the writers' room will change it quite a bit. Actually, that mostly just applies to the comedy. The dramatic moments I try to not mess with or punch up in the room. Drama needs to feel personal, and can't be written by committee.

CT: We definitely rewrite, but it's rare that we tear a script apart after the table read. We try to get it as close as we can by the time it table-reads— the goal is to basically just be beating jokes, making it funnier, not asking the question, "What story are we telling?!" That part needs to be figured out sooner, because the process of making a TV show just moves so fast. Cameras are rolling before you know it—so the story needs to be solid.

NL: What's your basic production schedule from script thru post?

CT: We break a story in the room on dry-erase boards (well, sometimes Carter or I come in with a two-three page beat sheet of a rough story idea and then go to the big boards). Then we send the writer out to do a rough outline, just to get the shape down, and usually have them come back into the room with that outline, which we fill in a bit more, answer questions that have come up from the process of putting it on paper. Once that is as clear as possible, we send the writer out for a week to do a first draft of a script. They turn that in, and Carter or I give them notes on it. Then they take a few more days to write a second draft. Then, we bring that into the writers' room and do a group rewrite prior to the table read. We table read it on a Monday, rewrite it, then do a run-thru onstage on Tuesday and rewrite it again. Then, Wednesday morning at 9:00 a.m., we start shooting until Friday.

NL: How much fine-tuning to jokes occurs right up 'til the last minute?

CT: We are always trying to beat the jokes, find the extra twist or surprise or a way to call something back that we never thought of until Tuesday night before shooting on Wednesday morning. And Carter and I also always have the writer onstage paired with either one of us or another writer watching every take so that they can tweak jokes and try out alts.

CB: Often, we'll fine tune jokes in the edit room, too. If a joke is too wordy, for instance, and could be funnier if it was faster, there's ways to shorten it through editing. And likewise, if a joke isn't landing because there isn't enough setup, you can use the narrator, or even record some off-camera dialogue, to make it clearer.

NL: Will your characters ever change, or will they continue to follow the golden rule of sitcoms that characters don't change, their situations do? Or am I wrong about that?

CB: I think there's an even bigger philosophical question there: do *people* change? Obviously the goal in creating any character is to make them feel real. Now, is the *reality* that after eight years of hooking up with random babes, Barney can become a new man who wants to settle down? Or is the *real* reality that a zebra can't change its stripes? I truly don't know the answer to that. I guess it depends on the person. So I don't know if I can even answer that question on a conscious level. Maybe the characters have changed over the course of the series, and maybe they haven't. If they have, it's probably because the people writing them have changed, and the actors playing them have changed, and to some degree even the people watching have changed.

Ultimately, I guess the answer is: If you're writing something that tries to draw from real life, you can't worry about how much or how little the characters change. You just write it and see what happens.

NL: Now that your show is a certifiable hit, how hands-on is the network with notes? Or do they leave you alone and let you and Carter do your thing?

CB: They're great. Really, really great. It took making a show for another network to really grasp that. The truth is, they *don't* leave us alone—they give us notes, and they're usually good notes at that—but they also trust us, and trust the process, and know how *not* to make a good show. If you try to micromanage the writing from outside the writers' room, you might as well just leave show business. That never, never, never works.

NL: Do you have a favorite episode of *HIMYM*?

CB: "Ten Sessions," aka the Britney Spears episode. I think thematically the episode encapsulates everything we try to do with the whole series. It's just about a guy trying to get a girl to fall in love with him. Trying over and over, failing over and over, but not giving up. And then when he does give up, his friends pick him up and give him the strength to keep going.

I love the last scene of the episode, in which Ted takes Stella on a two-minute date. It's a cab ride, a dinner, a movie, a cup of coffee and some cheesecake, and a walk home, all in one shot, on a sidewalk, in two minutes. What you don't see is everything going on off-camera—an entire crew working like a clock in perfect synchronicity making the shot work. It was one of those moments that makes TV writing feel like NASA in the 1960s. You come up with an idea that seems like it can't be done, then figure out how to do it, and have some really talented people work together to pull it off. Fifty years from now, that'll be the two minutes of *How I Met Your Mother* that make me smile the most.

CT: I always love the episodes that are surprisingly dramatic. I love that finale to season 1, with Ted comforting Marshall out in the rain on the stoop. That image gives me such a chill. I love the two episodes around the death of Marshall's dad. And purely comedically, I love all the Robin Sparkles episodes—Carter and I first started working together by writing music, so any episode where we can write a crazy song is extra joy.

NL: What's the worst/best thing about being a showrunner?

CB: The best thing by far is getting to write things that go out to a huge audience in very short order. It's not like any other medium in that respect, except perhaps journalism or blogging. In the movie business you spend years working on a movie that, if it does get made, lives or dies in a weekend. In TV, you have millions of people sitting around an enormous campfire waiting for you to start spinning a yarn, every single week. That's a beautiful thing.

The worst thing is the stress. It's stressful to the point of physical danger, and that's why I'm not sure I want to keep doing it after *How I Met Your Mother* ends. And that's also why, again, having a studio and network that doesn't support what you're doing makes it absolutely not worth doing. Because the blank page is stressful enough.

CT: The worst thing about being a showrunner is the pressure of the clock—come Wednesday morning, they're gonna shoot whatever we write. The best thing about being a showrunner is that come Wednesday morning, they're gonna shoot whatever we write.

See interview with **Don Roos and Dan Bucatinsky** *on the companion website:* http://www.focalpress.com/cw/landau

INDEX